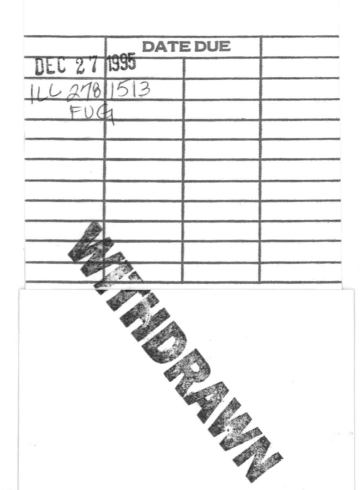

From Memex to Hypertext
Vannevar Bush and the Mind's Machine

From Memex to Hypertext:
Vannevar Bush and the Mind's Machine

James M. Nyce
Brown University
Providence, Rhode Island

Paul Kahn
Brown University
Providence, Rhode Island

ACADEMIC PRESS, INC.
Harcourt Brace Jovanovich, Publishers
Boston   San Diego   New York
London   Sydney   Tokyo   Toronto

ACADEMIC PRESS, INC.
1250 Sixth Avenue, San Diego, CA 92101

United Kingdom Edition published by
ACADEMIC PRESS LIMITED
24–28 Oval Road, London NW1 7DX

Library of Congress Catalog Card Number: 91-076751
International Standard Book Number: 0-12-523270-5

PRINTED IN THE UNITED STATES OF AMERICA

91 92 93 94   9 8 7 6 5 4 3 2 1

Contents

Part 1: The Creation of Memex

Part 2: The Extension of Memex

Part 3: The Legacy of Memex

Contributors

Colin Burke, Department of History, University of Maryland, Baltimore County, 5401 Wilkins Ave., Baltimore, MD 21228

Gregory Crane, Department of the Classics, Harvard University, Boylston Hall, Cambridge MA 02138

Douglas C. Engelbart, Bootstrap Project, Stanford University, Sweet Hall, Stanford CA 94305

Paul Kahn, Institute for Research in Information and Scholarship, Brown University, Box 1946, Providence RI 02912

Norman Meyrowitz, GO Corporation, 950 Tower Lane, Foster City, CA 94404

Theodor H. Nelson, Autodesk, 2320 Marinship Way, Sausalito CA 94965

James M. Nyce, Department of Anthropology, Brown University, Box 1921, Providence RI 02912

Tim Oren, Advance Technology Group, Apple Computer, 20525 Mariani Ave, MS 76-2C, Cupertino CA 95014

Larry Owens, Department of History, University of Massachusetts at Amherst, Amherst, MA 01003

Linda C. Smith, Graduate School of Library Science, University of Illinois, 1407 West Gregory Dr., Urbana IL 61801

Randall H. Trigg, Institute for Information, Aarhus Universitet, Niels Juelsgade 84, DK 8200, Aarhus N Denmark

Preface

This book focuses on one early and important figure in the history of computing—Vannevar Bush. Bush's contributions to engineering, higher education and science are well known. Bush was also one of the first Americans to design and use computing machines to solve mathematical and engineering problems. This book looks at these machines and particularly at Memex, a machine that was never built. While Memex was a visionary design, the documents and papers brought together here show how much Memex reflected the intellectual currents and the technology of the time. At the same time in writing about Memex, Bush argued that computing machines and machine intelligence would come to have an important place in man's intellectual life.

Much of the story about Memex concerns analogy computers. While Bush and his contemporaries thought analog machines had great promise, today this technology has been for the most part ignored or forgotten. We hope that through this book readers will gain a better understanding of the place analog machines have in the history of modern computing. In particular, we hope they will learn, as we have, something of the transitions and disjunctions that have characterized this history.

The seed for this book was planted at the 1987 Hypertext conference at Chapel Hill. The influence of Bush's essay "As We May Think" on the emerging field of hypertext was widely acknowledged. The year before, Bush had been discovered by the personal computing world at the first Microsoft CD ROM conference. However, we were struck by a discontinuity. People interested in hypertext, electronic libraries, and information retrieval, the very audience influenced by Memex, knew little or nothing about Bush as an engineer and pioneer of computing machines. People who knew Bush as an engineer and statesman had written little about Memex. We set out to determine what was known about Bush's Memex, to better understand the context from which it emerged, the ideas it represented, and to evaluate the impact it has had on the computer and information sciences.

The essays in Part One take us back to when the greatest technological innovations in machine calculation were occurring in the field of analog computing. In the first part of the book, **The Creation of Memex**, Larry Owens provides a history of several of Bush's analog computers—machines that set the stage for Memex. Our own essay describes Bush's speculative writings up through the publication of "As We May Think" in 1945 and tells the story of how this essay made its way into print. The balance of Part One is three essays by Bush, ending with a text of "As We May Think" that shows the variations between the versions published in *The Atlantic* and *LIFE* Magazine.

Bush's interest in Memex did not end with the publication of "As We May Think." The essays in Part Two show how Memex fared as digital machines and theory became the dominant technology. In Part Two, **The Extension of Memex**, our piece describes the essays Bush wrote in which he extended the Memex design and addressed questions of machine intelligence. Colin Burke sketches out the history of the Rapid Selector, a little-known machine whose technology helped inform the Memex design. "Memex II," in which Bush revisits the ideas and issues of the first Memex design, is published here for the first time. The remaining three essays, Bush's last published work about Memex, are taken from his collection of essays, *Science Is Not Enough*, and his autobiography, *Pieces of the Action*.

Part Three looks at the influence Bush's ideas have had on modern digital computing, particularly in the area of hypertext. We begin the third part of the book, **The Legacy of Memex**, by reprinting pieces by two pioneers in the field, Doug Engelbart and Ted Nelson. In their papers, Engelbart and Nelson discuss the continuity they recognized between their current work and Bush's ideas. Over a decade ago, Linda Smith examined through citation analysis the influence Bush's "As We May Think" has had—here she updates her research and findings. For many readers, Bush's essay "As We May Think" and his description of Memex there prefigures current research in several areas of computer and information science. The rest of Part Three traces out the relationship that exists between Memex and today's research in workstations, hypertext, and information retrieval. Norm Meyrowitz, the chief architect of Intermedia, uses Bush's ideas as a benchmark to assess today's technology and development efforts. Tim Oren of Apple surveys the current state of the art in information retrieval research and looks at how today's ideas relate to what Bush proposed. Randy Trigg, who helped develop NoteCards at Xerox, compares the idea of trails in Memex with guided tours and directed paths in current hypertext systems. Greg Crane, of Harvard's Perseus Project, looks at the research library, its history and importance, and relates this to today's projects in hypertext and information retrieval.

We are grateful for the support and interest shown in this project by Richard Bush, MD, executor of Vannevar Bush's estate. We also wish to acknowledge the support, both intellectual and technical, given to us by the Department of Anthropology and the Institute for Research in Information and Scholarship at Brown University. We particularly wish to thank Julie Launhardt, Marty Michel, George Landow, and Norm Meyrowitz at IRIS for reading drafts of our essays. The courtesy shown us by Sari Kalin, Jenifer Swetland, and David Pallai at Academic Press also needs to be mentioned.

Archival sources cited are given in the bibliographies of each paper. The correspondence to and from Bush mentioned in our own essays is from the Vannevar Bush Papers at MIT or the Library of Congress (in our first essay only letters from the Library of Congress appear). We sent copies of the essays and manuscripts by Bush reprinted here as well as "Man's Thinking Machine" and "Mechanization and the Record" to Crane, Oren and Trigg so that the volume's contributors would have a common set of documents to work from. We acknowledge the permission from the MIT Archives to cite these documents. We particularly wish to thank Helen Samuels and Elizabeth Andrews at the MIT Archives, Sally Beddow at the MIT Museum, and Jeff Flannery at the Library of Congress for their help. We would also like to thank Michael Buckland, Ph.D., Jeffrey Greenhut, Ph.D., and Michael Leavitt, Ph.D., for the interest they have shown in this project.

James M. Nyce and Paul Kahn

Part 1
The Creation of Memex

Vannevar Bush and the Differential Analyzer: The Text and Context of an Early Computer

Larry Owens

ONE DAY IN 1942, THE ROCKEFELLER DIFFERENTIAL ANALYZER was dedicated to winning the war. For the next several years this large mathematical machine, the centerpiece of MIT's Center of Analysis, labored over the calculation of firing tables and the profiles of radar antennas.[1] Weighing almost a hundred tons and comprising some two thousand vacuum tubes, several thousand relays, a hundred and fifty motors, and automated input units, the analyzer was the most important computer in existence in the United States at the end of the war.[2] (See fig. 1.) Wartime security prohibited its public announcement until 1945, when it was hailed by the press as a great electromechanical brain ready to tackle the problems of peace and to advance science by freeing it from the pick-and-shovel work of mathematics.[3]

The development of the analyzer had occupied Vannevar Bush and his colleagues at MIT for almost twenty years. In 1927, an early model made the front page of the *New York Times:* " 'Thinking Machine' Does Higher Mathematics; Solves Equations That Take Humans Months." In 1930, the group constructed a model which proved so successful that it inspired imitation around the world. In the United States, General Electric, Aberdeen Proving Ground, and the universities of Pennsylvania, California, and Texas all built analyzers. More were constructed abroad, in England at Manchester and Cambridge, and in Ireland, Germany, Norway, and Russia.[4] Bush's success prompted him to plan an analyzer more capacious, quicker in calculation, and more flexible in application, which would establish MIT as an international Center for the study of machine computation. He persuaded the Rockefeller Foundation in 1935 to finance the new machine, and in 1939 the Carnegie Corporation contributed money to help establish and maintain a center to serve as a site for the study of machine analysis. At the time, Bush's program seemed an adumbration of future technology. Harold Hazen, the head of the Electrical Engineering Department in

Reprinted from Technology and Culture, *Vol. 27, No. 1, (January 1986), pp. 63-95 with the permission of the author and University of Chicago Press.*

Fig. 1—The Rockefeller Differential Analyzer

1940 and a long-time colleague, predicted that the analyzer would "mark the start of a new era in mechanized calculus," and Karl Compton, MIT's president, declared in 1941 that the new machine would be "one of the great scientific instruments of modern times."[5]

Within five years of its announcement, however, the early enthusiasm which had marked the development of the analyzer had died, and the Center of Analysis had collapsed as a vital site for the study of computation.[6] In the early spring of 1950, Samuel Caldwell, the center's director and another of Bush's close colleagues in the development of the analyzer, came to the home of Warren Weaver to discuss the status of the machine and the program it had inspired. Weaver was the director of the Natural Sciences Division of the Rockefeller Foundation and a respected mathematician, and he had been intimately involved with the MIT project from its beginnings in the 1930s. The long meeting between the two men turned into an autopsy of the program begun fifteen years earlier with Rockefeller support. No one had expected in 1936, they admitted, that the whole field of "computer science" would so quickly overtake Bush's project. But things had indeed changed, and

Caldwell confessed to Weaver that the analyzer was "essentially obsolete" and the whole program had "become a real burden on MIT."[7]

What happened? Why did a twenty-year effort to create a computer fail when it did? The reasons, of course, are manifold. In the first place, the war released an unprecedented flood of federal money and spawned a multitude of laboratories at MIT, disrupting the simpler institutional environment in which the analyzer was conceived and nurtured. But if the war brought new public monies which overwhelmed the older tradition of private philanthropy that had sustained the analyzer, it also ushered in a variety of computational tasks, in the fields of large-volume data analysis and real-time operation, which were beyond the capacity of the Rockefeller instrument. The years around the war's end were marked by intense competition in computer development, and Bush's machine was quickly challenged by more capable computers incorporating radically different designs—by Eckert and Mauchly's ENIAC at the University of Pennsylvania, and by Jay Forrester's Whirlwind at MIT itself.[8] These new computers were electronic and digital rather than electromechanical, and to them belonged the future of computer technology. In brief, the Rockefeller Analyzer succumbed to technical obsolescence.

But are these suggestions of failure the most interesting features of this twenty-year project? In our rush to write the history of the most glamorous of modern technologies, we must be careful lest we find in older artifacts only anticipations of future developments, and overlook dimensions of meaning that open windows on the past. Warren Weaver indicated this extra dimension in the case of the analyzer when he remarked in a letter to Caldwell some days after their postmortem:

> [I]t seems rather a pity not to have around such a place as MIT a really impressive Analogue computer; for there is vividness and directness of meaning of the electrical and mechanical processes involved . . . which can hardly fail, I would think, to have a very considerable educational value. A Digital Electronic computer is bound to be a somewhat abstract affair, in which the actual computational processes are fairly deeply submerged.[9]

Weaver's insight can help us understand that the Rockefeller Analyzer was not so much an aborted beginning as the culmination of a series of inventions stretching back to Bush's undergraduate years at Tufts College. Furthermore, Weaver's reference to its vividness of meaning and educational value suggests that Bush's machines could be read as weighty "texts" embodying a variety of idioms—technical, intellectual, and ethical—ingredient in the culture of engineering in which he came of age. In the context of the early 20th-century engineering school, the analyzers were not only tools but paradigms, and they taught mathematics and method and modeled the character of engineering.

* * *

In the decade following the First World War, electrical engineers came up against severe mathematical difficulties in their studies of vacuum tubes, telephone lines, and especially long-distance power transmission lines. Given the large financial risks which accompanied the construction of power networks, it was imperative that engineers be able to predict the operating characteristics of proposed systems.[10] Consequently, between 1920 and 1925 the Research Laboratory of MIT's Electrical Engineering Department undertook a major assault on the mathematical problems involved in the study of long-distance lines. The attack was two-pronged and dealt, on the one hand, with the construction of artificial lines designed to reproduce on a laboratory scale the behavior of power networks, and, on the other, with the search for methods to handle the refractory equations generated by these networks.[11]

Much of the mathematics of long-distance lines had been developed by General Electric's Charles Steinmetz and the Bell Telephone engineer John Carson, but, while the derivation of the appropriate equations proved to be relatively straightforward, their solution was not. Of particular importance to MIT engineers worried about the stability of lines was the equation derived by Carson:

$$I = A(t)(E)\sin\theta + E p\cos(pt + \theta) \int_0^t \cos p\delta A \cdot (\delta)d\delta$$
$$+ E p\sin(pt + \theta) \int_0^t \sin p\delta A \cdot (\delta)d\delta,$$

where I is the entering current, and $E\sin(pt + \theta)$ the voltage suddenly applied to the sending end of an initially unenergized transmission line.

Normal procedure for the solution of this equation involved, first, the calculation of the products under the integral signs from tables of functions and their plotting by hand in graphic form, then the determination of the areas under the curves (and thus the integrals) with the use of an Amsler planimeter, and finally the necessary multiplication and addition of curves to give, in graphic form, I versus t.[12]

Early in 1925 Bush suggested to his graduate student Herbert Stewart that he devise a machine to facilitate the recording of the areas needed for the calculation of the Carson equation. In the course of his work, Stewart apparently discovered the series of papers that William and James Thomson had published in 1876 describing the disc-globe-and-cylinder integrator and its application to harmonic analysis. William Thomson explained the use of the integrator for calculating the integral

$$\int_0^x f(x)\phi(x)dx.$$

Stewart was properly intrigued, for the general form of the Carson equation was of the same type:

$$y(t) = F1(t)\int_0^t f(\delta)\theta(\delta)d\delta.$$

However, since this use of the Thomson integrator required knowledge of the integral

$$\int_0^x f(x)dx,$$

Stewart dismissed the device as unsuitable for his project, feeling that $f(x)$ might not, in the general case, be easily integrated. His dismissal of the Thomson integrator is ironic, for he might have found in the Thomson papers (which had been collected as Appendix B in Thomson and Tait's 1879 *Treatise on Natural Philosophy*) the essential insights that Bush would bring to fruition in the development of the mechanical integrator for which he had set Stewart searching.[13]

A colleague, F. D. Gage, suggested that Stewart interpret the equation electrically rather than mechanically. He then realized that the integration of the functional product could be performed with an ordinary watt-hour meter. Stewart intended to read the meter at appropriate time intervals, but Bush recommended linking the meter to a pen driven by a servomotor that would permit the integral's continuous recording. To generate the second-level product, Stewart turned again to the watt-hour meter until Bush pointed out that it could be accomplished more simply by an elementary mechanical linkage. Stewart received his master's degree in September 1925 for his work on this first Product Integraph.

Two more Bush students became involved with the Product Integraph. King Gould used the machine to study the temperature gradient along the heated filament of a vacuum tube.[14] Harold Hazen began the study of vacuum-tube circuits and soon realized that he could

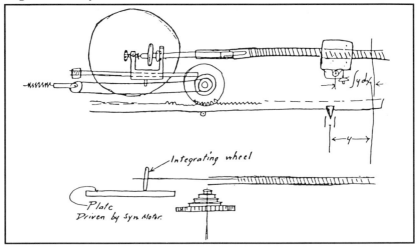

Fig. 2—The sketch by Harold Hazen of a second integrating element.

treat more complicated circuits if he had two levels of integration with which to work instead of one. He sketched out a second element for the integraph employing a wheel-and-disc integrator (a close cousin of the Thomson device), and showed his idea to Bush, who quickly recognized the generality of his innovation and generated a twenty-page memo outlining a new machine.[15] (See fig. 2.) After all, although first-order differential equations were encountered frequently in science, "it was once said that physics revolved about the second-order differential equation, and while recent developments have somewhat obscured this importance there is still much of physics thus described."[16] Under

Fig.3—(top) The revised Product Intergraph with Bush at the near end and, leading away, F.G. Kear, Harold Hazen, and R.D. Gage; (bottom) Bush seated at the output end of the intergraph with the disc integrator in front of him and the watt-hour meter, seen from the rear, to its right.

Bush's guidance, Hazen built a two-element machine capable of solving most second-order equations to an accuracy of several percent (fig. 3). In May 1928 the Franklin Institute awarded Bush its Levy Medal for his work on mechanical computation, with honorable mentions to Stewart, Gage, and Hazen.

The new model Product Integraph was applied to the study of vacuum-tube circuits, transmission lines, mechanical oscillations in synchronous motors, and electron orbitals.[17] Yet despite its successful applications, no one was satisfied with the new integraph. A hybrid machine that employed both an electrical and a mechanical device to perform the same function of integration, it suffered from the limitations of the former while failing to maximize the advantages of the

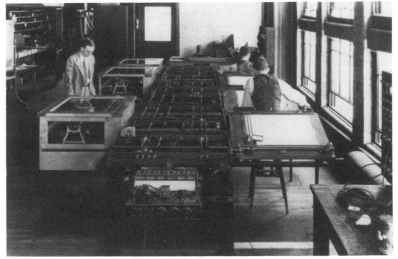

Fig. 4—The 1931 Differential Analyzer. Sam Caldwell can be seen at the left.

latter. The watt-hour meter was physically more complex and inherently less precise in its operation than a well-engineered mechanical integrator. Moreover, the meter was a more complex logical device in that it integrated the product of two functions, while the mechanical integrator, as will be seen, simply integrated $f(x)dx$. The combination of mathematical elegance and mechanical simplicity appealed to Bush, and by the fall of 1928 he had secured funds from the administration at MIT to build a new machine that would take advantage of the simple virtues of the wheel-and-disc integrator.[18]

The Differential Analyzer fulfilled Bush's expectations.[19] The new machine consisted of a long table-like framework crisscrossed by interconnectible shafts (fig. 4). Along one side were arrayed a series of drawing boards and along the other six disc integrators. Pens on some of the boards were driven by shafts so as to trace out curves on properly positioned graph paper. Other boards were designed to permit an operator, who could cause a pen to follow a curve positioned on a board, to give to a particular shaft any desired rotation. In essence, the analyzer was a device cleverly contrived to convert the rotations of shafts one into another in a variety of ways. By associating the change of variables in an equation with the rotations of shafts, and by employing an assortment of gearings, the operator could cause the calculator to add, subtract, multiply, divide, and integrate.

The disc integrator, the heart of the analyzer and the means by which it performed the operation of integration, is a variable friction-gear that consists of a disc resting on a wheel at a variable distance from its center (fig. 5*a*). The geometry of the integrator forces its constituent shafts to turn in accordance with the relationship

$$y = \int_a^b f(x)dx.$$

The precision of the disc integrator depends on eliminating slippage between the wheel and the disc when the wheel turns under load. In the Product Integraph Bush had reduced the load carried by the wheel shaft by the use of a servomotor which followed its rotations. In the Differential Analyzer, he accomplished the same end and continued his replacement of electrical by mechanical elements by incorporating another Hazen idea—the torque amplifier designed by C. W. Nieman of the Bethlehem Steel Corporation.[20] This was a purely mechanical device for the amplification of motion that depended on the winch principle (fig. 5*b*). By its use Bush was able to eliminate most of the torque load carried by the wheel shaft of the integrator and to supply the power needed to drive his calculating engine.

The use of the analyzer can be illustrated by an example based on one of Bush's own. Consider the equation of a falling body when the gravitational force *g* varies with the distance *x*:

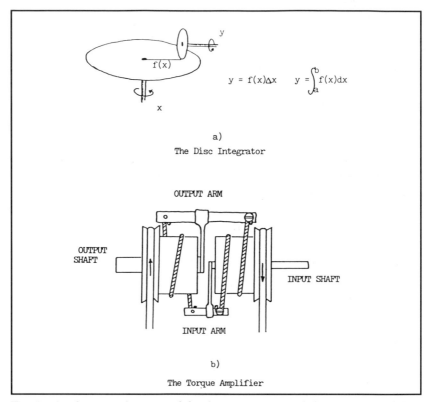

$$y = f(x)\Delta x \qquad y = \int_a^b f(x)dx$$

a)

The Disc Integrator

OUTPUT ARM

OUTPUT
SHAFT

INPUT SHAFT

INPUT ARM

b)

The Torque Amplifier

Fig. 5—A schematic diagram of the disc integrator and the torque amplifier.

$$\frac{d^2x}{dt^2} + k\frac{dx}{dt} + g(x) = 0,$$

or,

$$\frac{dx}{dt} = -\int \left[k\frac{dx}{dt} + g(x) \right] dt.$$

In Bush's words,

> A bus shaft is assigned to each significant quantity appearing in the equation. The several relations existing between these are then set up by means of connections to the operating units: a functional relationship by connecting the two corresponding shafts to an input table, a sum by placing an adder in position, an integral relationship by an integrator, and so on. When all the relationships which are involved have been thus

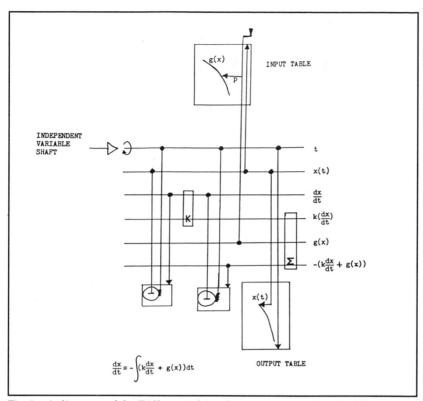

Fig.6—A diagram of the Differential Analyzer set up to solve the falling-body equation.

represented a final connection is made which represents the equality expressed in the equation. In the example above this connection is through an integrating unit . . . . When this has been done the machine is locked, and the rotation of the independent-variable shaft will drive everything else, thus forcing the machine to move in accordance with the expressed relationship . . . .[21]

A diagram of the analyzer connected to solve the equation of the falling body is shown in figure 6. The horizontal lines represent bus shafts, K and Σ multiplying and adding gears, and the integrators are represented by the indicated symbol. The terms of the equation associated with the rotations of particular bus shafts are noted at the side of the diagram. $G(x)$ would have been plotted earlier and an operator

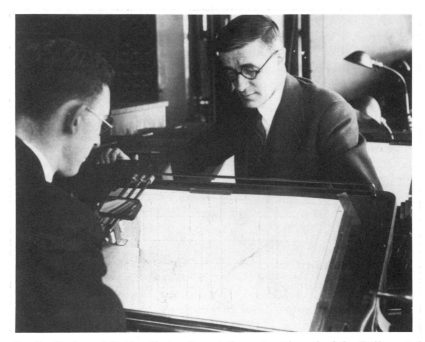

Fig. 7—Bush and Caldwell standing at the output board of the Differential Analyzer inspecting a family of curves produced during the solution to an equation.

stationed at the input table to keep the pointer p on the curve as the analyzer worked through the equation. The function $x(t)$, which expresses distance with respect to time, would be traced automatically on the output table. (See fig. 7.)

The Differential Analyzer did more, obviously, than compute $x(t)$. Through his elaboration of the mathematical possibilities inherent in the disc integrator and by the elimination of extraneous nonmechanical elements, Bush invented an elegant, dynamical, mechanical model of the differential equation. Articulated in a particular pattern, its shafts, gearboxes, integrators, pens, and drawing boards set in motion, the Differential Analyzer did not so much compute as kinetically act out the mathematical equation.

* * *

Between 1926 and 1935 the development and application of the analyzers generated four bachelors' theses, twenty-eight masters' theses, and four doctoral dissertations.[22] Among the students who worked on the analyzer project were a number destined to become influential figures at MIT—Harold Hazen, Sam Caldwell, Gordon Brown, and Harold Edgerton. Most of the problems studied with the help of the analyzers were drawn from the field of electrical engineering—but not all. By 1935 applications reflected the frontiers of scientific investigation and included studies in atomic physics, astrophysics, cosmic rays, and seismology. As early as 1932 Bush's colleague in the Physics Department, Philip Morse, used the analyzer to help thread his way through the computational thicket created by the quantum revolution of the 1920s.[23] The Englishman Douglas Hartree, a pioneer in the development of wave mechanics, visited Bush during the summer of 1933 to become familiar with the analyzer and used it for his calculation of the atomic field of mercury. Back at the University of Manchester, he constructed several analyzers modeled on the MIT machine, one of them from standard Meccano parts for a cost of some twenty pounds.[24]

Experience, mathematical skill, and sometimes days were required to translate difficult problems into forms that could be attacked by the calculator and then to connect the machine to perform the desired calculations. When Lemaitre and Vallarta calculated the trajectories of cosmic rays under the influence of the earth's magnetic field, it took five staff members and eighteen students thirty weeks to obtain the solutions.[25] (See fig. 8.) Nevertheless, the analyzer found an eager audience of scientists and engineers frustrated by impossibly difficult calculations. For these, the not-inconsiderable labors involved in work with the analyzer were inconveniences to be born lightly.

Success prompted Bush to plan yet another analyzer, one more precise in its calculations, convenient to operate, and with a larger universe of mathematical possibilities. The opportunity to pursue his plan presented itself in the person of Warren Weaver, who in the autumn of 1931 had become the director of the Natural Sciences Division of the Rockefeller Foundation. Weaver had first heard of the analyzer at a meeting in Paris with Sven Rosseland in 1932. Making plans for his new Institute of Theoretical Physics at the University of Oslo, Rosseland was interested in acquiring an analyzer with Rockefeller money to facilitate astrophysical calculations.[26] Weaver visited Bush in November to see the machine for himself, and he was "very much

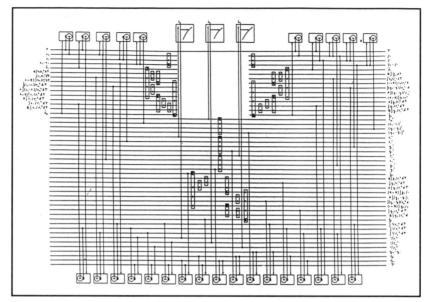

Fig. 8—Diagram of the Differential Analyzer set up to solve the Vallarta-Lemaitre cosmic ray problem.

impressed." An applied mathematician, Weaver was undoubtedly intrigued by the analyzer's practical applications as well as Bush's claim that a machine only twice as big could solve the three-body problem.[27] He came away from this first meeting with the feeling that it was "a matter of first-rate scientific importance for the Foundation to aid in disseminating knowledge concerning this new and extremely effective scientific device."[28]

Always ready to seize the moment, Bush began an active campaign to persuade Weaver that the analyzer project deserved large-scale support. "To dream in rather a definite way" was characteristic of Bush, and he made a point of keeping Weaver up-to-date on the progress of the three-body problem.[29] He shared as well his ideas concerning an improved computer, and reported that it was "going to become possible to produce something quite startling." Foremost was the possibility of enabling the analyzer to switch rapidly from one problem to another in the manner of the automatic telephone exchange.[30] He also shared with Weaver the prospect of unwelcome competition. The interest of men like Hartree and Rosseland provoked Bush to write that "with all modesty, I think that this radical development should be in my own hands," and foundation support would assure that. "It is rather hard . . . to appreciate the extent of the struggle which is necessary to overcome even simple mechanical difficulties in a device of this sort."[31]

The Depression discouraged the foundation from responding to Bush's overtures until the spring of 1935, when it awarded MIT a preliminary grant of $10,000 to complete the study of the improved analyzer.[32] Within the year Bush reported that the new machine was easily in reach and would incorporate three improvements: the automatic electrical interconnection of machine elements, increased precision in the working of the integrators, and a "function unit" designed to translate digitally coded mathematical functions into continuous electrical signals. The new machine seemed just over the horizon and he looked forward to the time when the institute, as he wrote to Weaver, would "become a center of analysis of a certain important type, to which research workers everywhere will turn for their solutions of their equations."[33] In March 1936 the foundation awarded MIT $85,000 for three years to build the Rockefeller Differential Analyzer.

The next few years were enthusiastic but frustrating. Bush's enthusiasm for invention was contagious, and the crew working on the new machine thoroughly enjoyed its work under him.[34] Yet his predictions proved overly optimistic. More precise integrators were developed with little difficulty, as were the servomechanisms needed to create the electrical connections between elements. But other problems with which the group had less experience proved more difficult. The function unit, as it turned out, was not complete even by the end of the war. The most frustrating problem involved automatic control. Intended to work on multiple problems simultaneously, the analyzer needed to be able to assign computing elements to different problems quickly, efficiently, and automatically, even as one problem finished and another began. The matter introduced "extraordinarily complicated difficulties" into the design of the machine.[35] In essence, the earlier devices had been dedicated machines, assembled anew each time an equation was to be solved. The automatic control of the new machine posed, in fact, a software problem, and it is not surprising that Bush and his team should have found it unsettling. Moreover, Bush had been MIT's vice-president and dean of engineering since 1932, and his duties were attracting more of his energies. In Bush's absence responsibility for the project fell on the shoulders of Sam Caldwell. Still, the project was in good hands and Weaver felt that "things were going exceptionally well."[36] When Bush announced he would leave MIT to become president of the Carnegie Institution of Washington, the project was dealt a serious blow.

Before he left for Washington, however, he brought to fruition his plans for a center of analysis. Along with James Conant, Frank Jewett, and Irvin Stewart, Bush was a member of the National Research Council's Committee on Scientific Aids to Learning. In February, Bush had received from Stewart a letter suggesting the publication of a catalog of important scientific instruments available to investigators. He informed Stewart of MIT's work on machine analysis, writing:

> There should be created in this country a center of mechanical analysis amply manned and equipped for such work, to turn out tables and solve actual problems for research workers everywhere. We have the ambition to create such a center.... To do this we will need support, but I can think of no place where support could be given to a program that would have more general benefit upon research programs in almost every branch of science throughout the country.[37]

The committee (which apparently received a portion of its funds from the Carnegie Corporation) submitted a proposal to the corporation on Bush's behalf. His maneuvers were successful and in January 1939 the corporation awarded MIT $45,000 for two years to establish a Center of Analysis with Sam Caldwell as its director. The center would house and coordinate the battery of computational devices developed at MIT over the years, with its centerpiece being the new Rockefeller Analyzer, undoubtedly the largest aid to learning the committee ever supported. The center was to provide assistance with problems of computation and foster research into computational and analytical tools.[38]

With Bush gone and development plaguing the engineers, progress on the new calculator slowed. While the older Differential Analyzer carried the growing load of the center's computations, Caldwell and his staff found the time to pursue other projects. In fact, by February 1941 work on a Rapid Arithmetical Computing Machine had come to occupy the major part of the center's research.[39] Bush had initiated study of an arithmetical machine at the end of 1936 in conjunction with cryptographic work for the government. Unlike the analyzers, this device was meant to deal with large volumes of arithmetic calculations at high speed. The design of the computer included a keyboard for entering data, an input unit for inserting numbers at appropriate moments in the process of computation, a control unit to coordinate machine operations automatically, an output unit, a storage unit for holding numbers temporarily during computation, and the computing unit. Bush attacked the problem of the high-speed computing element first with the help of a grant from the National Cash Register Company. By the fall of 1939, Bush, Sam Caldwell, Mark Radford, and others had devised a number of high-speed devices including vacuum-tube counting rings and a matrix switch that would utilize, in one of its forms, the magnetic properties of molybdenum or chrome permalloy rings.[40] (See fig. 9.)

By the time the first demonstration of the Rockefeller Analyzer was held on December 13, 1941, the project was two and a half years behind schedule. Convinced that Caldwell's staff was being distracted by other work and facing the imminent cessation of outside financing for the center, Karl Compton delivered an ultimatum: Make the analyzer self-supporting by October or the institute would suspend the project.[41] The president's concerns were undoubtedly aggravated by outside events. Six days before Caldwell's demonstration, the Japanese had bombed Pearl Harbor.

* * *

When Caldwell returned to peacetime work at the end of the war, he faced the challenge of revitalizing the center's programs. Given the transformations wrought at MIT by the war, this proved an impossible task. In the first instance, the war accelerated a generational change in the institute's staff. With both Caldwell and Hazen preoccupied with the affairs of the National Defense Research Committee, supervision of the center fell to Richard Taylor, the young assistant who had worked on the function unit and automatic control. When Caldwell tried to regain control after the war, he found that Taylor enjoyed running the center and felt he ought to go on doing so.[42]

These shifts in personal relationships were complemented by institutional changes. After the war, when Caldwell found his colleague

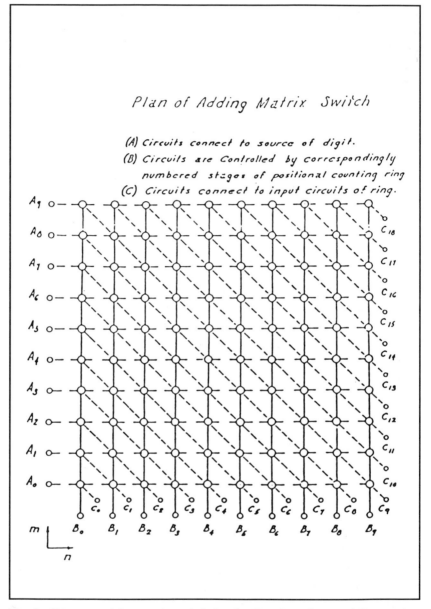

Fig. 9—Diagram of the matrix switch for the Rapid Arithmetical Computing Machine.

Gordon Brown promoted "over his head," he began to doubt the extent of administrative support for the center.[43] Be that as it may, Brown's success certainly had cause. He had served as the wartime director of the Servomechanisms Laboratory established in 1940 as an outgrowth of a training program for naval fire control officers. By the war's end the laboratory had a staff of almost a hundred and had developed considerable expertise in the field of fire control systems. Since these involved computing devices, the lab inevitably encroached on territory once occupied solely by the center and the Differential Analyzer. The Servomechanisms Lab is only one example of the massive institutional adjustments provoked at MIT by the war's demand for mission-oriented research and the consequent influx of federal defense money.[44]

Nevertheless, Caldwell worked hard to reinvigorate the Center of Analysis. His strategy was to turn, once again, to the Rockefeller Foundation. Spurred on by developments in digital computing at the University of Pennsylvania and at the Institute for Advanced Study in Princeton, Caldwell created a plan designed to reassert MIT's leadership in the field of computing. Aware that the center was no longer the sole repository of necessary skills, he proposed cooperation between the center, the Mathematics Department, and the Research Laboratory of Electronics established at the end of the war with the dissolution of the Radiation Lab. The center would be responsible for the design and construction of a new computer, the research lab for the basic electronic components, and the math department for the applied mathematics that was assuming greater importance in the design and construction of computers. In short order Rockefeller awarded Caldwell and the institute $100,000 to study computer design and the possibilities of the new electronic machines.[45]

Within these revised plans for the center, it is clear that Caldwell intended the Rockefeller Analyzer to play a continuing role. Indeed, in their 1945 account of the new machine, he and Bush had promised a series of future publications detailing innovations for which the present issue had lacked space. But for Taylor, the center and the science of computing had outgrown their dependence on mechanical analysis, despite Hazen's 1941 claim that the analyzer marked the start of a new era in mechanized calculus. As Taylor ironically noted in a memorandum outlining the new program, one of the analyzer's drawbacks reflected the sophisticated mathematics with which it dealt. Well-suited to differential equations, the analyzer bumbled arithmetic. Furthermore, the mechanical inertia of its operating parts limited its speed and accuracy.[46]

As it turned out, Caldwell's cooperative program failed to materialize. The Research Laboratory had its hands full with contract work funded by the military, and the mathematician central to Caldwell's plan, Norbert Wiener, proved a reluctant and irascible partner.[47] For Warren Weaver, who appreciated the need for first-rate mathematical help if MIT was to compete with such high-powered teams as John von Neumann, RCA, and the Institute for Advanced Study, the "time for mathematical thinking [was] fast slipping away."[48] Yet Caldwell's center would probably have been in trouble in any event. No longer occupying a privileged position in the study of computing, and with government support readily and generally available at other sites, the center could make only a token contribution to the vigorous and competitive boom in postwar computing. Not only was it ill-prepared to compete with ENIAC and the Princeton IAS computer, but it faced a fatal challenge within MIT itself.

In the winter of 1944, the institute and the navy had agreed to develop an Airplane Stability and Control Analyzer to serve as a universal flight simulator for the design of military aircraft. The mission fell within the province of the Servomechanisms Lab, and Gordon Brown assigned the project to Jay Forrester, a young research assistant from Nebraska. The original plans called for a cockpit with flight controls, an engineering station, and computing equipment. Forrester had first intended to use an analyzer as the computing element but soon realized, as had Taylor, that the mechanical principle of Bush's computer severely restricted its speed. The allure of computer building soon swept away the other elements of the plan, and Forrester and his team in the Servomechanisms Lab set out to develop a reliable, ultra-high-speed machine capable of operating in real time. The funding provided by the navy was generous. Whereas the Rockefeller Foundation had granted the Center of Analysis $100,000 for its computer study, in 1945-46 alone the navy alloted Forrester $875,000. In 1949 Forrester was spending the navy's money at the rate of $100,000 a month. By 1951 he had succeeded in constructing Whirlwind, the first real-time electronic digital computer.[49]

The Whirlwind project accentuated the inadequacies of the Center of Analysis and of the Differential Analyzer as significant influences in the study of computing. In the spring of 1946, only halfway through the center's two-year study, Compton returned to the foundation the $50,000 which the institute had so far spent. The Whirlwind project, he said, was fulfilling the objectives of the Rockefeller grant with such "vigor" and on such a substantially larger scale that the expenditure of foundation money for the same purpose was not only unjustified but "foolish."[50]

* * *

How does one tell the story of a machine? On what categories should the analysis rest, within what interpretive framework should one search for the meaning of engineering artifacts? However the historian chooses to answer these questions, utility must certainly play a role. Bush's analyzers were successful, to a large extent, because they were able to alleviate computational frustrations within electrical engineering and in scientific fields where theoretical advances had surpassed the stratagems of applied mathematicians. When faster machines based on a radically different technology became available after the war, in part as a consequence of new sources of funding, those who needed machine aids in computation could turn elsewhere. But there are other categories than utility, or, maybe, broader sorts of utility than so far invoked in our account. As John Kasson has shown us in *Amusing the Million* and *Civilizing the Machine,* machines exist not only as tools, but also as symbols. Bush's analyzers did indeed do more than simply compute *x(t)*. To flesh out our story of this particular machine, we must discover what this something else was.

Weaver was right when he reminded Caldwell that the analyzer had "a very considerable educational value." In 1928 Bush had attempted to justify the expense of the Product Integraph in the course of an article for the *Tech Engineering News.* The integraph, he said, enabled its users to cope with difficult mathematical equations. But it also provided "the man who studies it a grasp of the innate meaning of the differential equation." For this man "one part at least of formal mathematics will become a live thing."[51] Years later, Bush recounted an anecdote that made the same point. When the army wanted to build their own machine at the Aberdeen Proving Ground, he lent them a mechanic who had been hired as an inexperienced draftsman to help with the construction of the MIT calculator. The army wanted to pay the man machinist's wages; Bush insisted he be hired as a consultant with appropriate pay:

> I never consciously taught this man any part of the subject of differential equations; but in building that machine, managing it, he learned what differential equations were himself. He got to the point where when some professor was using the machine and got stuck ... he could discuss the problem with the user and very often find out what was wrong. It was very interesting to discuss this subject with him because he had learned the calculus in mechanical terms—a strange approach, and yet he understood it. That is, he did not understand it in any formal sense, but he understood the fundamentals; he had it under his skin.[52]

Studying the analyzers might help get the calculus under one's skin; but it taught something more as well. Continuing his justification of the integraph for his *Tech* audience of 1928, Bush struggled to put into words other tacit qualities expressed by the calculator:

> Before a man can build with his hands a seaworthy boat he must patiently learn to saw to a line and plane to an accurate surface .... The study of engineering mathematics becomes soul-satisfying only when one begins to grasp the power that lies in the ability to think straight in the midst of complexity, and visualizes the relationship between such reasoning and that engineering accomplishment which is useful and admirable, seaworthy and a thing of beauty.[53]

"To think straight in the midst of complexity." For young engineers coming of age in the glory years of Herbert Hoover, this was not the least of the lessons taught by the Differential Analyzer. Bush's expectations were not his alone. They were, in fact, constitutive of the early 20th-century culture of engineering.

The intellectual and ethical idioms embedded in the analyzers arose out of the classrooms, laboratories, and shops of the turn-of-the-century engineering school. Especially in the matter of mathematical pedagogy and in notions of graphic language do we discover precedents for Bush's claims regarding his computers. The historian can insinuate himself into the somewhat alien frame of mind of that early environment by listening in on a conversation which took place at Tufts

College between Samuel Earle and a student just a few years before Bush arrived as an undergraduate in 1909. Earle had been entrusted with the daunting task of teaching English composition to engineers, a new project at the time, and had established the practice of meeting his students in the shop or drafting room to discuss their writing exercises. One day he found himself having difficulty explaining to a student how his essay, in its attempt to portray the character of a man, had failed to convey any but his most superficial qualities. The drawing instructor, who had overheard the conversation, at some point interrupted with the question, "How about the dotted line?" The student, Earle tells us, saw the point at once.[54] Familiar with the use of dotted lines in mechanical drawings to depict invisible features and catalyzed by the remark of his drawing teacher, Earle's student was able to apply his knowledge of a more familiar language to one less familiar.

This anecdote suggests that the artifacts of engineering, particularly in the context of the school, can be interpreted as exercises in language. It suggests also that in the particular context of the turn-of-the-century engineering school the student was expected to move with facility between a number of different language communities serving as translator and interpreter; that the primary language on which the others, such as physics and mathematics, depended derived from the visual, tangible elements of the shop and laboratory. In such a setting the Graphic Language was a fundamental skill for the student engineer.

Gardner Anthony, for many years the dean of engineering at Tufts College, was an acknowledged master of mechanical drawing and graphics in the engineering curriculum. In 1922 in a small book with a long title, *An Introduction to the Graphic Language; the Vocabulary, Grammatical Construction, Idiomatic Use, and Historical Development with Special Reference to the Reading of Drawings,* Anthony summarized ideas he had been developing for over three decades and which formed the basis for the course he taught at Tufts. Drawing, he felt, was a universal language and possessed, like other languages, its own vocabulary, orthography, grammar, and literature. He first introduced his students to the vocabulary and idioms of simple pictorial graphics, continued to the more complex grammatical conventions of perspective drawing and descriptive geometry, and concluded his course with the topic of penmanship.

Anthony meant by penmanship not simply lettering, but the whole range of techniques by which ideas were transcribed from mind to paper with the help of such instruments as pencils, triangles, T-squares, compasses, graph paper, and drafting boards. Orthography, in fact, was an exercise in writing straight and in thinking straight. In the Graphic Language Anthony and fellow engineering educators found what they believed was "an exceptional cultural subject for strengthening the power and habit of exact thinking, that most difficult of all habits to fix, and for training the constructive imagination . . . to visualize quickly and accurately . . . ." "[I]t is the power and habit of observing accurately that marks one of the fundamental differences between the incapable man and the man of power." Ultimately drawing would promote not only clear thinking, but with the constructive power it evoked it would also become "drawing in relation to life."[55] When Bush claimed that the study of the Differential Analyzer, constructed from the material of the shop, laboratory, and drafting room, promoted the ability to think straight in the midst of complexity, he was echoing the virtues of Gardner Anthony's Graphic Language.

The penchant of engineers for the graphic idiom pervaded their notions of mathematical pedagogy. And here engineers found themselves in a dilemma which reflected the course of development of 19th-century mathematics. In the United States the community of mathematicians had acquired by the end of the century the rudiments of professional identity and were becoming noticed for activity in pure mathematics for the first time by European observers. Ironically, however, this maturation of the mathematical community threatened the traditional relationship between mathematics and the arts and sciences. Consequently, just when numerous recently established technical schools were discovering the need to teach their students more sophisticated mathematics like the calculus, many mathematicians were unable or unwilling to meet their practical demands.[56] While the disciplinary status of mathematics and engineering differed in Europe, there too the abstraction of modern mathematics frustrated the needs of engineers and experimentalists for adequate analytical tools.

The years around the turn of the century thus witnessed the growth of a movement to reform the teaching of mathematics. The movement was largely spearheaded by engineers and first took definite shape in

Britain with the work of the mechanical engineer and educator John Perry. His most important work was done at Finsbury Technical College in London after 1882, when he pioneered a course in practical mathematics for engineers that emphasized practical examples, the use of graph paper for the presentation of problems (a Perry innovation, apparently), and mechanical devices for measurement and computation. Contradicting the common opinion that calculus, given its essential formal rigor, was not a subject easily taught to engineers, Perry insisted that "there is no useful mathematical tool which an engineer may not learn to use. A man learns to use the Calculus as he learns to use the chisel or the file on actual concrete bits of work, and it is on this idea that I act in teaching the use of the Calculus to Engineers."[57] Perry's efforts helped modernize the teaching of mathematics in Britain, and by 1908 an observer could note the growing attention paid to mathematics "on its experimental and graphical side . . . exemplified by the use of drawing-boards, improved mathematical instruments, squared-paper," and the provision of mathematical laboratories "well-stocked with clay, cardboard, wire, wooden, metal and other models and materials, and apparatus for investigation of form, mensuration and movement. . . ."[58]

The "Perry Movement" percolated through the mathematics and engineering communities in the United States as well, encouraging the revision of curricula and the writing of new texts. The most eloquent proponent of practical mathematics in this country was E. H. Moore, the chairman of the mathematics department at the University of Chicago and a major figure in the American mathematical establishment. One of the architects of his discipline's new professionalism, Moore had nevertheless absorbed the concern of the great German mathematician Felix Klein that the increasing abstraction of modern mathematics threatened to impoverish the teaching of mathematics and its applications to science and engineering. In his presidential address to the American Mathematical Society in 1903, Moore proposed a program designed to revitalize mathematical pedagogy for students at all levels. Based on the methods of Perry and incorporating the approach of engineering educators, Moore's new curriculum centered around "arithmetic computations, mechanical drawing and graphical methods generally, in continuous relation with problems of physics and chemistry and engineering," and pursued in the mathematical laboratory. Educated in this tangible environment, the student would acquire "a feeling towards his mathematics extremely different from that which is met with only too frequently—a feeling that mathematics is indeed itself a fundamental reality of the domain of thought, and not merely a matter of symbols and arbitrary rules and conventions."[59] By 1910 the teaching of mathematics in most engineering schools thoroughly reflected the precepts of Anthony, Perry, and Moore. Practical mathematics and the Graphic Language complemented the practical demands of the schools and helped cultivate students whose thoughts about the world were composed of the symbols of shop and laboratory. This was an engineering curriculum which separated "the incapable man and the man of power" and discovered in the discipline of orthography the habit of thinking straight in the midst of complexity.

The early engineering school, then, was a repository of idioms which found expression in the Differential Analyzer. Looking closer, we can discover not only the idioms but also the first edition, so to speak, of the text that Bush and his colleagues would revise more than once before producing the most successful of their editions, the analyzer of 1931. During the course of his lectures on the Graphic Language, Anthony dwelt for a while on the vocabulary of topograpical maps, illustrating for his students contour lines and profiles of elevation. It is in a setting such as this that the young Bush might have been introduced to the problems faced by surveyors and the instruments they had at their disposal. Profiles were commonly obtained by running levels, and required several men, careful fieldwork, and tedious data reduction afterward. Bush set himself the task of mechanizing this job as an exercise for his master's thesis. His invention was an instrument box slung between bicycle wheels; as it was pushed along the path for which one desired a profile, a device within the box continuously recorded the required elevation onto a revolving drum (figs. 10, 11, and 12).

"It was quite a gadget," Bush admitted, and it earned him his degree. He patented the invention, which he called a Profile Tracer, and attempted to interest several companies in its manufacture. However, his entrepreneurial attempts flopped and he sagely charged the invention to experience. But if this first calculator failed in the commercial

Fig. 10—Bush testing the Profile Tracer near the reservoir at Tufts College.

market, it had a happier future. What Bush had in fact invented was an arrangement of gears, shafts, and servo-driven pens which translated mechanical motion into graphical mathematics. And the key mechanism was a disc integrator with which he would "have quite a lot to do."[60]

In 1919, after a year with General Electric and several more teaching at Tufts, Bush joined the staff of MIT's Department of Electrical Engineering. In many ways the institute he joined was like the college he left. The curriculum stressed mechanical skill, work in shop and laboratory, and mathematics and physics couched in the graphic idiom. The calculus was introduced to freshmen in a manner which emphasized graphical presentation and intuition over abstract rigor. In Joseph Lipka's Mathematical Laboratory, students could hone their problem-solving talents with graphical methods and mechanical methods of various kinds—slide rules, planimeters, a plethora of nomographic charts, and instruments for the mechanical integration of areas under curves.[61] All in all, the program at MIT still carried about it "the odor of the shop," a description Calvin Woodward had once applied to early electrical engineering.[62]

But in other ways MIT was very different, and a variety of forces were converging to transform the environment and enlarge opportunities when Bush arrived. First, the decade between the Great War and the Depression was a bull market for engineering. Enrollment in the Electrical Engineering Department almost doubled in this period.

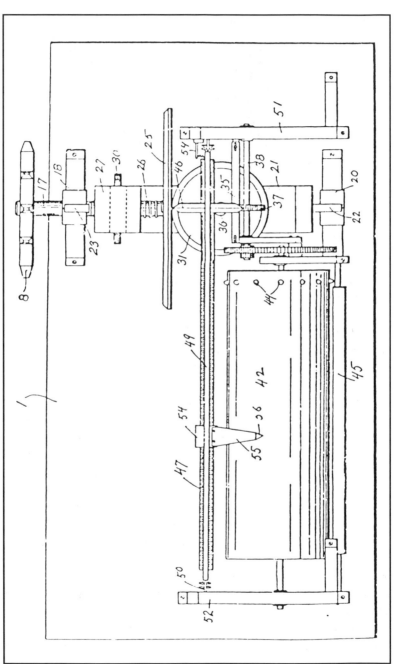

Fig. 11—A drawing from Bush's patent application illustrating the inner mechanism of the Profile Tracer.

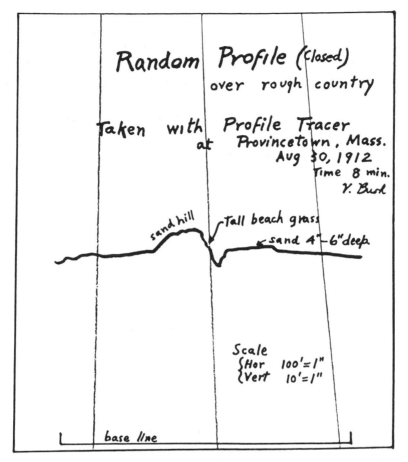

Fig. 12—A reproduction of a typical tracing found in Bush's master's thesis.

Furthermore, the decade witnessed the rapid expansion of graduate programs, especially in electrical engineering, which had been insignificant before the war.[63] Second, as we have seen, the development of electrical technology and the growing complexity of systems and circuits propelled the growth of circuit analysis and the aggressive search for methods of solution of mathematical equations beyond the scope of formal techniques. Third, the interwar years found corporate and philanthropic donors more willing to fund research and development within the university. All of these factors, as well as a diffuse public appreciation for the expert skills of the engineer which peaked in the 1920s, worked to Bush's advantage at MIT. The Profile Tracer might have flopped in the commercial market, but within the bull market of the engineering school where inventions, in addition to being useful, could be read as books, Bush's mathematical practice texts were a great success.

At this point our story becomes familiar. The technical success of the analyzers, the opportunities they provided for graduate research, the possibilities of new applications on the frontiers of science, and the availability of support from private foundations encouraged Bush to produce a bigger and better version of his popular 1931 computer. Ringed round by tantalizing problems in atomic structure and cosmic radiation, he and his colleagues labored to develop a new machine which would in a flash rearrange itself to tackle new and more difficult problems. But what is most significant about the Rockefeller Differential Analyzer is what remained the same. Electrically or not, automatically or not, the newest edition of Bush's analyzer still interpreted mathematics in terms of mechanical rotations, still depended on expertly machined wheel-and-disc integrators, and still drew its answers as curves. Differential equations and contours of elevation—Bush's computers were very much the offspring of the early Profile Tracer.

* * *

How does one tell the story of a machine? If nothing else, the evolution of the analyzers teaches us that there is more to machines than has met our eyes. Like all expensive investments, these machines were sensitive to the demands of utility, and when Weaver and Caldwell admitted in 1950 that the analyzer project had been overtaken by the whole new field of computer science, they conceded that such demands could be decisive. But Bush's machines inhabited another world as well, one where utility had a distinctively bookish aspect. Here, in the marketplace of the school, the analyzers were exercises in the language of early 20th-century engineering. Forged in the machine shop, the analyzers spoke the Graphic Language while they drew profiles through the landscape of mathematics. The student could find in these machine texts a catalog of his technical universe, lessons on the nature of mathematics and its instruments, and even expressions of the ethos which pervaded engineering education. Variations on the theme of mechanical analysis, the analyzers embodied an engineering culture belonging to the first decades of our century. When engineers and their new corporate and federal supporters turned to the problems of computation at the end of the Second World War, they discovered the need for new texts in a more modern idiom, composed by a younger generation of inventive authors.

Endnotes

1. The first demonstration of the still incomplete analyzer was held on December 13, 1941. By March 1943, when the staff and facilities of the center had been converted entirely to war work, about half of the analyzer was in operation. S. H. Caldwell to Warren Weaver, December 14, 1941. The letter is in the Rockefeller Archive Center, in RF1.1/224/2/25. See also Caldwell to Bush, April 19, 1943, Bush Papers, Library of Congress.
2. The small band of digital pioneers would argue this claim. But ENIAC did not become operational until some months after the war, and, while the Harvard-IBM Mark I was completed in mid-1944, both it and the Bell relay machine proved significantly slower than the analyzer for the computation of trajectories. The development of digital computers, especially as logic machines, seems to have been further along in Great Britain largely because of Alan Turing. For their history, see H. H. Goldstine, *The Computer from Pascal to von Neumann* (Princeton, 1972); Nancy Stern, *From ENIAC to UNIVAC: An Appraisal of the Eckert-Mauchly Computers* (Bedford, Mass., 1981); N. Metropolis, J. Howlett, and G. Rota, eds., *A History of Computing in the Twentieth Century* (New York, 1980); and Paul Ceruzzi, *Reckoners: The Prehistory of the Digital Computer, from Relays to the Stored Program Concept, 1935-1945* (Westport, Conn., 1983). For Turing and his interest in computing machines as a response to the crisis in the foundations of mathematics, see William F. Aspray, Jr., "From Mathematical Constructivity to Computer Science: Alan Turing, John von Neumann, and the Origins of Computer Science in Mathematical Logic" (Ph.D. diss., Univ. of Wisconsin, Madison, 1980); and Alan Hodges, *Alan Turing: The Enigma* (New York, 1983).
3. See *Life*, January 14, 1946; also, *Popular Science Monthly*, vol. 148 (1946).
4. For a valuable bibliography of analyzer literature, see the notes to chap. 5 of E. C. Berkeley, *Giant Brains, or Machines That Think* (New York, 1949).
5. MIT *President's Reports* for 1940, p. 101; and 1941, p. 28.
6. The analyzer and machines of a similar type did not, of course, disappear overnight. The Rockefeller calculator was not dismantled until 1954 (personal communication from Frank Verzuh, June 4, 1982). Descendants of Bush's analyzers still constitute a modest weapon in the armory of engineers, as can be surmised by a glance at the current texts on library shelves.

7. See Warren Weaver's project diaries for March 17, 1950. The diaries
    Weaver kept as a foundation officer are preserved at the Rockefeller
    Archive Center.
8. See Nancy Stern (n. 2 above) on ENIAC; for Whirlwind, see Kent Redmond
    and Thomas Smith, *Project Whirlwind, the History of a Pioneer Computer*
    (Bedford, Mass., 1980).
9. Weaver to Caldwell, March 27, 1950, in RF1.1/224/2/26.
10. The concern with such problems is obvious in the pages of the *Journal of
    the American Institute of Electrical Engineers*. In general, see Thomas Hughes,
    Networks of Power: Electrification in Western Society, 1880-1930 (Baltimore,
    1983). In particular, see for example V. Bush and R. D. Booth, "Power
    System Transients," *Journal of the American Institute of Electrical Engineers*
    44 (1925):229-240.
11. See the MIT *President's Reports* for the period; also, Herbert R. Stewart, "A
    New Recording Product Integraph and Multiplier," MIT master's thesis,
    1925; and Karl Wildes and Nilo Lindgren, *A Century of Electrical Engineer-
    ing and Computer Science at MIT, 1882-1982* (Cambridge, Mass., 1985).
12. Stewart; John Carson, "A Mathematical Discussion of the Building-up of
    Sinusoidal Currents in Loaded Lines . . ." (New York, 1925); C. P.
    Steinmetz, *Theory and Calculation of Transient Electric Phenomena and Oscil-
    lations* (New York, 1911).
13. During 1924-25, the development of the Product Integraph was the
    majority activity in the Research Division of the Electrical Engineering
    Department. For a description of the first Product Integraph, see V. Bush,
    F. D. Gage, and H. R. Stewart, "A Continuous Recording Integraph,"
    Journal of the Franklin Institute 212 (1927):63-84. My account of the origins
    of the integraph is based on materials in the MIT Archives and on
    discussions with Karl Wildes, April 12 and 13, 1984. It might be that
    Stewart never closely studied the Thomson papers. When Bush first
    suggested the project, he directed Stewart to Fred Dellenbaugh's 1921
    master's thesis as a fairly complete collection of "mechanical calculating
    contrivances which had been developed in the past" and in which he
    would have found a condensed description and diagrams of the Thomson
    integrator emphasizing its use in harmonic analysis, that is, with equa-
    tions of the form

$$\int f(x)g(x)dx.$$

Stewart to Bush, May 4, 1926, Hazen Papers, MIT Archives; Frederick
Dellenbaugh, "Harmonic Analysis, a Critical Compendium of Methods
and Devices for the Analysis of Complex Alternating Current Waves with
Suggestions for Improvements and Discussion of the Requirements of
Such Devices," MIT master's thesis, 1921. E. C. Berkeley and L. Wain-
wright, in *Computers, Their Operation and Application* (New York, 1956),

claim that Wainwright invented a "virtual prototype of the differential analyzer" in 1923 and communicated it to Bush in 1924. They cite his response to a later query: "I have become quite familiar with the literature of this subject, and as far as I know you [Wainwright] were the first person after Kelvin to proceed in study along these lines and the first to suggest a machine elaborated in detail for the handling of ballistic equations," pp. 114-15. Obviously, the analyzers incorporated the work of many people. As will become clear, however, their deeper origins lie not with Wainwright, Kelvin, Bush's colleagues, or even with Bush himself. They reflect a common universe of technical discourse that reaches back to the turn of the century and beyond.

14. V. Bush and K. Gould, "Temperature Distribution along a Filament," *Physical Review* 29 (1927):337-45.
15. Wildes (n. 13 above); Gordon Brown, "Eloge: Harold Locke Hazen, 1901-1980," *Annals of the History of Computing* 3 (1981):4-12; the sketch and Bush's memo are in the Hazen Papers, MIT Archives.
16. V. Bush and H. L. Hazen, "Integraph Solution of Differential Equations," *Journal of the Franklin Institute* 204 (1927):577.
17. For a list of topics, see n. 6 in V. Bush, "The Differential Analyzer," *Journal of the Franklin Institute* 212 (1931):447-88.
18. Wildes (n. 13 above).
19. Waldo Lyon, a departmental colleague, contributed the new name, apparently in response to the following: "We need some new names! The so-called product integraph was much more than an integraph. It was a machine for solving differential equations. . . . In token of appreciation to one who suggests a name which is accepted, the following procedure is proposed: The new machine will be set up to solve a differential equation, and the recording pencil will in this manner be caused to draw on the recording platen the name of the successful contestant. This will be accompanied by all due and proper ceremony." MIT Archives, AC13, Box 3, Folder 69. Dugald Jackson informs us that the Differential Analyzer cost MIT approximately $25,000. Jackson to Jackson, Jr., March 17, 1932. Jackson Papers, MIT Archives, Box 3, Folder 185.
20. Brown (n. 15 above); C. W. Nieman, "Torque Amplifier," *American Machinist* 66 (1927):895-97.
21. "The Differential Analyzer" (n. 17 above), p 459.
22. See the "List of Problems Studied with the Aid of the Differential Analyzer," attached to material sent by Bush to Warren Weaver, April 22, 1935, RF1.1/224/2/22.
23. P. M. Morse and W. P. Allis, "The Effect of Exchange on the Scattering of Slow Electrons from Atoms," *Physical Review* 44 (1933):269.
24. D. R. Hartree, "Approximate Wave Functions and Atomic Field for Mercury," *Physical Review* 46 (1934):738-43; also the Hartree citations in the Berkeley bibliography (n. 4 above).

25. See George Gray's draft, "A Roomful of Brains," returned by Caldwell to Weaver, December 17, 1937, in RF1.1/224/2/23. For the study, see Vallarta and Lemaitre, "On the Geomagnetic Analysis of Cosmic Radiation," *Physical Review* 49 (1936):719-26.
26. "Memorandum of Professor L. R. Jones' talk with Professor Sven Rosseland, Paris, July 6, 1932," in RF1.1/767D/2/19.
27. Weaver's diaries, November 21, 1932.
28. Weaver to Lauder Jones, December 6, 1932, in RF1.1/767D/2/19.
29. Bush to Weaver, January 6, 1933, RF1.1/767D/2/20; the phrase is Bush's.
30. Bush to Weaver, April 15, 1933, in RF1.1/767D/2/20.
31. Bush to Weaver, July 7, 1933, in RF1.1/224/2/22.
32. See the grant history in the Rockefeller files on the MIT Differential Analyzer Project.
33. Bush to Weaver, March 17, 1936, in RF1.1/224/2/23.
34. "To V. Bush, GREETINGS! 'To Doc' would perhaps be a better salutation for this note of farewell and Godspeed, for among ourselves we have always called you Doc as the title most appropriately expressing the affection and respect we have felt in working with you.

    "We would not have you leave without saying that it has been fun to build a Differential Analyzer with you. We think that you will agree that it has been fun, but we are not going to ask you to agree with some other feelings of ours, for of those we are better judges than you. We know, for example, the many ways in which we have felt your influence: in your generous praise for our successes, in your sympathetic analyses of our failures, in the enlivening breezes you have brought to our developmental doldrums. . . . The Differential Analyzer Staff." In RF1.1/224/2.
35. Weaver diaries, January 10, 1939.
36. Ibid.
37. Bush to Stewart, February 28, 1938, in the file on the "Support of a Center of Analysis at MIT" in the records of the Carnegie Corporation of New York.
38. Bush to Stewart, June 13, 1938; Stewart to Frederick Keppel, July 15, 1938, both in the Carnegie Corporation files.
39. Samuel Caldwell, "Report on Center of Analysis, July 1, 1939-February 1, 1941," in the Carnegie Corporation files.
40. W. H. Radford, "Research on A RAPID COMPUTING MACHINE," October 1939; copy from Perry Crawford, May 1982. Bush informed Weaver in October 1938 that equipment for carrying out arithmetical calculations at "almost unbelievably high rates" had already been constructed by the government and by the National Cash Register Company. Weaver diaries, October 28, 1938.
41. Weaver diaries, March 12, 1942; Caldwell to Weaver, March 13, 1942; Karl Compton to Weaver, March 14, 1942. In the event MIT, encouraged by

Weaver's offer of another $25,000, did not terminate the project. The letters are in RF1.1/224/2.

42. Weaver's diaries, April 11, 1946.

43. Ibid.

44. John Burchard, *Q.E.D., M.I.T. in World War II* (New York, 1948); Redmond and Smith (n. 8 above).

45. Excerpt, Caldwell to Weaver, January 16, 1946; grant history, both in RF1.1/224/4/31.

46. Richard Taylor, "Memorandum, Electronic Calculating Machine, 4/9/46," in RF1.1/224/4/31.

47. "Division 14, NDRC, MIT Research Laboratory in Electronics: Interim Progress Report, 3/15/46," in RF1.1/224/4/31; Weaver to Hazen, March 4, 1947; Hazen to Weaver, March 12, 1947; both in RF1.1/224/4/32.

48. Weaver to Hazen, March 4, 1947, in RF1.1/224/4/32.

49. Redmond and Smith (n. 8 above).

50. Compton to Weaver, June 26, 1947, in RF1.1/224/4/32.

51. V. Bush, "Mechanical Solutions of Engineering Problems," *Tech Engineering News,* vol. 9 (1928).

52. V. Bush, *Pieces of the Action* (New York, 1970), p. 262.

53. Bush, "Mechanical Solutions."

54. Samuel Earle, "English in the Engineering School at Tufts College," *Proceedings of the Society for the Promotion of Engineering Education* 19 (1911):44.

55. Thomas French, "The Educational Side of Engineering Drawing," ibid., vol. 21 (1913):109.

56. For an aging but valuable account of the history of mathematics in the United States, see: D. E. Smith and J. Ginsburg, *A History of Mathematics in America before 1900* (Chicago, 1934); the articles by Struik, Grabner, and Birkhoff in *The Bicentennial Tribute to American Mathematics, 1776-1976* (Washington, D.C., 1977), ed. J. Dalton Tarwater; *A History of Mathematics Education in the United States and Canada,* the 32nd Yearbook of the National Council of Teachers of Mathematics, 1970; and E. H. Moore's presidential address to the American Mathematical Society in 1903. For a new look at the way that limited mathematical training influenced the development of American science, see John Servos, "Taking the Measure of Nature: Mathematics and the Education of American Scientists, 1880-1930," paper read at the 1983 meeting of the History of Science Society in Norwalk, Conn. Complaints about the scarcity of mathematicians willing to take an interest in applications could be heard as late as 1941: "Though the United States holds a position of outstanding leadership in pure mathematics, there is no school which provides an adequate mathematical training for the student who wishes to use the subject in the field of industrial applications rather than to cultivate it as an end in itself. Both science generally, and its industrial application in particular, would be

advanced if a group of suitable teachers were brought together in an institution where there was also a strong interest in the basic sciences and in engineering." Thornton Fry, "Industrial Mathematics," *American Mathematical Monthly* 48 (1941):1-39. Most of the mathematicians working in industry, Fry noted, had been trained as physicists or as electrical or mechanical engineers.

57. John Perry, *Calculus for Engineers* (London, 1897), p. 5. For more on Perry, see William Brock and Michael Price, "Squared Paper in the Nineteenth Century: Instrument of Science and Engineering, and a Symbol of Reform in Mathematical Education," *Educational Studies in Mathematics*, vol. 11 (1980).

58. Brock and Price, p. 368.

59. E. H. Moore, (n. 56 above).

60. Bush, *Pieces of the Action*, pp. 155-57; see Bush's master's thesis, "An Automatic Instrument for Recording Terrestrial Profiles," Tufts College, January 1913. Bush might not have known of the disc integrator when he devised the Profile Tracer. However, variable friction gears much like the one he designed for the Profile Tracer were well known to engineers. See, e.g., the illustration of the deal-frame in *Knight's American Mechanical Dictionary*, vol. 1, 1876.

61. L. M. Passano, *Calculus and Graphs* (New York, 1921); Joseph Lipka, *Graphical and Mechanical Computation* (New York, 1918).

62. C. M. Woodward, "Report of the Committee on Technological Education—the Relation of Technical to Liberal Education," in *Addresses and Proceedings of the National Educational Association* (1894), p. 613.

63. See the MIT *President's Reports* for the period.

A Machine for the Mind: Vannevar Bush's Memex

James M. Nyce and Paul Kahn

VANNEVAR BUSH (1890-1974) IS REMEMBERED TODAY for many things. Bush was an engineer, an inventor, a teacher, a writer, and an administrator (for detailed biographical accounts, see Anon., 1951; Wiesner, 1979). Yet for readers today perhaps his most important work is the essay "As We May Think" (Bush, 1945a), which first described Memex. Bush's writings on Memex can be viewed as a proposal for an actual machine and as a body of essays that explore the potential utility and application of new kinds of machines for managing information and representing knowledge.

Computer and information scientists today recognize Bush's article as containing the earliest description of a machine designed to support the building of trails of association through vast stores of information. For this reason, a number of present-day products and research projects in the fields of hypertext, multimedia, and information retrieval look back to Bush's Memex as a prototypical first idea. D.J. Moore, for example, begins a recent essay on multimedia functionality in personal computers:

> A multimedia document need not be experienced in any predetermined sequence. Hypertext-like techniques allow a user to peruse a document in many directions. The selection of a word or an image may trigger the display of additional images and audio to reinforce the subject. . . . This possibility was conceived in the mind of Vannevar Bush in 1945, including an imagined implementation using components that were then available. (Moore, 1990:494)

This is fairly typical of how Bush's writings are used today. However, such statements suggest that Bush had something very much like hypertext or multimedia software in mind. Was Bush prescient enough to prophecy combinations of digital information on personal computers? Why did Bush propose his ideas and where did he think they would lead?

Because "As We May Think" was published in the summer of 1945, at the end of the war effort in which Bush played a major role (Kevles,

1978:296-301), most readers make the understandable mistake of associating his ideas with the post-War information boom. In fact Memex,
both as a machine and as a vehicle for innovation and change, was a
product of the technological environment of the 1930s. This essay will
explain why Bush created the Memex and what he hoped to accomplish
with it.

We will start by examining the machines being built by Bush in the
1930s and the problems they were designed to solve. We will show how
Bush's writings on Memex were informed by both the scientific literature of the time and the American utopian tradition. In particular, we
will look at the largely forgotten role microfilm played in both these
traditions. We will then trace out the process by which Bush's Memex
essay found its way into print and discuss the impact its publication had
in 1945. We will show that the central theme of the Memex essays was
to describe a machine for locating and representing knowledge. Bush
believed Memex was the best model for such a machine because it
represented the best effort to describe a mechanical analogy to the
human brain.

The MIT Rapid Selector

The notes of the October 14, 1937 Massachusetts Institute of Technology
(MIT) Patent Committee meeting, which Bush chaired, record work on
"the Rapid Selector developed by Dr. Bush and designed to be immediately applicable in libraries and having other broader ramifications
principally in business machinery." The following spring Bush reported that "twenty-five thousand dollars have been donated to [MIT's
Research Corporation] jointly by the National Cash Register Company
and the Eastman Kodak Company for the development of apparatus for
rapid selection, on which patent applications are pending" (Patent
Committee, April 7, 1938). Bush's graduate assistant, John H. Howard,
was to head the research team for this project, which also included
Russell Coile, John Coombs, Lawrence Steinhardt, and Claude Shannon (Coile, 1954:2). Shannon, who was one of the early pioneers in
information research, later became one of Bush's major sources on
concepts of machine intelligence.

The rapid selector proposal specified that the research would be divided into three stages:

> 1. Construction of experimental equipment to test the feasibility of a device which would search reels of coded microfilm at high speed and which would copy selected frames on the fly, for printout and use.
> 2. Investigation of the practical utility of such equipment by experimental use in a library.
> 3. Further development aimed at exploration of the possibilities for introducing such equipment into libraries generally. (Bagg and Stevens, 1961:18)

A stated intention of the project was to determine how information stored on microfilm could be used in a library (see Burke, this volume, for other unstated aspects of the research agenda). Bush was not concerned in 1938 with then common applications, such as finding better ways to copy and store business records. He wanted to know if a university library's contents could be effectively delivered and used on microfilm. This was also a concern of Watson Davis and others in the documentation movement (Farkas-Conn, 1990).

At the same time, Bush was involved in the development of mechanical and photographic mechanisms for text composition. At the June 8, 1938 Patent Committee meeting, Bush read a letter from Frederick G. Fassett, the editor of *Technology Review*, "relative to a photocomposing machine whereby it was proposed to transfer typing directly to microfilm by optical means." Bush then was interested and actively pursuing the relationship between the output function of selecting information from microfilm and recording textual information onto the same media in his laboratory. Later in his career, Bush helped promote phototypesetting as a standard technology in the print and publishing industries. Here, as with the rapid selector, Bush's research involved photographic reproduction, optics, and registration issues, areas he remained interested in throughout his career. These all supported his ideas for Memex.

Bush became president of the Carnegie Institute of Washington in 1939, bringing his career as an MIT professor to a close. Carroll Wilson took over supervision of the microfilm rapid selector and photocomposer projects. By the time Bush left MIT, the parts of Memex had come together in his own mind. From Washington he wrote the first essay that described Memex in detail, "Mechanization and the Record."

The Information Problem: Design and Synthesis

In the 1930s, Bush recognized that the scientific literature was expanding faster than man's ability to understand, let alone control, it.

> There is much evidence that we are becoming bogged down today, as specialization extends and research is quickened. There is a growing mountain of research results; the investigator is bombarded with the findings and conclusions of thousands of parallel workers which he cannot find time to grasp as they appear, let alone remember; specialization becomes increasingly necessary for genuine progress, and effort [sic] to bridge between disciplines correspondingly superficial. Still we adhere rather closely, in our professional efforts, to methods of revealing, transmitting, and reviewing results which are generations old, and now inadequate for their purpose. (Bush, 1939:9)

He sought to address this problem by applying mechanization to the written record of scientific knowledge. The first step towards this design was the microfilm rapid selector. In his own words what he did at this time was to "see a public need . . . and scurry about to find a way of meeting it" (Bush, 1970:172). Having identified the problem, Bush, like the engineer he was, surveyed the existing technology, borrowed from it, and came up with a design. But Memex, the solution he proposed, required more than the microfilm rapid selector could promise. In designing Memex he drew upon analytic devices of the time (his own and others), photography, tube electronics, and mass production techniques (to insure reliability and lower unit costs).

The genesis of Memex came early in the 1930s. From the description and context, the machine with "a thousand volumes located in a couple of cubic feet in a desk, so that by depressing a few keys one could have a given page instantly projected before him" in "The Inscrutable 'Thirties" (Bush, 1933:126) seems to be its earliest image. Further, Bush himself dates Memex to 1932. His autobiography, *Pieces of the Action* (Bush, 1970:190), and "Memex Revisited" tell us that he began his work on Memex in the early thirties. In addition, there is lengthy description

of a Memex-like device in an April 14, 1937 proposal Bush sent Warren
Weaver at the Rockefeller Foundation (Bush, 1937). Reflecting back on
the matter of origins in "Memex Revisited" (Bush, 1967a:76), Bush
gives, with some arithmetic, a date of 1932. However, in none of his later
essays does Bush explore why he felt such a device was needed.

As Bush puts it in a letter to Edward Weeks at *Atlantic Monthly*, "I
do not ordinarily call myself a scientist but rather an engineer" (June 1,
1945). He elsewhere reminds us that the "applying science in an
economic manner to the needs of mankind is its [engineer's] broad
field" (Bush, 1946:137). While he recognized that the technological
details had yet to be worked out, for Bush, the engineer, Memex was a
pragmatic solution to a particular problem (for the relationship between science and engineering in America, see Layton, 1976; for Bush
as an engineer, see McMahon, 1984 and Owens, 1987). However, we
will also show that Memex was more than this.

The rapid selector machine being built at MIT (Figure 1) was a
device that combined several different technologies. The parts and even
the basic concept of the rapid selector may not have been original to

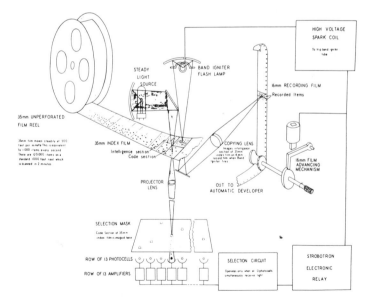

Figure 1. Schematic Diagram of Bush Rapid Selector (Bagg and Stevens,
1961:20).

Bush and his MIT team. As Buckland (forthcoming) argues, the basic concept of selecting frames from microfilm reels by means of optical sensors can be traced to the earlier work of Emanuel Goldberg in Germany. The strobotron electronic replay and capture, controlled by the photocell-driven selection circuit, was derived from work being done by MIT's Harold Edgerton.

The description of Memex in "Mechanization and the Record" comes from the same methodology Bush used to design the rapid selector: combine lower-level technologies into a single machine with a higher level function. The Memex-like machine proposed in Bush's 1937 memo to Weaver shows how much the two machines have in common. In the rapid selector, low-level mechanisms for transporting 35mm film, photo-sensors to detect coded dot patterns, and precise timing mechanisms combined to support the high-order task of information selection. In Memex, microfilm, photo-optic selection devices, keyboard controls, and dry photography would be combined to create a high-order machine that mirrored and supported the process of the human mind.

A good example of how Bush imaginatively synthesized a new machine appears in his description of how to add voice interaction to Memex. The American Telephone and Telegraph exhibit at the 1939 New York World's Fair featured "Pedro the Voder" (Voice Operation Demonstrator), an electronic human voice synthesizer which "produced . . . English-language speech using 50 phonemes" (Wurts *et al.*, 1977:39). With Memex, Bush, who either saw or read about the Voder, brought together this speech generator, a speech recognizer he knew was under development at Bell Laboratories, and the stenography and shorthand techniques then used in courtrooms and business—much like Levi-Strauss's bricoleur (1966[1962]:16-18). Bush predicted that users would accommodate themselves to limitations of the machine's linguistic abilities. He even suggests that human language should change to better accommodate mechanization.

> Our present languages are not especially adapted to this sort of mechanization, it is true. It is strange that the inventors of universal languages have not seized upon the idea of producing one which better fitted the technique for transmitting and recording speech. Mechanization may yet force the issue, especially in the scientific field; whereupon

scientific jargon would become still less intelligible to the layman. (Bush, 1945a:104)

By describing an imaginary machine, Bush selected from the existing technologies of the time and made a case for how they should develop in the future. He also speculates on the consequences that such an innovation might have. For example, in his 1937 memo he discusses how a device like Memex could both support and change academic libraries and everyday work routines at the university (Bush, 1937:5-9). In these ways, Bush's advances are not confined to normal practice or design. At the same time, Bush's work with Memex, in which he essentially combined a set of technologies, represents a middle ground between evolution and revolution in design (Vincenti, 1990:8).

Utopian Fiction and Speculative Engineering

While influenced by real machines, Memex was a machine that existed entirely on paper. The impulse to create such a speculative machine can be traced to a clear shift in Bush's writings. In 1933 Bush was about to turn 43, having risen through faculty ranks to become head of an important laboratory, dean of the School of Engineering and, a few years later, vice president of MIT, the institution that was becoming the most important technical university in America (for his career at MIT, see Wildes and Lindgren, 1985). As Owens tells us (this volume), Bush's development of the Differential Analyzer and related analog computers had placed him in the forefront of the emerging discipline of computing (for other discussions of these devices, see Birkhoff, 1980 and Bromley, 1990). The term "computer" was about to shift meaning from "a person doing manual calculations" to a machine that alone could do most of this work (Shurkin, 1984). It is at this time, in "The Inscrutable 'Thirties," which appeared in the January 1933 issue of *Technology Review*, that we find the beginnings of Memex.

"The Inscrutable 'Thirties" is an anomaly among Bush's early writings. Up to this time Bush wrote technical articles, alone or with others, in the fields of electrical and mechanical engineering. These articles were straightforward scientific writing. "The Inscrutable 'Thirties," by contrast, was a literary satire, an ironic description of the present seen from an imaginary future when an appreciation of the "difficulties surrounding a former generation" would lead the reader "to marvel that so much was accomplished with so little" (1933:123). The inversion of the time frame creates an ironic distance from which to describe the present. The result is a prophetic form, well known in utopian literature.

In the tradition of utopian literature, a prophetic author foresees the future in order to criticize the present. Thus, in "The Inscrutable 'Thirties" the narrator judges the 1930s because he already knows the future. A similar literary device had a major impact in American letters a few years before Bush was born, when Edward Bellamy published the enormously successful utopian social prophecy *Looking Backward 2000-1887* (Bellamy, 1887). Bellamy's hero, an upper-class Bostonian from 1887, awakens from an hypnotic trance to find himself in Boston 113 years later, in a nation transformed by technological advances and social reforms. By describing the positive transformations that were to take place in the future, Bellamy was able to critique late nineteenth-century America. Bellamy's work was no isolated case, and, as Kasson has pointed out (1976:183), his fiction was part of a tradition of social critics such as H. G. Wells, John Ruskin, William Morris, and Samuel Butler, who all used a dislocation in time and/or space to create a place from which to criticize the present.

As the nineteenth century came to a close, utopian fiction, initially driven by concerns about social and moral transformation, turned to technology as a medium and agent for cultural innovation. Bellamy's imagined future included innovations such as centrally broadcast music, which replaced the piano in private homes, and goods delivered from central storehouses via pneumatic tubes instead of trips to individual merchants. Segal (1985:98-99) suggests that the shift from the creation of utopian communities to the writing of utopian fiction in late nineteenth-century America was a function of the increasing social complexity of the period. The utopian imagination, which needed a fictional landscape as context in which to express its ideas and technology, became in this literature an agent of social change. Segal notes that a number of social issues of the time that inspired the utopian imagination (conservation, corporate and government reorganization, city and national planning, scientific management and technocracy) all seemed more possible through technological innovation.

Bush's writings about Memex have a place in this American tradition of technological utopianism. Americans see engineering as offering the possibility of elaboration and extrapolation from current *technology,* that dynamic combination of *structures* like buildings and roads and *machines* such as motors and automobiles (Segal, 1985:12-13). As the nineteenth century came to an end, utopian authors understood that writing about future technology "provided richer possibilities than [real] communities both for conceiving alternatives to existing society and for attracting popular support to the alternatives" (Segal, 1985:99). Extrapolations of technology from the present to the future provided a compelling and persuasive literary strategy. In the 1939 manuscript "Mechanization and the Record," Bush himself acknowledged the usefulness of this strategy:

> Undoubtedly man will learn to make synthetic rubber cheaply, undoubtedly his aircraft will fly faster, undoubtedly he will find more specific poisons to destroy his internal parasites without ruining his digestion, but what can he do to mechanically improve a book? The quandary can hardly be dodged, if one is to write more than vague generalities; and there is only one way out: frank prophesy, the attempt to preduct [sic] the future of scientific application in the implementation of thought, by extrapolation of recent trends. (Bush, 1939:6)

Bush's ideas about how technology should support intellectual work or make information more widely available were grounded in the machines being developed in his laboratory, but neither these machines nor his technical writings could entirely represent the ideas he wanted to convey. Like the utopian communities of the previous century, Bush's laboratory machines and technical writings had reached their limits. To influence the direction of the future, Bush turned to "frank prophecy," a speculative, imaginative engineering. Bush sought to trace out and explore in his essays the implications of as yet unrealized technology.

Bush's writings about Memex should be viewed as part of both the utopian impulse to envision a perfect future world and the scientocratic impulse to place the technological, scientific elite atop the cultural and political hierarchy. This kind of argument drives or is also implicit in much of Bush's later writings on public affairs (Kevles, 1978). Wagar (1988:117) argues that authors such as Bellamy and Wells represent a tradition in modern social thought that he calls "scientocracy—the vision of a technologically advanced society governed by the masters of science and applied science." Much the same can be said of Bush, though in his case the pragmatism of the engineer and a certain idealism about public service and the common good tempered these impulses. Nevertheless, Bush is quite clear that the scientific elite should, if not hold power, at least advise those who do (for Bush's contributions to national science policy, see Kevles, 1978:345-365 and Sapolsky, 1990:29-36). In fact, considerations of this kind strongly influenced where and why Bush wanted to publish his essays on Memex.

In "The Inscrutable 'Thirties" Bush does not seek quite so distant a vantage point as Bellamy's (in fact he does not specify what future he is looking back from), nor quite so broad a critique of the world as Wells'. Instead, what he wants to do is turn a fresh eye on the technology that permeates a professor's life at "some northern urban university" (i.e., MIT) and comment on the general lack of appreciation for techno-logical innovation.

His message was two-fold. First, the dirty, noisy, and imprecise technology of the 1930s affected every aspect of urban life. The ad-vances in technology during this "time of transition" were rapid and enormous. In the same year that "The Inscrutable 'Thirties" appeared, H. G. Wells published his future history of the twentieth and twenty-first centuries, *The Shape of Things To Come* (Wells, 1933). Like Bush, Wells characterized the 1930s as the "Age of Frustration" due to the period's enormous social, economic, and political turmoil, obvious even as the decade began. Bush catalogs technological innovations in transportation, telecommunications, clothing, and housing. Whereas social critics such as Wells railed against the economic inequities of the time, Bush was content to note that the world was in "the midst of the last great economic readjustment." The current economic situation may make no sense, but in Bush's view logic and a rationalism derived from science would triumph eventually.

Second, Bush wanted his readers to understand a particular source of frustration for scientists and engineers: that state of the art in the early 1930s was crude when measured against what might be possible as technology advanced.

Many of us well remember the amazing incredulity which greeted the first presentation of the unabridged dictionary on a square foot of film. The idea that one might have the contents of a thousand volumes located in a couple of cubic feet in a desk, so that by depressing a few keys one could have a given page instantly projected before him, was regarded as the wildest sort of fancy. This hesitation about accepting an idea, the basic soundness of which could have been tested by a little arithmetic, is worthy of more than passing notice. (Bush, 1933:126)

The real problem, he told us, was that people in the 1930s understood so little about the technology of the period they could not distinguish the *possible* from the virtually *impossible*.

The Promise of Microfilm

Stepping back from the fiction, we can see that the technological advance prompting this example of "a thousand volumes located in a couple of cubic feet" was microfilm. Neither microphotography nor the concern with improving and augmenting intellectual resources was new. While microphotographic technology derived from nineteenth-century experiments, a number of engineering advances in the 1920s leading to the use of microfilm to record canceled checks helped to redefine it as an important technical and information resource. Today, when microfilm is usually thought of as an awkward technology, it is important to remember that such was not always the case. In the 1930s many believed that microfilm could make information universally accessible and thus spark an intellectual revolution (Farkas-Conn, 1990:16-22). Bush, like others at the time, was exploring the possibilities inherent in microfilm in his writing and his MIT laboratories.

Thomas C. Bagg and Mary Elizabeth Stevens have traced out this aspect of the history of microfilm. They note that as early as 1926 Watson Davis and Edwin Slosson proposed using microfilm to reproduce scientific literature so that it might reach a wide audience (Bagg and Stevens, 1961:15). Davis, who helped establish the Science Service and later the American Documentation Institute (an ancestor of the American Society of Information Science), was both an evangelist of science information and a proponent of worldwide document organization. He was among the pioneers in subject indexing, a fundamental issue in information retrieval. Davis left notes of a meeting with Bush on November 15, 1932. At this meeting, they discussed how to index information recorded on microfilm (Bagg and Stevens, 1961:32). Although Bush does not mention Davis in his writings, both men clearly believed, as did others at the time, that microfilm provided the technology that could support the miniaturization, distribution, and selection of scientific and technical information.

On this topic, Davis managed to inspire H. G. Wells. For example, in *World Brain* (1938), a collection of talks given between 1936 and 1938, Wells argued for a "Permanent World Encyclopedia" that would unify and embody all the world's knowledge and cultures. This internationalist, progressive proposal was based on microfilm:

> By means of microfilm, the rarest and most intricate documents and articles can be studied now at first hand, simultaneously in a score of projection rooms. There is no practical obstacle whatever now to the creation of an efficient index to all human knowledge, ideas and achievements, to the creation, that is, of a complete planetary memory for all mankind. And not simply an index; the direct reproduction of the thing itself can be summoned to any properly prepared spot. A microfilm, coloured where necessary, occupying an inch or so of space and weighing little more than a letter, can be duplicated from the records and sent anywhere, and thrown enlarged upon the screen so that the student may study it in every detail. (Wells, 1938:60)

Microfilm promised miniaturization, complete fidelity of reproduction, freer access to rare and original materials, and transportability. In a later speech, Wells invokes Davis, who had been promoting microfilm at various international gatherings, to support his argument that his World Encyclopedia need not have to reside in a single place. Equating the encyclopedia with what he came to call the "world brain," Wells wrote:

> Plainly we have to make it a centralized and uniform organization but, as Mr. Watson Davis is here to remind us, it need not have any single local habitation because the continually increasing facilities of photography render reduplication of our indices and records continually easier. In these days of destruction, violence and general insecurity, it is comforting to think that the brain of mankind, the race brain, can exist in numerous replicas throughout the world. (Wells, 1938:63)

Bush was interested in neither Wells' progressive ideas nor Davis' mission—to support by microfilm the popular dissemination, both national and world wide, of library and institutional resources. In fact, when Bush did take this problem up (and this was later), he framed it differently. For example, Bush believed the control and exchange of scientific, technical resources that Wells and Davis concerned themselves with should be left to scientists, the scientific community (both national and international), and its academies. Bush did share with Davis, Wells, and others their assumptions about "the continually increasing facilities of photography" and the importance that the intellectual, scientific record—its use, transfer and preservation—had to man's survival and progress. In the years when Wells was proposing the world brain and its distribution through microphotography, Bush at MIT was designing a machine he believed would advance knowledge transfer and improve the scientific record. In Bush's design, this machine brought together a number of innovations in microfilm and photo-optics.

Bringing Memex to Print

Bush's writings and correspondence show that several forces motivated his push toward technological innovation in the area of information management. In a March 5, 1939 letter to F. P. Keppel at the Carnegie Corporation of New York, Bush outlined how he thought foundation monies should best be spent to support scientific research.

> I would not be at all surprised if developments of new methods . . . and new ways of making . . . material for research workers readily available, would have much effect on ultimate progress . . . than many a direct effort. In fact, I would go further. Unless we find better ways of handling new knowledge generally as it is developed, we are going to be bogged down by its very mass. I suspect we now have reincarnations of Mendel all about us, to be discovered a generation hence if at all.

Bush likely received a sympathetic hearing from Keppel, who that year published a speculative essay "Looking Forward, a Fantasy," in an American Library Association symposium, *The Library of Tomorrow*.

With echoes of both Washington Irving and Edward Bellamy, Keppel wrote of how a librarian, Rippina Van Winkle, might awaken in 1958 after a twenty-year slumber to find the role of her profession transformed by technological innovations. He imagined his heroine being told by another librarian old enough to remember the 1930s that "[a]s soon as a book or journal has had its active day, it is no longer kept to gather moss, but is replaced by a film, and a film in a pill box doesn't take much space" (Keppel, 1939:5). The use of microfilm as a technology to support innovation in knowledge transfer and storage was much in the air.

Once Bush conceived of Memex as a solution to this problem, he began to solicit others to obtain a hearing for his device. On December 7, 1939, Bush wrote to Eric Hodgins, the publisher of *FORTUNE*, enclosing a draft of "Mechanization and the Record." Bush described his draft in typical understatement as "...a rough manuscript. I would not feel free to place it before you in its present state . . . . Yet I have an idea that if I could get the thing in shape the thought is worth enunciating just at this time."

This forty-five page typescript repeated and expanded upon the issues Bush raised in his letter to Keppel. In addition, here he used the name Memex for the first time, described it in detail, and argued that the machine was a solution to the problem of managing the record.

This draft contains all the material that was to appear under the title "As We May Think" some six years later. However, this original draft contained a different introduction and conclusion. "Mechanization and the Record" begins by stating that human intellect has influenced the progress of civilization in four distinct ways:

First: increasing man's "control over his material environment";

Second: increasing his "control of his own biological processes";

Third: increasing the effectiveness of warfare so that it is now "more complex, more rapid in effect, more inclusive of whole populations, and much more destructive";

Fourth: supporting and improving "man's processes of thought." Bush argues that "this fourth influence is the truly fundamental one." It is tied to our means of communication and is more fundamental to the building and maintaining of civilization than is control of natural forces, disease, or warfare (Bush, 1939:2-3).

[The fourth influence] provides for the acceleration of the other three, and furnishes a compressed time scale for a shrunken world. It is a matter of mechanisms, taking these in the broadest sense to include the printing press and also the book itself. . . . The future means of implementing thought are hence fully as worthy of attention by one who wonders what comes next as are new ways of extracting natural resources, or of killing men, or even of prolonging life. (Bush, 1939:3)

Essentially, Bush was measuring the importance of committing new technological energy to address the management of information against the importance of committing similar energy to developing better defense against military threats. The threat in 1939 to what Bush meant by "civilization" from new developments in military technology was very real. As he stated in his conclusion:

The third influence of science . . . threatens to destroy more of material benefit than is created by the use of science to overcome poverty, to make more misery than is relieved by the application of science to heal the sick, to stop in its tracks the trend toward a broader outlook on the mission of the race which might well come were the full record truly grasped. (Bush, 1939:42-43)

He offered the hope that the destructiveness of this "third influence" could be neutralized by equally powerful technological defenses, and that the "fourth influence" would help mankind "grow in the wisdom of race experience."

That Bush framed his presentation of machines to help scientists and engineers take control of their intellectual materials in terms of its relative importance to warfare and the development of military technology shows just how intertwined these matters were. In the months before he was to begin his own career as a manager of national scientific research, first as the science advisor to Franklin Delano Roosevelt and then as director of the Office of Scientific Research and Development, Bush was arguing that mankind should reorganize its priorities to build better ways of managing libraries of written records rather than better bombers and submarines.

Upon reading Bush's manuscript, Hodgins wrote back, "I found the reading of your manuscript one of the most exciting events of all my life in the publishing business. . . . If anyone had told me that the future of filing and reference systems could be made the subject of such a bold

. . . attack, I would have laughed at him prior to my reading of your essay." Hodgins asked Bush if he would rewrite and submit the piece to *FORTUNE* (December 14, 1939). On December 18, 1939, Bush replied and expressed a lack of interest in publishing the piece there.

> I admit a prejudice against *Harpers* and *The Atlantic*. It probably comes from having been an engineer in Boston. [But] I don't think the men I want to reach read them. . . . You reach many of them; but I was entirely honest when I told you I felt free to consult you because the thing is off your beat, and it still strikes me that way.

The matter seems to have rested here for almost a year until Richard Wood, an editor at *FORTUNE*, picked it up again. On May 15, 1940, he wrote Bush, "I want to apologize to you for having taken so long over this manuscript," and he once again asked Bush to publish the piece in *FORTUNE*. Bush responded:

> The prospect, therefore, after the large amount of delay . . . [already of] . . . further delay while you look over the article . . . is not especially attractive. I think it may be better . . . to abandon the idea of publishing this particular essay in *FORTUNE*. . . . I hesitate to do this for . . . I might reach through *FORTUNE* the people I would really like to reach [but] . . . Before making any decision . . . I will try to get in touch with Eric Hodgins as soon as the pressure of national defense matters allows. (May 16, 1940)

Hodgins (May 17, 1940) suggested that he could distribute reprints of the article to people who did not see the piece in *FORTUNE*. While still uncertain about whether *FORTUNE* could attract the interest and support necessary to launch Memex and caught up in America's war preparations, Bush wrote to Hodgins five days later. "When the present pressure releases a little, if it does, let's get at this Memex . . . . Never mind about . . . the reprints. . . . I [just] would like to get the article in good shape and published . . . for the sake of getting a new thought into the heads of people that I would like to reach" (May 22, 1940).

Bush described the audience he wanted to reach in a brief essay sent to Hodgins on April 10, 1941, titled "Memorandum regarding Memex." His choice of an audience is not fortuitous—it expresses his belief that a scientist must make himself heard by the nation's elite if he truly wants to improve society. "In particular, it seemed worth while [sic] to try to influence the thinking of trustees of foundations, educational and scientific institutions, and those concerned with governmental support . . . of scientific effort" (Bush, 1941:1). Technology like Memex, Bush argued, could not only assist, but also improve, the practice of science. In short, as an engineer, he wanted others to know that technology need not be just gadgetry nor need technology's effects be trivial or destructive. Further, Bush believed that, as it has in the past, technology would continue to contribute significantly to man's mental development (Bush, 1941:1, 6).

However, three years later Bush still had not published his Memex essay. As he complained in a letter on March 15, 1944 to Frederick Fassett, who had now moved from MIT to join Bush at Carnegie in Washington, "I still have that blooming article I wrote on Memex. I never did a thing with it except to take it up with Eric Hodgins." In September, he wrote Fassett again about the paper. "I could go back to *FORTUNE* . . . . However, I do not think they reach many people who really read their stuff and I am not enthusiastic about them anyway" (September 15, 1944). In this letter, he brought up the *Atlantic Monthly* as a possibility.

By October 1944, Fassett, Bush, and Edward Weeks, editor of the *Atlantic Monthly,* were discussing how best to edit "Mechanization and the Record" for publication. In an October 6, 1944 letter to Fassett, Bush returned to the question of who its audience should be. He explained:

> [I wish to] reach the proper people at the proper time with a statement which I think will aid them in becoming reoriented into useful channels, possibly with a re-stimulated enthusiasm which may well be badly needed. I rather think that the *Atlantic* will reach a fair fraction of those I would like to appeal to, but it certainly will not reach all of them. . . . However, I do think I ought to secure enough reprints so that I can pass them around . . . should I find that the article creates enough interest to warrant [this].

As for the essay's thesis and its importance, Fassett's November 2, 1944 letter to Bush explains it this way:

> The three of us [Fassett, Weeks and associate editor Charles Morton of the *Atlantic Monthly*] agreed (1) that the piece should be published as one unit in one issue; (2) that it should be preceded (and this is most

unusual, if not extraordinary, in the *Atlantic*) by an editorial paragraph
in which the *Atlantic* expresses its high esteem of the fact that the
document is appearing; (3) that your . . . central message, is that . . . the
broad problem of implementing the intelligence in order that it may
cope adequately with the increased complexity of the loads placed
upon it by modern civilization is at once the most important and the
most challenging opportunity to face scientists as they turn away from
war.

Having posed the problem, Bush also attempted to resolve it in some
way. Once more, Bush turned to technology to do so and again he
offered Memex as a solution.

Memory and Association

In all versions of the Memex essay (Bush, 1939, 1945a, 1945b, 1967a)
Bush begins his description of the machine with a critique of how
information was currently organized in libraries. He asserted that
scientific research "involves the entire process by which man profits by
his inheritance of acquired knowledge" (Bush, 1945a:105) and went on
to say that before knowledge could be used it had to be selected and
retrieved. In fact, Bush argued that knowledge that cannot be selected
was lost. For Bush, what was most problematic was this act of selection.

> The real heart of the matter of selection, however, goes deeper than a
> lag in the adoption of mechanisms by libraries, or a lack of develop-
> ment of devices for their use. Our ineptitude in getting at the record is
> largely caused by the artificiality of systems of indexing. When data of
> any sort are placed in storage, they are filed alphabetically or numeri-
> cally, and information is found (when it is) by tracing it down from
> subclass to subclass. It can be in only one place, unless duplicates are
> used; one has to have rules as to which path will locate it, and the rules
> are cumbersome. Having found one item, moreover, one has to emerge
> from the system and re-enter on a new path.
>
> The human mind does not work that way. It operates by associa-
> tion. With one item in its grasp, it snaps instantly to the next that is
> suggested by the association of thoughts, in accordance with some
> intricate web of trails carried by the cells of the brain. It has other
> characteristics, of course; trails that are not frequently followed are
> prone to fade, items are not fully permanent, memory is transitory. Yet

the speed of action, the intricacy of trails, the detail of mental pictures, is awe-inspiring beyond all else in nature. (Bush, 1945a:106)

These paragraphs are central enough that they appeared verbatim in all four versions of the Memex essay. Nevertheless, the relationship between the two paragraphs is often ignored. For example, the subhead added by the *LIFE* editors read "The human brain files by association— the Memex could do this mechanically" (Bush, 1945b:121). In a recent reprint of "As We May Think" in *CD ROM: The New Papyrus*, the editors added a call-out that read "The human mind operates by association" (Bush, 1986:15). Although these do not necessarily misrepresent Bush's words and intentions, the result has been to overlook the central contrast he makes between conventional methods of indexing information and the mental associations Memex was to support.

It was clear as early as the 1930s that the process of locating items through conventional indexing could be improved through mechanization. Although others also recognized this problem and believed its solution lay in technology, what separated Bush from information retrieval pioneers such as Luhan, Taube, and Mooers were his ideas on how to represent, define, and sort information. In brief, Bush was not only interested in improving work flow and output but in inventing a technology that would directly aid, even add to, the mental processes of classification and knowledge representation. Memex got its name because it was to support and extend the powers of human memory and association.

Memex was defined as a private file and library, emphasizing its personal nature and its scope. At this time, information management and retrieval research dealt primarily with institutional, generic issues (Farkas-Conn, 1990; Nelson, this volume). With Memex, Bush worked through quite a different set of issues, i.e., how particular and individual knowledge requirements could be supported. Unlike the scenario sent to Weaver in 1937, where the microfilm selector resided in a research library operated by library staff, Bush described this device as a personal work desk with viewing screens, a keyboard, sets of buttons and levers. Storage of printed materials of all kinds was accomplished using microphotography. He expected this storage technology to be so compact that new material could easily be added at the rate of an additional two million pages per year for "hundreds of years" (Bush,

1945a:107). Prerecorded documents were entered via microfilm. Material could also be entered through dry photography or keyboarding. One could type an index code or move levers to bring page images one wanted into view.

Any two items in the Memex could be permanently coded for associative selection. Bush called this coded association "a trail," analogous to the trail of mental association in the user's mind. It is this principle, this direct modeling of the brain and neural pathways, that sets Bush's work apart from others of his time, this and the promise this principle has for personalizing and linking information. In a letter suggesting some additions to "As We May Think," Bush pushed this analogy further, and its terms and claims became quite clear.

> When items are thus tied together in a chain, when any item in the chain can be caused to be followed by the next, instantly and automatically, wherever it may be, there is formed an associative trail through the material. It is closely analagous [sic] to the trails formed in the cells of the brain, and it may be similarly employed. (November 19, 1944)

Unlike mental associations, however, trails in Memex would not fade over time. Once recorded, this trail could be followed at any time without the need for going up and down the hierarchies of conventional indexing.

Picturing the Memex

When "As We May Think" was finally published in the closing months of the Second World War, it generated considerable interest. Hodgins wrote to Bush, "I was in the offices of *The Atlantic* two days ago and my old friend . . . Donald Snyder, now its Publisher, flipped a telegram to me . . . 'Associated Press using 800 words Bush story. . .'. I gnashed my teeth at Snyder and told him my own version of why and how *FORTUNE* had missed a great . . . opportunity" (June 22, 1945). Not only did the Associated Press pick up the story, a news story ran in *TIME* magazine (Anon., 1945) and *LIFE* requested permission to reprint a condensed version of the essay itself.

The *LIFE* version was to be illustrated and the assignment to draw the Memex went to Alfred D. Crimi, an artist who had been working for

Sperry Gyroscope Company. Crimi was chosen because some of his drawings of Sperry computer machines had appeared in an earlier issue of *LIFE*. As Crimi recalls,

> It was August 13, 1945, the day Japan surrendered to the United States. I was at the MacArthur Air Field in Long Is., working on an aerial view of the Sperry Experimental Laboratory in flight. That memorable day I received a letter from Allan McNab from the Art Dep't of *LIFE* Magazine, asking if I would make some drawings for that publication. (Crimi to Nyce, January 21, 1988)

Crimi made two sketches based solely on the description of Memex in "As We May Think." He then went to Washington with McNab to talk to Bush. The two men spent much of one day discussing Bush's ideas, and Crimi took notes. Back in New York he produced the four drawings, two of Memex, which were to accompany the essay. These drawings were later approved by Bush (Crimi to Nyce, March 7, 1988).

The first Memex drawing was a cutaway view of a machine with two viewing screens that showed the mechanisms and photoelectric devices hidden in the desk (Bush, 1945b:123). Although Bush specified "slanting translucent screens on which material can be projected for convenient reading" (Bush, 1945b:121), he did not specify how many screens Memex was to have. Since Bush wrote that when a user builds a trail he has before him "the two items to be joined, projected onto adjacent viewing positions" (Bush, 1945b:123), Crimi included two viewing screens in both drawings. The second illustration (Bush, 1945b:124) showed "Memex in use." The essay offered an example of a researcher creating a trail of information about the Turkish bow and the English longbow. In this scenario, the user creates a trail between the two pages, and this was noted in the caption to the second illustration. The illustration showed related images on two viewing screens, and the user's hand was shown writing an annotation directly on the image of one of these pages. Crimi notes that he did his research for this illustration in the New York Historical Society "where I chose some Indian Symbols which I found interesting as illustrations for the transparent screen" (Crimi to Nyce, March 7, 1988). A close examination of this illustration reveals that the figures actually look more like Iroquois warriors than English or Turkish soldiers.

Personal Associations in the General Record

Bush's correspondence also reveal some early objections to Memex. Immediately after "As We May Think" appeared, John H. Weakland wrote to Bush. While Weakland was clearly impressed by the article, he offered these objections:

> (1) Wouldn't the fact that association patterns are thoroly [sic] individual make a general use of the memex difficult? (2) How would the tremendous bulk of information already recorded be made usable, especially for a searcher who wants to branch into lines of thought and knowledge that are quite new and unfamiliar to him? (Weakland, August 27, 1945)

Weakland here anticipated two fundamental issues that were to appear again in hypertext system design. How could the personal associations of the general record be generally useful, Weakland asked, and how could a researcher find things that he did not already know about in such a system? The issue here was selection, as Bush puts it, and the heart of the matter was whether access and use of the record should be based on abstract general principles or on personal, i.e., individual associations. This has been a major issue separating information retrieval systems from hypertext. In a talk from the 1970s on Bush's ideas, Theodor H. Nelson elaborated on this point:

> It is strange that "As We May Think" has been taken so to heart in the field of information retrieval, since it runs counter to virtually all work being pursued under the name of information retrieval today. Such systems are principally concerned either with indexing conventional documents by content, or with somehow representing that content in a way that can be mechanically searched and deciphered. (Nelson, 1973:442)

Nelson's argument, that information retrieval research has focused on characteristics of the record that can be objectively analyzed, be it keywords, full text, or bibliometrics, was certainly accurate. Linda C. Smith (1981 and this volume) traces the various influences Bush's essay has had in the information retrieval research literature. She found only a fraction of these citations focuses on Memex as a "personal information system." However, for Bush, and later for Nelson and others engaged in hypertext research, Memex represented a very personal tool. As Bush himself wrote,

> In that essay ["As We May Think"] I proposed a machine for personal use rather than the enormous computers which serve whole companies. I suggested that it serve a man's daily thoughts directly, fitting in with his normal thought processes, rather than just do chores for him. (Bush, 1967a:76)

While over time the analog devices originally envisioned were left behind, the idea of a personal computer with the storage capacity of a major library providing easy and personalized access to large stores of information did not go away. After many of Bush's technologies, such as microfilm, were discarded, the idea Memex represented continued to inform the pioneering work of Nelson and Engelbart (Engelbart and English, 1968), who brought hypertext to digital computers in the 1960s.

An Analog to the Brain

Although essentially an electro-optical device, Memex is a direct descendant of the analytical machines Bush invented. Bush's interest in these machines and analog technology in general goes back to his college years. In 1921, Bush patented a surveying machine based on this technology (Bush, 1970:155-157). Whereas the relationship between Memex and Bush's other machines cannot be taken up here at length, all Bush's analytic devices clearly relate to each other (see Owens, this volume). What has to be kept in mind is that what ties these machines together, Memex included, is that they were all analog devices.

In the 1930s, mechanical analog technologies represented the state of the art (Burks and Burks, 1988:263, 272). Further, for ten years or so, Bush had helped develop this technology, and he was deeply committed to analog machines (Shurkin, 1984:96, 145). Bush found these machines attractive because they were literal models of existing phenomena. In other words, they directly mirrored, with some simplification, the thing itself. Bush saw analog machines as a combination of mechanical or electrical elements designed to act exactly in the same manner as the thing itself (Bush, 1970:181). They follow the same physical laws and in effect were concrete embodiments of a phenomenon (Bush, 1967a:83-84).

Furthermore, as Owens (this volume) argues, Bush's Differential Analyzer and other machines were not simply elegant, mechanical reproductions of things or phenomena. They also, he notes, kinetically act out and so represent those processes that constitute and define the thing itself. Further, they represent a triumph over a tendency in mathematics and science to idealize and typify the frustrated engineers of the time (Owens, this volume; Layton, 1976), and this may be why these machines appealed to Bush. In other words, these machines express directly and vividly what they represent.

Bush's interest in directly representing biological processes in vivid mechanical terms appears in the kinds of parallels he draws between Memex and the brain. Although Bush's computing machines were quite good at what they did (Wiener, 1956:235), Bush also wanted to design machines bound neither to nor by mathematical, logical operations. Throughout his life, Bush was fascinated by and sought out parallels between mechanics and natural processes. For example, in a paper that describes several advances in electrocardiography, Bush does not just describe the heart as a pump, he translates its action and effect into quantitative, material terms. Total up all the human hearts in the United States, he tells us, and the output will equal some 70,000 horsepower, enough to light up and power Boston (Bush and Reid, 1932:159). The paper then discusses the heart as a generator, and here electricity, not mechanics, links the two together. For Bush, an electrical engineer, electricity was a universal force, common to both biology and mechanics. However, electricity was not just a universal property, it was a metaphoric principle. To be more specific, Bush used electricity to draw strong parallels or sets of analogies between mind/brain and machine. He not only thought with and in these terms—Bush set up and built technological projects with them. In a 1944 letter to Weeks, for example, he first argued that "a great deal of our brain cell activity is closely parallel to the operation of relay circuits" (Bush, November 6, 1944). Again based on electricity, Bush concluded that "one can explore this parallelism and the possibilities of ultimately making something out of it almost indefinitely" (November 6, 1944).

With Memex, Bush thought and designed in terms of analogies between brain and machine, between electricity and information. This kind of project reflected some central research interests and agendas of the time. For example, Wiener and McCulloch, both at MIT, looked for and worked from parallels they saw between neural structure and process and computation (Wildes and Lindgren, 1985:243, 263; Birkhoff, 1980:26). Unlike Bush, they did not do this with the intention of constructing a mechanical analog to the brain.

Bush's intention was to use machines to innovate by improving on parts of the imperfect biological process he was attempting to model. For example, Bush thought of human memory as information stored in the relay circuits and neural substrate of the brain. He proposed reels of coded microfilm and a selection mechanism as an analogy for this. He hoped that this analog technology could improve upon the means by which a person worked with information. Modern technology, Bush believed, would help make this device more reliable and more dependable than the biological mechanism it modeled (Bush, 1970:185-186).

While Bush finally published "As We May Think" some twelve years after he first conceived of Memex, he did not during this time alter its basic design. He did alter the design, however, after the essay's publication. Bush himself recognized that "the digital machine is on the peak of the wave of progress in analytical machinery, and the analog machines for the purpose are now to some extent overshadowed" (Bush, 1954:12). In other words, the analytical devices favored by Bush, "have been crowded out by the great success of the digital machine" (Bush, 1967a:84). At the same time, Bush was not much interested in digital computers and professed to know little about them. For example, in a letter to R. C. Gibbs, who chaired a post-war National Research Committee on high speed machines, Bush wrote, "I would very much like to discuss the subject with him [von Neumann] even though I know I cannot contribute to a field that is moving as rapidly as this one with much study" (September 19, 1946). "If I mixed with it" Bush wrote later, "I could not possibly catch up with the new techniques, and I did not intend to . . . become a patriarch emitting dull generalities on the subject" (Bush, 1970:208).

Nevertheless he continued to work with these ideas throughout his life. After "As We May Think" appeared, Bush re-engineered Memex using new technology, some of it derived from digital computers, as described in our essay in the second part of this volume. Yet, what had little impact on Memex was digital theory. In short, despite the new technology, Memex remained an analog machine. Bush looked to the future, beyond the digital computers he saw, for technologies that might support Memex. He wrote "I believe we shall advance in our mastery over the records we create, rendering them easier to consult by means which would now seem strange and bizarre to us" (Bush, 1955:304).

References

Anonymous (1945). A Machine That Thinks, *TIME*, 46(4), 93-94.

Anonymous (1951). Biography of Vannevar Bush, Medalist for 1951, *Supplement to John Fritz Medal Book*, New York.

Bagg, T. C., and Stevens, M. E. (1961). *Information Selection Systems Retrieving Replica Copies: A State-Of-The-Art Report*, Washington, DC: National Bureau of Standards, (Technical Note 157).

Bellamy, E. (1887). *Looking Backward 2000-1887*, Boston: Houghton Mifflin.

Birkhoff, G. (1980). Computing Developments 1935-1955, as Seen from Cambridge, U.S.A., in N. Metropolis, J. Howlett, and G. Rota (editors), *A History of Computing in the Twentieth Century: A Collection of Essays* (pp. 21-30), New York: Academic Press.

Bromley, A. G. (1990). Analog Computing Devices, in W. Aspray (editor), *Computing Before Computers* (pp. 156-199), Ames, IA: Iowa State University Press.

Buckland, M. (forthcoming) Emanuel Goldberg and the Antecedents of Vannevar Bush's Memex.

Burks, A. R., and Burks, A. W. (1988). *The First Electronic Computer: The Atanasoff Story*, Ann Arbor: University of Michigan Press.

Bush, V., and Reid, W. D. (1932). The Human Power Plant: Peak Capacity of American Hearts over Half a Million H.P., *Technology Review*, 34(4), 159-162, 188.

Bush, V. (1933). The Inscrutable 'Thirties, *Technology Review*, 35(4), 123-127.

Bush, V. (1937). *A Reference Selector: Description of a Possible Method for Facilitating the Preparation and Use of Evaluated Bibliographies*, [Rockefeller Archives], RG 1.1 224D 2 23.

Bush, V. (1939). *Mechanization and the Record*, [Vannevar Bush Papers, Library of Congress], Box 138, Speech Article Book File.

Bush, V. (1941). *Memorandum regarding Memex*, [Vannevar Bush Papers, Library of Congress], Box 50, General Correspondence File, Eric Hodgins.

Bush, V. (1945a). As We May Think, *Atlantic Monthly, 176*(1), 101-108.

Bush, V. (1945b). As We May Think: A Top U.S. Scientist Forsees a Possible Future World in Which Man-Made Machines Will Start to Think, *LIFE, 19*(11), 112-124.

Bush, V. (1946). The Qualities of a Profession, in *Endless Horizons* (pp. 132-145), Washington, DC: Public Affairs Press.

Bush, V. (1954). *Today's Research and Tomorrow's World,* [Vannevar Bush Papers, MIT Archives], MC78, Box 23.

Bush, V. (1955). Communications—Where Do We Go from Here?, *Mechanical Engineering, 77*(4), 302-304.

Bush, V. (1967a). Memex Revisited, in *Science Is Not Enough* (pp. 75-101), New York: William Morrow.

Bush, V. (1967b). The Gentleman of Culture, in *Science Is Not Enough* (pp. 31-49), New York: William Morrow.

Bush, V. (1970). *Pieces of the Action,* New York: William Morrow.

Bush, V. (1986). As We May Think, in S. Lambert, and S. Ropiequet (editors), *CD ROM: The New Papyrus* (pp. 3-20), Redmond, WA: Microsoft Press.

Coile, R. C. (1954). Scientific Aids to Documentation, *University of Kentucky Libraries Occasional Contribution.* (No. 61).

Engelbart, D. C., and English, W. K. (1968). A Research Center for Augmenting Human Intellect. *AFIPS Conference Proceedings, 1968 Fall Joint Computer Conference, 33* (pp. 395-410), Montvale, NJ: AFIPS Press.

Farkas-Conn, I. S. (1990). *From Documentation to Information Science: The Beginnings and Early Development of the American Documentation Institute-American Society for Information Science,* New York: Greenwood Press.

Kasson, J. F. (1976). *Civilizing the Machine: Technology and Republican Values in America 1776-1900,* New York: Grossman Publishers.

Keppel, F. P. (1939). Looking Forward, a Fantasy, in E. M. Danton (editor), *The Library of Tomorrow* (pp. 1-11), Chicago: Amerian Library Association.

Kevles, D. J. (1978). *The Physicists: The History of a Scientific Community in Modern America,* New York: Alfred A. Knopf.

Layton, E. T. (1976). American Ideologies of Science and Engineering, *Technology and Culture, 17*(4), 688-701.

Levi-Strauss, C. (1966[1962]). *The Savage Mind,* Chicago: University of Chicago Press.

McMahon, A. M. (1984). *The Making of a Profession: A Century of Electrical Engineering in America,* New York: IEEE Press.

Moore, D. J. (1990). Multimedia Presentation Development Using the Audio Visual Connection, *IBM Systems Journal, 29*(4), 494-509.

Nelson, T. H. (1973). As We Will Think, *Online 72: Conference Proceedings of the International Conference on Online Interactive Computing, 1* (pp. 439-454), Uxbridge, England: Online Computer Systems Ltd.

Owens, L. E. (1987). Straight-Thinking Vannevar Bush and the Culture of American Engineering, Ph.D. diss., Princeton University.

Sapolsky, H. M. (1990). *Science and the Navy: The History of the Office of Naval Research*, Princeton: Princeton University Press.

Segal, H. P. (1985). *Technological Utopianism in American Culture*, Chicago: University of Chicago Press.

Shurkin, J. (1984). *Engines of the Mind: A History of the Computer*, New York: W. W. Norton & Company.

Smith, L. C. (1981). 'Memex' as an Image Potentiality in Information Retrieval Research and Development, in R. N. Oddy (editor), *Information Retrieval Research* (pp. 345-369), London: Butterworths.

Vincenti, W. G. (1990). *What Engineers Know and How They Know It: Analytical Studies from Aeronautical History*, Baltimore: Johns Hopkins University Press.

Wagar, W. W. (1988). Dreams of Reason: Bellamy, Wells, and the Positive Utopia, in D. Patai (editor), *Looking Backward, 1988-1888: Essays on Edward Bellamy* (pp. 106-125), Amherst: University of Massachusetts Press.

Wells, H. G. (1933). *The Shape of Things To Come*, New York: Macmillan Company.

Wells, H. G. (1938). *World Brain*, London: Methuen & Co.

Wiener, N. (1956). *I Am a Mathematician*, Cambridge: MIT Press.

Wiesner, J. B. (1979). Vannevar Bush, March 11, 1890-June 28, 1974, *Bibliographic Memoirs of the National Academy of Sciences, 50*(8), 89-117.

Wildes, K. L., and Lindgren, N. A. (1985). *A Century of Electrical Engineering and Computer Science at MIT, 1882-1982*, Cambridge: MIT Press.

Wurts, R. *et al.* (1977). *The New York World's Fair 1939/1940 in 155 Photographs*, New York: Dover Publications.

The Inscrutable 'Thirties

Reflections Upon a Preposterous Decade

Vannevar Bush

This essay first appeared in M.I.T.'s Technology Review *in January, 1933. The editor's note preceding the essay read: "This article is presented as a preprint of a paper that might be found many years hence among the literary effects of the present Vice-President of the Massachusetts Institute of Technology, or else as a paper that may be written by some future Vice-President of M.I.T. and printed in this magazine when the present decade has receded into the 'landscape of the past.'" A slightly revised version, "The Inscrutable Past", published in 1946 appears here.*

A REVIEW OF THE MODE OF LIVING OF OUR FOREFATHERS, if it is to be useful, should be sympathetic in its attitude. The lapse of time often obscures the difficulties surrounding a former generation, and we are apt to smile at crudities when a just estimate should rather leave us to marvel that so much was accomplished with so little.

It is especially pertinent that we should review the technical accomplishments of another period only in the light of the contemporary science. Otherwise, we may well be guilty of a patronizing complacency, and as a result lose the benefit to be derived from a really analytical view of history.

Take the early Nineteen-Thirties as an example. From this distance the mechanical aspects of that time certainly appear grotesque; but, when we realize that this was the period when physics was in the throes of conflicting and essentially independent theories, the fact that applications were made at all is remarkable.

We read of the trials of the men of that day and wonder that they could have been apparently content with their mode of life, its discomforts, and its annoyances. Instead, we should admire them for having made the best of a hard situation, and treasure the rugged qualities which they exemplified. It is possible that by taking our minds back, divesting them of their modern knowledge, and then studying these

Reprinted from Vannevar Bush's Endless Horizons, *(Washington, 1933), pp. 1-15, by permission of Public Affairs Press and Richard Bush, MD.*

bygone days in an attempt really to appreciate their true worth, we should lose some of our satisfaction with respect to the technical accomplishments of our own generation, and be better prepared for advance. At least it is worth the attempt.

Those were interesting times when the second Roosevelt was elected, and the world was in the midst of the last great economic readjustment. It was a time of transition, evident enough as we now regard it, but perhaps not wholly appreciated at the moment. It was marked by great extremes; the United States were just emerging from the prohibition experiment, and international affairs were chaotic. The system of distribution had nearly broken down, and there was little real control of production. No one really understood the monetary system under which the civilized world then tried to operate, and which was based on the curious process of laboriously digging gold out of one hole in the ground in order equally laboriously to bury it in another. Hence, it is illuminating to review the life of a plain citizen of the period and the nature of his environment.

The Hardships of Daily Existence

Consider, for example, a professor in some northern urban university, and let us attempt to appreciate the sort of life he led, with a sympathetic attempt to evaluate the extent to which his efforts were circumscribed by the hardships and discomforts of his daily existence.

It is necessary at the outset to realize that he was in the peculiar position of being regarded by many of his fellow countrymen as of outstanding intellect; while at the same time his scale of living was decidedly middle-class. Yet he had much of comfort, in the way that comfort was then regarded, and undoubtedly he considered himself well off.

He probably owned an automobile, for example, and in this he proceeded from his home to his work. In many ways his car was embryonic, for it was, of course, a relatively new development. To get it under way, he first started the engine turning over while entirely free from any operative connection with the vehicle, and then he had to go through 14 separate motions with his hands and feet before getting the car up to full speed. It seems hard to realize that this situation could have been long tolerated, but actually it persisted for years. Moreover, these motions, of various pedals and a hand lever, had to be carried through in a rigid sequence and with a fairly careful timing of the operations. A clumsiness, such as performing one act out of proper sequence, would spoil the whole affair, and the professor would practically have to start all over. Yet people of all degrees learned this ritual and drove cars everywhere. Nor were these motor cars of the Nineteen-Thirties toys, for in a curious delusion that weight and riding qualities were inseparable, even the better grades of automobiles were built so heavy that they weighed several hundred pounds per passenger, a total weight of as much as 4,000 pounds being not unusual.

On nearly all highways traffic moved in both directions at the same time! Moreover pedestrians crossed these roads at the same level. There was no drying of streets in the cities, so that they were often wet, and, in extreme weather, covered with ice. Car speeds seldom got above 60 miles per hour, but under conditions which then obtained, there was a carnage and literally tens of thousands were killed yearly in the country. Right in the hearts of cities there were grade intersections of important streets and practically no elevated arteries. The law officer who was often stationed at points where important arteries intersected on a level, and who attempted to regulate traffic by whistling and waving his arms, was often a diverting spectacle. His antics are still recalled with amusement by some of my elderly colleagues. No wonder our professor arrived at work with his nerves somewhat frayed, and that the scientific writings of the time reflect a sort of general nervousness and a haste to publish fragmentary findings.

It is hard to suppress untoward amusement and to preserve the sympathetic attitude when one considers the clothing which our professor wore. It was put on in layers, and, while the lower layer was periodically washed, the other layers were often worn practically continuously until they disintegrated, with only infrequent dips into various solvents. In spite of this intentional protection of the top layers from contact with water, they sagged and stretched, and this tendency was ineffectually combated by occasional pressing by a highly heated metal implement. If caught out in the rain—for accidental sprinkling accelerated this process of deformation—the professor would don still another layer called a raincoat, so designed that it drained the water principally into his shoes. These shoes, by the way, were never thoroughly washed or even cleansed with solvents. They were daubed over occasionally with an impermanent varnish, which was given some specular reflection by rubbing with a cloth, but which was not really waterproof. The shoes were of natural leather, close-fitting and entirely unventilated, and fastened in position with lacing cords, which frequently became entangled. The fastening of his clothes generally was by buttons. Even though sleeves did not open, buttons were still retained in position at his wrists, where they were actually quite inconvenient, as a sort of atrophied appendage. He wore a collar about his neck, kept meticulously white by frequent changing, as a sort of obvious presentation of one thoroughly clean portion of clothing. Some of his collars were rendered stiff and irritating by saturation with vegetable starches. They were surrounded by highly colored ornamented bands which he tied in intricate knots and adjusted with careful precision.

The lenses by which his vision was corrected were wired to his ears, or else held on by pincers which gripped his nose. As his accommodation was faulty he carried two sets of lenses which he alternated in position on his face, carrying the spare in a little metal box. Some of his colleagues wore both sets of lenses at the same time, made into a combination called bifocals, so that they could produce the effect of changing lenses by tipping the head and inclining the eyeballs. Of course with this arrangement they went about with their feet and the ground in their vicinity in a perpetual haze.

In his office the professor ordinarily found other conditions hardly conducive to logical thought. Right in the midst of his most careful musings, anyone, not merely his chosen friends and col-leagues, but literally anyone, could interrupt instantly by calling him on the telephone. A bell would ring in his office and convention demanded that he should immediately cease everything else and answer. There was no provision whatever by which a conversation ensued only when both parties had indicated willingness; even tradesmen in the city could initiate the ordeal. In answering, it was necessary that the professor practically wrap himself up in an instru-ment. He would hold one gadget to his ear and another to his mouth, and entangled in the connecting wires, proceed to try to talk. Some forms of equipment, then just going out, but strangely enough persisting longest in this country, even required the use of both hands as well as the vocal organs.

The sounds heard over the telephone of the day were recognizable, but hardly natural, for only a fifth of the useful frequency spectrum, or even less, was transmitted. In fact, people habitually listened to radio music in which there was less than one-third the spectrum present, although scant enthusiasm for the result has come down to us, except in the amusing and rhapsodic advertising of the times.

Our professor was bound to be fairly uncomfortable for other reasons. His office was heated in winter, of course, but in summer was left to its own devices with the window open to admit the dirt and noise of the city and the hot, humid air. Even in winter, while there might possibly have been some control of air temperature aside from his own chance manual regulation, there certainly was none of humidity. Also the walls of his office, with none too certain thermal insulation from the outside conditions, took up almost any temperature whatever, and the conditions for his bodily radiation varied in a wide and erratic manner. It is strange that these matters were so completely ignored, for they are hardly mentioned in the technical literature of the time, although certainly engineers should have been somewhat conversant with the laws of radiation, if not of biophysics.

Somewhere on the premises of the college there was a heating plant, which probably consisted of simply a coal fire with some distribution medium such as steam. For every thermal unit released by burning coal, there was transmitted into the building actually less than a thermal unit, so that the process was highly inefficient. Thermal pumps were in the early stages of development, and the central stations played little part in the heating of a city except perhaps to operate coal-burning heating plants of their own and sell steam.

The most striking feature of our professor's day, however, and one which he considered an important part of his work, was the giving of lectures. He would stand up in front of a group of 50 students or so and orally recite a bit of scientific matter, perhaps meanwhile drawing crude diagrams on a large flat black surface with a white crayon. This was done not alone in the presentation of new thoughts and researches, but as a means of imparting well-known information to students. It would not disturb him in the least that a hundred other professors in various parts of the country might be doing exactly the same thing at the same time. It was the custom of the day that he should appear personally for this ceremony, although it would have been possible even then to prepare a much more finished presentation by vocal cinema, realizing of course that it would not have been stereoscopic and that the articulation might have been a bit crude. Thus a fair fraction of our professor's time was occupied in a rehash of the well-known before large groups, where anything approaching Socratic dialogue was patently impossible. Another amusing feature of these lectures was the so-called taking of notes by the students, who attempted by simple pencil and paper to reproduce important ideas as the affair proceeded. The results were naturally fragmentary, but we must remember that under the then existing system a word once spoken was lost unless recorded in some such manner.

At noon the professor might take a walk, either because of assumed benefit to the functioning of his organic processes, or more likely as a temporary means of escape from the distractions of his office. If the latter incentive was his reason, the attempt was likely to be unsuccessful. The streets were heavy with the odor and smoke which nearby factories poured freely into the air almost without restraint. The price paid by the public for thus distributing unburned fuel on the breeze, and later abstracting it from draperies and clothing, was startling. One statistically-inclined person computed that no less than 70,000,000 tons of soot fell on the country every year, so that all the buildings were soon dingy and the sun was at times obscured.

He would also meet with din and confusion. Electric cars on rails, with hard steel wheels and steel spur gears, were still used for urban traffic. They made so much noise that one could literally be heard a mile away on a still night. Every automobile carried noise-making apparatus, usually in the form of a diaphragm operated by an electric vibrator, ostensibly for the purpose of cautioning pedestrians, although one wonders how an incautious one could have been extant. Automobile engines, burning highly volatile refined hydrocarbons, filled the air with carbon monoxide due to faulty combustion. Worse yet, there was a furor at about this time for the use of admixtures of anti-detonants.

These were really useful in view of the nature of the fuel on the market commercially and its complete admission before compression, and a very popular type incidentally consisted of tetraethyl lead. Apparently these exhaust gases did little real harm to the pedestrians, although the data on the point were then incomplete, but the knowledge of their presence in the air was disturbing, at least to the scientifically minded.

An airplane or two may have roared overhead with unmuffled exhausts during this noon-hour walk, for there were quite a few planes in use. The professor probably watched these with a bit of trepidation. In the event of even minor power-plant difficulty they were obliged to land immediately and precipitately at high ground speed. There were no landing spots on buildings, nor could they have been used if present, for the planes of the commercial routes came to the ground while still traveling as much as 60 miles an hour. The slightest fog was a serious matter, for it could not be dissipated, and there was no way in which the pilot of the usual commercial plane could get his position accurately with respect to the field except by visual observation. In order to travel by plane one usually had first to make an intricate automobile trip from the center of the city out to a field in the country, and then, if there were fog or heavy rain, the trips would be cancelled. In spite of all these enormous handicaps a few courageous pioneers operated passenger lines and succeeded in giving acceptable service.

Of course the existing competition in the field of long-distance transportation had its disadvantages. Electrification of railroads had not proceeded far, and it was a common sight to see a great steam locomotive belching smoke and steam, radiating expensive heat units broadcast, and puffing away at its load. The driver leaned out of a side window in the rear, one end of him baked and the other end frozen. When the track curved the right way, he could see ahead. In order to start a train—for roller bearings were just appearing on railroad cars— the locomotive would first back up to take up the slack in couplings, and then go ahead with a great bumping and crashing, much to the discomfort of passengers. Air conditioning was also in its infancy, and the atmosphere in the rear coaches of a train on a hot, dry summer day rocking across the country on uneven wood-ties and an unoiled road-bed may be imagined. The picture is more unattractive if one considers that sanitary arrangements were still somewhat barbarous.

Trains were enormously heavy and when well up to speed required a long distance in which to stop, for brakes were simply pieces of cast iron pressed onto the steel wheels by air pressure. There were many highway crossings at grade, some of them actually without any automatic protection except a bell brought down from the old horse-drawn carriage days and inaudible to an automobile driver except when actually abreast, and not even then in a high wind. The locomotives carried shrieking whistles which blew almost constantly, much to the discomfiture of the countryside, but there were of course many grade crossing accidents.

Lunch for our professor was a ceremony of a sort. Nearly all the ingredients were of natural origin with very little in the way of synthetics or products of the biological industries. The foods were attractive in their way, but chosen almost at random, and served in circumstances that were somewhat appalling. To the discomforts noted in his office were added in the dining room a complete intermixture of the odors of all the several dishes and usually such incomplete ventilation that a blind man could have told the instant he entered the door of a restaurant. In fact he would not have had to depend upon his olfactory sense, for the dishes were of various glasses and ceramic materials (as well as in some cases the tables themselves), so that there was plenty of noise from the impact of hard materials.

On his return to the office, the same hectic round would continue. Perhaps in the afternoon the incessant clatter of typewriters would be especially annoying. For letters were written on typewriters, and there was a great deal of letter writing. That was the only way of practically conveying ideas outside of the archaic telephone and personal visit.

The library, to which our professor probably turned, was enormous. Long banks of shelves contained tons of books, and yet it was supposed to be a working library and not a museum. He had to paw over cards, thumb pages, and delve by the hour. It was time-wasting and exasperating indeed. Many of us well remember the amazing incredulity which greeted the first presentation of the unabridged dictionary on a square foot of film. The idea that one might have the contents of a thousand volumes located in a couple of cubic feet in a desk, so that by depressing a few keys one could have a given page instantly projected before him, was regarded as the wildest sort of fancy. This hesitation about accepting an idea, the basic soundness of which could have been tested by a little arithmetic, is worthy of more than passing notice. For the tenor of the age was to welcome new inventions and theories. In fact the man on the street was wont to visualize scientific triumphs as *faits accomplis* even as they were being hatched in the laboratory. He combined a simple credulity on some things, not erased even by the singeing of the Big Bull Market of the late 'Twenties, with a strange resistance to others. It seemed that the greater the technical difficulties which accomplished some really revolutionary proposition, the more casually the ordinary citizen accepted its consummation as being temporarily delayed but a fortnight or so.

Television was a case in point. To read the contemporary popular accounts one would suppose that the basic problem was solved at least once a month for several years. Yet the public seemed not to mind this crying of wolf, and quietly ignored simple analyses which showed that to transmit the image of a man's face in recognizable fashion would require 50 times the amount of communication channel adequate to transmit his voice. And when the progress of television proved to be exceedingly slow (like many other things which in the 'Thirties were asserted to be just around some corner), the layman was positive that the retardation was because of some corporation's machinations.

Somewhat the ordinary fellow of the 'Thirties, though he was by no means so witless as he deemed himself when he counted up his stock market losses in the earliest years of the decade, was quite muddled in his thinking process as seen from our present vantage point. He would, as I have said, readily accept the solution of such a complex thing as television to be imminent—as something he might find poking its way into his bedroom unawares on a bright Sunday morning. But he would consider a reasonable improvement in such an elementary thing as the arrangement of sleeping car space (it was really being tried by the railroads at the time) as incapable of realization for a couple of generations at least.

All about him he could see bridges, viaducts, steamships, engines, and so on, being built in hitherto unprecedented sizes. And, if some publicity agent issued an optimistic statement to the press that in the coming year they would be built twice as large again, he'd accept such a radical prediction with little emotion. Yet, when it was proposed to make it practicable for those who were neither too fat nor abnormally tall to undress in an upper berth, his reaction was likely to be expressed in the quaint vernacular of the day by some such expletive as "boloney" which, it seems, signified intense incredulity and an impatient skepticism.

As afternoon wore on the lights in the college buildings would be started. These were undoubtedly of the incandescent type in which a wire of tungsten in a gas-filled globe was heated by direct passage of current. About 95% of the energy furnished the lamp went into heating the room. The color was yellowish, and, as the sources were usually concentrated and small, there was formed a complex system of shadows. Lights would be forced on his attention again as he drove home, for there were no polarizers and the full beams of an approaching car would often strike in his eyes and temporarily blind him.

The professor's home had been built in position by the hand work of men of a dozen trades, who obtained materials by small-sized purchases from as many dealers, and cut and fit these materials on the site. It had meant an expensive capital outlay, and as much as a fifth of his income went into fixed charges on it. It had a cellar. This cellar, by way of explanation, was a large hole dug in the ground under the residence, and was a relic from the days when heating appliances required a cellar for their distribution pipes, which were so dirty that it was well to put them underground, and when thermal insulation was so imperfect that a ground floor of a house without a cellar was expected to be cold. Although these factors had ceased to be determining, the cellar with its expensive excavation had been continued as a sort of tradition.

Of course the house was immobile, and the idea of disassembling and transporting a house to a new site would have been considered quite radical. The heating plant was as crude as the one at the office, and even less efficient on account of its small size. Rooms were not soundproofed, hence many noises could be heard all over the house. This was particularly true of the plumbing fixtures, which made quite a racket. The floors were covered with fabric rugs, with their store of lint and dirt which was sometimes removed with a suction cleaner— incidentally the noisiest implement in the place. Some of the furniture was also fabric-covered and stuffed with natural horsehair as a sort of pseudo-elastic filling. It is not pleasant to contemplate in retrospect.

The excess of noise has been mentioned often in this review. One would think there would have been general protest, but the subject was only mildly mentioned in the contemporary newspaper. There was, in fact, some indication that the people generally liked to have a lot of noise about; at least they may have considered that its presence was conducive to intense activity in some manner. In no other way can we explain, for example, a turnstile which had been installed in large numbers in subways, and which was purposely arranged to give a loud clack whenever it was operated. This same peculiar love of noise was also exemplified in the contemporary music, which throws so much light on the strained mass psychology of the period.

The typical newspaper of the Nineteen-Thirties was a large affair, which reached truly ponderous proportions on Sunday. A single edition would then contain as much as 500 square feet of fine print. Of course no single individual could read all of this, and most people read much less than one per cent. Yet the forests were denuded—for paper was still made from pulp obtained from fair-sized trees—in order to print this mass of waste material. Bulky newspapers were one extravagance chargeable against the mania for advertising which had reached grotesque proportions. Nowhere were its extent and its methods more ludicrous than in the advertising of such things as cigarettes. A single phrase, usually quite absurd, would be repeated thousands of times in newspapers as well as on large placards placed by the roadsides (of course entirely out of harmony with the scenery), in trolley cars, and everywhere where space could be found. All this was done at enormous expense and without relief from the monotony of the repetition. One would expect there might have been a protest in the form of a boycott of any article thus intrusively offered, but, on the contrary, such methods apparently succeeded in their purpose. The cost of distribution to a public with so little true discrimination was, as we might expect, a heavy economic burden.

Peculiar Pastimes

Our professor, after his dinner, had many possible diversions. It is very likely that he participated in one of the peculiar popular pastimes which swept the country in sudden waves at about this period in history, exemplifying again the inexplicable mass psychology in force. One of these was a game called contract bridge, which persisted for several years and which was regarded with great seriousness by its devotees. It was participated in by both sexes, although it is hard to understand how their joint adherence to what was essentially a cult for mental exercise came about. Very complicated and artificial rules controlled the action, and the whole procedure must have been wearying, although it was indulged in by large sections of the population, sometimes to the substantial exclusion of all other mental activity. The force of mass opinion was so strong and individualism so repressed, that not to follow the public whim of the moment was to lose social caste. One of the strangest of these pastime manias occurred when over $100,000,000 was spent in the building of small gardens in which the participants knocked little white balls about among various obstacles. This lasted, as would be expected, for only a few months.

An epidemic of jig-saw puzzles also swept the land. Though they were harmless in themselves, the distress of elderly people and children alike when some piece or pieces dropped to the floor and became hidden in some out-of-the-way place, was apt to be expressed in fitful bursts of temper.

It is little wonder that under such hectic conditions many professors developed otherwise unaccountable tendencies, and that the science of the times was disjointed, heterogeneous, and very much an opportunist affair. There should be the greatest of admiration for one who could do any constructive thinking at all when thus badgered about during the Nineteen-Thirties.

Today, quite correctly, we realize that all of the desirable modifications of our natural environment, which are possible through simple mechanical means, have been accomplished. Even 20 years ago there were significant indications that the door to progress along such lines was fast closing. About that time the standing Congressional Committee, appointed to consider the scope of the world's scientific and technical progress with special reference to its bearing upon matters to be discussed at a proposed conference to be convened for the further discussion of inter-governmental debts, was able to include in its preliminary report the convincing statement that everything worth while had been done.

What a contrast to the Nineteen-Thirties! Then it should have been possible, even by the most rudimentary of analyses, to disclose attractive avenues for constructive effort.

It may be asked why, with all this opportunity, we had to wait so long for the obvious. It could not have been because of a lack of leisure; for there were emphatic contemporary complaints that leisure engendered by the quickening of production had become both burdensome and notoriously unwelcome. Perhaps it was ascribable in a measure to the prevailing social code which then forced all men to dress alike and, to some extent, to think alike. Or, it may have been that the pressure of advertising propaganda had induced a mass psychology which led people to believe they had arrived at some sort of mechanical Utopia with which they were in duty bound to be content.

These few suggestions are typical of the myriad of hypotheses contained in the extensive literature dealing with this quite amazing decade in the history of the Republic. From all the thought given to the subject but one solitary fact emerges: the Nineteen-Thirties still remain inscrutable.

Memorandum Regarding Memex
Vannevar Bush

This manuscript is in the Vannevar Bush Papers at the Library of Congress. It is attached to a letter Bush sent Eric Hodgins April 10, 1941. Hodgins was then the publisher of FORTUNE.

THE GENERAL OBJECTIVE IN WRITING THE ARTICLE was to influence in some small way thinking regarding science in the modern world, and to do so in an interesting manner. The secondary objective was to emphasize the opportunity for the application of science in a field which is largely neglected by organized science.

The audience aimed at was the group of active thinkers who are taking part in affairs, rather than those who are developing a philosophy concerning the relation of science to human progress or the like. Hence the decidedly objective approach. In particular it seemed worth while to try to influence the thinking of trustees of foundations, educational and scientific institutions, and those concerned with governmental support or control of scientific effort.

The concern was primarily with the physical sciences, rather than the natural sciences as a whole, for the conflict as to what constitutes a reasonable attitude centers principally on physics and chemistry and their engineering applications.

The main thesis is that science and its applications are not, on the whole, evil. A secondary thesis is that gadgetry is not necessarily trivial, and that in particular it may contribute substantially to man's mental development in the future as it has in the past.

The attitude of the intended audience had gone through much transformation during the previous two decades.

There was much naive praise of the benefits of science in all sorts of fields up to the last war. After the war this became intensified, and applying science in the American way was about to solve all the ills of mankind, increase the standard of living all around, and leave us all prosperous and happy.

This was sublimed by the idealism that abounded. All war was over. We could leave those evil uses we had indulged in, and turn to higher things, such as air conditioning and four wheel brakes.

Held by the Vannevar Bush Papers, Library Congress (Box 50, General Correspondence File, Eric Hodgins), the manuscript is published here by permission of Richard Bush, MD.

Then came a disillusionment and a reaction. The grand economic idea came a cropper. The reaction extended to the applications of science; we had indulged in too much change in our ways of life and should become simple. Technocracy convinced many people that the machine meant unemployment.

The idealism persisted in a new form. If it were evil to devise new material things for ordinary use, it were [sic] still more evil to make new devices for war. We should show a fine example and forget all such things. We nearly did.

The effect was principally with older men, and with laymen. Youngsters still tried to become aeronautical engineers, and physicists were as keen on cracking the atom as ever. Foundations, however, radically cut their support of the physical sciences at this time. They never had participated much in the applications of physical science, leaving that for those having a commercial motive, and now they abandoned this field entirely. This was true even though there were plenty of possible applications which had little commercial incentive attached, but which were nevertheless of much potential benefit. For example, the foundation never thought of doing a fine job, beyond that which would be caused by a profit motive, in producing good mechanical music. It was left out because it was mechanical. Rather the foundations turned to the biological sciences, which could satisfy man's craving for knowledge without doing him any harm, and in particular to the medical sciences which could cure his ills, sometimes without inquiring too deeply into the ultimate results. They also turned to the social sciences, often with a hope that was entirely unjustified by the state of advancement of the disciplines in that category. They turned heavily to art, to adult education, and so on. Many new foundations were created, with very great sums in the aggregate at their disposal, and almost uniformly they avoided the physical sciences and their applications. The attitude of foundations exemplified a more general attitude which tended to frown upon physicists and all their works.

This was the situation when the Memex was first written; and this was the attitude which it was intended indirectly to combat. Publication was delayed, principally because it took a long time to write.

Then came the present war and attitudes changed in a hurry. Where there had been a feeling that we had too much physics, there arose the

cry for more and very active physicists to devise war gadgets. The shift in attitude has not been made by all. Most men on the active list have shifted, if they ever needed to. Many a philosopher hasn't, and of course many thoughtful people do not really know there is a war on. But the change of attitude has been profound.

The idealism has largely gone. We are living in a real and tough world. It is no longer regarded as wicked to devise a means for shooting an airplane, in a world where it suddenly appears that men will actually ride in airplanes, and drop bombs. It is not even wicked to work out more powerful bombs to drop on someone else. It is being realized with a thud that the world is probably going to be ruled by those who know how, in the fullest sense, to apply science, whatever their other attributes may be.

Part of the original thesis no longer needs demonstration. If [sic] may now be all the more necessary to emphasize the rest.

The long-range pursuit of scientific knowledge is now being pressed aside by the needs for defense research. This is as it should be, but it will be highly important to swing back again, when the pace is not so breathless, to the sound development of fundamental science and the widespread acquaintanceship with scientific matters which goes with this. There is real danger, when peace comes, if we still have a free and orderly civilization that is controlled by mass public opinion, that we will again lapse into dreamland.

The application of science to war is now getting its emphasis. Along with this, and partly as a consequence after the emergency, it is more probable that there will come an increased emphasis at least for a time, on applications to transportation, food, clothing and all the other aspects of living in a mechanical way. It may therefore still be pertinent to argue that there are possible applications to the things of the mind that are not negligible.

It is a question of timing. People will even now read an interesting story. It may even carry a new realization that there is a neglected field worth cultivating. But the field cannot be cultivated now, and by the time it can the story, if published now, will undoubtedly have been forgotten. Even so, it may now be cheering to contemplate the application of science to something more satisfying than weapons. Perhaps it is worth telling for that reason. It was originally constructed to produce

an effect, and the need to do so still remains. It seems too bad to tell it at a time when it can probably accomplish little of its original purpose. Yet if merely allowed to wait it probably will not last until it could be told in an atmosphere which would admit its full effectiveness, whatever that might turn out to be.

It is certain, however, that, if it is to be anything more than an amusing tale, it needs to be revamped to bring it in line with changed times. Just how to do this is a puzzle. Another thing to do would be to say "when this was written...." and then tell a yarn for the sake of telling a yarn, which is not a very serious undertaking. My hearn [sic] to influence the attitude toward science would then have to be approached from an entirely new direction when and if it were possible to do so.

As We May Think
Vannevar Bush

Bush's most well-known essay on Memex was published in two forms during 1945. It first appeared in the Atlantic Monthly *in July and a condensed, illustrated version came out in* LIFE *early in September.* LIFE's *editors added a subtitle, "A Top U.S. Scientist Foresees a Possible Future World In Which Man-Made Machines Will Start To Think." They also replaced the* Atlantic Monthly *numbered sections with headings and added illustrations. The essay first appeared in book form the following year in Bush's* Endless Horizons *(Washington: Public Affairs Press), where the* Atlantic Monthly *text was reprinted, but without section numbers and with different headings than those* LIFE *used.*

Both magazines provided introductory remarks describing Bush's role in the war effort and the essay as a call for peacetime research goals.

The next two pages reprint the introductory remarks that led off the essay. To show the reader the difference between the two versions, the text that appeared in the Atlantic Monthly *but was omitted from* LIFE *is printed in italics here. All additional words inserted in the* LIFE *piece are printed in* **bold**. *The* LIFE *illustrations and captions follow the text of the essay.*

Reprinted from the Atlantic Monthly *, Vol. 176, No. 1 (1945), 641-649, and* LIFE, *Vol. 19, No. 11 (1945) 112-114, 116, 121, 123-124, by permission of Alfred D. Crimi, the* Atlantic Monthly, *and Richard Bush, MD.*

Editor's Note, *Atlantic Monthly*

As Director of the Office of Scientific Research and Development, Dr. Vannevar Bush has coördinated the activities of some six thousand leading American scientists in the application of science to warfare. In this significant article he holds up an incentive for scientists when the fighting has ceased. He urges that men of science should then turn to the massive task of making more accessible our bewildering store of knowledge. For years inventions have extended man's physical powers rather than the powers of his mind. Trip hammers that multiply the fists, microscopes that sharpen the eye, and engines of destruction and detection are new results, but not the end results, of modern science. Now, says Dr. Bush, instruments are at hand which, if properly developed, will give man access to and command over the inherited knowledge of the ages. The perfection of these pacific instruments should be the first objective of our scientists as they emerge from their war work. Like Emerson's famous address of 1837 on "The American Scholar," this paper by Dr. Bush calls for a new relationship between thinking man and the sum of our knowledge—The Editor

Editor's Note, *LIFE*

Dr. Vannevar Bush is head of the Office of Scientific Research and Development, which marshaled the scientific brains of the U.S. in the service of the war. As such he has performed one of the greatest, though most secret, jobs of the war, as important in its sphere as that of the Army chief of staff. Under his direction 6,000 scientists worked on such projects as the development of radar and the atomic bomb.

In the July issue of the *Atlantic Monthly* Dr. Bush published an article in which he set a great task for men of science in the peacetime world. Man has piled up a staggering body of knowledge—so staggering, in fact, that men of learning have great difficulty in finding and using the parts they want. It is the task of science, Dr. Bush says, to make this store of knowledge more available, to aid the human memory. Says the *Atlantic*, "Like Emerson's famous address of 1837 on 'The American Scholar,' this paper by Dr. Bush calls for a new relationship between thinking man and the sum of our knowledge."

LIFE is indebted to the editors of the *Atlantic Monthly* for permission to bring a condensed version of this important article to its larger audience.

What Dr. Bush Foresees

Cyclops Camera

Worn on forehead, it would photograph anything you see and want to record. Film would be developed at once by dry photography.

Microfilm

It could reduce *Encyclopaedia Britannica* to volume of a matchbox. Material cost: 5¢. Thus a whole library could be kept in a desk.

Vocoder

A machine which could type when talked to. But you might have to talk a special phonetic language to this mechanical supersecretary.

Thinking machine

A development of the mathematical calculator. Give it premises and it would pass out conclusions, all in accordance with logic.

Memex

An aid to memory. Like the brain, Memex would file material by association. Press a key and it would run through a "trail" of facts.

THIS HAS NOT BEEN A SCIENTIST'S WAR; it has been a war in which all have had a part. The scientists, burying their old professional competition in the demand of a common cause, have shared greatly and learned much. It has been exhilarating to work in effective partnership. *Now, for many, this appears to be approaching an end.* What are the scientists to do next?

For the biologists, and particularly for the medical scientists, there can be little indecision, for their war work has hardly required them to leave the old paths. Many indeed have been able to carry on their war research in their familiar peacetime laboratories. Their objectives remain much the same.

It is the physicists who have been thrown most violently off stride, who have left academic pursuits for the making of strange destructive gadgets, who have had to devise new methods for their unanticipated assignments. They have done their part on the devices that made it possible to turn back the enemy. They have worked in combined effort with the physicists of our allies. They have felt within themselves the stir of achievement. They have been part of a great team. Now, *as peace approaches,* one asks where they will find objectives worthy of their best.

Of what lasting benefit has been man's use of science and of the new instruments which his research brought into existence? First, they have increased his control of his material environment. They have improved his food, his clothing, his shelter; they have increased his security and released him partly from the bondage of bare existence. They have given him increased knowledge of his own biological processes so that he has had a progressive freedom from disease and an increased span of life. They are illuminating the interactions of his physiological and psychological functions, giving the promise of an improved mental health.

Science has provided the swiftest communication between individuals; it has provided a record of ideas and has enabled man to manipulate and to make extracts from that record so that knowledge evolves and endures throughout the life of a race rather than that of an individual.

There is a growing mountain of research. But there is increased evidence that we are being bogged down today as specialization extends. The investigator is staggered by the findings and conclusions of thousands of other workers—conclusions which he cannot find time to grasp, much less to remember, as they appear. Yet specialization becomes increasingly necessary for progress, and the effort to bridge between disciplines is correspondingly superficial.

Professionally our methods of transmitting and reviewing the results of research are generations old and by now are totally inadequate for their purpose. If the aggregate time spent in writing scholarly works and in reading them could be evaluated, the ratio between these amounts of time might well be startling. Those who conscientiously attempt to keep abreast of current thought, even in restricted fields, by close and continuous reading might well shy away from an examination calculated to show how much of the previous month's efforts could be produced on call. Mendel's concept of the laws of genetics was lost to the world for a generation because his publication did not reach the few who were capable of grasping and extending it; and this sort of catastrophe is undoubtedly being repeated all about us, as truly significant attainments become lost in the mass of the inconsequential.

The difficulty seems to be, not so much that we publish unduly in view of the extent and variety of present-day interests, but rather that publication has been extended far beyond our present ability to make real use of the record. The summation of human experience is being expanded at a prodigious rate, and the means we use for threading through the consequent maze to the momentarily important item is the same as was used in the days of square-rigged ships.

But there are signs of a change as new and powerful instrumentalities come into use. Photocells capable of seeing things in a physical sense, advanced photography which can record what is seen or even what is not, thermionic tubes capable of controlling potent forces under the guidance of less power than a mosquito uses to vibrate his wings, cathode ray tubes rendering visible an occurrence so brief that by comparison a microsecond is a long time, relay combinations which will carry out involved sequences of movements more reliably than any human operator and thousands of times as fast—there are plenty of mechanical aids with which to effect a transformation in scientific records.

Two centuries ago Leibnitz invented a calculating machine which embodied most of the essential features of recent keyboard devices, but it could not then come into use. The economics of the situation were against it: the labor involved in constructing it, before the days of mass production, exceeded the labor to be saved by its use, since all it could accomplish could be duplicated by sufficient use of pencil and paper. Moreover, it would have been subject to frequent breakdown, so that it could not have been depended upon; for at that time and long after, complexity and unreliability were synonymous.

Babbage, even with remarkably generous support for his time, could not produce his great arithmetical machine. His idea was sound enough, but construction and maintenance costs were then too heavy. Had a Pharaoh been given detailed and explicit designs of an automobile, and had he understood them completely, it would have taxed the resources of his kingdom to have fashioned the thousands of parts for a single car, and that car would have broken down on the first trip to Giza.

Machines with interchangeable parts can now be constructed with great economy of effort. In spite of much complexity, they perform reliably. Witness the humble typewriter, or the movie camera, or the automobile. Electrical contacts have ceased to stick when thoroughly understood. Note the automatic telephone exchange, which has hundreds of thousands of such contacts, and yet is reliable. A spider web of metal, sealed in a thin glass container, a wire heated to a brilliant glow, in short, the thermionic tube of radio sets, is made by the hundred million, tossed about in packages, plugged into sockets—and it works! Its gossamer parts, the precise location and alignment involved in its construction, would have occupied a master craftsman of the guild for months; now it is built for thirty cents. The world has arrived at an age of cheap complex devices of great reliability; and something is bound to come of it.

A record, if it is to be useful to science, must be continuously extended, it must be stored, and above all it must be consulted. Today we make the record conventionally by writing and photography, followed by printing; but we also record on film, on wax disks, and on magnetic wires. Even if utterly new recording procedures do not appear, these present ones are certainly in the process of modification and extension.

New Ways To Extend The Record—The Cyclops Camera And Dry Photography

Certainly progress in photography is not going to stop. Faster material and lenses, more automatic cameras, finer-grained sensitive compounds to allow an extension of the minicamera idea, are all imminent. Let us project this trend ahead to a logical, if not inevitable, outcome. The camera hound of the future wears on his forehead a lump a little larger than a walnut. It takes pictures 3 millimeters square, later to be projected or enlarged, *which after all involves only a factor of 10 beyond present practice.* The lens is of universal focus, down to any distance accommodated by the unaided eye, simply because it is of short focal length. There is a built-in photocell on the walnut such as we now have on at least one camera, which automatically adjusts exposure for a wide range of illumination. There is film in the walnut for a hundred exposures, and the spring for operating its shutter and shifting its film is wound once for all when the film clip is inserted. It produces its result in full color. It may well be stereoscopic, and record with two spaced glass eyes, for striking improvements in stereoscopic technique are just around the corner.

The cord which trips its shutter may reach down a man's sleeve within easy reach of his fingers. A quick squeeze, and the picture is taken. On a pair of ordinary glasses is a square of fine lines near the top of one lens, where it is out of the way of ordinary vision. When an object appears in that square, it is lined up for its picture. As the scientist of the future moves about the laboratory or the field, every time he looks at something worthy of the record, he trips the shutter and in it goes, without even an audible click. Is this all fantastic? The only fantastic thing about it is the idea of making as many pictures as would result from its use.

Will there be dry photography? It is already here in two forms. *When Brady made his Civil War pictures, the plate had to be wet at the time of exposure. Now it has to be wet during development instead. In the future perhaps it need not be wetted at all.* There have long been films impregnated with diazo dyes which form a picture without development, so that it is already there as soon as the camera has been operated. An exposure to ammonia gas destroys the unexposed dye, and the picture can then be taken out into the light and examined. The process is now slow, but someone may speed it up, and it has no grain difficulties such as now keep photographic researchers busy. *Often it would be advantageous to be able to snap the camera and to look at the picture immediately.*

Another process now in use is also slow, and more or less clumsy. For fifty years impregnated papers have been used which turn dark at every point where an electrical contact touches them, by reason of the chemical change thus produced in an iodine compound included in the paper. They have been used to make records, for a pointer moving across them can leave a trail behind. If the electrical potential on the pointer is varied as it moves, the line becomes light or dark in accordance with the potential.

This scheme is now used in facsimile transmission. The pointer draws a set of closely spaced lines across the paper one after another. As it moves, its potential is varied in accordance with a varying current received over wires from a distant station, where these variations are produced by a photocell which is similarly scanning a picture. At every instant the darkness of the line being drawn is made equal to the darkness of the point on the picture being observed by the photocell. Thus, when the whole picture has been covered, a replica appears at the receiving end.

A scene itself can be just as well looked over line by line by the photocell in this way as can a photograph of the scene. This whole apparatus constitutes a camera, with the added feature, which can be dispensed with if desired, of making its picture at a distance. It is slow, and the picture is poor in detail. Still, it does give another process of dry photography, in which the picture is finished as soon as it is taken.

It would be a brave man who would predict that such a process will always remain clumsy, slow, and faulty in detail. Television equipment today transmits sixteen reasonably good pictures a second, and it involves only two essential differences from the process described above. For one, the record is made by a moving beam of electrons rather than a moving pointer, for the reason that an electron beam can sweep across the picture very rapidly indeed. The other difference involves merely the use of a screen which glows momentarily when the electrons hit, rather than a chemically treated paper or film which is permanently altered. This speed is necessary in television, for motion pictures rather than stills are the object.

Use chemically treated film in place of the glowing screen, allow the apparatus to transmit one picture only rather than a succession, and a rapid camera for dry photography results. The treated film needs to be far faster in action than present examples, but it probably could be. More serious is the objection that this scheme would involve putting the film inside a vacuum chamber, for electron beams behave normally only in such a rarefied environment. This difficulty could be avoided by allowing the electron beam to play on one side of a partition, and by pressing the film against the other side, if this partition were such as to allow the electrons to go through perpendicular to its surface, and to prevent them from spreading out sideways. Such partitions, in crude form, could certainly be constructed, and they will hardly hold up the general development.

Reducing The Written Record To Manageable Size— Microphotography

Like dry photography, microphotography still has a long way to go. The basic scheme of reducing the size of the record, and examining it by projection rather than directly, has possibilities too great to be ignored. The combination of optical projection and photographic reduction is already producing some results in microfilm for scholarly purposes, and the potentialities are highly suggestive. Today, with microfilm, reductions by a linear factor of 20 can be employed and still produce full clarity when the material is re-enlarged for examination. *The limits are set by the graininess of the film, the excellence of the optical system, and the efficiency of the light sources employed. All of these are rapidly improving.*

Assume a linear ratio of 100 for future use. Consider film of the same thickness as paper, although thinner film will certainly be usable. Even under these conditions there would be a total factor of 10,000 between the bulk of the ordinary record on books, and its microfilm replica. The ENCYCLOPAEDIA BRITANNICA could be reduced to the volume of a matchbox. A library of a million volumes could be compressed into one end of a desk. If the human race has produced since the invention of movable type a total record, in the form of magazines, newspapers, books, tracts, advertising blurbs, correspondence, having a volume corresponding to a billion books, the whole affair, assembled and compressed, could be lugged off in a moving van. *Mere compression, of course, is not enough; one needs not only to make and store a record but also be able to consult it, and this aspect of the matter comes later. Even the modern great library is not generally consulted; it is nibbled at by a few.*

Compression is important, however, when it comes to costs. The material for the microfilm BRITANNICA would cost a nickel, and it could be mailed anywhere for a cent. What would it cost to print a million copies? To print a sheet of newspaper, in a large edition, costs a small fraction of a cent. The entire material of the BRITANNICA in reduced microfilm form would go on a sheet eight and one-half by eleven inches. Once it is available, with the photographic reproduction methods of the future, duplicates in large quantities could probably be turned out for a cent apiece beyond the cost of materials. The preparation of the original copy? That introduces the next aspect of the subject.

The Author Need Not Write—He Could Talk His Thoughts To A Machine

To make the record, we now push a pencil or tap a typewriter. Then comes the process of digestion and correction, followed by an intricate process of typesetting, printing, and distribution. To consider the first stage of the procedure, will the author of the future cease writing by hand or typewriter and talk directly to the record? He does so indirectly, by talking to a stenographer or a wax cylinder; but the elements are all present if he wishes to have his talk directly produce a typed record. All he needs to do is to take advantage of existing mechanisms and to alter his language.

At a recent World Fair a machine called a Voder was shown. A girl stroked its keys and it emitted recognizable speech. No human vocal chords entered into the procedure at any point; the keys simply combined some electrically produced vibrations and passed these on to a loud-speaker. In the Bell Laboratories there is the converse of this machine, called a Vocoder. The loud-speaker is replaced by a microphone, which picks up sound. Speak to it, and the corresponding keys move. This may be one element of the postulated system.

The other element is found in the stenotype, that somewhat disconcerting device encountered usually at public meetings. A girl strokes its keys languidly and looks about the room and sometimes at the speaker with a disquieting gaze. From it emerges a typed strip which records in a phonetically simplified language a record of what the speaker is supposed to have said. Later this strip is retyped into ordinary language, for in its nascent form it is intelligible only to the initiated. Combine these two elements, let the Vocoder run the stenotype, and the result is a machine which types when talked to.

Our present languages are not especially adapted to this sort of mechanization, it is true. It is strange that the inventors of universal languages have not seized upon the idea of producing one which better fitted the technique for transmitting and recording speech. Mechanization may yet force the issue, especially in the scientific field; whereupon scientific jargon would become still less intelligible to the layman.

One can now picture a future investigator in his laboratory. His hands are free, and he is not anchored. As he moves about and observes, he photographs and comments. Time is automatically recorded to tie the two records together. If he goes into the field, he may be connected by radio to his recorder. As he ponders over his notes in the evening, he again talks his comments into the record. His typed record, as well as his photographs, may both be in miniature, so that he projects them for examination.

Simple Repetitive Thought Could Be Done By Machine, Following Laws of Logic

Much needs to occur, however, between the collection of data and observations, the extraction of parallel material from the existing record, and the final insertion of new material into the general body of the common record. For mature thought there is no mechanical substitute. But creative thought and essentially repetitive thought are very different things. For the latter there are, and may be, powerful mechanical aids.

Adding a column of figures is a repetitive thought process, and it was long ago properly relegated to the machine. True, the machine is sometimes controlled by a keyboard, and thought of a sort enters in reading the figures and poking the corresponding keys, but even this is avoidable. Machines have been made which will read typed figures by photocells and then depress the corresponding keys; these are combinations of photocells for scanning the type, electric circuits for sorting the consequent variations, and relay circuits for interpreting the result into the action of solenoids to pull the keys down.

All this complication is needed because of the clumsy way in which we have learned to write figures. If we recorded them positionally, simply by the configuration of a set of dots on a card, the automatic reading mechanism would become comparatively simple. In fact, if the dots are holes, we have the punched-card machine long ago produced by Hollorith for the purposes of the census, and now used throughout business. Some types of complex businesses could hardly operate without these machines.

Adding is only one operation. To perform arithmetical computation involves also subtraction, multiplication, and division, and in addition some method for temporary storage of results, removal from storage for further manipulation, and recording of final results by printing. Machines for these purposes are now of two types: keyboard machines for accounting and the like, manually controlled for the insertion of data, and usually automatically controlled as far as the sequence of operations is concerned; and punched-card machines in which separate operations are usually delegated to a series of machines, and the cards then transferred bodily from one to another. Both forms are very useful; but as far as complex computations are concerned, both are still in embryo.

Rapid electrical counting appeared soon after the physicists found it desirable to count cosmic rays. For their own purposes the physicists promptly constructed thermionic-tube equipment capable of counting electrical impulses at the rate of 100,000 a second. The advanced arithmetical machines of the future will be electrical in nature, and they will perform at 100 times present speeds, or more.

Moreover, they will be far more versatile than present commercial machines, so that they may readily be adapted for a wide variety of operations. They will be controlled by a control card or film, they will select their own data and manipulate it in accordance with the instructions thus inserted, they will perform complex arithmetical computations at exceedingly high speeds, and they will record results in such form as to be readily available for distribution or for later further manipulation. Such machines will have enormous appetites. One of them will take instructions and data from a whole roomful of girls armed with simple keyboard punches, and will deliver sheets of computed results every few minutes. There will always be plenty of things to compute in the detailed affairs of millions of people doing complicated things.

The repetitive processes of thought are not confined, however, to matters of arithmetic and statistics. In fact, every time one combines and records facts in accordance with established logical processes, the creative aspect of thinking is concerned only with the selection of the data and the process to be employed, and the manipulation thereafter is repetitive in nature and hence a fit matter to be relegated to the machines. Not so much has been done along these lines, beyond the bounds of arithmetic, as might be done, primarily because of the economics of the situation. The needs of business, and the extensive market obviously waiting, assured the advent of mass-produced arithmetical machines just as soon as production methods were sufficiently advanced.

With machines for advanced analysis no such situation existed; for there was and is no extensive market; the users of advanced methods of manipulating data are a very small part of the population. There are, however, machines for solving differential equations—and functional and integral equations, for that matter. There are many special machines, such as the harmonic synthesizer which predicts the tides. There will be many more, appearing certainly first in the hands of the scientist and in small numbers.

If scientific reasoning were limited to the logical processes of arithmetic, we should not get far in our understanding of the physical world. One might as well attempt to grasp the game of poker entirely by the use of the mathematics of probability. The abacus, with its beads strung on parallel wires, led the Arabs to positional numeration and the concept of zero many centuries before the rest of the world; and it was a useful tool—so useful that it still exists.

It is a far cry from the abacus, **with its beads strung on parallel wires,** to the modern keyboard accounting machine. It will be an equal step to the arithmetical machine of the future. But even this new machine will not take the scientist where he needs to go. Relief must be secured from laborious detailed manipulation of higher mathematics as well, if the users of it are to free their brains for something more than repetitive detailed transformations in accordance with established rules. A mathematician is not a man who can readily manipulate figures; often he cannot. He is not even a man who can readily perform the transformations of equations by the use of calculus. He is primarily an individual who is skilled in the use of symbolic logic on a high plane, and especially he is a man of intuitive judgment in the choice of the manipulative processes he employs.

All else he should be able to turn over to his mechanism, just as confidently as he turns over the propelling of his car to the intricate mechanism under the hood. Only then will mathematics be practically effective in bringing the growing knowledge of atomistics to the useful solution of the advanced problems of chemistry, metallurgy, and biology. For this reason there will come more machines to handle advanced mathematics for the scientist. Some of them will be sufficiently bizarre to suit the most fastidious connoisseur of the present artifacts of civilization.

The scientist, however, is not the only person who manipulates data and examines the world about him by the use of logical processes, although he sometimes preserves this appearance by adopting into the fold anyone who becomes logical, much in the manner in which a British labor leader is elevated to knighthood. Whenever logical processes of thought are employed—that is, whenever thought for a time runs along an accepted groove—there is an opportunity for the machine. Formal logic used to be a keen instrument in the hands of the teacher in his trying of students' souls. It is readily possible to construct a machine which will manipulate premises in accordance with formal logic, simply by the clever use of relay circuits. Put a set of premises into such a device and turn the crank, and it will readily pass out conclusion after conclusion, all in accordance with logical law, *and with no more slips than would be expected of a keyboard adding machine.*

Logic can become enormously difficult, and it would undoubtedly be well to produce more assurance in its use. The machines for higher analysis have usually been equation solvers. Ideas are beginning to appear for equation transformers, which will rearrange the relationship expressed by an equation in accordance with strict and rather advanced logic. Progress is inhibited by the exceedingly crude way in which mathematicians express their relationships. They employ a symbolism which grew like Topsy and has little consistency; a strange fact in that most logical field.

A new symbolism, probably positional, must apparently precede the reduction of mathematical transformations to machine processes. Then, on beyond the strict logic of the mathematician, lies the application of logic in everyday affairs. We may some day click off arguments *on a machine* with the same assurance that we now enter sales on a cash register. But the machine of logic will not look like a cash register, even of the stream-lined model.

How To Consult The Record—Machines Examine The Files and Select Related Items

So much for the manipulation of ideas and their insertion into the record. Thus far we seem to be worse off than before—for we can enormously extend the record; yet even in its present bulk we can hardly consult it. This is a much larger matter than merely the extraction of data for the purposes of scientific research; it involves the entire process by which man profits by his inheritance of acquired knowledge. The prime action of use is selection, and here we are halting indeed. There may be millions of fine thoughts, and the account of the experience on which they are based, all encased within stone walls of acceptable architectural form; but if the scholar can get at only one a week by diligent search, his syntheses are not likely to keep up with the current scene.

Selection, in this broad sense, is a stone adze in the hands of a cabinetmaker. Yet, in a narrow sense *and in other areas,* something has already been done mechanically on selection. The personnel officer of a factory drops a stack of a few thousand employee cards into a selecting machine, sets a code in accordance with an established convention, and produces in a short time a list of all employees who live in Trenton and know Spanish. Even such devices are much too slow when it comes, for example, to matching a set of fingerprints with one of five million on file. Selection devices of this sort will soon be speeded up from their present rate of reviewing data at a few hundred a minute. By the use of photocells and microfilm they will survey items at the rate of a thousand a second, and will print out duplicates of those selected.

This process, *however*, is simple selection: it proceeds by examining in turn every one of a large set of items, and by picking out those which have certain specified characteristics. There is another form of selection best illustrated by the automatic telephone exchange. You dial a number and the machine selects and connects just one of a million possible stations. It does not run over them all. It pays attention only to a class given by a first digit, then only to a subclass of this given by the second digit, and so on; and thus proceeds rapidly and almost unerringly to the selected station. It requires a few seconds to make the selection, although the process could be speeded up if increased speed were economically warranted. *If necessary, it could be made extremely fast by substituting thermionic-tube switching for mechanical switching, so that the full selection could be made in one one-hundredth of a second. No one would wish to spend the money necessary to make this change in the telephone system, but the general idea is applicable elsewhere.*

Take the prosaic problem of the great department store. Every time a charge sale is made, there are a number of things to be done. The inventory needs to be revised, the salesman needs to be given credit for the sale, the general accounts need an entry, and, most important, the customer needs to be charged. A central records device has been developed in which much of this work is done conveniently. The salesman places on a stand the customer's identification card, his own card, and the card taken from the article sold—all punched cards. When he pulls a lever, contacts are made through the holes, machinery at a central point makes the necessary computations and entries, and the proper receipt is printed for the salesman to pass to the customer.

But there may be ten thousand charge customers doing business with the store, and before the full operation can be completed someone has to select the right card and insert it at the central office. Now rapid selection can slide just the proper card into position in an instant or two, and return it afterward. Another difficulty occurs, however. Someone must read a total on the card, so that the machine can add its computed item to it. Conceivably the cards might be of the dry photography type I have described. Existing totals could then be read by photocell, and the new total entered by an electron beam.

The cards may be in miniature, so that they occupy little space. They must move quickly. They need not be transferred far, but merely into position so that the photocell and recorder can operate on them. Positional dots can enter the data. At the end of the month a machine can readily be made to read these and to print an ordinary bill. With tube selection, in which no mechanical parts are involved in the switches, little time need be occupied in bringing the correct card into use—a second should suffice for the entire operation. The whole record on the card may be made by magnetic dots on a steel sheet if desired, instead of dots to be observed optically, following the scheme by which Poulsen long ago put speech on a magnetic wire. This method has the advantage of simplicity and ease of erasure. By using photography, however, one can arrange to project the record in enlarged form, and at a distance by using the process common in television equipment.

One can consider rapid selection of this form, and distant projection for other purposes. To be able to key one sheet of a million before an operator in a second or two, with the possibility of then adding notes thereto, is suggestive in many ways. It might even be of use in libraries, but that is another story. At any rate, there are now some interesting combinations possible. One might, for example, speak to a microphone, in the manner described in connection with the speech-controlled typewriter, and thus make his selections. It would certainly beat the usual file clerk.

The Human Brain Files By Association—The Memex Could Do This Mechanically

The real heart of the matter of selection, however, goes deeper than a lag in the adoption of mechanisms by libraries, or a lack of development of devices for their use. Our ineptitude in getting at the record is largely caused by the artificiality of systems of indexing. When data of any sort are placed in storage, they are filed alphabetically or numerically, and information is found (when it is) by tracing it down from subclass to subclass. It can be in only one place, unless duplicates are used; one has to have rules as to which path will locate it, and the rules are cumbersome. Having found one item, moreover, one has to emerge from the system and re-enter on a new path.

The human mind does not work that way. It operates by association. With one item in its grasp, it snaps instantly to the next that is suggested by the association of thoughts, in accordance with some intricate web of trails carried by the cells of the brain. It has other characteristics, of course; trails that are not frequently followed are prone to fade, items are not fully permanent, memory is transitory. Yet the speed of action, the intricacy of trails, the detail of mental pictures, is awe-inspiring beyond all else in nature.

Man cannot hope fully to duplicate this mental process artificially, but he certainly ought to be able to learn from it. In minor ways he may even improve, for his records have relative permanency. The first idea, however, to be drawn from the analogy concerns selection. Selection by association, rather than by indexing, may yet be mechanized. One cannot hope thus to equal the speed and flexibility with which the mind follows an associative trail, but it should be possible to beat the mind decisively in regard to the permanence and clarity of the items resurrected from storage.

Consider a future device for individual use, which is a sort of mechanized private file and library. It needs a name, and, to coin one at random, "memex" will do. A memex is a device in which an individual stores all his books, records, and communications, and which is mechanized so that it may be consulted with exceeding speed and flexibility. It is an enlarged intimate supplement to his memory.

It consists of a desk, and while it can presumably be operated from a distance, it is primarily the piece of furniture at which he works. On the top are slanting translucent screens, on which material can be projected for convenient reading. There is a keyboard, and sets of buttons and levers. Otherwise it looks like an ordinary desk.

In one end is the stored material. The matter of bulk is well taken care of by improved microfilm. Only a small part of the interior of the memex is devoted to storage, the rest to mechanism. Yet if the user inserted 5000 pages of material a day it would take him hundreds of years to fill the repository, so he can be profligate and enter material freely.

Most of the memex contents are purchased on microfilm ready for insertion. Books of all sorts, pictures, current periodicals, newspapers, are thus obtained and dropped into place. Business correspondence takes the same path. And there is provision for direct entry. On the top of the memex is a transparent platen. On this are placed longhand notes, photographs, memoranda, all sorts of things. When one is in place, the depression of a lever causes it to be photographed onto the next blank space in a section of the memex film, dry photography being employed.

There is, of course, provision for consultation of the record by the usual scheme of indexing. If the user wishes to consult a certain book, he taps its code on the keyboard, and the title page of the book promptly appears before him, projected onto one of his viewing positions. *Frequently-used codes are mnemonic, so that he seldom consults his code book; but when he does, a single tap of a key projects it for his use.* Moreover, he has supplemental levers. On deflecting one of these levers to the right he runs through the book before him, each page in turn being projected at a speed which just allows a recognizing glance at each. If he deflects it further to the right, he steps through the book 10 pages at a time; still further at 100 pages at a time. Deflection to the left gives him the same control backwards.

A special button transfers him immediately to the first page of the index. Any given book of his library can thus be called up and consulted with far greater facility than if it were taken from a shelf. As he has several projection positions, he can leave one item in position while he calls up another. He can add marginal notes and comments, taking advantage of one possible type of dry photography, and it could even be arranged so that he can do this by a stylus scheme, such as is now employed in the telautograph seen in railroad waiting rooms, just as though he had the physical page before him.

Building "Trails" Of Thought On The Memex—Unlike Memory, They Would Never Fade

All this is conventional, except for the projection forward of present-day mechanisms and gadgetry. It affords an immediate step, however, to associative indexing, the basic idea of which is a provision whereby any item may be caused at will to select immediately and automatically another. This is the essential feature of the memex. The process of tying two items together is the important thing.

When the user is building a trail, he names it, inserts the name in his code book, and taps it out on his keyboard. Before him are the two items to be joined, projected onto adjacent viewing positions. At the bottom of each there are a number of blank code spaces, and a pointer is set to indicate one of these on each item. The user taps a single key, and the items are permanently joined. In each code space appears the code word. Out of view, but also in the code space, is inserted a set of dots for photocell viewing; and on each item these dots by their positions designate the index number of the other item.

Thereafter, at any time, when one of these items is in view, the other can be instantly recalled merely by tapping a button below the corresponding code space. Moreover, when numerous items have been thus joined together to form a trail, they can be reviewed in turn, rapidly or slowly, by deflecting a lever like that used for turning the pages of a book. It is exactly as though the physical items had been gathered together from widely separated sources and bound together to form a new book. It is more than this, for any item can be joined into numerous trails.

The owner of the memex, let us say, is interested in the origin and properties of the bow and arrow. Specifically he is studying why the short Turkish bow was apparently superior to the English long bow in the skirmishes of the Crusades. He has dozens of possibly pertinent books and articles in his memex. First he runs through an encyclopedia, finds an interesting but sketchy article, leaves it projected. Next, in a history, he finds another pertinent item, and ties the two together. Thus he goes, building a trail of many items. Occasionally he inserts a comment of his own, either linking it into the main trail or joining it by a side trail to a particular item. When it becomes evident that the elastic properties of available materials had a great deal to do with the bow, he branches off on a side trail which takes him through textbooks on elasticity and tables of physical constants. He inserts a page of longhand analysis of his own. Thus he builds a trail of his interest through the maze of materials available to him.

And his trails do not fade. Several years later, his talk with a friend turns to the queer ways in which a people resist innovations, even of vital interest. He has an example, in the fact that the outranged Europeans still failed to adopt the Turkish bow. In fact he has a trail on it. A touch brings up the code book. Tapping a few keys projects the head of the trail. A lever runs through it at will, stopping at interesting items, going off on side excursions. It is an interesting trail, pertinent to the discussion. So he sets a reproducer in action, photographs the whole trail out, and passes it to his friend for insertion in his own memex, there to be linked into the more general trail.

Wholly new forms of encyclopedias will appear, ready-made with a mesh of associative trails running through them, ready to be dropped into the memex and there amplified. The lawyer has at his touch the associated opinions and decisions of his whole experience, and of the experience of friends and authorities. The patent attorney has on call the millions of issued patents, with familiar trails to every point of his client's interest. The physician, puzzled by a patient's reactions, strikes the trail established in studying an earlier similar case, and runs rapidly through analogous case histories, with side references to the classics for the pertinent anatomy and histology. The chemist, struggling with the synthesis of an organic compound, has all the chemical literature before him in his laboratory, with trails following the analogies of compounds, and side trails to their physical and chemical behavior.

The historian, with a vast chronological account of a people, parallels it with a skip trail which stops only on the salient items, and can follow at any time contemporary trails which lead him all over civilization at a particular epoch. There is a new profession of trail blazers, those who find delight in the task of establishing useful trails through the enormous mass of the common record. The inheritance from the master becomes, not only his additions to the world's record, but for his disciples the entire scaffolding by which they were erected.

Thus science may implement the ways in which man produces, stores, and consults the record of the race. It might be striking to outline the instrumentalities of the future more spectacularly, rather than to stick closely to methods and elements now known and undergoing rapid development, as has been done here. Technical difficulties of all sorts have been ignored, certainly, but also ignored are means as yet unknown which may come any day to accelerate technical progress as violently as did the advent of the thermionic tube. *In order that the picture may not be too commonplace, by reason of sticking to present-day patterns, it may be well to mention one such possibility, not to prophesy but merely to suggest, for prophecy based on extension of the known has substance, while prophecy founded on the unknown is only a doubly involved guess.*

All our steps in creating or absorbing material of the record proceed through one of the senses—the tactile when we touch keys, the oral when we speak or listen, the visual when we read. Is it not possible that some day the path may be established more directly?

We know that when the eye sees, all the consequent information is transmitted to the brain by means of electrical vibrations in the channel of the optic nerve. This is an exact analogy with the electrical vibrations which occur in the cable of the television set: they convey the picture from the photocells which see it to the radio transmitter from which it is broadcast. We know further that if we can approach that cable with the proper instruments, we do not need to touch it; we can pick up those vibrations by electrical induction and thus discover and reproduce the scene which is being transmitted, just as a telephone wire may be tapped for its message.

The impulses which flow in the arm nerves of a typist convey to her fingers the translated information which reaches her eye or ear, in order that the fingers may be caused to strike the proper keys. Might not these currents be intercepted, either in the original form in which information is conveyed to the brain, or in the marvelously metamorphosed form in which they then proceed to the hand?

By bone conduction we already introduce sounds into the nerve channels of the deaf in order that they may hear. Is it not possible that we may learn to introduce them without the present cumbersomeness of first transforming electrical vibrations to mechanical ones, which the human mechanism promptly transforms back to the electrical form? With a couple of electrodes on the skull the encephalograph now produces pen-and-ink traces which bear some relation to the electrical phenomena going on in the brain itself. True, the record is unintelligible, except as it points out certain gross misfunctioning of the cerebral mechanism; but who would now place bounds on where such a thing may lead?

In the outside world, all forms of intelligence, whether of sound or sight, have been reduced to the form of varying currents in an electric circuit in order that they may be transmitted. Inside the human frame exactly the same sort of process occurs. Must we always transform to mechanical movements in order to proceed from one electrical phenomenon to another? It is a suggestive thought, but it hardly warrants prediction without losing touch with reality and immediateness.

Presumably man's spirit should be elevated if he can better review his shady past and analyze more completely and objectively his present problems. He **[Man]** has built a civilization so complex that he needs to mechanize his records more fully if he is to push his experiment to its logical conclusion and not merely become bogged down part way there by overtaxing his limited memory. *His excursions may be more enjoyable if he* *can reacquire the privilege of forgetting the manifold things he does not need to have immediately at hand, with some assurance that he can find them again if they prove important.*

The applications of science have built man a well-supplied house, and are teaching him to live healthily therein. They have enabled him to throw masses of people against one another with cruel weapons. They may yet allow him truly to encompass the great record and to grow in the wisdom of race experience. He may perish in conflict before he learns to wield that record for his true good. Yet, in the application of science to the needs and desires of man, it would seem to be a singularly unfortunate stage at which to terminate the process, or to lose hope as to the outcome.

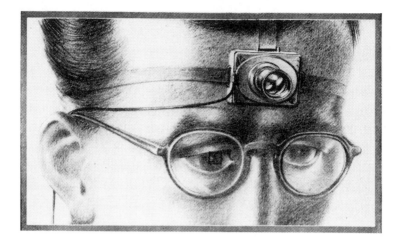

A scientist of the future records experiments with a tiny camera fitted with universal-focus lens. The small square in the eyeglass at the left sights the object (*LIFE 19*(11), p. 112).

Supersecretary of the coming age, the machine contemplated here would take dictation, type it automatically and even talk back if the author wanted to review what he had just said. It is somewhat similar to the Voder seen at the New York World's Fair. Like all machines suggested by the diagrams in this article, it is not yet in existence (*LIFE 19*(11), p. 114).

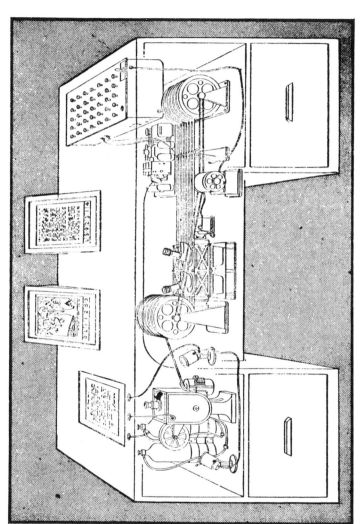

Memex in the form of a desk would instantly bring files and material on any subject to the operator's fingertips. Slanting translucent viewing screens magnify supermicrofilm filed by code numbers. At left is a mechanism which automatically photographs longhand notes, pictures and letters, then files them in the desk for future reference (*LIFE 19*(11), p. 123).

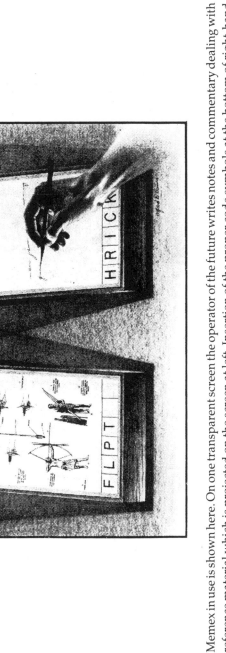

Memex in use is shown here. On one transparent screen the operator of the future writes notes and commentary dealing with reference material which is projected on the screen at left. Insertion of the proper code symbols at the bottom of right-hand screen will tie the new item to the earlier one after notes are photographed on supermicrofilm (*LIFE 19*(11), p. 124).

Part 2
The Extension of Memex

The Idea of a Machine: The Later Memex Essays
Paul Kahn and James M. Nyce

Introduction

THE PUBLICATION OF "AS WE MAY THINK" in the summer of 1945 was by no means the end of Bush's involvement with the idea he called Memex. During the remaining three decades of his life he returned to many of the issues raised in that essay. We have gathered the most significant of Bush's writings on this topic in this section of the book to present, in a chronological fashion, how he continued to develop the Memex design up through the 1960s.

What did Bush hope to accomplish in his later writings about Memex? In the late 1930s when he wrote "Mechanization and the Record," Bush was in the forefront of engineering fields such as microfilm and dry photography. Two decades later it was still unclear what role a technology like microfilm would play in mechanizing libraries and how the digital computer would be harnessed to store and retrieve information. We will show that the later essays contain a decreasing attention to engineering detail in their proposals for how to deal with information handling issues and a concomitant increase in the attempts to discuss the moral and evolutionary implications of machine intelligence, leading to questions of whether consciousness and free will are even within the realm of scientific enquiry.

We will explore whether there was any relationship between the series of microfilm rapid selectors developed during this period and the ideas expressed in Bush's later essays. This period saw the dramatic rise of digital computing, beginning with a few experimental machines in the early post-war years and developing into widespread mainframe computing for data processing in American business. At the same time there was an explosive growth in the use of television and other electronic methods of communication throughout the United States. While in the 1950s the analog machines that Bush pioneered had been largely eclipsed in the area of mathematical computing, microfilm was still very much a viable technology. As a method for storing and retrieving information in libraries and related archives, microfilm was still in constant use. Did Bush continue to think microfilm would play an important role in the future? How aware was he of the new issues in computer science, and how did he account for the changes in technology in these later essays?

To answer these questions we will first trace the history of how and in what context these later essays were composed. In the process, we will analyze what materials are shared among these essays and how certain themes are developed.

Further, there had always been a fundamental tension between the problems of institutional management of the public record embodied in the rapid selector and a Memex that managed associated memories and ideas, often those of one individual. We will show how Bush used Memex as a vehicle over a period of three decades to present his ideas about the possible relationship between mechanization and human thought, particularly in reference to what might be called the personalization of information.

The Rapid Selector(s) in Use

The startling predictions of "As We May Think" were not the only artifacts of Bush's 1930s work at MIT to resurface at the end of the war. In October 1946, Bush, at that time the director of the Carnegie Institution of Washington, received a letter from Ralph R. Shaw, the librarian of the U.S. Department of Agriculture. Shaw had read "The Rapid Selector," a document dated July 1940 describing a mechanism for selecting items from reels of microfilm. Shaw was impressed by the idea of applying such a machine in his library work. He wrote, "I should like, if feasible, to experiment with its application to the organization of knowledge in a great research library" (Shaw to Bush, October 5, 1946). He wanted to know from Bush whether anyone had produced such a machine, and if not, whether he could "borrow the prototype for experimental use in the Department of Agriculture . . . ."

Bush's response was indirect but positive. He wrote a note to Frederick G. Fassett, Jr., his former MIT student and then director of publications for the Carnegie Institution of Washington. Bush scrawled the unequivocal "delighted if they would use it" in the first paragraph, asking Fassett to respond. Fassett's letter to Shaw clearly conveys Bush's permission to go ahead, with the information that the prototype in question was not patented and had been "cannibalized to some extent during wartime shortages of components" (Fassett, November 12, 1946). Both Bush's note and Fassett's letter identify John Howard, the former MIT student who had led the engineering effort on the first rapid selector, as the most likely source to develop a new machine along these lines. Fassett put Shaw in touch with Howard's firm, Engineering Research Associates, Inc. (ERA), and the development of a series of microfilm rapid selectors associated with Bush's earlier design was set in motion.

At the same time there were inquiries from the Office of Technical Services (OTS) of the Department of Commerce to Eastman Kodak concerning that company's current plans, if any, for the rapid selector technology they had funded at MIT. Kodak evidently had no plans to exploit the technology. On December 24, 1946, E.S. Farrow of Kodak wrote to MIT vice president J.R. Killian that Kodak saw no direct relationship between a patent they did hold on a method of recording and selecting items from film based on sound tracks (U.S. Patent #2,295,000, Morse) and "the Rapid Selector which was developed at MIT before the war." Both MIT, the government agencies, and their contractors were free to exploit the research without a challenge from the photography giant. John C. Green of OTS corresponded directly with Bush on the matter (Green, March 31, 1947) and received confirmation that the Morse patent presented no obstacle. Bush himself assured Green that there was no way the Morse patent "can possibly stand [in] the way of the use of the Rapid Selector by the Department of Commerce, which is what we are interested in" (Bush, April 2, 1947).

The MIT Rapid Selector prototype machine, described in our earlier chapter and by Burke (this volume), was based on a mechanism for selecting and rephotographing items from a reel of microfilm. Selection was done by optically matching dot patterns on the film with a mask placed over photocells. When Bush had written in "As We May Think" that most of the Memex contents "are purchased on microfilm ready for insertion," he clearly had this kind of coded microfilm in mind. Now it appeared that there was an opportunity to put into service some of his ideas for attacking the problem of selecting information in a library. Bush clearly wanted to see this happen.

A little over two years later, on June 22, 1949, Ralph R. Shaw gave the first public demonstration of his Rapid Selector at the Department of Agriculture Library. The public demonstration of the machine attracted some attention in the library and electronics press. Shaw himself published several articles (1949, 1951a, 1951b) describing this Rapid Selector as the latest step in a progression of machines designed to solve bibliographic management and sorting problems.

Shaw, for his part, never seemed concerned with the more far-reaching aspect of the Memex design. For Shaw, the Rapid Selector was a solution to a problem in information management. Shaw sought to address only two of the many features in the design: miniaturization and automatic selection. He developed and sent to Bush a table comparing various information storage technologies, the point of which was to show that the Rapid Selector had the greatest "order of efficiency" (Shaw, 1951b:208).

Bush does not appear to have been impressed. In an undated note about Shaw to Fassett he confessed, "I can't discourage him on his rapid selector, even although [sic] it will supplement and not replace books." His response to Shaw was more polite. "I thank you for sending me the table on storage of text and index entries," Bush wrote. "It is interesting to see in this record that the printed book, for all its difficulties, still rates pretty high" (Bush, March 16, 1950). Bush's eye was attracted not to the fact that Shaw rated the Rapid Selector as having the best "order of efficiency" for the storage of text and index entries, but to the fact that printed books were rated better or not much worse than various Hollerith and catalog card methods.

There was clearly a shift in Bush's thinking by this time about the usefulness of the microfilm selector technology itself. There is no indication that Bush thought that Shaw's Rapid Selector or any of the later microfilm selector devices that were created in the 1950s could offer an effective alternative to traditional publication and book storage as a means of distributing, locating, and indexing information. But this temporary lack of success in the field, so to speak, did not keep him from suggesting in his speeches and his writings that the Rapid Selector *as an idea* held great promise. As each succeeding Rapid Selector seemed to prove only how ineffective technology was at solving these problems,

Memex still remained as a model for what should be possible. It was essentially a concept or a model that was good to think with. In fact, what changed in Bush's writings over time was that the number and kinds of issues Memex was good to think with expanded.

In a speech given in January 1953 to the 23rd annual Scientific Assembly of the Medical Society of Washington, D.C. (Bush, 1953), he discussed the problem of overspecialization in professions such as medicine, accompanied by an increase in technical publications. Because of these two forces, as his title stated, "We are in danger of building a Tower of Babel." At this time he still envisioned new methods of publishing on the technological horizon.

> The day of metal type, which has served so long, may be nearing an end. New electronic photocomposition machines are beginning to produce books, and this is by no means the final step in a revolution of methods of printing. (Bush, 1953:151)

In 1953, Bush still saw some form of interaction between electronics and photographic reproduction and miniaturization as the key technology, and he offered the Rapid Selector as a positive example.

> There is a little used machine in existence—the rapid selector—which can review items on a strip of microfilm at the rate of 1,000 items a second and print those which are selected in accordance with a code set on a keyboard. It could, for example, review the case histories of half a million hospital patients in 10 minutes and present for aid in diagnosis printed copies of the few cases which corresponded to an unusual set of symptoms and complications. I say it could, but as yet it does not. (Bush, 1953:151)

The fact that Bush offered as an example this kind of automated diagnosis shows that he was still considering ways in which a machine that calculates and sorts could be used to support professional work. But the ability to sort medical data at high speeds based on signs and symptoms was not the most important problem he sought to address. He was still deeply concerned about the weaknesses of subject classification. It was here, in fact, that Bush may have felt that Shaw's work with the Rapid Selector had failed. Projects such as Shaw's had not really addressed this more fundamental problem and had proceeded on the assumption that mechanization, rather than a radical re-thinking of how information and knowledge is ordered, was sufficient. The boundaries between these classifications were increasingly out of touch with emerging disciplines such as biochemistry, neuropathology, and clinical psychiatry. These synthetic disciplines were just the places where important information was going to be lost due to rigid classification systems, particularly in areas that dealt with the mind and brain. Again this concern with crossovers, spillovers, from discipline to discipline and the possible losses and gains was characteristic of the time (cf. Heims, 1977).

> The rapid selector mentioned above will select according to an established code, but the code must be developed on a rational principle so that it can be effectively operated. No system of coding or of indexing under established subject heads can efficiently serve to guide us through the written thoughts or findings of scientists when the very science in which they work will not submit to definition. We can only wish—the optimists among us may hope—that a way will be found for converting into some form of mechanism the kind of fluid indexing and cataloging that takes place in our minds. There is here a feature which man has not yet introduced into his machinery, a feature of great power, the pursuit of paths through a complex record by means of association of ideas. Modern electronics can do for us almost anything we ask in the way of rapid, involved operations upon masses of data. But we still tell our research findings to one another in much the same old way, and we record our research results in a mass of paper from which their extraction becomes increasingly laborious. (Bush, 1953:151)

Bush was still searching in the early 1950s for a way to create in the form of a machine an analog to the way information was stored, categorized, and retrieved by the human mind. This search for biological analogies, and applying them to models and mechanisms of computation, were not uncommon (MacCormac, 1984; MacKay, 1962). The rapid selector could do only a small part of the job, and it was now clear to Bush that the part that it did was just not that important. Mechanical sorting of data at high speeds could be done, but the design of a machine that could build trails of association and later use those trails for retrieval remained an important but illusive goal.

Redefining the Memory Machine

In December of 1958 Bush wrote the first drafts of an essay he titled "Memex II." He had returned to Belmont, Massachusetts, after retiring as director of the Carnegie Institute of Washington in 1956. His relationship to MIT was now one of an honorary trustee. He served on the boards of several corporations in the Boston area.

Throughout the late 1940s and 1950s he had been writing essays on issues of science and public policy (for an appreciation of this, see Reingold, 1987 and Smith, 1965). By the end of 1958 he had returned in his writing to those issues raised in "As We May Think" that remained largely unresolved. He was aware that the Memex was based on what was now twenty-year-old technology. Bush clearly wanted to bring his projections up to the present.

He had begun to work with Eric Hodgins, the man who in 1938 had been the publisher of *FORTUNE* and an enthusiastic reviewer of his Memex ideas. Hodgins was now with Elmo Roper and Associates, placing articles and book manuscripts with New York publishers. By the mid-1960s Hodgins was to develop his own program for Bush's writing, but in 1958 Hodgins was to Bush simply an old friend and an agent, encouraging Bush and finding places for the manuscripts he received.

A draft of "Memex II" was sent to Hodgins on December 16. Bush had returned to the issue of miniaturization, seeking to account for how microfilm and analog machines had given way to magnetic tape and digital computers. He noted that the development of magnetic tape was particularly significant, as it not only led to further compression of data but also:

> can be erased or added to almost instantaneously, without the sort of development and delay inherent in conventional photographic processes. It is essentially the equivalent of the system of dry photography then sought, and in fact it is better for our purposes. (Bush, 1959:5)

He saw greater possibilities for miniaturization as well. "Memex II" from the very first draft contains a proposal for using organic crystals to record data by means of phase changes in molecular alignment. Recording and erasing data would be accomplished by scanning each crystal with different wavelengths of radiation. In many ways this proposal is similar to the "phase change" technology used today in erasable optical storage media. Bush proposed crystal storage as the ultimate miniaturization, for it was an improvement in terms of information density over the human brain, based on the neuroscience of the time (Bush, 1959:6-7).

Bush also saw in the transistor more evidence for the superiority of machine memory over human memory. Compared to the thermionic tube with which Bush had built machines, the transistor was far smaller, had far greater capacity, and needed no power to be renewed. Bush saw such machines as impermeable to time. As he put it, "Records and controlling devices in crystals and metals do not fade" (Bush, 1959:9).

He also saw new possibilities in areas such as voice recognition. From an examination of his papers, it does not appear Bush did any typing. His typescripts were prepared by a secretary and his revisions were added in longhand. He had already noted in the earlier essays the machine synthesis of voice by the Vocoder and had connected this with the rapid machine recording of speech by stenographers. He suggested that in time man would finesse the larger problems of machine recognition of natural speech by adopting what Bush termed a "phonetic shorthand." Bush imagined that the machine would type out what we said, allowing a person to record ideas by speaking rather than typing. In this case, man would accommodate himself to the limits of the machine and "undoubtedly we shall some day learn to read such [phonetically-spelled] records as readily as we now read our cumbersome language" (Bush, 1959:9).

These ideas, both crystal storage and voice interaction, were repeated in the later essays. However, while Bush could envision in 1958 the goal as well as the means and the technology to affect that goal, in later years he stopped writing about the means. He grew increasingly unsure of, or perhaps uninterested in, how the technology would achieve the goal he sought.

Within a week of this draft of "Memex II," Bush was adding refinements and examples, which were typed and sent off to Hodgins on December 30, 1958. "I collared the needed added idea, and here it comes," said his note accompanying the second draft to Hodgins.

The ideas Bush was adding included examples of how Memex could be used in New World archaeology and diagnostic medicine, both of which found their way into the final draft. The example of medical diagnosis support was an elaboration of the one used in his address to the Medical Society of Washington (Bush, 1953).

He was also beginning to specify boundaries between what he saw as the different realms of human judgment (Figure 1). The pioneer of the analog calculating machine could see that mathematical calculation could be relied on to solve only a limited class of problems. But the potential of machine-support for mental processes seemed larger than what Bush was to call the realm of quantitative science, where definitions of data were precise and mathematical logic could be employed

Realm of

Quantitative Science	Reasonable Judgment	Emotional Judgment
Control exercised by		
precise definition	experience	human emotion
explicit hypothesis	comparison	spiritual feelings
logic		art

Data becomes increasingly imprecise

Figure 1. Bush's Schema for Human Judgment

with assurance. This was the area in which his own analog machines had proved successful, and it was also the area in which digital computers were dwarfing that earlier success.

But now Bush was trying to redefine what lay beyond the boundary of explicit hypothesis. His focus on the operations of the human mind led him to a concern for how memory and judgment appear to interact and support each other. He was familiar with the early work on machine learning by Claude Shannon. Much of the pioneering work in this area was done at MIT (for a discussion of this research, see Wildes and Lindgren, 1985), and Bush indirectly and directly referred to much of it in his later writings on Memex. He proposed a second realm beyond the simple machine learning produced thus far, "a region in which judgment enters, and in which man's decisions and acts are based on experience and comparisons rather than logic" (Bush, 1959:29). In this realm, reasoning is the result of access to stored experience and the ability to compare the current situation with information in this experience store.

Beyond this, he hypothesized a third realm of emotion and spirit. Just as Bush wanted to suggest where mechanization would now expand, he also wanted to suggest where it would not. "How far can the machine accompany and aid its master along this path?" Bush asked, rhetorically. His answer was meant to clarify the upper limit in the relationship between man and machine.

> Certainly to the point at which the master becomes an artist, reaching into the unknown with vision and versatility, erecting on the mundane thought processes a structure of beauty, or inspiration. This region will always be barred to the machine. (Bush, 1959:29)

Bush's strategy in his later work was to map out which domains and competencies machine intelligence would not be able to emulate. As he increased the powers he proposed for machines, he countered those powers with assurances of what machines could not be. Describing those powers, which Bush believed to be uniquely human, became increasingly important in his later essays. This rhetorical strategy essentially exempted for the machine certain of man's cognitive, intellectual, and higher order abilities. In the end this reasserted man's position over the machine, however much those machines worked from or resembled biological principles.

The first Memex was primarily a memory extender. It recorded data in an explicit and permanent fashion, much as Bush thought the brain did, but improved on the "fading" quality of human memory. It also supported the explicit recording of "trails of association," something Bush saw as an attribute of human memory also prone to fading in its non-mechanical form. The Memex II, or "Memex Mark II" as he occasionally referred to the new design, still had all these qualities. But with Memex II, a new emphasis on machine learning appears. With this machine a person could still record and access his or her memory, but now the machine itself could also record and reuse its master's experience. This led to a proposal of active symbiosis between machine and human memory.

> The machine's primary service lies . . . in extending the mass of recollection . . . . Its trails are formed deliberately, under full control of the user, ultimately in accordance with the dictates of experience in the

art of trail architecture. This, in turn, remolds the trails of the user's brain, as one lives and works in close interconnection with a machine of scanned records and transistors. For the trails of the machine become duplicated in the brain of the user, vaguely as all human memory is vague, but with a concomitant emphasis by repetition, creation and discard, refinement, as the cells of the brain become realigned and reconnected, better to utilize the massive explicit memory which is its servant. (Bush, 1959:21)

As the human molds the machine, so the machine "remolds" the human mind. This early expression of co-evolution was not to find its way into the later published essays. But once again Bush was not alone in looking at how machine use could influence man, right down to the level of biology. J.C.R. Licklider published his landmark paper, "Man-Computer Symbiosis," in 1960, stating as his premise the same kind of evolutionary relationship. As Licklider put it,

The hope is that, in not too many years, human brains and computing machines will be coupled together very tightly, and that the resulting partnership will think as no human brain has ever thought and process data in a way not approached by the information-handling machines we know today. (Licklider, 1960:4)

Licklider was writing as a leading researcher in digital computing. It is clear from later evidence that neither man was aware of the other's work at this time. Licklider certainly had not read Bush's unpublished manuscript and by his own account was aware of but had not read "As We May Think" (Licklider, 1965:preface). Bush was not to be introduced to Licklider's work until the planning meeting for Project Intrex in 1965 (see below). Yet it is worthwhile to compare the issues Licklider reviewed in 1960 with what Bush wrote at roughly the same time. Licklider identified the things men could do and machines could do. He saw some promise in the early work in artificial intelligence. He assessed the projected capabilities of digital computing speed and memory and even reviewed advances in both machine language and speech recognition. Bush was doing much the same thing in "Memex II," but his goal was quite different. He sought to develop a machine that mirrored and recorded the patterns of the human brain. While the pioneers of digital computing understood that machines would soon accelerate human capabilities by doing massive calculations, Bush continued to be preoccupied with extending, through replication, human mental experience. However, it was this concern with analogy that became more explicit during the 1960s, and consequently Bush responded to the issues of the day quite differently than his contemporaries. It is Bush's continued reliance on analog mechanism and theory that separated him from his peers.

The initial response Bush received to the manuscript of "Memex II" was enthusiastic. Caryl P. Haskins, his successor as president of the Carnegie Institution of Washington, sent him glowing comments on January 12, 1959. Haskins discussed recent research on the physical organization of the brain, the number of cells and the way they are arranged, mentioning a recent conference "on self-organizing machines and neural-and-brain-analogues." He was particularly enthusiastic about Bush's speculations on the application of machine learning. He urged Bush to continue his focus on "the 'association-trail-following' concept" and the "matter of memory storage," which Bush had pushed from coded microfilm into three-dimensional arrays and crystalline structures.

In February, the second draft of "Memex II" was sent to *The Atlantic Monthly*, where Bush had published several public policy essays since the appearance of "As We May Think" fourteen years before. Ted Weeks, who was still editor, responded enthusiastically. "Your paper which we think of calling The Memory Machine is fully as absorbing and we think better written than its predecessor," he wrote to Bush (Weeks to Bush, February 13, 1959). However, from the beginning Weeks made it clear that the essay was too long. Weeks turned the editing tasks over to Emily Flint, the managing editor who had only recently come to the magazine from her position at the MIT library. Bush responded with a third draft in early March, adding, rather than cutting, material.

This draft seems to have languished on Weeks' desk until late July, when a letter from Bush prompted a response from Flint. Weeks was out of the country for a month on a State Department-sponsored trip to the Soviet Union, she wrote, but he intended to use the essay in their November 1959 issue (Flint to Bush, August 4, 1959). Flint returned the March draft to Bush, asking for a new draft by the end of August, suggesting a maximum length of 7,500 words.

Bush had other plans. He wanted neither to reduce the size of the essay nor to edit it himself. He was also, once again, concerned with the size and composition of the audience he would reach by publishing in the *Atlantic*. Flint seemed to be unaware of the fact that Bush had already discussed with Weeks a repeat of the arrangement reached between the *Atlantic* and *LIFE* in 1945. Bush wanted the essay to appear in the *Atlantic* and then be reprinted in *LIFE*, thereby reaching the largest possible audience.

Given the awkward situation she was in, Flint responded on August 19 with a great deal of tact. She accepted the manuscript back from Bush. "What I shall do first," she wrote Bush, "is to reread MEMEX I [i.e., "As We May Think"], and I hope to have some helpful suggestions for you in two or three days." She assured him that the *Atlantic* intended to give the essay adequate space, but in the matter of making an arrangement with *LIFE*, she pointed out that the matter was out of her hands. In the case of "As We May Think," the request to reprint came from *LIFE*. In matters between publishers, she wrote to Bush, "I do not really see how the initiative can come from the *Atlantic*."

The following week, Flint sent Bush the results of her edits. She had reduced the essay by her own account "from about 9500 words to about 8500 words." She enclosed an outline she had created, dividing the essay up into seven sections. She raised objections to the passage where Bush described the machine being trained to read a book and also felt that the example of medical diagnosis was too clinical for a lay audience (Flint to Bush, August 25, 1959).

Bush responded on August 27 by sending Flint what was to be the final draft of the essay. He accepted most of her editorial changes but did not remove or change either of the passages to which she objected. What seemed to concern him more than further edits to the essay was its possible appearance in *LIFE*. He recognized now that the initiative for this would have to be his own, and on the same day he sent the manuscript to John Jessup, *LIFE*'s chief editorial writer.

In his letter to Jessup, Bush made it clear that the manuscript was what he termed a "modernization" of "As We May Think." Since *LIFE* had gone out of its way by reprinting the original essay in 1945, Bush wrote that he "did not feel right to just plow ahead and publish along the same lines elsewhere." He was offering *LIFE* the same opportunity, this time by showing them the manuscript in advance.

When Bush finally heard from Jessup at the end of September, the response was a negative one. Jessup's colleagues judged the essay "too strange and difficult for *LIFE*'s readers," and so he assured Bush that any obligation he might have to *LIFE* was fulfilled (Jessup to Bush, September 23, 1959). He did not return the manuscript, however. Instead he informed Bush that it had been sent on to Francis Bello, an editor at *FORTUNE*, on the chance that he would be interested in publishing it.

Bush wrote to Weeks the day he heard from Jessup, informing Weeks that *LIFE* had turned down the opportunity. "This leaves us free if you still want to use the article in the *Atlantic*," and he offered to do some further work on the essay which he felt "was not by any means as good as it ought to be." A few days later Bush received a second letter from Jessup returning the manuscript. Bello had read it and turned it down. As Jessup explained it, the rejection was a matter of *FORTUNE*'s role rather than the essay's content.

> At *FORTUNE* these days . . . they regard their chief job in the field of information storage and retrieval as being that of reporting directly on the considerable work in progress in various laboratories, much of it stimulated by your provocative ideas. In doing this reporting job, *FORTUNE* would find it easier to refer to your ideas than to carry a full and authoritative statement of them. (Jessup to Bush, September 29, 1959)

Bush responded to Jessup's September letter by saying that the *Atlantic* now planned to publish "Memex II" in their January 1960 issue, giving him "a chance to polish it a bit, which it badly needs" (Bush to Jessup, October 6, 1959). However, nothing seems to have happened. At the end of November, Bush was writing to Weeks, asking what had become of their plans to publish "Memex II" at all. He himself admitted to not having done any work on it.

In the end, the essay did not appear. It is possible that the response Bush received from Jessup discouraged him from overcoming the dissatisfaction he expressed over this third draft. If he originally hoped to repeat his 1945 feat, when "As We May Think" reached millions and generated news stories carrying his name and ideas around the world, he was to be disappointed.

In addition, the technology was not the only thing that had changed in the intervening fourteen years. Bush's political and scientific position had changed as well. Further, his prestige had been tarnished because of his largely unsuccessful attempts to direct, some might say dictate, science policy in the United States (for a review of his attempts to establish science policy, see Kevles, 1977). He was a *former* MIT dean and vice president, *former* head of O.S.R.D., and most recently *former* president of the Carnegie Institution of Washington. His charisma as the scientific hero whose research efforts had "secretly won the war" was largely forgotten, as was the sense of awe at the potential of new technologies that greeted Bush's predictions in 1945. Speculative computing machines were no longer news, and *FORTUNE* was now reporting on, rather than predicting, a data processing industry. Computer technology was a reality, and the reading public had developed a new set of expectations for what a computer might or might not do. The ideas in "Memex II" that Jessup's colleagues had termed "too strange and difficult" were no stranger than the Vocoder and the forehead camera described in "As We May Think." However, the new essay was likely judged "too strange and difficult" because the machines it described did not resemble the direction the industry was taking in the 1950s.

As if to illustrate this very point, the following year Francis Bello did exactly what Jessup suggested he might. He published in the September 1960 issue of *FORTUNE* an article on the new information retrieval (I.R.) industry entitled "How to Cope with Information." He projected a rosy future for "I.R. systems," noting that "I.R. in 1960 is just about where E.D.P. [electronic data processing] was ten years ago" (Bello, 1960:163). The only mention of Bush was a quote from "As We May Think" about the information problem and a reference to the controversy that occurred over patents associated with the Rapid Selector, based on an interview with Ralph Shaw. Bello does not refer to Bush's ideas about associative indexes, trails, and machine learning, which are quite different from the work with term and subject descriptor indexes being commercially developed by Luhn, Taube, and Mooers in the fledgling I.R. industry of the late 1950s.

Whatever the reason for its rejection and abandonment, Bush was clearly dissatisfied with "Memex II." He expressed that dissatisfaction in several letters written the following year. On April 6, 1960, he wrote to Leverett Saltonstall, then chairman of the Senate Armed Services Committee, in response to a request for information on the subject of "the mechanization of libraries," which he characterized as "an exceed-

ingly difficult" subject to assess. In this letter he described the MIT
Rapid Selector developed before the war. He noted that the device had
been "used by some of the people who were interested in breaking
enemy codes" and that after the war the Department of Commerce had
built a similar machine in Washington. He also mentioned Kodak's
Minicard machine, which he recognized as related to this early research
at MIT. He sent Saltonstall "an old article of mine on this general subject,
called MEMEX," which he called "a sort of Jules Verne affair." The
enclosure was presumably a copy of "As We May Think." There is no
mention in the letter to Saltonstall of "Memex II" or any recent revision
of the ideas contained in the older essay.

In October, Bush received a letter from Scott Spangler, an engineer
at the General Electric Flight Propulsion Division, enquiring about the
current state of the Memex design. Spangler was inspired by "As We
May Think" and wrote Bush to ask if he had "written more articles on
the subject . . . ." Bush's response was perhaps a fair assessment of his
feelings about the essay he had put aside.

> Sometime over a year ago I sat down and wrote an article in which I tried
> to bring MEMEX up to date, but I did not get a satisfying result and
> hence discarded it. I may try it again before long, but it is a difficult thing
> to do. (Bush to Spangler, October 14, 1960)

Two years later, in May 1962, Bush received a letter from Douglas
C. Engelbart (this volume). Engelbart was preparing a report at Stanford
Research Institute for a U.S. Air Force contract and, like Spangler, he
wrote Bush in response to "As We May Think." Engelbart included a
draft of this report, which outlined an ambitious program for using
computers to "augment human intellect." This draft later became the
basis for "A Conceptual Framework for the Augmentation of Man's
Intellect," (Engelbart, 1963) the first publication stating the ideas
Engelbart was later to embody in the pioneering computer system,
oNLine System (NLS) (Engelbart and English, 1968). That Bush's writings had inspired Engelbart is well known, and Engelbart's statement
of his program goals in the 1963 paper makes this even more evident:

> By "augmenting man's intellect" we mean increasing the capability of
> a man to approach a complex problem situation, gain comprehension to
> suit his particular needs, and to derive solutions to problems. . . . And by
> "complex situations" we include the professional problems of diplo-

mats, executives, social scientists, life scientists, physical scientists, attorneys, designers—whether the problem situation exists for twenty minutes or twenty years. We do not speak of isolated clever tricks that help in particular situations. We refer to a way of life in an integrated domain where hunches, cut-and-try, intangibles, and the human "feel for a situation" usefully coexist with powerful concepts, streamlined terminology and notation, sophisticated methods, and high-powered electronic aids. (Engelbart, 1963:1)

In the draft enclosed with his May 24 letter, Engelbart cites Bush as one of "several researchers. . . [who] have pointed out the gains offered by close integration of modern information-handling equipment with the human problem solver" (Engelbart, this volume). Others on the list include B.F. Skinner and J.C.R. Licklider. In his published paper Engelbart repeats the acknowledgment, referring to Bush's essay as "the earliest and one of the most directly stimulating" precursors of his own work (Engelbart, 1963:26). It is easy to see why Bush's Memex was an inspiration to Engelbart, who emphasized in his writings the real-life application of computers over game playing and laboratory simulation of machine intelligence.

Bush never replied to Engelbart's letter. His secretary sent a brief note granting the requested permission.

The Moral Issues of Thinking Machines

Bush returned to the subject of thinking machines early in 1963. On February 5 he sent a draft of an essay titled "Man's Thinking Machines" to Eric Hodgins at Elmo Roper and Associates in New York and to Merle Tuve in Washington. Tuve, a physicist, had been a colleague of Bush's at O.S.R.D. during the war, and was now director of the Department of Terrestrial Magnetism at the Carnegie Institution of Washington.

In his letter to Tuve, Bush describes his new essay as "an article on the ways in which the field of analytical machinery affects man's thinking about the deep subject of free will." He invited Tuve "to pick me up on places where I am discussing modern physics, or anywhere else for that matter" (Bush to Tuve, February 5, 1963). It is clear from the letter that Bush was also looking for advice from a fellow senior scientist as to whether such an essay was advisable at all.

The letter to Hodgins is just as blunt, but focuses on Bush's sense of vulnerability at writing an essay that moved out of his own areas of expertise (science, engineering, and public policy) and into philosophy and religion. Until now, Bush had stayed pretty close to the ground in his writings.

> It does not disturb me at all that, if I publish any such thing, I would be promptly attacked by philosophers for talking about philosophical subjects without belonging to the group. I would probably also be attacked by theologians, but that offhand would seem to be an attractive incident if it should occur. Seriously, I have worked hard on this thing and have had it in mind for two or three years before trying to write. (Bush to Hodgins, February 5, 1963)

Bush's first "attack" on philosophy was in "Memex II" where he argued that the application of Aristotelian logic to certain domains of experience represents the worst kind of reductionism. The most important results, he argues, are to be found in higher-order relationships that are essentially beyond logic. Philosophy suffers from the "application of the rules which had their inception in Aristotle, to premises which never became precisely defined, which, in fact, were incapable of definition" (Bush, 1959:22). Here, he is pointing out that the application of logic, by man or machine, can only produce results derived from the raw data to which the logic is applied.

In this new essay Bush once again takes up the theme of what machines can and cannot do. This once again is a characteristic concern of his time (cf., for example, Wiener, 1950). As he did in "Memex II," he gives a list of machine accomplishments. Machines can be used to apply mathematics in any place man can imagine. They can provide results in numeric, graphic, musical, or linguistic forms. They can be taught to write, predict outcomes based on statistical probabilities, detect their own malfunctions, and to some extent learn from their own experience. They have the now familiar property of memories that "are precise and do not fade" though now Bush adds that "one can erase a machine memory" (Bush, 1963:4). He goes on to enumerate the accomplishment of machines in fields such as chemical engineering, process control, airplane and missile guidance, noting the failure of libraries to use the same information processing technology that has proven so useful in business.

After completing this survey, Bush returns to another theme found in "Memex II," defining what machines "cannot do, now or in the future." Before proposing to define truly complex machine intelligence, Bush, as he did before, defines the limits within which such machines will operate. The crux of the argument he uses here revolves around distinctions between devices engineered out of organic rather than inorganic materials. It is a distinction that separates brain from machine and essentially delimits, by an appeal to differences of a more fundamental kind, what machines and machine intelligence are capable of. We have already observed that Bush sought to define a mechanical analog for the human brain. The answer to the question "are machines alive?" will be more difficult to answer, he noted, "if man had built aids to his thinking out of chemical rather than physical elements" (Bush, 1963:13). Such a chemical machine would be truly "complex" and so a better analog to the human brain itself. Presumably this would be because its organic base truly mirrored the physical structure and nature of the brain.

The description of the "really complex machine" is largely copied from the earlier Memex II essay, though the term "Memex" is never used. However, the details match quite closely. Memory is stored in the form of "crystal structure." The machine consults this memory array

> by ordinary indexing methods, or by rapid selection of items in accordance with specifications, and in the process it would evaluate resemblances. But also it would thread through the maze of records by building trails of association. Some of these would be built by directions of its master, as he guided it from one spot to another, in search of an obscure item. There would be no delays; it could move from one spot to another almost instantly. It would of course remember all these trails, to follow them later when ordered. It would also adopt trails developed elsewhere, and add them to its equipment; those built by distant scholars as they examined a subject, those accompanying a book which added to its store. The set of trails would then become complex, intersecting, intertwined. (Bush, 1963:16-17)

All the familiar elements of the Memex are present here. Bush states once again that this new machine will "become a partner to man," extending all his mental powers in the same fashion that industrial development extended his physical powers. Essentially Memex was to bridge differences between biological and mechanical structures and in this way enable man to augment or extend his intellectual competence and capacity. But to this assertion he attaches a new one, that the machine will also "profoundly affect man's philosophy." As in the earlier essay where Bush had reserved the realm of emotional judgment, spirituality, and art to man, this calls for a defense of what is intrinsically human.

We can understand a major part of the motivation behind Bush's concerns in this area. Bush was the son of a Unitarian minister. He wanted to assert, if not prove, that an acceptance of the new knowledge from nuclear physics, biochemistry, and genetic engineering, combined with the development of thinking machines, would not lead to atheistic materialism. Instead, he argues that a profound appreciation of scientific knowledge can lead to a new appreciation of man's "free will," a term which Bush's Unitarian background approximates with human spirituality. To add another layer of context, this essay was written at a high point in the Cold War, a time when a nuclear conflict between the United States and the Soviet Union was on everyone's mind. Bush insists that all this technological and philosophical speculation

> is a practical, in fact a pressing subject. The world is divided into two armed camps, facing each other with nuclear weapons. One camp professes materialism as its philosophy. It considers a modified materialism which produced in man a free will. It denies the existence of any ethical or moral code beyond the law of the jungle, it justifies any form of deception, cruelty, barbarism ruled to be in the service of the State. In the other camp is a wide variety of religions, Bhuddism, Mohammadanism, [sic] Christianity, and a host of others. They spread and diverge in their theological detail. But all of them depend, in the last analysis, upon the free will of man, and upon some form of moral responsibility beyond the bounds of mere expediency. (Bush, 1963:34)

In effect, what Bush wants to show is that new developments in science are not playing into the hands of communist dogma. This was certainly a popular concern, and Hodgins saw in the manuscript a piece that could be placed in any number of magazines, the first one that came to his mind being *FORTUNE*. His April 1 reply to Bush made it clear that he thought the draft should be expanded into a book-length manuscript and that he had already shown it in confidence to an editor at *FOR-*

TUNE. Bush's reply indicated that Tuve had provided him with "some nice comments" and indicated that none of the science in the draft had been called into question. However, he did not like Hodgins' suggestion to expand the draft into a book, nor did he think *FORTUNE* "the right audience for the purpose I have in mind" (Bush to Hodgins, April 5, 1963). Bush showed no great enthusiasm for *Science* or the *Atlantic Monthly* as alternatives.

Hodgins countered a few months later with suggestions to expand the essay by adding material on "poverty, wars and the profound upcoming social changes to be wrought by 'the machine' before . . . [plunging] still deeper, and into philosophy" (Hodgins to Bush, August 20, 1963). However, what was most on his mind was an opportunity to present the draft to H. R. Luce, the founder of Time, Inc. Due to a change in Luce's health, the meeting did not take place. While Hodgins reported that, based on his verbal description, Luce was enthusiastic about the essay, it is unlikely that anyone at *TIME* or *LIFE* ever read it. Bush produced a fifth and final draft of the essay in October 1963. Hodgins continued to suggest that an expanded version of the essay should become the basis for a book. While Bush never took this suggestion seriously, some of the material contained in this final draft was to find a home in a later essay.

The Final Revisions: "Dr. Bush's Dream about Memex"

Vannevar Bush produced two books during the last decade of his life. The first, *Science Is Not Enough*, was his final collection of essays. It contained several essays that had previously appeared in magazines, as well as several chapters written specifically for the book. The second, *Pieces of the Action*, an autobiography or memoir, was his last publication. Both books were certainly Bush's own writings, but their shape was determined largely by his relationship to two longtime associates, Eric Hodgins and Frederick G. Fassett, Jr.

Beginning in early 1964, Eric Hodgins began to develop specific plans for several books by Bush. In a January 18 letter he described them as "BUSHBOOK I, II, and III." The first was to be a collection of essays, similar in format to *Endless Horizons* (1946). The second was the book he hoped would expand from "Man's Thinking Machines" and address the technical developments America could expect in the coming years, told from the point of view of "The Engineer (of whom you are America's prime exemplar) . . . ." The third was to be a collaboration between the two men, creating in a question and answer format an autobiographical summary of Bush's life and career.

Science Pauses

By later that year, only the first and third of these projects survived. Soon to be known as "Bush Book Junior" or just BBJ, the collection of essays was taking shape. Bush had reorganized the material in "Man's Thinking Machines" and fashioned a shorter and simpler essay titled "Science Pauses." This essay focused on the conflict between science and religion, with technology playing a secondary role. By October 19 Hodgins had been circulating drafts of the essay to prospective magazine publishers. The latest rejection had come from Hobart Lewis of *Reader's Digest*. Lewis assured Hodgins that he would likely publish a part of it once the essay had been published elsewhere. Hodgins suggested that he would ask Helen King, an editor for William Morrow, to place the essay in *LOOK*, a rival to *LIFE*. *Scientific American*, *Harpers*, and the *Atlantic* were also mentioned.

An almost complete draft of "Science Pauses" is dated December 15, 1964. While Bush often expressed dissatisfaction with the essays that preceded this one, "Science Pauses" seems to have fallen into place quickly, and the result was something that Bush felt he could live with. A brief discussion of machine intelligence appears about midway through the essay. The description of what such machines *should be* had disappeared entirely. Bush simply states the accomplishments ("They search through their vast memories in a flash to produce a desired item") and limitations ("They translate languages, badly, and write poetry, badly") of contemporary machines and reduces the revised Memex design to a single paragraph. From this it is clear that Bush was still fundamentally uncomfortable with digital electronics as a means to create the machine intelligence. The examples he gives only emphasize how unbrainlike these machines were:

> Not yet have machines appeared which operate as the brain does. *Transistors, magnetic toroids, tape recorders, electric circuits, lead more naturally to a digital procedure, before which thus far everything else bows.* The

brain does not operate by reducing everything to indices and computation. It follows trails of association, flying almost instantly from item to item, bringing into consciousness only the significant. The trails bifurcate and cross, they become erased in disuse, and emphasized by success. Ultimately the machine can do this better. Its memory will be far greater and the items will not fade. Progress along trails will be at lightning speed. The machine will learn from its own experience, refine its own trails, explore in unknown territory to establish trails there. All this it will do under the orders of its master, and as his slave. (Bush, 1964:14-15)

The second sentence (the italics are ours) was removed from the essay before its publication in *FORTUNE*. Otherwise, the paragraph occurs in the published version with only minor changes. By removing this one sentence, Bush, or one of his editors, eliminated the only engineering details that remained in the essay. Nevertheless, Bush recognized the fundamental limitations, despite pressures towards the contrary, of the digital machine and digital intelligence. He wanted Memex to both embody and improve the biology of the mind. These essays lead us to believe that Bush felt digital technology was fundamentally unsuited to form the basis of complex machine intelligence.

The philosophical theme of this essay was more explicit than in any of his earlier ones. Bush was defending against materialism, and he did this by placing limitations not only on machines but on science as a whole. "Science never proves anything, in an absolute sense," he states at one point. Later he draws the line on what science cannot prove squarely through the definition of mental process. The realm of science approaches "the questions of consciousness and free will—and there it [science] stops" (Bush, 1967a:22, 27). Across this line, the place where "science pauses," Bush asserts that man needs humility, a sense of awe, and faith.

The essay appeared in the May 1965 issue of *FORTUNE*, illustrated by a full-page portrait of Bush (1965a). The publication generated a news story in the May 5 issue of *TIME*. Bush ordered a large number of reprints from *FORTUNE* to send out to friends, reminiscent of his plan in 1945 to send out reprints of "As We May Think" so that the essay could reach beyond the *Atlantic's* readership. He received a great deal of highly favorable unsolicited mail, much of it from clergymen, including many invitations to speak to church groups around the country.

While the publication of "Science Pauses" in 1965 was a popular success, it did not update the Memex design. His technological projections had been reduced to a few general paragraphs, and his theme had changed from what a machine to support the "mental revolution" should be like to the limitations of science and the importance of faith.

Memex Revisited

The summer of 1965 was the occasion of an important planning meeting on a subject that was clearly relevant to the Memex: library automation. MIT was about to embark on Project Intrex, an ambitious set of "information transfer experiments" designed to test the application of computer technology for the delivery of information in a library setting (Overhage, 1974). The planning meeting was held at Woods Hole, Massachusetts, and was attended by many major figures in the fields of library and computer science. Bush was invited to attend the planning session and to open the meeting.

That summer, Bush was at his home on Cape Cod, hard at work on new essays, preparing to make another try at revising the Memex design. The Intrex meeting could have provided an interesting public occasion to test out these ideas. But Bush did not use the occasion for this. His brief remarks at the conference are most notable for what was left unsaid.

Evidence of Bush's influence on and lack of contact with the principal figures in Project Intrex can be found in J.C.R. Licklider's *Libraries of the Future*. The book was the result of a multi-year study Licklider had begun at Bolt Beranek and Newman to explore "the use of computers in information storage, organization, and retrieval" (Licklider, 1965:1). The book's foreword, by Verner Clapp of the Council on Library Resources, begins by quoting Bush's statement of the information problem in "As We May Think." Clapp there refers to the article "in which he [Bush] invented the 'Memex,' the private memory device in which all a man's records may be stored, linked by associative indexing and instantly ready for his use." In short, the relationship between Memex and Licklider's work was clear enough to Clapp. It was also clear to Carl Overhage, the director of Intrex, for Licklider's preface to the book reads:

> Perhaps the main external influence that shaped the ideas of this book had its effect indirectly, through the community, for it was not until Carl Overhage noticed its omission from the References that I read Vannevar Bush's "As We May Think." . . . I had often heard about Memex and its "trails of reference." I had hoped to demonstrate Symbiont [a program developed by Licklider] to Dr. Bush as a small step in the direction in which he had pointed in his pioneer article. But I had not read the article. Now that I have read it, I should like to dedicate this book, however unworthy it may be, to Dr. Bush. (Licklider, 1965:xii-xiii)

Despite this dedication, neither Licklider nor MIT Press sent Bush a copy of the book. It was only when Overhage invited Bush to the meeting that he requested and received a copy. Bush wrote a letter to Licklider in response; judging from Licklider's response it was a very positive one (Licklider to Bush, July 22, 1965).

Bush's statement to the Intrex meeting gives the impression of a man quite removed from "competition with a lively group of younger men" engaged in a new science of which he was not a master. There is not even a direct mention of Memex in his remarks, only a plea that the "benefits of the great advance in analytical machinery" reach beyond its current impact on "business, science, and engineering" and expand to "revolutionize the methods of every professional group, in law, medicine, the humanities" (Bush, 1965b:1-3). The short law example he offers, however, is characteristic of the scenarios found in all the Memex essays. For Bush, the body of knowledge in a library is always a evolving, coherent space through which one travels intellectually. So in this example, the lawyer finds "comments and criticisms of his colleagues who had passed that way before." It does point out, as with Memex, how the recorded addition of personal associations in the public record would enhance professional communication.

The result of the Intrex meeting was a planning document, which Bush received in September, outlining the areas to be addressed in the experiments. The equipment that Intrex planned to use represented a hybrid of both the new digital computing technology, which Licklider described in his study (cathode-ray tube terminals and teletypewriters connected to time-sharing computers with high-speed magnetic memory), and microfilm data-handling machines similar in some ways to the equipment Bush had developed thirty years earlier (Overhage, 1974:163).

While Bush never mentioned Memex at the Intrex meeting, Memex was on his mind. The month before the conference, Bush was writing the first drafts of the essay that was to become "Memex Revisited." The work of revising the essay began in a five-page letter to Hodgins on July 6, 1965. In this letter he notes that the original essay's "main prediction still remains unrealized, but attracts more interest now than it did then." The main prediction is the building of an analog to the human mind, complete with memory, trails of association, and the ability to learn from experience. In this new essay, Bush states his intention to take "a longer look ahead than there was twenty years ago, not on technical details, but more broadly." As we have seen, this is consistent with the direction Bush took in his essays over the last several years. In this way Bush stated to Hodgins the problem he now faced in rethinking Memex. While he was aware of the newer technologies, he no longer worked with them as he had in the 1930s.

This letter was followed within a week by more prose and then quickly by a complete manuscript. By mid-July, Bush and Hodgins had a forty-page manuscript with the working title of "Memex Revisited." This manuscript contained the basic shape of the essay as it was published. It begins with the example of Mendel, restates "our present ineptitude at getting at the record" by paraphrasing passages from the original essay, and then quotes directly the original description of Memex up to and including the example of the researcher building a trail about the Turkish bow. The remainder of the essay reviews new recording technology such as magnetic tape and video tape that offered some advantage over the reels of microfilm proposed in the original design. The unambiguous theme of this essay is to revisit his own prophecy of a "personal machine." The phrase appears over and over again, a "personal machine" designed to fit in with a person's daily thoughts, entirely unlike "the enormous computers which serve whole companies." This interest in a personal machine separated Bush from those who worked with and wrote about digital computers at the time. The idea of a personal computer to support and augment individual work and thought had no present examples and no champion.

Work on this and other writing projects was slowed by Hodgins' poor health. By early 1966, Bush turned to Fredrick Fassett for assistance. Fassett, who had returned to MIT after his years with Bush at Carnegie in Washington, was now retired and living in Maine. On

March 31, 1966, Bush wrote him a note which contains perhaps his most unequivocal acknowledgment of the success of Memex as an idea:

> That old memex paper finally turned out to be a bit of a classic in its field. It is remarkable that, even now, it looks to the future. These machine nuts are pretty slow after all.

In the same note he informed Fassett that Hodgins was in the hospital. By summer, Fassett had taken over as Bush's editor, and all the manuscripts Hodgins had prepared for BUSH BOOK JUNIOR were sent to Fassett. In his cover letter to Fassett on September 13, Hodgins remarks that

> "Memex Revisited" will take a hell of a lot of work because its original publication in *The Atlantic* under the title "As We May Think" is now twenty years ago, and a great deal of what Van was then talking about as possible moon stuff has now become hardware. It's tough to be a prophet whose prophecies turn out correct.

Responding to Hodgins that the essay was "dangerously repetitive and too long" (Fassett to Hodgins, October 4, 1966), Fassett agreed that there was much work to be done on the manuscript. To Bush he offered concrete suggestions as to how the essay might be refocused and condensed. He cut some of the opening pages and inserted a "flash back paragraph . . . in order to make clear that 'Memex' was conceived of speculatively some while ago" as well as suggesting that the material lifted directly from the original essay be set apart as a quotation (Fassett to Bush, October 13, 1966). Over the next several months Fassett continued to edit and condense "Memex Revisited." He pointed out material that overlapped with "Science Pauses," then eliminated it, making the role of the Memex design in the final version of "Science Pauses" even more subtle than what had appeared in *FORTUNE*.

Bush hoped that the new Memex essay would replace the old one. A clear indication of this is found in a letter he sent to William Orr in June 1967. Orr had sent him a request to republish "As We May Think," the sort of request that Bush had granted on several occasions. At this point, however, Bush refused to allow the earlier essay to be reprinted, saying that he had recently "revised this, in order to bring it up to date, and it is now in the form of one chapter in a book of essays on which I have just sent the manuscript to the publisher" (Bush to Orr, June 5,

1967). Bush suggested that Orr wait until the book comes out and then secure republication rights for "Memex Revisited," though he never mentioned the essay by name.

At roughly the same time, Bush was writing additional material on another topic he was struggling to address: extrasensory perception (ESP). In early 1965 he had sent a manuscript to Hodgins on the "sixth sense" and early checklists of the essays to be included in BUSH BOOK JUNIOR include an essay on ESP, which Hodgins had cut by the time he passed the manuscripts on to Fassett. Now in December 1966, Bush sent Fassett a new manuscript titled "Material for Memex or Earlier" ("Earlier" refers to another essay, which was to be included in the book, called "It Is Earlier Than We Think"). The link between ESP and Memex goes back to the passage in "Mechanization and the Record" and "As We May Think" that speculates on a more direct form of man-machine communication. Equally important here is a concern with how man's capabilities and competencies could be extended.

> By bone conduction we already introduce sounds into the nerve channels of the deaf in order that they may hear. Is it not possible that we may learn to introduce them without the present cumbersomeness of first transforming electrical vibrations to mechanical ones, which the human mechanism promptly transforms back to the electrical form? With a couple of electrodes on the skull the encephalograph now produces pen-and-ink traces which bear some relation to the electrical phenomena going on in the brain itself. True, the record is unintelligible, except as it points out certain gross misfunctioning of the cerebral mechanism; but who would now place bounds on where such a thing may lead? (Bush, 1945:108)

Now in 1966, Bush continued to speculate whether the interaction between man and machine might cause new senses to evolve in the human organism as well as new capacities in the machine. The advent of radio and television had demonstrated that electrical impulses serve "as a bridge between the senses of sight and sound," but Bush wondered "whether other senses could be employed usefully in communication, and in fact whether new and specialized senses could be developed for the purpose" (Bush to Fassett, December 30, 1966). This interest is best explained by Bush's lifelong fascination with the electrical correlates of thought and mind and the elusive nature of consciousness.

Bush sent a copy of the ESP essay to James B. Conant, chemist, former president of Harvard University, and member of the O.S.R.D., for comments in April 1967, and Conant wrote back with a very positive response. He applauded Bush for having taken ESP "out from under the rug and put in the front parlor, so to speak" (Conant to Bush, April 14, 1967). While neither man thought of himself as a spiritualist, they both agreed that the nature of thought and consciousness was a misunderstood frontier and that it needed to be investigated scientifically. Bush wrote back thanking Conant for his encouragement.

> How will our mental processes advance? I have not a ghost of an idea, and tried to make it clear I have not. More biological evolution may be involved. Science, in its broadest sense, is certainly far from completed. (Bush to Conant, April 24, 1967)

Both men had seen enormous advances in their respective fields during their lifetimes and Bush's theme that science and man's progress were "far from completed" struck a responsive chord.

Despite Conant's encouragement, the ESP material did not find its way past Bush's editors into either of the essays included in the book. The dual themes of the essays collected in *Science Is Not Enough* are stated first in the book title, which Fassett and Helen King, the editor at William Morrow (Fassett to Bush, April 4, 1967) chose, and second in the title of the essay which Bush and Conant discussed, "It Is Earlier Than We Think." For Bush, science alone is not enough to give meaning to human existence, and faith in higher forces should not be abandoned in favor of scientific materialism. Bush wanted his readers to understand that the advances of science that had shaped the century were themselves only in early stages of a long evolutionary process. The advances in physics, astronomy, and medicine only showed mankind how little we understand.

Helen King sent Conant proofs of the book in June for comment, and Conant praised it. He recognized that "Dr. Bush's dream about Memex" was one of the book's main themes.

> The reader will find here something for a variety of tastes. One can look into the future and see the use of new technology to supplement and enlarge one's memory. In so doing, he or she will learn something about the new computer technology. The younger ones, at least, may live long enough to see Dr. Bush's dream about *Memex* come true. (Conant to King, July 5, 1967)

The task remaining for both Bush and Fassett was to finish BUSH BOOK SENIOR, the other manuscript Hodgins had begun. These autobiographical essays became Bush's last book, *Pieces of the Action*. It had begun as a dialog between Bush and Hodgins, with the latter supplying the leading questions and Bush supplying recollections about his career and the figures of his time.

Memex found its way into this book as well, as did the Rapid Selector. Fassett and Carroll L. Wilson, the professor who had supervised John Howard's work on the MIT Rapid Selector, urged Bush to mention the project in his book. Bush needed reminding about what had actually been done by whom during the development period of the late 1930s and how important it was. Bush's original draft lacked sufficient detail, prompting Fassett to write,

> I acknowledge the piece on the rapid selector, and have to agree with your stricture that 'it is not very good.' I do agree with CLW [Carroll L. Wilson] that it ought to be in the book and I hope you will go ahead and rewrite, giving perhaps more detail on the actual original device—how it worked, what it looked like. I think the man helping you may have been John H. Howard, VI SM 1939. (Fassett to Bush, May 17, 1968)

This is the only place where Bush gives a detailed description of the Rapid Selector itself. He wrote about it separately from the "analytic machines" built for computational work. After describing the mechanism of high-speed movie film, delay circuits, and strobes employed in the MIT Rapid Selector, Bush stated his view of the relationship between the machine he actually built and the machine he was never able to realize.

> Something more than thirty years ago, pondering these latter problems in the light of the work in the selector as well as the analytical machines, I conceived the idea of a machine that should be an extension of the personal memory and body of knowledge belonging to an individual, and should work in a fashion analogous to the working of the human brain—by association rather than by categorical classification. I called the device a memex, and published a discussion of it in the *Atlantic Monthly* in July 1945. . . .
> No memex could have been built when that article appeared. In the quarter-century since then, the idea has been with me almost constantly,

and I have watched new developments in electronics, physics, chemistry, and logic to see how they might help to bring it to reality. That day is not yet here, but has come far closer, as I set out in an essay, "Memex Revisited," published in 1967. (Bush, 1970:190)

This was a rather cool conclusion, but also a realistic assessment of where Memex stood. Bush had put his energies in these later years into updating and publicizing his predictions. He had been able to realize further advances in areas such as medical technology, where his engineering skills could still be applied. But in areas such as digital electronics, a technology he understood but never mastered, he was not to see a satisfactory realization of his ideas. At the end of Bush's life, Memex remained what it had been in the 1930s, "the idea of a machine."

References

Bagg, T. C., and Stevens, M. E. (1961). *Information Selection Systems Retrieving Replica Copies: A State-Of-The-Art Report*, Washington, DC: National Bureau of Standards (Technical Note 157).

Bello, F. (1960). How to Cope with Information, *FORTUNE, LXII*(3), 162-167, 180, 182, 187, 189, 192.

Bush, V. (1945). As We May Think, *Atlantic Monthly, 176*(1), 101-108.

Bush, V. (1946). *Endless Horizons*, Washington, DC: Public Affairs Press.

Bush, V. (1953). We Are in Danger of Building a Tower of Babel, *Public Health Reports, 68*(2), 149-153.

Bush, V. (1959). *Memex II*, [Vannevar Bush Papers, MIT Archives], MC78, Box 21.

Bush, V. (1963). *Man's Thinking Machines*, [Vannevar Bush Papers, MIT Archives], MC78, Box 21.

Bush, V. (1964). *Science Pauses*, [Vannevar Bush Papers, MIT Archives], MC78, Box 22.

Bush, V. (1965a). Science Pauses, *FORTUNE, LXXI*(5), 116-119, 166-169.

Bush, V. (1965b). *Project Intrex*, [Vannevar Bush Papers, MIT Archives], MC78, Box 20.

Bush, V. (1967a). Science Pauses, in *Science Is Not Enough* (pp. 14-30), New York: William Morrow.

Bush, V. (1967b). Memex Revisited, in *Science Is Not Enough* (pp. 75-101), New York: William Morrow.

Bush, V. (1970). *Pieces of the Action*, New York: William Morrow.

Engelbart, D. C. (1963). A Conceptual Framework for the Augmentation of Man's Intellect, in P. D. Howerton and D. C. Weeks (editors), *Vistas in Information Handling, Volume 1* (pp. 1-29), Washington, D.C.: Spartan Books.

Engelbart, D. C., and English, W. K. (1968). A Research Center for Augmenting Human Intellect, *AFIPS Conference Proceedings, 1968 Fall Joint Computer Conference, 33,* San Francisco, CA (pp. 395-410), Montvale, NJ: AFIPS Press.

Heims, S. J. (1977). Gregory Bateson and the Mathematicians: From Interdiscinpinary Interaction to Societal Functions, *Journal of the History of the Behavioral Sciences, 13,* 141-159.

Kevles, D. J. (1977). The National Science Foundation and the Debate Over Postwar Research Policy, 1942-1945, *ISIS, 68,* 5-26.

Licklider, J. C. R. (1960). Man-Computer Symbiosis, *IRE Transactions on Human Factors in Electronics,* March, 1960, 4-11.

Licklider, J. C. R. (1965). *Libraries of the Future,* Cambridge: MIT Press.

MacCormac, E. R. (1984). Men and Machines: The Computational Metaphor, *Technology In Society, 6,* 207-216.

MacKay, D. M. (1962). The Use of Behavioral Language to Refer to Mechanical Processes, *British Journal for the Philosophy of Science, 13*(50), 89-103.

Overhage, C. F. J. (1974). Project Intrex: A General Review, *Information Storage and Retrieval, 10*(5/6), 157-188.

Reingold, N. (1987). Vannevar Bush's New Deal for Research: or The Triumph of the Old Order, *Historical Studies in the Physical and Biological Sciences, 17*(2), 299-344.

Shaw, R. R. (1949). The Rapid Selector, *Journal of Documentation, 5*(3), 164-171.

Shaw, R. R. (1951a). Machines and the Bibliographical Problems of the Twentieth Century, in L. N. Ridenour, R. R. Shaw, and A. G. Hill (editors), *Bibliography in an Age of Science* (pp. 37-71), Urbana: University of Illinois Press.

Shaw, R. R. (1951b). Management, Machines, and the Bibliographic Problems of the Twentieth Century, in J. H. Shera and M. E. Egan (editors), *Bibliographic Organization: Papers Presented before the Fifteenth Annual Conference of the Graduate Library School, July 24-29, 1950* (pp. 200-225), Chicago: University of Illinois Press.

Smith, A. K. (1965). *A Peril and a Hope: The Scientists' Movement in America, 1945-47,* Chicago: University of Chicago Press.

Wiener, N. (1950). *The Human Use of Human Beings: Cybernetics and Society,* Cambridge: Houghton Mifflin.

Wildes, K. L., and Lindgren, N. A. (1985). *A Century of Electrical Engineering and Computer Science at MIT, 1882-1982,* Cambridge: MIT Press.

A Practical View of Memex: The Career of the Rapid Selector

Colin Burke

WHILE VANNEVAR BUSH NEVER BUILT HIS MEMEX, the hardware on which it would have depended was quite real. The Rapid Selector and the Bush Comparator, the machines it was to be based on, were the technological foundation for Memex. Their story is a complex one, stretching over several decades and involving a number of government, academic, and private institutions. When this history is taken into account, why the machine Bush described in "As We May Think" was never built will become intelligible to today's readers.

The history of Memex begins in the 1930s. In those years, Bush completed his internationally famous Differential Analyzer—a huge gear and shaft analog machine that took such devices to their limits. The Analyzer was a great success, and it brought Bush and MIT international fame. Unfortunately, little money followed, and Bush found himself without the resources to progress beyond the Analyzer. The Depression intensified the problem of funding academic research and development and Bush, even though beginning his climb to power in American science, had to scramble for money to support MIT, his department, and his students.[1]

As soon as the Analyzer was announced to the public in 1931, Bush began to contact foundations and possible corporate sponsors with no results. He realized that he would need a grand strategy that would fit with the predispositions of a wide range of possible donors. Bush focused on the idea of creating a world-class center for modern calculation at MIT. To make it competitive with the other emerging academic centers in the United States and Europe and to avoid conflicts with companies such as IBM, Bush decided to base the Center of Analysis around innovative new calculating machines. By creating new devices, he thought both corporate and foundation sponsors would be attracted.

Using the previous experiences of his MIT colleagues as a base, Bush decided to exploit three new basic technologies: microfilm, photoelectricity, and digital electronics. All three were just emerging but, unlike the fragile magnetic recording his students were exploring, they appeared to be ready to use in calculation machines. Microfilm would provide ultra-fast input and inexpensive mass memory, photoelectricity would allow high-speed sensing and reproduction, and digital electronics would allow astonishingly fast and inexpensive control and calculation.[2]

As important as these technologies were in themselves, Bush also wanted MIT to apply those technologies in the areas of digital calculation and record management. Bush sensed opportunity here. While the needs of scientists and bureaucrats were increasing, the technology had not moved much beyond the Hollerith tabulator and electromechanical calculators. Bush was also aware of the market for file management devices and thought he could raise money for development if he had designs for super-fast data retrieval machines. He was not going to abandon those who continued to need analog calculation, however. He planned to create a super-analyzer relying upon the three new technologies.[3]

In the early 1930s Bush took his proposal to all those he thought might sponsor his work. He approached the Navy about building a very fast film-optic-electronic cryptanalytic machine. He called on foundations with his ideas for the next analyzer. He searched for someone in the emerging documentalist field with funds to help sponsor a super-fast microfilm document selection and reproduction device. He also contacted the FBI and the Patent office about versions of a document selector. He let his contacts in foundations know that he had some solid ideas for a bibliographic machine that would revolutionize the library. And he began to formalize his ideas for an electronic digital computer making inquiries about its possible financing.[4]

After a time, Bush looked much like a man who was willing to put any combination of the three basic technologies together for any sponsor who might help him create machines for MIT's calculation center. However, if he had sketched out his concept of Memex at this time, he kept it to himself. He saw little chance that someone would provide funds for such a speculative device.

He had no luck until late 1935 when the Navy came to him for advice on machines to crack coding devices like the new Japanese cipher machines. The Navy wanted to begin a long-term project to give the United States the most technically advanced cryptanalytic capabilities in the world. Bush agreed for a $10,000 fee to help as a consultant. He was expected to shape a project to build a series of revolutionary optical-film-electronic counting machines that would use new statistical methods to unravel these Enigma-like machines. He thought the project would be a chance to refine his ideas for a document selector based on the same technologies. The Navy's Comparator would transfer to the Selector because it was a close match to the document retrieval machine's architecture and technology.[5]

The Navy Comparator

The Comparator was to be a super-fast machine to count the coincidences of letters in two messages or copies of a single message. Using the new electronic circuits first introduced in radiation measuring devices, it was planned to be at least twenty, hopefully one hundred-fifty, times faster than the best tabulating equipment the Navy was using. Bush rightly saw it as the first electronic data-processing machine.[6]

Almost immediately, two things happened that changed the history of the Comparator and the Selector. The Navy refused at first to accept Bush's demands for an unusual contract. Resolution of the conflict took more than a year.[7] Meanwhile, Bush received some good news: the Rockefeller Foundation, which favored analog over digital calculation models, agreed to provide nearly $100,000 for MIT to build a partially electronic version of the Differential Analyzer (see Owens, this volume). Bush promised delivery in three years, which meant that all the resources of his department had to be shifted to the new Analyzer. Unfortunately for the Comparator and the future Selector, by the time the Navy accepted most of Bush's terms for the cryptanalytic Comparator, Bush had overextended himself.

Bush began the project for the Navy in mid-1937 and agreed to do his best to deliver a machine by the next summer, although the contract did not require the construction of any hardware. Immediately, there were problems. Bush had probably planned to design the Comparator around the use of microfilm, but it had too many "bugs". It was decided to use paper tape with minute holes, although paper was only one-twentieth as effective as microfilm. Then, Bush had to tell the graduate students working on the Comparator's major components to hurry so they could return to the hard-pressed Analyzer project. They did and turned over very unreliable components to the manager who, as the only full-time man on the project, had to put the parts together and make the machine function. Bush, busy with other projects and with growing responsibilities in the academic community, had almost no time to give to the Comparator.[8]

Nothing seemed to work well. The high-speed tape transport mechanism to carry the two message tapes had problems, such as being unable to reliably shift one tape a single space relative to the other tape at the end of every pass through the machine's reading station. There were also deficiencies in the optical readers that were to register whether or not the tapes had coincident holes in them, which indicated matching letters. Also, the electronic counters, probably the first to be used in a data processing machine, were poorly designed. They had to be improved in order to keep accurate tallies of the cryptological patterns found during the runs. If there were wrong counts, an analysis would be worthless. However, the simplest components gave them the most problems. The punch for the message tapes and the small adding machine used to print the results of each run of the tapes past the reader refused to work long enough to be useful.

The young manager did his best, but he was injured in a game and for many weeks was unable to work. Despite that, Bush decided to go by the letter of the Bureau of Ships[9] contract and ended the MIT work before the machine was functioning as a complete unit. Being told the machine would need some fine tuning, the Navy agreed to pay the young manager to come to Washington for three months. The Comparator was shipped to Washington without him, however. He had decided to get married and the Navy had to wait a few months for him. Also not arriving in Washington for many weeks were the tape punch and printer.

When the machine was unpacked in Washington, it would not even start up. As a result, the Navy had serious worries about the entire project. When the young MIT engineer finally arrived he got the machine running again. But, with Bush's tacit approval, he soon left Washington refusing to stay on with the project. Within a very short time the machine again would not function and was sent to a back room tended only by a part-time technician.[10]

The Comparator had contributed little to the Navy. Meanwhile, Bush had requested that he be excused from any contact with the

Navy's project at least for a year. Then, something much more important than the Comparator died. The Navy's project to develop more and
better cryptanalytic computers was suspended, if not cancelled, just a
few years before Pearl Harbor.[11]

The Selector

About this time, Bush's plans for a Center of Analysis at MIT were being
fulfilled and he was becoming a major force in the national scientific
community. In addition to the Rockefeller project, Bush had secured
support to develop an electronic, programmable digital computer, for
research into magnetic recording, and for two large, optically based
analog measuring-calculating devices. He even arranged for money to
finance the center itself. As well, Bush finally gained financing for the
Rapid Selector.

Bush had been looking for support for a Memex-like device for
years, hoping to gain funds from a foundation interested in the compi-
lation of scientific bibliographies and in modernizing the library to
make it more useful to technical researchers. He had visited major
foundations with his plans for the library of the future, with depressing
results. Then, he contacted two corporations that were old friends of
MIT, Eastman Kodak, and the National Cash Register Company. They
gave him $25,000 to spend two years developing a machine, with hints
that more support would follow.[12]

Bush's career then took a turn that would interfere with the Selector's
development. As he fixed the design of the machine, Bush began to
ready himself to leave Cambridge and move to head the Carnegie
Foundation's Institute in Washington, one of the two most influential
sponsors of research in the nation. As a consequence, Bush soon had to
concentrate on defining America's science policy rather than on developing any specific technology.

Just as the Comparator was sent to Washington in the spring of
1938, Bush brought together a new team of graduate students to build
the first Selector. He turned the project over to three young men who
became central to the history of the Rapid Selector and the Comparator.
John Howard, Lawrence Steinhardt, and John Coombs would spend
more than a decade involved with the device. Bush spelled out their

work and held them to a tight schedule. The project was to construct a prototype machine based on his outline and to prepare patent reports for the Selector. After the completion of the prototype, which was to take no more than two years, they were to find an application for the device and then revise the machine based on the experience gained during the application phase.[13]

Almost as soon as it was begun, the Selector project drifted away from its original purpose and began to show some telling weaknesses. First, it lost some dynamism because Bush was busy preparing to move to Washington. More importantly, although no one was conscious of it, the Selector was becoming more of a business than a Memex or a library machine. In fact, Bush seems to have suggested to one of his student assistants in the fall of 1938 that the Selector would eventually be turned into a statistical machine.[14] And, Bush kept the project isolated from those outside the MIT, Eastman Kodak, and NCR circles. Although he continued to tell colleagues that he was building a machine for the library of the future, and described the Selector to others as a statistical tool for a new calculation center for genetic research, he severed whatever ties he had with librarians, documentalists, and outside statisticians.[15] Bush was so confident of his own circle's advantage and his previous work that he did not launch a major patent search in 1938. This was to be a serious error.[16]

In Bush's design, abstracts of documents were to be microfilmed on half frames of 35mm film, reduced in size by a factor of twenty-five. The other half of the frame was to contain twelve code letters, the *associations*.[17] Each code was represented by a minute transparent dot, one to a field. Bush planned to spin long rolls of 35mm film containing the codes and abstracts past a photoelectric sensing station so fast, at speeds of six feet per second, that 60,000 items could be tested for selection in one minute. This was at least one hundred-fifty times faster than the mechanical tabulator.[18] Bush was sure that the raw speed of the machine would make it effective and attractive.

The Selector's scanning station was much like that used in the Comparator. There were major differences between the two machines, however. In the Comparator, the medium containing the items to be matched was itself a moving film; in the Selector it was to be a stationary card containing the code of the subject of interest to a researcher. A perfect match between the codes on an abstract and the codes on the card triggered the selection circuit. In the Comparator, light penetrating through overlapping holes in the two tapes activated a set of counters while a complete coincidence in the Selector was to activate an Edgerton super-fast flash and camera system to reproduce the desired abstracts.

Of great importance, the allied circuitry in the Selector was less complex and allowed fewer choices than the Comparator. The Selector demanded a complete match between a code submitted by a researcher and the codes associated with the abstract, while the Comparator used some simple "and/or" logic and circuitry. Although Bush wanted to incorporate a means to short-circuit the Selector's photocells for code areas that were blank, thus avoiding the need to have all the photocells active during a search, it is not certain that he saw this as a way to facilitate generic searches.

More radical, useful, and perhaps necessary to the Selector was another feature Bush suggested but did not pursue. He mentioned that a Selector should contain more than one scanner, with as many as five. With that number, he stated, each run could select several different items. Although he may not have discussed it with his students, he might also have realized that multiple scanner-selectors, with appropriate plugboards or selection circuits, would allow one individual to search multiple categories per run, thus using a more flexible "or" search logic. Such a feature might have helped overcome the limitations of a machine designed to do just serial searching. For whatever reason, this suggestion was not implemented.

Bush and the others associated with the project, it seems, were so entranced with the speed of microfilm tape scanning that little attention was paid to coding schemes. Apparently, Bush did not realize how limiting serial processing or a coding scheme without hierarchy or code-position significance could be.

In Bush's scheme, a researcher would place, in any of the twelve code fields, a letter indicating a subject contained in an abstracted article or book. The code might also indicate an association, a tie to another subject. Bush's examples usually filled all twelve fields. This and the single-scanner architecture of the Selector made particular kinds of searching difficult, if not impossible.[19] Even with the short-circuit feature, a general subject or an "association" search would have been very tedious. For example, if a code system was using 'L' to indicate the abstracted document was relevant to the study of languages, a search for all 'L' abstracts on a roll of film would have to use a unique selection mask for each of the twelve possible positions of the 'L' and short-circuit or black-out all but the target cell during the separate runs. When a search was concerned with, say, two matches, such as the conjunction of 'L' and 'S', the number of required runs would have increased dramatically.

Although Bush saw the Memex as a personal machine, for the use of one scientist, the Selector was to serve communities of researchers. It was to be the mechanical part of a system in which specialists wrote abstracts of articles and then coded them by content and by their relevance to other areas of interest. The coded abstracts would be submitted to a central data entry facility, then added to the roll(s) of film by either splicing or recopying a roll. Apparently, Bush planned to have separate rolls of film for each abstractor's subject areas.

Bush did not describe how the specialists in various fields would arrive at common meanings for their codes. He wanted the encoders to use up to twelve letters to represent the contents of an article, leading to complex and difficult to remember keys like DMUHCORMENVS. He did not explain how a searcher was to arrive at such lengthy and non-memorable keys, and his few references to code books did not really answer questions about the logistics and economics of indexing. Nor did Bush deal with the economics of data entry, storage, or retrieval before beginning to build the Selector.[20]

As well, in part to avoid delaying the project, potential improvements to Bush's original design were rejected. In early 1939, Eastman Kodak's A. F. Sulzer notified Bush and his men of an invention made by one of Eastman's team in Rochester. Like NCR, Eastman Kodak had its own group working on microfilm reading and recovery. Its R. S. Morse had just completed a sophisticated selection system that Eastman Kodak thought avoided problems of film shrinkage and distortion and the misreading of codes because of dust.[21] More significantly, Morse's system, centered around multiple *sound tracks* for codes, allowed a much more flexible use of code categories than Bush's coincident dot arrangement. Further, it allowed generic and hierarchal searches, the use of cross-classifications, and the weighted searches such as the selection of an item if four out of five categories fit a searcher's request.

Bush consulted with Harold Hazen at MIT, then advised Eastman Kodak he thought Morse's idea unsuited to the MIT project.[22]

In fact, during the two development years, John Howard, the student in charge, made only those changes dictated by practical engineering problems. The one major departure from Bush's original design was made for this reason. Instead of reproducing a selected document on paper, a roll of 16mm film was to be the output of the machine. Moving the paper at a speed fast enough to prevent having to slow the master film proved impossible.[23]

The young men completed the machine on schedule and some $10,000 under budget.[24] As far as possible, they had followed Bush's original specifications. But in the summer of 1940, Howard and his team became less optimistic about the Rapid Selector.

Problems with the Selector

The machine that emerged in 1940 was not the elegant, desk-size, and affordable Memex that Bush had envisioned and started to write about in the early 1930s. It included a seven-foot high relay rack, which housed the film drives, scanner, and reproduction apparatus. Electronics took another cabinet. The modified electric typewriter for the abstracts, which used long rolls of paper advanced by a stepping mechanism to ensure alignment in the later filming process, was itself desk-size.

There was another large component. Because of technical problems, Howard substituted a set of sliders attached to the side of the filming desk for the proposed typewriter-like device for code entry. The operator of the camera, who filmed the abstracts from the rolls of paper produced on the special typewriter, had to read the codes written at the beginning of an abstract then set twelve sliding metal tabs so that holes in the tabs corresponded to the intended code letters. In addition, the selection mask, once planned to be a card, was changed to a drum with sliding bands. That change made off-line preparation and storage of retrieval orders impossible.

As well, the machine had to be appreciably slowed down to accommodate the weaknesses of the mechanical and electronic components. Also there were problems using 16mm film to reproduce selected abstracts. The mechanism to shift the film at a rate that would avoid a slowing of the master film proved unworkable. If selected items were too close together on a roll, they would be skipped. The only solution the MIT team could devise was an unhandy one. To avoid skipping selected items, all abstracts had to be checked to make sure that ones with identical codes (or, by implication, ones with the same generic codes) were spaced at least ten frames apart. That, Howard realized, was a serious handicap even if searches were restricted to infrequently occurring twelve-code items. But Howard did not propose a solution to any of the problems related to selecting or sorting on microfilm.

Further, Howard found it difficult to justify the Selector's cost. Even with the use of student labor, the prototype had cost $10,000, a sum equivalent to the salary of four engineers. The economic issues went deeper, however. No one seems to have surveyed the cost of typing the document abstracts but Howard gave enough information to suggest that just the filming step might be financially prohibitive. It took an average of thirty seconds to set the code tabs and film one typed abstract. Thus, the filming of one roll of microfilm alone would call for 1,000 hours of work. And unless several filming and coding stations and several workers were used, the preparation of one roll of film could take six months.

There were also problems with the patents. Based on earlier work at the Institute, Bush had filed patent claims in late 1937. By 1939 the MIT group had begun to worry about producing a machine that would not infringe on established patents. Only one of their twenty-some claims had been allowed, and the list of relevant patents held by others continued to grow.[25] The situation was so tangled that, on November 1, 1940, Bush abandoned the 1937 claims and filed a new and more inclusive set of patents. Howard had spent much of his time preparing those forty new claims during 1939 and 1940, but he was soon confronted by a critical patent examiner. Worse, during World War II neither Howard nor Bush had time to challenge the patent office.[26]

There was more depressing news. During the first half of 1940 Howard had spent time exploring possible applications for the Selector. What he wanted to find was an application that would both test and promote the system. But he was as much or more interested in the device's long-term commercial possibilities. Given the new sponsors of the project, Eastman Kodak and NCR, it was not surprising that Howard spent little time seeking a library or bibliographic application. The purpose of the machine Bush first sketched out in the 1930s had changed, and now the Selector had little to do with Memex.[27]

Howard, in fact, focused on government and commercial markets. He went back to the FBI and the Patent Office. He thought about using the Selector at the Mayo Clinic's X-ray center.[28] At least twice he tried to convince Bush that the Selector could find another sponsor if it were applied to cryptanalytic work. Bush, unable to tell Howard about the Comparator project, had to argue that intelligence agencies would neither be interested in nor have any use for the Selector.[29]

Howard continued without success to search for a use for the document retrieval machine. At the deadline for finding an application, he reported the results of his survey of business applications. Using Social Security files as an example, he had very disturbing news for Bush.[30]

In this report, Howard described three typical data retrieval situations, and he concluded that for them, older techniques and methods were more efficient than the Selector. Howard's first scenario was one in which the search was for what he termed a "single item," the logic of each test being a binary, yes or no. In this trial, records for individuals had to be located by name and date of birth with a complete match being required. Howard compared the time a serial search with the Selector would take with the time needed by the alphabetically arranged Social Security filing system. With 52,000,000 records, the Selector would take fourteen hours, the Social Security system one minute. For looking up telephone numbers, Howard found that the telephone books were more effective than the Selector. Howard also discovered that library card files were much better in cases in which classification codes were hierarchal. Two other trials of what were essentially generic searches confirmed that manual searches and card files were faster than the Selector.

In his general evaluation of the Selector, Howard wrote that what had to come first was a categorization-coding scheme. After that had been developed, machines to fit the scheme might be constructed. That was a bold statement for a young man who had been directed by Bush to think of hardware first. Then, Howard took a much more positive tone and recommended something that would have direct consequences for the Selector, the Comparator, and the history of America's war against its enemies' secret communications.

The Statistical Machine

Howard recommended the Selector be turned into a statistical machine and applied to census work. He wanted it to be changed from selecting and reproducing documents to incrementing counters when "cross-classifications" of census material had to be done. Without asking for design details necessary to allow flexible cross-classification analysis, Bush, just made the head of America's scientific research agency for the coming war, the NDRC, concurred.[31] The Selector and Memex were abandoned. Howard did not know it, but the Selector was about to change into an improved version of the Comparator. Bush, however, remained optimistic about the eventual use of the Selector in bibliographic and library work. Nevertheless, he advised Harold Hazen to concentrate on converting the Selector to a counting device.

While Howard and his team were busy preparing new patent applications and turning the Selector into a statistical machine, Bush was becoming the czar of American science. Appointed to head the National Defense Research Committee, he had at his disposal millions of dollars for research and development. The NDRC freed scientists from bureaucratic control. Under Bush they would select projects and carry them through until they were turned over to the military.

One of the first things Bush did at NDRC was rescue the Comparator, which had sat unused at the Navy yard for almost two years. Prompted by the officers who had first contacted him in 1935, Bush agreed to refurbish the original machine and to design a more advanced model. He decided to use NDRC, not Navy, funds and people.[32]

Because of the war, the behind-schedule and over-budget Rockefeller project, and the shortage of men at MIT, the Selector project was cancelled and the machine was put into storage in Boston. In the winter of 1940, John Howard's team was instructed to use all they had learned on the Selector to repair the Comparator and to produce a new model based not on paper tape but on microfilm. The old Comparator was shipped back to MIT for repairs, and the cryptanalysts were told they would soon see a technical breakthrough. Bush planned to make the new Comparator project an example of how much scientists could accomplish when they were left free of outside control.[33]

It took a year to repair the old Comparator, and it arrived back in Washington some three weeks after Pearl Harbor. No one had thought of how it was to be set up and used, and again it sat in its crates until floor space and an engineer to assemble it became available. It was put to use but its remaining flaws, especially the paper punch, limited its use.[34]

Howard and his men had spent much of the year designing a Comparator that would be at least twenty times faster than the first version. The use of microfilm was the key. With densely packed data, the limitations of tape-drive speed could be overcome. At the same mechanical speed, the machine could match the potentials of photoelectricity and electronic counting. Howard was certain that the scanner could be made small enough to handle the new density and the minute microfilm code dots. In a November 1941 meeting Howard told the cryptanalysts that such a machine could be built, one with even more features and better electronics than originally thought. It seemed that at least the Comparator was to have a future.[35]

Then, just two days later, Howard had to inform the Navy that the MIT group had been wrong. The microfilm, said Howard, would deform and could not be aligned so that coincidences could be identified. A microfilm Comparator would probably not work.[36]

Because there continued to be problems with the paper-tape Comparator's punch, Howard suggested that a version of the microfilm plates MIT's men had explored for the Institute's electronic computer project be used instead. While glass plates would not deform, Howard had to tell the Navy that the use of such plates would radically change the new Comparator. It would no longer be a digital counting machine that could handle messages thousands of characters long on a run. Holding at most 1,000 characters, it would just be a hand-operated analog device. In its eventual design, an analyst would slide two message plates across each other and above a light source. When "enough" dots were coincident, a photocell system signalled the analyst, who then had to locate and hand count the overlaps.

The disappointment over the Comparator and the reorganization of the Navy's cryptanalytic branch led to an end to the direct role of the NDRC. The project was taken over by the Navy despite Bush's protest.

The MIT group was disbanded, and its three young engineers were ordered to be consultants to the Navy while they awaited their commissions.[37] The new Comparator project had not become a model academic university research project.

With adequate funding for the first time in their history, the Navy cryptanalysts in OP20G ordered an all out search for useful machines. Eastman Kodak, NCR, and other contractors were asked to flesh out the outlines provided by Howard and the other engineers drafted into OP20G's new research branch. While almost every combination of the optical, film, paper-tape, digital and analog electronic technologies were explored, most of the machines that were produced during World War II were not even as universal and advanced as the Bush Comparator. There were too little time and too many critical code-breaking tasks to allow much experimentation.[38]

Most of the many different machines produced during the war were, in a sense, retrogressions, using photocells and electronics in an analog fashion. Tapes or films were run until "enough" coincidences were identified, then the machine would signal the location of the tapes at the point of sufficient overlap. Revised and updated versions of the Bush and Eastman Kodak comparators were built, and they did count, but both continued to have problems with misaligned holes in the tapes and poor data registration on microfilm.[39]

Worse, none of the machines was ready until the fall of 1943. In fact, the only active electronic machine the Navy had during the first two years of the war was the 1938 Bush Comparator. The continued delays and machine failures account for why the Navy, in early 1943, allowed the cryptanalytic group to break free of the Bureau of Ships and form its own machine development section. But even this team, which included Howard and his men, and which had, in effect, its own research and manufacturing facility at NCR, could not make up for all the lost time.[40]

Because of these delays, the Selector briefly reappeared. Because of an emergency problem with Japanese codes, the Selector was taken out of storage in Cambridge and rushed to Washington in the spring of 1942. It was stripped of many of its functions and run as something of a pattern locator. But with the end of the cryptanalytic crisis, and because it was unreliable, it was put back into storage in Washington. So many parts were pulled out that the machine was never again operable.[41]

The ERA and Later Selectors

In 1945, Bush, librarians, documentalists, and a group of ex-Navy men, including the original MIT Selector team, began a campaign to create and market a new Selector. But, like the earlier efforts, this campaign was not very successful. Although by 1945 as much had been invested in the development of Selector-like devices as in building ENIAC, the Selector still could not be turned into a useful device.

At the end of World War II, the Navy's cryptanalytic machine group joined with other military scientists to form a company to do secret work for the armed forces. Engineering Research Associates (ERA) included the three MIT engineers from the Selector project. Its first contract was with the Navy to improve all of the cryptanalytic devices built during the war. In 1946 its work focused on Bush's trinity of technologies (microfilm, photoelectricity, and digital electronics). Given Bush's desire to restart the Selector project, the unwillingness of MIT to take on such projects, and ERA's advanced work on even more complex but similar machines, it seemed natural for Howard to think of taking up the Selector, if sponsors could be found.[42]

A sponsor did appear after a year of searching, and this time it was one involved with what had been one of Bush's major concerns in the 1930s, scientific bibliography. World War II had led to a deluge of classified scientific reports and captured German scientific documents. One of the documentalists who Bush knew during the 1930s, Ralph Shaw, of the Agricultural Library, had been able to convince the government to make as many of the reports public as soon as possible. The Department of Commerce set up the Office of Technical Services (OTS) to collect and distribute the declassified materials. Shaw played an informal but important role in OTS, shaping its policies and methods, and he was able to convince its director, John Green, to finance both a study of indexing and the construction of a new Bush Selector at ERA.[43]

A contract was promised to ERA and to Shaw, and work began in 1947 with Bush, Green, and Shaw looking forward to a machine and a system within a year. Almost immediately, however, some old problems reappeared. Patents were mismanaged, deadlines missed, and contracts misunderstood. By the time ERA found that both Bush's and its newer patent claims were invalid, only Vannevar Bush was holding the project together, and he had to put pressure on the company and John Howard to produce a machine for Shaw and Green.[44]

After spending at least $100,000, ERA did ship a device to Washington in early 1949. This device and Shaw's absolute match, seven-digit codes did not work. The machine, built around a single scanner and unable to use and/or logic, also had a number of mechanical problems. Bush again appeared. He helped to find a high speed camera to replace the overly-complex mechanism that ensured that closely spaced abstracts were not skipped. He also arranged for the Atomic Energy Commission and the Carnegie Foundation's Institute to rebuild the machine and to further explore the use of microfilm in scientific documentation. Perhaps another $50,000 was invested.[45]

Green asked the National Bureau of Standards (NBS) to redo the ERA Selector. NBS staff worked on the machine and returned it to Shaw who, after a short time, abandoned it. Shaw's Selector may have gone to NBS to be used as a source of spare parts. At that point another sponsor appeared, the Central Intelligence Agency (CIA). It had inherited the files of the wartime OSS and had built its own indexed database on world political, economic, cultural, and military systems. A small CIA-connected group at Yale was given a contract to build a Selector. It contacted NBS, set up a group of student engineers at the university, and built a prototype of a complex scanner and a new reproduction camera. But, this Selector was never finished.[46]

Once again, Bush stepped in. After decades of trying, he had succeeded in establishing a project to revise the American patent system, including the way patents were indexed and retrieved. He asked the NBS for help on a Selector. Using parts from the Yale machine, NBS built a prototype only to find that the patent project's men had lost interest.

Perhaps the only "working" Selector ever built was for, ironically, the Navy's Bureau of Ships. In the late 1950s its overload of microfilmed manuals and blueprints led it to finance NBS's construction of another Selector. That machine's history is unclear but it may have stayed in operation for some years. However, by the time this $100,000 machine was delivered in the early 1960s, the modern digital computer and magnetic storage had gained the upper hand. Others continued to build special data retrieval machines but, like IBM's Walnut for the intelligence agencies, they were more like the digital computer than the Selector.[47] The cryptanalytical agencies had been among the first to turn to the modern digital computer. In fact, one reason ERA had problems with its version of the Selector was that it was busy designing and constructing one of the very first modern computers, the Atlas.[48]

It is clear that Bush's view of Memex changed over the years, especially his tendency to talk less and less in terms of hardware. In the 1940s he had an artist depict his workstation as a desk-size machine that coordinated four or more reels of microfilm and allowed the selection and complex updating and addition of records in a timely and efficient way. By the 1960s the project and machine failures associated with the Selector, it seems, made it difficult for Bush to think about Memex in concrete terms (for a discussion of Bush's later writings on Memex, see Kahn and Nyce this volume). The history of the Selector adds a practical and sad dimension to the Memex story.

Endnotes

1. On the Analyzer and the history of MIT during the era, see Bernard O. Williams, "Computing By Electricity" (Ph.D. diss., University of Kansas, 1984), and, Karl Wildes and Nilo A. Lindgren, *A Century of Electrical Engineering and Computer Science at MIT, 1882-1982* (Cambridge: MIT Press, 1985). On Bush's influence see his *Pieces of the Action* (New York: Murrow, 1970).
2. A very useful general history of computer development is Michael R. Williams, *A History of Computing Technology* (Englewood Cliffs, NJ: Prentice-Hall, 1985). Of importance is Charles S. Bashe, *et al., IBM's Early Computers* (Cambridge: MIT Press, 1985).
3. On the previous work at MIT, Smithsonian Institution, History of Computers Project, Interview with Gordon S. Brown, January 27, 1970; Charles Babbage Institute, Interview by William Aspray with Dr. Frank M. Verzuh, February 20 and 24, 1984. On microfilm, Frederick Luther, *Microfilm: A History 1839-1900* (Annapolis: National Microfilm Association, 1959), and, William White, *Subminiature Photography* (Boston: Focal Press, 1991).
4. Hagley Museum and Library, Sperry Trial Records: August 8, 1937, Bush to Deeds, "Selector."
5. National Security Agency, RAM File, Chief of Naval Operations to Chief of Bureau of Engineering, 18 November 1931, and, NARA

RG457, SRH355 Part 1, " Naval Security Group History to World War II," p. 269.

6. C. E. Wynn Williams, "The Scale of Two Counter," *The Year Book of the Physical Society*, 1957: 56-60.

7. NARA SRH355, pp. 269-70; and, NSA RAM File, Bureau of Engineering to OP20G, July 7, 1936.

8. 551 NSA RAM File, "Brief Description of RAM Equipment"; NSA RAM File, December 10, 1938, Safford to Bush; and, interviews with W. S. MacDonald and Jeff Wenger, 1988-91.

9. At the time Bush was dealing with the Bureau of Engineering but it merged with an allied Navy bureau to become the Bureau of Ships on the eve of World War II.

10. NARA RG457 SRH355, pp. 270 and 300; NSA RAM File, 19 November, 1940, Safford to Admiral Hooper; December 10, 1938, Safford to Bush; November 2, 1940, Safford to Radio Division, Bureau of Ships; Library of Congress, Papers of Vannevar Bush, MacDonald File, July 25, 1939, MacDonald to Bush.

11. NSA RAM File, 19 November 1940, Safford to Hooper; November 2, 1940, Safford to Bureau of Ships; April 25, 1938, Wenger to DNC; August 22, 1939, Safford to Bureau of Ships; and, December 10, 1938, Safford to Bush.

12. Hagley Museum and Library, Honeywell v. Sperry Records; May 19, 1938, Bush to Deeds; August 13, 1937, Bush to Deeds; March 1, 1938, Bush to Deeds. Thomas C. Bagg and Mary Elizabeth Stevens, *Information Selection Systems: Retrieving Replica Copies: A State of the Art Report* (Washington, DC: National Bureau of Standards, Technical Note 157, December 31, 1961), 18.

13. Rockefeller Archives, Diaries of Warren Weaver, October 28, 1938, Bush Visit. RF RG 1.1 224D 2 23, April 14, 1937, "A Reference Selector."

14. U. S. Library of Congress, Papers of Vannevar Bush, Box 49, Folder 1184, July 13, 1940, Sulzer/Howard, "Progress Report on the Rapid Selector Research," p. 4.

15. Rockefeller Archives, Diaries of Warren Weaver, March 24, 1938, and October 28, 1938, Bush Visits.

16. Hagley Museum and Library: Unprocessed ERA Material from Sperry Archives; "Memo to File," Selector Infringement Search, November 1, 1949, and, Honeywell v. Sperry Records; Bush to Deeds, August 13, 1937; and, Research Corporation to Deeds, October 25, 1937.

17. Rockefeller Archives, RG1.1 224D 2 23, April 14,1937, "A Reference Selector."

18. Library of Congress, Papers of Vannevar Bush, Box 49, Folder 1184, July 13, 1940, John Howard, "Progress Report on the Rapid Selector Research." Tabulators read about two cards a second, but one-field sorters read about three times faster in the 1930s.

19. Library of Congress, Papers of Vannevar Bush, Box 95, March, 12, 1940, Howard and Steinhardt to C. L. Wilson, "General Description of the Rapid Selector and the Apparatus for Preparing the Index Film," p. 2.
20. Bush later claimed that he had examined and discussed at least multidimensional "sorting" at the beginning of the project. Library of Congress, Papers of Vannevar Bush, Box 95, Bush to Carroll L. Wilson, April 15,1940, "Howard's Memorandum."
21. Hagley Museum and Library, Honeywell v. Sperry Records; February 6, 1939, Sulzer to Bush; "Morse Rapid Selector". R. S. Morse, Patent 2,295,000; "Rapid Selector Calculator," filed June 23, 1936.
22. Library of Congress, Papers of Vannevar Bush, Box 35, March 6, 1939, Bush to Sulzer.
23. Library of Congress, Papers of Vannevar Bush, Box 35, April 4, 1939, Howard to Sulzer, "A Brief Progress Report on the Rapid Selector Research."
24. Library of Congress, Papers of Vannevar Bush, Box 95, May 24, 1940, Hazen to Bush, ".Rapid Selector."
25. Hagley Museum and Library: Sperry Archives, Unprocessed ERA Material, Project 1045 (E-45) "Memo to File," November 1, 1949 , p. 2. L. G. Townsend, Patent 2,121,061, filed July 6, 1936, and, Hagley Library and Museum, Honeywell v. Sperry Records; Bush to Carroll L. Wilson, October 30, 1939, "Patents."
26. Hagley Museum and Library: Sperry Archives, Unprocessed ERA Material, Project 1045 (E-45), "Memo to File," November 1, 1949, p. 2.
27. Library of Congress, Papers of Vannevar Bush, Box 95, May 24, 1940, Hazen to Bush, "Rapid Selector". This also shows that Bush had asked an MIT faculty group to find a scientific application, which they could not. Wiener, in fact, rejected the premises of the Selector.
28. Library of Congress, Papers of Vannevar Bush, Box 52, November 29, 1939, Howard to Bush.
29. Interview with J. Wenger, 1991.
30. Library of Congress, Papers of Vannevar Bush, Box 95, April 3, 1940, Carroll L. Wilson to Bush; and Howard to Wilson, "Discussion of Possible Applications of the Rapid Selector."
31. Library of Congress, Papers of Vannevar Bush, John Howard File, April 15, 1940, Bush to Carroll L. Wilson, "Selector."
32. NARA RG457 SRH355 Part I, *Naval Security Group History to World War II*, 405.
33. Library of Congress, Papers of Vannevar Bush, Box 52, Howard to Killian, March 21, 1946, "Rapid Selector," and, Box 49, November 22, 1940, Hazen to Sulzer.
34. NSA RAM File, January 1, 1942, Safford to Howard, and, NARA RG457 SRH355, 440.

35. NSA RAM File, 5 November 1941, Safford, "Memorandum for OP20A," and November 14, 1941, Bureau of Ships to Howard.
36. NSA RAM File, Bureau of Ships to Howard, November 14, 1941. Note that Bush, in reply to Sulzer's inquiry about Morse's invention, had stated that microfilm would not deform. Library of Congress, Papers of Vannevar Bush, Box 35, Bush to Sulzer, March 6, 1939.
37. Hagley Museum and Library, Honeywell v. Sperry Records; March 28, 1942, Harrison to NCR; March 16, 1942, Stewart to Harrison. NARA RG457 SRH355, p. 440.
38. NSA RAM File, Ralph Meader to J. N. Wenger, "Report of 14 Days Training Duty, 21 January, 1949."
39. For example, NSA RAM File, MAC Outlines #17, 70mm Comparator, April 1947.
40. NSA RAM File, January 21, 1949, Meader to Wenger.
41. NARA RG457 SRH355, p. 240; Library of Congress, Papers of Vannevar Bush, Box 52, March 21, 1946, Howard to Killian.
42. Erwin Tomash, "The Start of an ERA: Engineering Research Associates, Inc., 1946-1955," in N. Metropolis *et al.* (editors), *A History of Computing in the Twentieth Century* (New York: Academic Press, 1980), 485-496.
43. Ralph R. Shaw, "The Rapid Selector," *Journal of Documentation,* 5(1949): 164-71; Pamela Spence Richards, "Information Science in Wartime: Pioneer Documentation Activities in World War II," *JASIS,* 39(1988):301-306; Irene S. Farkas-Conn, *From Documentation to Information Science,* (New York: Greenwood Press, 1990), 88, 111-3.
44. Library of Congress, Papers of Vannevar Bush, John Howard File, March 16, 1948, Bush to Howard.
45. James L. Pike and Thomas C. Bagg, "The Rapid Sector and Other New Document Retrieval Studies," in,Vernon Tate (editor), *Proceedings of the National Microfilm Association Eleventh Annual Meeting and Convention* (Annapolis, Maryland, 1962), 212-222; Ralph R. Shaw, "High Speed Intermittent Camera," *American Documentation,* 1(1950):194-6; Claire K. Schultz and Paul L. Garwig, "History of the American Documentation Institute," *American Documentation* 20(1969):157.
46. Thomas C. Bagg and Mary Elizabeth Stevens, *Information Selection Systems: Retrieving Replica Copies: A State of the Art Report* (Washington, DC: National Bureau of Standards, Technical Note 157, December 31, 1961), 25.
47. "IBM Demonstrates Walnut," *Computing News* 9(1961):201-9.
48. Tomash, "Start of an ERA,", p. 490.

Memex II
Vannevar Bush

This is reprinted from the last manuscript draft of "Memex II" found in the Vannevar Bush Papers at the MIT Archives. Dated August 27, 1959, this draft had been edited by Bush and Emily Flint of the Atlantic Monthly *and was submitted to John Jessup at* LIFE.

THE INDUSTRIAL REVOLUTION ENABLED US to make more of the things we need or desire, to raise our standard of living. It is based on the concept that a machine can perform any repetitive operation a man can do with his hands, and do it faster, more precisely, and with far more strength. Today there is another revolution under way, and it is far more important and significant. It might be called the mental revolution. It is also based on the concept that fully defined repetitive processes may be relegated to the machine. This time steps in the thought processes are becoming mechanized and this is far more significant than the mere mechanization of mechanical processes.

Existing machines for mental aid may be grouped into two overlapping classes: data handling and computation. Machines, such as punched card devices, search and sort data. The great digital computing machines perform the four operations of arithmetic upon data which they can extract from storage, or be given to work upon. The digital computers have precise memories in which to accumulate partial results. Their great power lies in the fact that even the most abstruse mathematical analyses, in their application to concrete problems, involve a mountain of hack work of this sort, which the machine can be told to perform, and on which its response can be far more rapid and accurate than that of a human computer with his pencil and paper, his reference data, and the feeble computing aids which preceded the comprehensive digital machines.

There are also analogue machines. These are devices, sometimes complex, which in their motions or their electrical variations obey the same laws as the phenomenon under investigation, so that they can be made to record their performance as an explicit solution of a technical problem, by imitating nature, or rather the simplified concept of the natural process which is adopted. And there are machines which are a

Held by the Vannevar Bush Papers, MIT Archives (MC78, Box 21), the manuscript is published here by permission of Richard Bush, MD.

bit more general, and behave in accordance with particular mathematical relations.

Both the data handling machines and the computers are advancing rapidly and, of course, in combination. Modern business could not function without accounting machines; modern science and technology now proceed much more rapidly with the use of machines, especially in cases where the mental labor of applying current hypotheses would become prohibitive if it had to be done non-mechanically. We thus enter a new revolution, where the power of man's thought is enhanced, for he is learning to train machines to relieve his mind of much that is formulated and repetitive.

Still there is an almost untouched area in the field of data handling. The individual, in his diverse ponderings is aided only remotely and at intervals as he strives to rationalize and create. This, I believe, is because in bringing machines to man's aid, we have thus far built them on patterns which fitted the technical elements at hand and our habitual ways of doing things, rather than to cause them to imitate and extend the actual processes by which the brain functions. Many years ago I described a machine, called the Memex*, which I conceived of as a device that would supplement thought directly rather than at a distance. It abandoned the usual indexing schemes in handling data, and substituted the construction through the data of trails of association which it included in its memory. It has never been built for a number of reasons. For one thing, its development would have been enormously expensive, no worse than that of shooting a rocket at the moon perhaps, but exorbitant. I extrapolated freely as I wrote, and implied the existence of various technical elements and devices which were actually then in embryo, or even practically impossible with current technology. The object was not to propose a practical device, but to try to take a long look ahead.

The time has come to try it again. In the interval since that paper was written, there have been many developments of significant technical elements. Steps that were then merely dreams are coming into the realm of practicality. Moreover, thanks to the psychologists and the neural physiologists, we have a clearer conception of how the brain actually functions, and hence a better chance of joining it with a machine which can truly supplement because it does things in much the same way.

The professional man of tomorrow, seated before his desk, which contains Memex I, would have before him two screens and a set of keys and switches. Stored in the desk would be his records, correspondence, technical papers, books, all compressed on microfilm, so that the complete works of Winston Churchill, for example, would occupy less than a cubic inch. By pressing his keys he could call up any page of this material, which would promptly appear on a screen. When there it would not look like a movie projection, it would look like a printed page, better illuminated and easier to read than the present printed pages. His longhand notes would appear also. Moreover, he could thus project two pages simultaneously, and, by touching a key, tie them together by a code. Thereafter, on viewing one of them, he could shift to the other merely by moving a lever. In this way he would gradually build trails of association through his material, and at any time could follow a chosen trail and add to it. This is the heart of the machine, for, where the brain reasons and ponders, searching its memory as it does so, the process it employs is this identical one of following trails of association.

Memex I was a crude device, even although [sic] it involved the use of techniques not then developed. Much has occurred since then, and we may now become more sophisticated in our look forward.

One significant development has been rapid advance in the recording of data on magnetic tape. This is important, not merely because it will ultimately involve further compression in the volume necessary for the record, but more to the point because the magnetic record can be erased or added to almost instantaneously, without the sort of development and delay inherent in conventional photographic processes. It is essentially the equivalent of the system of dry photography then sought, and if fact it is better for our purposes.

A recent form shows its versatility. This is the recording of scenes, speech, and music directly on magnetic tape, so that it can be reproduced for motion pictures and television. A television show of a half hour involves the projection, one after another and at a rate of 30 pictures a second, of 54,000 complete views of a scene in considerable detail, together with accompanying sound. All this goes onto a tape which occupies a volume of about fifty cubic inches. The information contained is equivalent to about 100 medium sized books if they were reproduced by facsimile, and several times as many if reproduced by code. The information is placed on the tape, during the taking of the scene, by a varying magnetic field, controlled by the light received as the scene is scanned. It is taken off, and converted into pictures and sound, by scanning with a magnetic pickup device. There is a lot of storage available here in small space.

Yet we are by no means at the limit of what can be accomplished in this general direction. The present devices are two dimensional, that is the record is on a tape or a sheet of magnetic material, and this is moved bodily as it is scanned. There are other forms of record which are electrostatic rather than magnetic, used as memories in digital computers, in which reading off is done by an electron beam without the movement of any massive part. There are also arrays of minute magnetic toroids, used for the same purposes, which are three dimensional, that is, in which storage is in a volume, rather than spread out on a plane.

There is no telling where this technological trend will lead. The ultimate might be something along the following lines. A cubic single crystal would be made up of rather large and complex molecules, probably organic in nature. These would have the property of altering a bond when subjected to radiation within a narrow range of wave lengths and above a sharp threshold of intensity. When acted upon by similar radiation, but of a different wave length, the bond connections would revert, and in so doing react appreciably upon the source. Recording would be done by scanning by the first wave length, and reading off by the second, in each case focussed sharply on a chosen plane of the crystal. By such a method, even allowing for very large molecules, storage of information could be made more compact, even, than in the brain itself, and the brain, which contains some ten billion cells, is capable of storing all the scenes one sees, and all that one hears, through a long lifetime.

The difficulty with the brain is that the record is vague, and it fades, unless it is periodically renewed by a process of review. The records in our crystal brain will be exact in detail, and will not fade, when properly protected, although they may intentionally be erased and alterations and substitutions made. My colleagues will charge that I have glossed over some very serious practical difficulties in the way of realization of such a device. So I have, and no doubt, development when it comes will take a different form than the dream above, and it may not progress as far. But we are safe in assuming, for the purposes of Mark II, that ample storage will be available in small space, that this will all be readily and instantaneously accessible on call, and that it can be supplemented and altered at will.

Some time ago there was developed a device called a rapid selector. It could review records at the rate of one thousand per second, and pick out and reproduce those indicated by a code. The record in this case was on motion picture film, one item to a frame, and the code in the form of transparent dots on this same film. By using 20 dots one may make 1,248,576 different specifications, and pick out all the items which correspond to any one of them. In this device the film moved, and much more speed could be secured if the record were on a crystal and only a scanning beam moved. Of course, given a specification in a code, one would not scan the entire record to find it. Rather a system such as appears in national dialing in the telephone system would be used. Here, if one is dialing from Boston for a number in Southern California, the first three numbers dialed connect one to the right area of the country, the next three to the right exchange, and the last four to one individual telephone among some sixty million.

Similarly in Memex II, when a code on one item points to a second, the first part of the code will pick out a crystal, the next part the level in this, and the remainder the individual item. This should not require more than a few milliseconds. In the telephone system there are other features. A complete record of the call is automatically made for billing purposes. If one route to the desired station is busy another is automatically chosen. We will need some similar provisions in Mark II. We may then assume that our entire record can readily be interconnected by codes, and will be accessible throughout at ample speed.

In the interval since Mark I the transistor has come of age. A little unit the size of a pea or smaller, it can perform most of the functions of the thermionic tube. Moreover, it does so with the consumption of very little power, and it is utterly reliable and will last indefinitely. One of the marvelous features of the human brain is that a record placed in it by interconnections between brain cells, a complicated record such as the detailed appearance of a human face by which it can by distinguished among thousands, can be recalled almost intact after the lapse of fifty years, and found by following a trail of association impressed in the same way in fragile material which had undoubtedly been completely replaced many times over the years. The wonder remains even when one accepts the hypothesis that the record is preserved by periodic reimpression and enhancement.

But a transistor will need no renewal. Even if it lies inactive for years, it will respond in a microsecond when activated, and will do so in precisely and specified manner [sic]. Records and controlling devices in crystals and metals do not fade. Some of the control circuits in modern digital computers are decidedly complex, controlling as they do the arithmetic processes on large numbers drawn from storage, and doing so in a matter of microseconds, or even when necessary in a fraction of a microsecond. We may assume that the control devices of Mark II will be positive and rapid in action, and that they will go into small space.

Another development is highly suggestive. Machines are now made which will write down what we say to them. In particular, we can speak words to a machine and it will type them out, not well as yet, but still intelligibly. It is much easier to make a machine which will write in a language which is natural to the machine, a sort of phonetic short-hand, and undoubtedly we shall some day learn to read such records as readily as we now read our cumbersome language. If we wish, such a record may readily be made to talk back to us. Also, when one can do this it is readily possible to make a complex mechanical machine which will perform its various operations on the receipt of vocal orders. When a machine receives a spoken syllable and writes down a corresponding symbol it is making a translation of codes.

Many paths are opened up by such a concept. For example, there is now developed a machine for composing in the Chinese language. By stroking a series of only 20 keys, corresponding to the strokes in an ideograph, one selects one of thousands of those in storage, and this is then promptly printed. A relay bank translates the impressions it receives from the key sequence, perhaps 5 or 10 impulses, into a code which selects the correct ideograph by giving its two dimensional location in the storage. Thus, with Mark II, we will not always go through the cumbersome process of pushing keys and levers. We will talk to it and our words will be recorded in intelligible shorthand, and may also be translated into a code which will take us promptly to a specified location in the enormous record.

Finally, there are now machines that learn from their own experience, and we can use this concept to render Mark II more responsive to our wishes, without the burden of giving it detailed instructions of the performance expected of it. A striking form of self adaptable machine is Shannon's mechanical mouse. Placed in a maze it runs along, butts its head into a wall, turns and tries again, and eventually muddles its way through. But, placed again at the entrance, it proceeds through without error making all the correct turns. During its first exploration it stored in its memory, a bank of relays in this case, all its experience, and used this to select correct performance on its second attempt. There are far more sophisticated machines than this one, and very simple useful ones. Spraying a red hot bathtub with glaze used to be a disagreeable job. But a machine will now observe carefully as a skilled mechanic works the spray gun, whereupon it will repeat all of his motions exactly on subsequent units. This is mere imitation, suggestive of the way in which the chimpanzee learns. But the machine can go far beyond this. It can weigh the successes and failures, not just on a good or bad basis, but on a graduated scale; it can correlate closely similar but differing attempts; in short, it can come very close to exercising judgment. The engineer who designs the machine instructs it exactly on the procedures it will follow in so doing, and from these it will never depart.

Memex II will have an enormous memory. Into it may be inserted voluminous material, through a lifetime, and this will remain until called for. It does not need to get in the way, for it will remain quiescent unless and until a trail is purposely followed which leads into its interrelated mass. It will be useful to be able to distinguish recent from ancient trails, and color may be used for this purpose. An item is projected before a man's personal memex, say a letter from a friend received some years before, and inserted and coded by his secretary. On the margins of the item are a dozen code areas, a few of them active. One leads to other correspondence with the same individual laid on a trail in chronological order. Another leads off to a report referred to by the writer. A third, inserted much later, leads to recent correspondence with another individual on the same subject. At each code area is a colored dot. A recent entry is bright red, an older one yellow, a very old one blue. These colors shift through the spectrum as time goes on. So the recent trails do not get confused with the old ones.

To follow a trail there will be a trail lever. Pushing it in the direction of a chosen code area on an item picks out that trail. The further it is deflected the faster the trail is traveled. Starting with the letter above, the operator may wish to consult later correspondence. He pushes the lever toward the chronological code area, and, since it is a long correspondence, pushes it way over. Items zip by at a hundred a second. He lets up a bit and they appear two or three a second, just pausing long enough to be recognized. He goes past the spot he wanted, so he backs the lever in the opposite direction and steps back slowly to the desired item. In a few seconds he has his information before him. But this has a code for a trail on a subject on which he has had correspondence with many people. So he alters the direction, in which he moves the lever, and steps along a trail that brings the thoughts of them all. On some of the letters appear his own comments, and he adds to these from time to time, speaking his thoughts, which the machine then inscribes on the item in its phonetic shorthand.

The letters were inserted in the record one by one as received, by placing them on a recording platen and pressing a key, which made the record and also brought that letter into projection for addition of codes. The books in the record, however, he bought, and they were sent to him on a piece of tape, which he then inserted for transfer to his record. In fact, he bought a set of books, a dozen on the same subject, and they came all coded for sequential examination, and also cross coded wherever paragraphs treated the same detailed subject. So, when his letter carried him across to a book reference he found himself in a whole network of trails which he could follow at will.

Professional societies will no longer print papers. Instead they will send him lists of titles with brief abstracts. And he can then order individual papers or sets to come on tape, complete, of course, with photographs and diagrams. In fact, if he is in a hurry, he can dial a telephone call to the society, and then dial further to identify a paper, whereupon it will be transmitted over his phone connection and entered into his record immediately and directly, by facsimile transmission. The societies will do much more than process individual papers. In each society will be maintained a master memex on the professional field of interest. This will contain all papers, references, tables, and the like, intimately interconnected by trails, so that one may follow a detailed matter from paper to paper, going back into the classics, recording criticism in margins. It will be so coded that new papers will immediately fit the pattern. Our Memex user can order a whole section of this record, to become his personal affair. And, as he reviews it he will add his own thoughts and comments as he goes, speaking them into the record. Massive records, such as those of the law and medicine, thus will become at last really accessible. Even the confused morgue of a magazine should yield to treatment of this sort, and become practically useful.

Reference books, handbooks and the like, will be bought with special coding. On calling up such a book by title, one step leads to the index. One can then press keys to indicate a page number, and the machine will step rapidly to that page. In fact, one may do better than this, for the machine can read numbers as well as the operator can. So, when a pointer is moved to the item desired, the machine will read and step to it.

There will be special organizations making a speciality of reference books. They will tie all the useful ones together, so that, having found an item in one book, the Memex user will be able to step directly to related items in others. For example, in connection with patents, one may have a complete file in storage of all those in an area of interest, added to as new patents appear, and completely threaded through horizontally by trails which connect all points of identity or resemblance. The chemists should have a particularly interesting time, for their morass of hundreds of thousands of compounds will be interconnected, not merely by chemical analogy, but also by chosen physical properties, therapeutic action, and the like, and every important compound may have side trails leading off to give its preparation or synthesis, its history, costs, sources.

In addition to the specialized libraries, in professional societies and publishing organizations, there will be central libraries where all these are collected in massive memexes, and where the staff builds trails among them, and constructs trails in the literature where there are no specializing groups engaged. One may then, under proper controls, dial by telephone directly into the memex of such a library, and use it from a distance, browsing about along trails, and transferring items of interest to the private store. This involves rapid facsimile transmission over the telephone wires, so that library items may appear on one's own screen, but this is no such task as the transmission of television by wire, where 30 complete pictures have to be transmitted each second. Many individuals may thus consult the library store simultaneously. When they meet on trails there will need to be special means provided so that they can pass one another.

The private memex needs a special provision so that it may be entered readily. Here there are a number of interesting possibilities. One method of entry would naturally be by a name index, called up by pressing a button, and stepped through in the usual manner. Each name would have a code attached, and, when this was indicated by a pointer, the machine would step directly to the corresponding trail in storage. In fact, it would project at once the latest item entered in that name, doing so by first finding the trail at any point by code, presumably the point at which the trail was first constituted, and then stepping rapidly, that is at hundreds of items a second, to the latest entry.

Since names are not readily handled phonetically, this index is in ordinary type and alphabetically arranged. To add a name one projects simultaneously the corresponding part of the index, and the newly entered item. With the pointer at the point where the new name is to be inserted between existing ones, the name is then typed on ordinary typewriter keys. Then a coding key is pressed. The machine itself selects a code, not then used, and appropriate to the region of the storage in which the new item appears, and thus ties the item and the index together. It does not matter that there may be no room on the index sheet for the new name. The machine can readily copy its own material, and needs only a few seconds per page to do this, so it copies and inserts alphabetically. Similar schemes may, of course, be used for lists of materials, or devices, or subjects.

A more interesting index is one that is itself connected by association. This is just a list of words, not alphabetically arranged, but strung out in accordance with shades of meaning, much as the headings in a thesaurus. Practice in this regard would differ in various fields of scholarship. It need not be a simple line, the main sequence could be a list of main headings, from each of which side lists lead off. New words will be added from time to time, and there will be cross ties to the alphabetical lists.

This method of entry is not for the individual seeking something specific, it is rather for the man who has a vague idea, is trying to pin it down, and does not quite know where he is headed. He knows that he has read a very fine statement, by some prominent person whose name he forgets, a definition of nobility or something of the sort, and he wants it. So, in his thesaurus index, he slides along by nobility, kingship, etc. until he sees gentleman. That was it, it was about gentlemen. So he hits the trail on gentlemen. This brings him at once to an encyclopedia discussion of the origin of the term, its alteration in usage in England, and the like. In fact, strung along, are dictionary definitions, book references, etc. He has been along this trail before.

Ah, here is a side trail, and on it are a sequence of striking remarks, by friends, authors, even himself, in which the concept of gentleman is part of the central theme. And, along this path appears the statement by Cardinal Newman of the definition of gentleman, as the term should apply in modern society. This is what he sought. And it gives him what he needs to pursue the line of thought which caused him to enter. So he pins a side trail onto the Newman quotation, and speaks some of his own elaborations of the thought into the record. And, in succeeding days, as his concept develops, he follows that same trail again several times, and adds new matter, of his own, and that he has garnered elsewhere. Can he find it again after a lapse of years? In several ways, by remembering an individual there quoted, from his subject index, or just by again browsing vaguely as he did before.

After years of use the record will be everywhere permeated by a complex network of trails. These intersect at a multitude of points, a single item of importance may be tied into a dozen trails that pass through it for one reason and another. On a new exploration one may often just follow one of these old trails, the machine stepping along slowly [sic] and automatically from item to item as the user recalls what is there. But also he will at times move through the network in some novel way, following one trail for a time, branching off to another, taking false trails and promptly backing up, tying together on the path he traces through the maze a whole new association of ideas which has become of importance to him. Here is where the ability of the machine to learn can help.

Let us say that our scholar is a student of archaeology, and that, over the years he has accumulated the principal literature on the Mayan, Aztec, Incan societies. These are more or less separated, and each has trails following out subjects of social organization, pottery, history, migrations and so on. Now he becomes interested in systems of counting, and in calendars, and specifically in the extent to which the development of these became tied in with the planting and harvesting of crops. He builds himself a new trail on this subject cutting across through the whole collection. It permeates the Mayan literature first, following one trail, then branching to another, moving over to the Aztec area on a parallel point, and so on. At times a side trail is followed for a bit, and then found unfruitful, so he backs up and tries another lead. Finally, he has mapped a trail through the whole affair tying in his new interest. But this is composed of pieces of old trails, together with new material which he has inserted as he proceeds. He wants to preserve this new path.

So when he has finished the trip, he indexes back to the point where he began, and presses a button which tells the machine "repeat that last trail." This it does, at the speed he specified, taking all the correct turns, removing any side trip where he found nothing and backed up. He can watch it, if he wishes, as items remain projected only long enough to be recognized, and he may modify and add further material as he does so. Then when he is satisfied he presses the button which says "repeat that trail ten times" and he goes about other business.

For the machine remembers what it has been caused to do. Thus, when left to itself, stepping along some indicated trail, it will pause and explore a side trail if that has been its experience often when the trail was followed under orders. At an important bifurcation it will take the path that has most frequently followed, and it can even give more weight to recent orders than to earlier ones, in making its decisions. Of course, it can always be halted in its course and ordered to turn at will. Also it can be told, by another button, "de-emphasize that last trail you followed, and leave it as it was first introduced for I have finished with it." Then, too, trails, or parts of them, can be cancelled, as new material supersedes the old. One way of doing this is to project an item, place the new item on the recording platen, and cause a substitution, without removing codes.

Our archeologist now has his path through his storage to bring out all he has accumulated on calendars. He speaks a summary, and some of his conclusions, and tacks it on at the head of the trail. It may remain indefinitely. But, if his interest transfers to other aspects, he can reduce or eliminate the emphasis he placed on this complex path, so that its presence will not confuse the machine as it pursues some of the older trails.

The reading of a book can also be aided by machine memory. This is assumed to be a serious treatise, worth reading, and not a reference book. After insertion it is read for a first time throughout. Reading is better absorbed when one is comfortable, so there is a light portable projection screen, together with essential controls, connected by a cable so that one may take it to an easy chair. There a button turns pages. And, at points of importance, one may insert marginal comments, locating them opposite the pertinent part of the page. This can be done by speaking and thus inserting the comment in phonetic shorthand. Or, for common notes, one may merely insert a symbol by pressing a key, signifying "important," "doubtful," "not proved," "requires further examination," or even "preposterous," "plagiarized," "fine writing which says nothing." Thus for a first reading. But on a second reading the machine can be turned loose. It will pause where pauses were made before, and skip where skipping was done. It is still under control, so that its actions may be modified, and it will thus learn faster how to handle that particular book. Or it may be caused to run through rapidly, and pause only where importance, or some other characteristic, was indicated. All this, of course, in addition to tying the text in by codes to associated material and trails. A book thus becomes controlled to reflect the interests, and for that matter the personality, of the owner.

What will be accomplished by Memex II? Going beyond the extension and ordering of man's memory, it can also touch those subtle processes of the mind, its logical and rational processes, its ability to form judgments in the presence of incomplete and contradictory data, as these become facilitated by better memory. The machine's primary service lies primarily in extending the mass of recollection, and in rendering this explicit rather than vague. It also provides a memory which does not fade, and by causing it to be more promptly accessible than by the somewhat haphazard trails of association in the brain itself.

Its trails are formed deliberately, under full control of the user, ultimately in accordance with the dictates of experience in the art of trail architecture. This, in turn, remolds the trails of the user's brain, as one lives and works in close interconnection with a machine of scanned records and transistors. For the trails of the machine become duplicated in the brain of the user, vaguely as all human memory is vague, but with a concomitant emphasis by repetition, creation and discard, refinement, as the cells of the brain become realigned and reconnected, better to utilize the massive explicit memory which is its servant.

Two mental processes the machine can do well: first, memory storage and recollection, and this is the primary function of the Memex; and second, logical reasoning, which is the function of the computing and analytical machines. These latter can operate only when furnished with data which is precise, and they can then apply the rules of formal logic, and all of the intricate ramifications of mathematical treatment which rest upon these rules. But this is a limitation of the human mind as well as of the machine. Unless definitions and data are precise, formal logic has no meaning; it is in fact worse than useless because it delivers apparent but specious relationships, and these have led men astray throughout history.

The absurdity of much which parades as classic philosophy is due to a downright, and often egotistical, application of the rules which had their inception in Aristotle, to premises which never became precisely defined, which, in fact, were incapable of definition. A large part of the mathematical progress of this century has been due to pinning down definitions exactly, which is often hard to do, and to ridding logical processes of some of the fallacies and vagueness. But neither man nor the machine can develop, out of a mass of data and a set of premises, by the use of logic, more than is implicitly contained therein; they can merely present relationships which are new and valuable only because they are revealed in a form which the mind cannot grasp from the raw data itself.

The advantage of the great computing machines is that they can do this very rapidly, and without making mistakes. In order to function they need to be given the data, and the rules to be used in operating upon it, together with instructions as to the progress of transformation which it is believed will produce useful results. In most cases the data is numerical, the rules used are those of arithmetic, and the program involves using these to apply complex mathematical reasoning.

The number given can represent anything which can be measured or specified, and the program may involve choice of alternatives. For example, the machine which plays chess is furnished, after each move of the opponent, the numerical data specifying the nature and position of each piece on the board. The machine is instructed to use definite rules in regard to the allowed movement of each type of piece. It can then, rapidly, examine every possible move under the existing condition of the board. But then, its most interesting function, it can evaluate each resulting configuration for its relative value. It can do so only because it has been given a set of criteria for measuring values. The machine can go beyond one move, it can look ahead for two or three moves, evaluate all the possibilities, and finally choose the one which its stored criteria of comparison dictates is the most favorable.

Still, a good chess player can beat the present machines. The complications are so great that the examination of all possibilities, with their consequences through several moves, bogs down even the machine with its rapid microsecond operation, so that it takes too long for it to figure a move. The human chess player prevails because he joins judgment with logic. He does not examine every possibility by any means; he follows only promising leads. Moreover, he can visualize the future position of the board, not in minute detail, but in essentials.

Two questions thus arise—first, can types of machines be linked to advantage and, second, can machines be taught to use judgment when data is incomplete or indefinite?

On the first point there is little doubt. Memex as thus far described is after all not an ambitious project; it merely supplements a memory, does so precisely and comprehensively, and aids the process of recollection. It performs little reasoning, only as it modifies its performance a bit in accordance with its experience. But it can act as storage and data ordering source for any type of machine with which it may be linked. And its facility in this regard may enable other machines to elaborate their performance.

The greatest accomplishment of the human mind is the exercise of judgment. Yet it is difficult to specify just what this function is, and how it is performed. If the race had been constrained to advance only so far as strict logic would carry it, it would not have moved far. For the things which can be specified exactly are limited, and the situations with which man deals are manifold. When logic falters, when data are vague or missing, when the mass of conditions surrounding a problem are far too numerous and nebulous to be reduced to equations and figures, man still somehow muddles his way through, often coming to absurd conclusions, but still arriving at decisions on which to move, if not always forward, at least with conviction.

Judgment matures from the modification of thought processes in accordance with experience. Once developed, in spite of faulty data, in spite of violations of logic, it works surprisingly well, and it governs most of human relations. Can the machine be made to imitate? For this purpose Memex needs to graduate from its slavish following of discreet trails, even as modified by experience, and to incorporate a better way in which to examine and compare the information it holds.

Let us turn to an example, with which to explore the possibilities, and to an example where judgment, based on inadequate and some-times conflicting evidence, is paramount; let us turn to the problem confronting the medical diagnostician of the future. His Memex will contain the case histories of thousands of patients, the symptoms, the physical data of the individual, the results of numerous clinical tests, the diagnosis, prognosis, and treatment, the course of the disease, the final outcome, and sometimes the results of autopsy. All this may be called up in the usual form of records, but it is all also coded in much the way in which punched cards carry codes, but far more elaborately. All this is supplied by the medical societies, complete with trails running through the mass, kept up to date as new information develops. Through the mass also run trails built by the individual diagnostician as he has explored in different cases, with his comments on the validity and meaning of the individual cases. With this he can accomplish much. But, can the machine be caused to step beyond this to explore for him, to accept and reject evidence? In short, can it be caused to exercise judgment, at least tentative judgment, and present its conclusions and its supporting evidence for his review?

The core of this procedure is the following of trails with concurrent evaluation. For this purpose there will be an evaluation network incorporated in Memex, revised and added to from time to time, compared occasionally with the evaluation criteria of other diagnosticians. It contains the results of correlation studies of groups of symptoms and tests, the relative significance of ranges of measurements. In particular, it contains significant warnings, positive and negative, on unusual combinations indicating either unusual emphasis or discarding as unreliable.

The procedure is as follows: The diagnostician, having a patient with a puzzling case before him, placed the beginnings of the case history in his record. This contains merely the symptoms with an indication of intensity, the results of laboratory measurements, physical characteristics such as age and sex, and the preceding therapy. All this appears both in visual record and in code. He then places the machine on a trail, usually one which ties together the case histories in which development of the case eventuated in a disease suspected in the case before him. The machine steps along this trail. At each case it pauses and refers to the evaluation network, comparing only the data recorded for the new case. For each symptom and measurement it compares and assigns a weight, and then combines these into an overall weight, all in accordance with the dictates of the evaluation network, paying particular attention to symptoms present in one case and absent in the other. When it has completed the trail, involving some hundreds of cases, it is ready to report. The whole procedure has taken only a minute or two while the physician and patient conversed.

Now, on order, the machine projects the significant cases it has found, beginning with those most heavily weighted. If the physician is satisfied he advises accordingly, if not, he starts the machine on another trail. At the next visit of the patient the whole procedure is repeated, in the light of the added data and the results of the advised therapy. The physician exercises the final judgment, and Memex is his slave. But the machine can examine and compare hundreds of cases in the time it would take him to find and compare one, and its basis of comparison may be far more elaborate than can be remembered and applied when trusting only human fallibility.

Now, can the machine learn from its own experience and thus improve its judgment? It certainly can. And it can have plenty of unattended experience on which to alter, or to recommend alteration of the criterion in its evaluation network. Left to itself it can be instructed to review a trail, and also to compare it with an alternative trail. And it can be told to put its mind at work on the weights to give in correlation of a particular symptom.

After a dozen reviews it is ready to report. This sounds like a complicated performance, and it is, so complicated that it would take a corps of human computers months to carry it out, but the machine can do several such reviews when left by itself overnight, and be ready to report in the morning. In doing so it presents the criteria it has used, together with the degree of sureness it has obtained in their use. Of course, it could then automatically incorporate the preferred criterion into its evaluation network, but it pauses for the consent of its master.

In much the same way it can explore and recommend the alteration of trails. Given an arbitrary set of data, it can follow a dozen related trails and gather weights, thus occasionally locating cases in unexpected places which should be tied in. In fact, it can be made to review the entire mass of thousands of cases and prepare lists of cases where high correlation is found, and which therefore should be trail connected and, on order, it can then so connect them.

What can be done in medical diagnosis can also be done in branches of the profession of law, or in many of the sciences. Whenever judgment can be based on explicitly stated criteria, the machine can judge more precisely, and far more rapidly, than any group of men. It becomes relatively helpless when both the data and the criteria are vague. That is where human judgment, fallible though it is, must enter when decision is imperative. But the machine can prepare the way for this, when the problems are complex, the data of experience massive, and the criteria of correlation intricate. To this extent the machine can learn from its experience and exercise primary judgment.

Memex II is a modest extrapolation, and it is still crude. To control it, one still has to speak to it, and to guide it by pushing buttons on moving levers. It would be more intimate if it could be controlled without this necessity for translating thoughts and wishes into pulses in the motor nerve system, and thus into muscular action. The ultimate is far more subtle than this. Memex III may respond without this crudity of involving nerve systems which have no real part in cerebration. But this will have to wait until the psychologists and neurologists know far more than they do now, and until the advent of devices and instruments, of which the encephlograph [sic] is only a faint beginning, which can sense the activity of a brain without interfering with its action.

Quantitative science stops at the boundary where precise definition and the formulation of explicit hypotheses become impossible. Beyond this is a region in which judgment enters, and in which man's decisions and acts are based on experience and comparisons rather than logic. As the conditions become still more tenuous, especially as human emotions enter to modify or control, we enter the region of art, and the affairs of the spirit. How far can the machine accompany and aid its master along this path? Certainly to the point at which the master becomes an artist, reaching into the unknown with vision and versatility, erecting on the mundane thought processes a structure of beauty, or inspiration. This region will always be barred to the machine. But, moving with his slave more surely and comprehensively through the definable regions, who knows, man may indeed practice his unique arts in new and higher ways.

The race progresses as the experience and reasoning of one generation is handed on to the next. Can a son inherit the memex of his father, or the disciple that of his master, refined and polished over the years, and go on from there? In this way can we avoid some of the loss which comes when oxygen is no longer furnished to the brain of the great thinker, when all the pattern of neurons so painstakingly refined becomes merely a mass of protein and nucleic acid? Can the race thus develop leaders, of such power of intellect, and such forces of conviction, that the world can be saved from its follies? Can science and technology, as they support and extend man's power of thought, bring us nearer to social wisdom, rather than merely to extend the control over the forces of nature for good or ill? This is an objective, of far greater importance than the conquest of disease, even than the conquest of mental aberrations. The path toward the objective has only recently been entered upon. Progress along the path depends upon the advent of new technical instrumentalities, and still more upon greater understanding of how to use them.

Speed along the path is accelerating, as one discipline reacts upon another, and as success in modest accomplishments invites attack upon tougher problems. The next decade or two will witness a new revolution, as the hack work, the repetitive work, of the brain is relegated to the machine. It will be of much greater influence upon our destiny than the revolution which followed the machine supplementation of man's muscles, his vision, and his speech. No man can now visualize the ultimate outcome.

Science Pauses
Vannevar Bush

This essay first appeared in FORTUNE *in May, 1965. The text of this essay is based on the version reprinted in 1967 as Chapter II of* Science Is Not Enough.

PEOPLE HAVE LONG HELD QUEER IDEAS ABOUT SCIENTISTS. Once they were regarded as long-haired idealists, likely to wear one black shoe and one tan. Some days they ate two lunches, and some days none, for their thoughts were not on mundane things.

Then came the A-bomb. Now scientists are regarded as supermen. They can do anything, given enough money. If America wants to put a man on the moon, which is really a tough engineering job, just gather enough thousands of scientists, pour in the money, and the man will get there. He may even get back.

In such moonbeams there is a misconception about scientists and the nature of science. But carried within this there is still another misconception, much more serious. This is the misconception that scientists can establish a complete set of facts and relations about the universe, all neatly proved, and that on this firm basis men can securely establish their personal philosophy, their personal religion, free from doubt or error.

Much is spoken today about the power of science, and rightly. It is awesome. But little is said about the inherent limitations of science, and the two sides of the coin need equal scrutiny. The impact of science on men's minds has been long in the making, but the age of Galileo gives us one place to start.

Galileo did not, as the ENCYCLOPAEDIA BRITANNICA for so many years asserted, drop heavy and light weights from a tower and watch them fall together. (They would not have fallen together if he had.) He *did* roll balls down inclined grooves and time their progress. In so doing he developed the first laws of nature, if we wish to call them that, based on observation and calculation. He was not alone, but he was pre-eminent in his time.

Galileo caused quite a bit of turmoil in intellectual circles. Some of his colleagues refused to look through the telescope he had fashioned.

Reprinted from Vannevar Bush's Science is Not Enough, *(New York, 1967), pp. 14-30, by permission of William Morrow and Richard Bush, MD.*

Some looked and refused to believe what they saw—moons swinging around Jupiter, for example. The Church frowned upon him, but did not burn him. He personified a new spirit, and carried with him a new intellectual freedom rising throughout Europe. Here was a new liberty of thought to contend with—and to suppress if possible.

No doubt many, or most, of those who tried to prevent this awakening were moved by a desire to perpetuate the privileges of an organized priesthood. But, along with them in the effort at prevention, there were honest men as well, and the point of view which these took was most understandable, even if shortsighted and doomed.

For centuries men had been indoctrinated in a complex system of myths, built on what had originally been a simple religion but had been embroidered through the years by tradition and the human tendency to elaborate and ornament. Upon this was erected a rigid code of conduct, enforced by authority based upon asserted superior knowledge and upon the fear of Hell. The only science admitted was the science of Aristotle—including its absurdities. The only reasoning permitted about men or nature followed the strict logic of Aristotle—including its fallacies. The scholastics argued learnedly about angels. But they did not open an egg and observe the growth of an embryo.

If, it was reasoned at the time, man now began to learn about nature himself, if he were moved to cut even part way loose from authority and throw out some of the old myths, the code of ethics would go overboard also, whereupon the mass of men would revert to savagery. This at any rate was the conviction held by many devoted persons. It was indeed a courageous adventure that began when men decided to try to understand nature on their own and embark on the hazardous endeavor of building a philosophy of life upon observed facts. We have not yet seen the end of this experiment. It was no wonder that intelligent men, with sincere and worthy motives, hesitated to take the plunge.

Another jolt to entrenched tradition came when Newton and Leibnitz invented the calculus, and when such geniuses as d'Alembert, Euler, Lagrange, and Gauss built an amazing structure of dynamics and optics. A sparkling assemblage of equations, developed with marvelous ingenuity, could predict the movements of the planets with precision, or the precession of a gyroscope, or the path of light through an assemblage of lenses. Nowhere in the whole history of human thought has there been a finer example of the power of the intellect than in this seventeenth- and eighteenth-century burst.

This burst of analysis is important to ponder today because it led, widely, to a philosophy of materialism, and an especially unattractive form of it. Soon man would be able to understand all of nature, this philosophy ran. Everything would be controlled by a neat set of equations. Merely by observing the present state of things, one could predict all the future. All the history of the universe, all of man's part in it, was, so it seemed, controlled by causal, mechanistic laws. Man was merely an automaton. His fancied choice of acts was an illusion; he merely carried out what was inevitable in the light of his nature and nurture. Pride of intellect never went further.

The extremes of materialism that flowed from these beginnings did not touch the mass of men. But later there came an upheaval that wrenched even the common man loose from his moorings. Darwin did not originate the theory of evolution, but his meticulous observation and exposition made it more readily credible. Herbert Spencer drew from it a great sweep of disquieting speculation. And the man in the street was suddenly confronted with the assertion that he was descended from an ape.

Worse was to come: it soon appeared that princes and people alike were even descended from a bacterium. Mythology came apart, and the question of the spontaneous origin of life was fiercely debated. If all living things had descended from some minute organism in a primeval soupy sea, did that organism itself appear by the chance joining of chemical constituents in that complex environment? Much of the reasoning and the experiment to try to prove or disprove the thesis of spontaneous generation was absurd. Men sealed up gooey liquids in glass tubes, heated them to destroy all life, and then argued that spontaneous generation was impossible, because no new life appeared. But there was no accepted definition of "life."

How does a spider know how to spin?

Today we are calmer, at least on that front, and it is generally accepted that life began with the appearance of the first self-reproducing molecule. This is merely a chemical capable of assembling, from chemical fragments about it, an exact duplicate of itself. One can grasp what would happen when such a molecule appeared in a warm, complex sea, full of all sorts of simple nonliving chemical structures, existing there by virtue of chemical processes and photochemical effects. These structures would have included such things as amino acids and nucleotides. (In the laboratory it has been demonstrated that such things show up when light shines on a chemical soup, chosen to be like the primeval seas as we envisage them.) A single molecule, able to build a twin from such a mess, would proliferate prodigiously until it had used up all the available primary material with which it could combine. It would not be interfered with by predators since, for a time, it would be all alone. But the process would not stop there. By chance, other replicating molecules would appear. Some of these would proliferate by seizing upon material already combined; thereupon the great process of evolution would be on its way. After millenniums, cells with all their internal intricacy would appear, then organisms made up of cells in combination, then fish and plants and mammals, and finally man.

This account is persuasive because so much of life, as we observe it today, depends upon replicatory molecules. All of heredity, as we now depict it, depends on the genes, which are self-duplicating nucleic acids. These pass the characteristics of an individual from one generation to the next. They control the development of an organism, from sperm and egg to adult, by molding messenger chemicals, which in turn mold the proteins: the hormones, enzymes, and the structural materials that constitute the body; those chemicals form and control your body and mine. The code by which the gene signals and controls is just now being deciphered in hundreds of laboratories. There is some question whether all this is sufficient to explain, for example, the linkages in the brain of a spider by which it knows how to spin a web without being taught, and so we may be taking only the first step on a very long road. But there is no doubt that the molding of one molecule by another lies at the basis of the wealth of life we see about us.

Man has not yet succeeded in creating life as here defined, but there is little doubt that he soon will. Some very simple short-chain nucleic acid, synthesized from inert matter and placed in a chemical soup, will suddenly assemble accurate images of itself and the job will be done.

We seem, thus, to have arrived at a concept of how the physical universe about us—all the life that inhabits the speck we occupy in this universe—has evolved over the eons by simple material processes, the sort of processes we examine experimentally, which we describe by equations, and call the "laws of nature."

Except for one thing! Man is conscious of his existence. Man also possesses, so most of us believe, what he calls his free will. Did consciousness and free will too arise merely out of "natural" processes? The question is central to the contention between those who see nothing beyond a new materialism and those who see—Something.

The enthusiasm, the exuberance, that properly accompanies the great achievements of science, the thrill of at last beginning to understand nature and the universe about us, in all their awesome magnificence, continues to lead many men all over the world, especially young men, on to this new materialism. In taking what they imagine to be their final steps, they conceive that they are merely following the dictates of science and carrying them to their inevitable and logical conclusion. In Russia, of course, materialism is the state religion. But the new materialism is by no means confined to those who further the communistic organization of society. The philosophy of existentialism, with its powerful appeal to young men, takes many forms, but in every form there is a concern for what the existentialist believes to be science, which leads, more often than not, to a rigid atheism. Under whatever name or state they go, there is cause for much concern over those who follow science blindly, or relapse into a hopeless pessimism.

Immortality in a machine

A relatively new development, and a potent one, gives support to the chain of ideas we need, today, to examine.

Long ago man built machines to supplement or replace his muscles or those of his beasts. He also built devices to supplement and extend his vision, so that he can now see the very small: the virus that preys on his flesh, and the very distant: the galaxy a billion light-years away. Instruments also extend his voice, so that he can speak across a continent, or to a satellite, which repeats his voice across an ocean. No longer content with the form of the materials he finds on the earth, he produces new metals and new chemicals. Dissatisfied with the sources of energy in fossil fuels, he taps the internal energy of the atom, and may soon find nearly inexhaustible resources in the sea. Beyond this he creates devices that control and guide his machines, so that they perform in concert to produce the things he needs or desires: automation with all its current problems and its future promise. Still further, he is learning to understand his own physical self, to make new chemical entities to cure his ills; some day in similar manner he will conquer the grosser malfunctioning of his brain. All this creates modern civilization, with its comfort and its health, limited as yet to the few, but capable of encompassing all mankind if the race acts with wisdom and uses its new powers for the benefit of man's true interests.

Now man takes a new step. He builds machines to do some of his thinking for him. These are still in their infancy, but their significance is great. It is one thing to supplement muscles and senses. It is a far more profound thing to supplement intellectual power. We are now in the early stages of doing just this, and in its success, if it is to succeed, we shall have a revolution that can make the industrial revolution, so called, seem a mere episode in mankind's onward march.

Even the machines that have been built and used thus far do interesting things. They do in a minute a computation that would take an unaided man a year. They conduct the accounting of vast businesses. They search through their vast memories in a flash to produce a desired item. They translate languages, badly, and write poetry, badly. They will do better when they have been taught better. They compose music, still not interesting, but they will some day compose well. They refine the design of a bridge for an engineer, and take over the labor of drawing his concepts. They have not yet solved the problem of our libraries, about to be swamped by the deluge of printed matter, but some day they will.

But no machine has yet appeared that operates as the brain does. The brain does not operate by reducing everything to indices and computation. It follows trails of association, flying almost instantly from item to item, bringing into consciousness only the significant. Its associative trails bifurcate and cross, are erased by disuse and emphasized by success. Ultimately we shall produce a machine that can do all this. Its memory will be far greater and the items will not fade. It will progress along trails at lightning speed. The machine will learn from its own experience, refine its own trails, explore in unknown territory to establish trails there. All this it will do under the orders of its master, and as his slave.

When Mercury was found to wobble

Thus our speculations lead us: if scientists can settle the ancient question of the spontaneous generation of life by repeating the process in their laboratories, will not scientists also settle the next question by building machines that are conscious and that exhibit free will?

We can hardly approach this tremendous possibility directly. Rather let us consider how science operates, and hence what are its limitations.

Science never proves anything, in an absolute sense. It works by processes of induction, and of deduction. Let us take them in order. Science accumulates data, by observation and measurement. Today its observations are likely to be in the form of the positions of needles on dials, or the optical density of photographic film, or the count of particles arriving in a chamber, for most of the things observed are not accessible to the unaided senses. The scientist attempts to select phenomena in which only the variables to be studied are present, with extraneous influences excluded. From an assemblage of such data he constructs a hypothesis, a formula that expresses the relationships he finds. With this he predicts, and then measures to determine whether his prediction is valid. If there is general confirmation, and no facts appear in contradiction, he, and scientists generally, accepts the hypothesis and proceeds on his way. But at any time thereafter a single confirmed measurement found to be in flat contradiction with the hypothesis destroys it completely. The attempt is then made to refine the theory and remove the contradiction.

This has happened hundreds of times in the history of science. A good example lies in celestial mechanics. The observations of the planets by Tycho Brahe enabled Kepler to calculate that they moved about the sun in ellipses, and to formulate rules of their motions. Newton, with his treatment of gravitation, verified all this, and showed that the whole procedure could be calculated if one merely assumed that bodies attracted each other with forces proportional to their masses and inversely proportional to the square of the distances of their separation. He also assumed that geometry on the earth, the Euclidean geometry that harassed us in school, holds also in the wide spaces of the universe. The hypothesis, the theory if you will, held up under tests of prediction. By the use of it alone, an eclipse could be predicted, the region of the earth where it would be seen, and the time of its advent at a particular spot. In fact, it held up marvelously; the prediction could be made to a second. Yet today it is regarded as merely an approximation, good enough for many purposes, but by no means refined enough to apply generally.

What has happened? First, the planet Mercury was found, if one measured closely enough, to wobble in its flight—i.e., not to follow *exactly* the orbit that theory predicted. Second, the application of Euclidean geometry for the vast universe was shown to be only one assumption among three possible ones. When Einstein produced his general relativity theory, he cured the gross imperfections that had escaped the notice of Kepler and Newton—and the old theory became simply a special case adequate for most local needs. Few believe Einstein's formulation is the last word, although no one has yet done better. But as for Newton's assumption that Euclid's geometry held throughout all his range of thought, this involves deductive reasoning, and deduction is more subtle than inductive reasoning.

More than one geometry

Deduction uses the rules of logic to proceed from a set of assumptions to their consequences. But we have troubles here. Logic itself is by no means a perfect tool and, even if it were, it could do no more than transfer the question of the validity of a deduced relationship to the question of the validity of the premises on which it is based. And these premises are merely statements that are assumed to be valid for the purposes of the argument: simple statements, so simple that they cannot be expressed in terms of statements which are more simple.

This is well illustrated by the history of geometry. Various Greeks, with admirable diligence and insight, developed logical reasoning about matters of geometry. Euclid compiled these thoughts into a form that lasted for two thousand years. He based his reasoning on a set of axioms, assumed to be self-evident, needing no proof or even examination. One of these was the so-called parallel postulate, the statement that if two perpendiculars are erected to a given line they will remain equidistant no matter how far extended. To the scholars of centuries ago this seemed fair enough. On the basis of these axioms it was proved, for one result, that the sum of the angles of a triangle is two right angles.

In the great age of analysis this parallel postulate was questioned by Gauss, Bolyai, Lobachevski. Gauss was so moved by what he found, perhaps appalled by what his colleagues might say, that he did not publish. The others did. In fact, they worked out whole systems of geometry, non-Euclidean geometry, based on the other possibilities. One is that if the perpendiculars are extended, perhaps out to the most distant regions of the universe, they will diverge. The other is that they will finally intersect. We cannot, at least today, settle by measurement which assumption is more probable. And we have no instinctive reason for believing in *any* of the three premises. Triangles made of straight lines extending out among the stars need no longer have as the sum of their angles two right angles. In fact, on one assumption we can conceive of a triangle with all of its three sides parallel, or asymptotic, in pairs, a triangle nevertheless of a specific area. On the other assumption, if we enlarge a triangle indefinitely it will approach the form of a circle, although its sides will still be straight lines. Space may be curved, an idea that it is hard to visualize with our limited three-dimensional outlook. The universe may be closed, but unlimited; there may be a longest line. We have no evidence that three dimensions are all that exist. Perhaps we observe merely a three-dimensional cross section of a four-dimensional universe.

The whole long process of deduction that built Euclidean geometry revealed fascinating relations, useful ones also, which enabled man to sail the wide seas, or to build telescopes of great power. But it proved none of these relationships; it merely transferred the question of their validity to that of the axioms upon which everything rested. And one of these axioms was shown to be merely one of three equally reasonable assumptions.

Stepping outside the system

Even prevailing logic itself came under closer scrutiny. Aristotle was found not to be so infallible as he had been considered for over a thousand years. Russell, and others, labored to remove the paradoxes and to straighten out the semantics. The subject became even more difficult when Gödel showed that no closed logical system could be proved to be free of contradictions unless one stepped outside the system.

Fortunately, a scientific endeavor does not have to be perfect in order to yield results. The magnificent structure of dynamics was based on a differential calculus that was, logically, full of holes. Mathematics, on a much firmer basis today, starts with simple assumptions, and produces unexpected and beautiful conclusions. Theorems that glitter, often quite useless when they appear and treasured for their aesthetic appeal, sometimes later become of direct utility. In exploring the nucleus of the atom today, with all its galaxy of particles, and its wholly mysterious relations, mathematics is used that was originally the prized possession of mathematicians alone.

Science's use of logic becomes more and more demanding: the symbolic logic of Russell and Whitehead has been one answer to this demand. Logic can proceed only when the entities with which it is concerned are strictly defined. Science can proceed only when it can observe with precision, and when it can measure. Mathematics becomes useful only when the quantities it manipulates have precise meaning. Many, most, of the classic philosophers sinned badly in this regard. They dreamed dreams, which was well, and constructed systems that were often fascinating. But then they dressed these up with logical arguments based on elements that they did not define, or even on elements that were undefinable. And they often announced their systems with dogmatism and an assumed superiority. Philosophy has come far since those days. It has had to.

Science, too, has come a long way, in delineating the probable nature of the universe that surrounds us, of the physical world in which we live, of our own structure, our physical and chemical nature. It even enters into the mechanism by which the brain itself operates. Then it comes to the questions of consciousness and free will—and there it stops. No longer can science prove, or even bear evidence. Those who base their personal philosophies or their religion upon science are left, beyond that point, without support. They end where they began, except that the framework, the background, against which they ponder is far more elaborate, far more probable, than was the evidence when an ancient shepherd guided his flock toward the setting sun, and wondered why he was there, and where he was going.

Science proves nothing absolutely. On the most vital questions, it does not even produce evidence.

But is all the labor of science vain to the thinker, the seeker after a sure harbor, amid the mystery, evil, cruelty, majesty, that surrounds us? By no means. Science here does two things. It renders us humble. And it paints a universe in which the mysteries become highlighted, in which constraints on imagination and speculation have been removed, and which becomes ever more awe-inspiring as we gaze.

A belief larger than a fact

The first men who pondered did so on a small earth, which did not extend far beyond the horizon, for which the stars were mere lamps in the skies. Now, we are no longer at the center; there is no center. We look at congeries of stars by light that left them before the earth had cooled.

Among the myriads of stars we postulate myriads of planets with conditions as favorable to life as is our earth. We puzzle as to whether the universe is bounded or extends forever; whether, indeed, it may be only one universe among many. We speculate as to whether our universe began in a vast explosion, whether it pulsates between utter compression and wide diffusion, whether it is self-renewing and thus goes on unchanged forever. And we are humble.

But science teaches more than this. It continually reminds us that we are still ignorant and there is much to learn. Time and space are interconnected in strange ways; there is no absolute simultaneity. Within the atom occur phenomena concerning which visualization is futile, to which common sense, the guidance from our everyday experience, has no application, which yield to studies by equations that have no meaning except that they work. Mass and energy transform one into another. Gravitation, the solid rock on which Newton built, may be merely a property of the geometry of the cosmos. Life, as its details unfold before us, becomes ever more intricate, emphasizing more and more our wonder that its marvelous functioning could have been produced by chance and time. The human mind, merely in its chemical and physical aspects, takes on new inspiring attributes.

And what is the conclusion? He who follows science blindly, and who follows it alone, comes to a barrier beyond which he cannot see. He who would tell us with the authority of scholarship a complete story of why we exist, of our mission here, has a duty to speak convincingly in a world where men increasingly think for themselves. Exhortation needs to be revised, not to weaken its power, but to increase it, for men who are no longer in the third century. As this occurs, and on the essential and central core of faith, science will of necessity be silent.

But its silence will be the silence of humility, not the silence of disdain. A belief may be larger than a fact. A faith that is overdefined is the very faith most likely to prove inadequate to the great moments of life. The late Mr. Justice Holmes said, ". . . the faith is true and adorable which leads a soldier to throw away his life in obedience to a blindly accepted duty, in a cause he little understands, in a plan of campaign of which he has no notion, under tactics of which he does not see the use." Young men, who will formulate the deep thought of the next generation, should lean on science, for it can teach much and it can inspire. But they should not lean where it does not apply.

Modern philosophy divides, roughly, into two parts. One pores through the ancient record and attempts to recover from it thought that is worth preserving and to present this in modern dress. The other labors to refine our logical processes and our language, that we may reason more assuredly. This is not all that philosophy can do. It can return to its mission in its day of glory. It can dream and it can guide the dreams of men. To do so it will need to present its visions humbly, and in the concepts of the universe that science offers. There are a few who labor to do just this. Their task is difficult, for the universe that science presents as probable is continuously altering, and grasping it depends upon mathematics that requires deep study for many years. Nevertheless, the opportunity is there to present wide-sweeping thought that will sway the minds of men.

And the theologian. He can accept the aid of science, which draws for him a wide universe in all its majesty, with life in all its awe-inspiring complexity. He can accept this, knowing that on the central mysteries science cannot speak. And he can then step beyond to lead men in paths of righteousness and in paths of peace.

And the young man. As always he will build his own concepts, and his own loyalties. He will follow science where it leads, but will not attempt to follow where it cannot lead. And, with a pause, he will admit a faith.

Memex Revisited
Vannevar Bush

*While this essay was completed in 1965, it was not published until 1967
as* Chapter V of Science Is Not Enough.

AN AUSTRIAN MONK, GREGOR MENDEL, published a paper in 1865 which
stated the essential bases of the modern theory of heredity. Thirty years
later the paper was read by men who could understand and extend it.
But for thirty years Mendel's work was lost because of the crudity with
which information is transmitted between men.

This situation is not improving. The summation of human experience is being expanded at a prodigious rate, and the means we use for
threading through the consequent maze to the momentarily important
items are almost the same as in the days of square-rigged ships. We are
being buried in our own product. Tons of printed material are dumped
out every week. In this are thoughts, certainly not often as great as
Mendel's, but important to our progress. Many of them become lost;
many others are repeated over and over and over.

A revolution must be wrought in the ways in which we make, store,
and consult the record of accomplishment. This need holds true in
science, in the law, in medicine, in economics, and, for that matter, in the
broadest subjects of human relations. It is not just a problem for the
libraries, although that is important. Rather, the problem is how creative men think, and what can be done to help them think. It is a problem
of how the great mass of material shall be handled so that the individual
can draw from it what he needs—instantly, correctly, and with utter
freedom. Compact storage of desired material and swift selective access
to it are the two basic elements of the problem.

I began worrying over this matter more than a quarter century ago,
and some twenty years ago published an essay about it, called "As We
May Think." Next in this present discussion I want to present some
thoughts from that earlier paper. Then we will have a look at what has
happened during the past two decades and try to see if we are any closer
to the means of the needed revolution.

In that essay I proposed a machine for personal use rather than the
enormous computers which serve whole companies. I suggested that it

Reprinted from Vannevar Bush's Science is Not Enough, *(New York,
1967), pp. 75-101, by permission of William Morrow and Richard
Bush, MD.*

serve a man's daily thoughts directly, fitting in with his normal thought processes, rather than just do chores for him.

If it is to fit in with his normal thought processes, the heart of the matter is selection. Our present ineptitude in getting at the record is largely caused by the artificiality of systems of indexing. When data of any sort are placed in storage, they are filed alphabetically or numerically, and information is found (when it is) by being traced down from subclass to subclass. It can be in only one place, unless duplications are used; one has to have rules as to which path will locate it, and the rules are cumbersome. Having found one item, moreover, one has to emerge from the system, like a dog who has dug up a buried bone, and then re-enter the system on a new path. This is a serious handicap, even with the high-speed machinery just now beginning to be applied to the problem of the libraries.

The human mind does not work that way. It operates by association. With one item in its grasp, it snaps instantly to the next that is suggested by the association of ideas, in accordance with some intricate web of trails carried by the cells of the brain. The mind has other characteristics, of course: trails not frequently followed are apt to fade; few items are fully permanent; memory is transitory. Yet the speed of action, the intricacy of trails, the detail of mental pictures, is awe-inspiring beyond all else in nature.

Man cannot hope fully to duplicate this mental process artificially. But he can certainly learn from it; in minor ways he may even improve on it, for his records have relative permanency. But the prime idea to be learned concerns *selection*. Selection by association, rather than by indexing, may yet be mechanized. Although we cannot hope to equal the speed and flexibility with which the mind follows an associative trail, it should be possible to beat the mind decisively in the permanence and clarity of the items resurrected from storage.

To turn directly to that earlier discussion:

Consider a future device for individual use, which is a sort of mechanized private file and library. It needs a name. To coin one at random, "memex" will do. A memex is a device in which an individual stores all his books, records, and communications, and which is mechanized so that it may be consulted with exceeding speed and flexibility. It is an enlarged intimate supplement to his memory. What does it consist of?

It consists of a desk. Presumably, it can be operated from a distance, but it is primarily a piece of furniture at which an individual works. On its top are slanting translucent screens, on which material can be projected for convenient reading. There is a keyboard, and sets of buttons and levers. Otherwise, memex looks like an ordinary desk.

In one end is its stored reference material. The matter of bulk can be well taken care of even by present-day miniaturization. Only a small part of the interior of the memex is devoted to storage, the rest to mechanism. Yet if the user inserted 5,000 pages of material a day it would take a hundred years to fill the repository. So he can be profligate, and enter material freely.

Most of the memex contents are purchased on tape ready for insertion. Books of all sorts, pictures, current periodicals, newspapers, are thus obtained and dropped into place. And there is provision for direct entry. On the top of the memex is a transparent platen. On this our user places longhand notes, photographs, memoranda, all sorts of things. When one is in place, the depression of a lever causes it to be recorded on a blank space in a section of the memex memory.

Memex has, of course, provision for consulting the record by the usual scheme of indexing. When the user wishes to consult a certain book, he taps its code on the keyboard, and the title page of the book promptly appears before him, projected onto one of his viewing positions. Frequently-used codes are mnemonic, so that he seldom consults his code book; but when he does, a tap of a key or two projects it for his use. Moreover, he has supplemental levers. By deflecting one of these levers to the right he runs through the book before him, each page in turn being projected at a speed which just allows a recognizing glance at each. If he deflects the lever further to the right he steps through the book 10 pages at a time; still further speeds scanning to 100 pages at a time. Deflection to the left gives him the same control backwards. A special button transfers the user immediately to the first page of the index. Any book of his library can thus be called up and consulted with far greater facility, comfort and convenience than if it were taken from a shelf. And his personal library is voluminous; if he had it present in paper it would fill his house or office solidly.

He has several projection positions; hence he can leave one item in position while he calls up another. He can add marginal notes and comments, for the nature of his stored record is such that he can add or erase, quite as readily as though he were adding notes to the page of a book.

So far, all this is conventional; a mere projection forward of present-day mechanisms and gadgetry. It affords an immediate step, however, to *associative* indexing, the basic idea of which is a provision whereby any item may be caused at will to select another, immediately and automatically. This is the essential feature of the memex; the process of tying items together to form trails is the heart of the matter.

When the user is building a trail, he names it, inserts the name in his code book, and taps it out on his keyboard. Before him, projected onto adjacent viewing positions, are the items to be joined. At the bottom of each there are a number of blank code spaces; a pointer is set to indicate one of these on each item. The user taps a single key, and the items are permanently joined. In each code space appears the code word. Out of view, but also in the code space, is automatically placed a set of dots as a designation; and on each item these dots by their positions designate the index number of the other.

Thereafter, at any time, when one of these items is in view, the other can be instantly recalled merely by tapping a button adjacent to the code space. Moreover, when numerous items have been thus joined together to form a trail, they can be reviewed in turn, rapidly or slowly, by deflecting a lever like that he used for turning the pages of a book. It is exactly as though the physical items had been gathered together from widely separated sources and bound together to form a new book. But it is more than this; for any item can be joined into numerous trails, the trails can bifurcate, and they can give birth to side trails.

To give you a simple example, the owner of the memex, let us say, is interested in the origin and properties of the bow and arrow. Specifically he is studying why the short Turkish bow was apparently superior to the English long bow in the skirmishes of the Crusades. He has dozens of possibly pertinent books and articles in his memex. First he runs through an encyclopedia, finds an interesting but sketchy article, and leaves it projected. Next, in a history, he finds another pertinent item; he ties the two together. Thus he goes, building a trail of many items. Occasionally he inserts a comment of his own either linking it into the main trail or joining it, by a side trail, to a particular item. When it becomes evident to him that the elastic properties of available materials had a great deal to do with the superiority of the Turkish bow, he branches off on a side trail which takes him through text books on elasticity and tables of physical constants. He inserts a page of longhand analysis of his own. Thus he builds a trail of his interest through the maze of materials available to him.

His trails do not fade. Several years later, his talk with a friend turns to the queer ways in which a people resist innovations, even of vital interest. He has an example in the fact that the Europeans, although outranged, still failed to adopt the Turkish bow. In fact he has a trail on it. A touch brings up the code book. Tapping a few keys projects the head of the trail. By lever, the user runs through it at will, stopping at interesting items, going off on side excursions. It is an interesting trail, pertinent to the discussion. So he sets a reproducer in action, records the whole trail, and passes the record to his friend for insertion in his own memex, there to be linked to a more general trail.

Now, is this all a dream? It certainly was, two decades ago. It is still a dream, but one that is now attainable. To create an actual memex will be expensive, and will demand initiative, ingenuity, patience, and engineering skill of the highest order. But it can be done.

It can be done, given enough effort, because of the great advances which have been made in mechanization, the instruments which have already been built in great numbers to aid man's computations and his thoughts, the devices already used for storing and consulting masses of data, the ingenious elements of electric and magnetic circuits which have been developed during the last two decades.

New and powerful instrumentalities have come into use to help it on its way toward birth. Highly sensitive photocells capable of seeing things in a physical sense; magnetic tapes that instantly record with utter faithfulness music or vision; advanced photography which can record not only what is seen but also what is not; transistors capable of controlling potent forces under the guidance of less power than a mosquito uses to vibrate his wings; cathode ray tubes rendering visible an occurrence so brief that by comparison a microsecond is a long time; transistor combinations which will carry out involved sequences of operations more reliably than any human operator and thousands of times as fast; miniaturization of solid-state devices which will put the complex circuitry of a radio set into the volume of a pinhead; video tapes which put the moving episodes of a football game onto a little strip of film, and instantly reproduce it—there are plenty of mechanical aids with which now to effect a transformation.

So it *can* be done. Will it be done? Ah, that is another question. The great digital machines of today have had their exciting proliferation because they could vitally aid business, because they could increase profits. The libraries still operate by horse-and-buggy methods, for there is no profit in libraries. Government spends billions on space since it has glamor and hence public appeal. There is no glamor about libraries, and the public do not understand that the welfare of their children depends far more upon effective libraries than it does on the collecting of a bucket of talcum powder from the moon. So it will not be done soon. But eventually it will.

To look forward to memex we will lean on what has already been done. Machines of today fall into two great divisions, first those that supplement man's muscles and his senses, and second those that aid his mind. We do not need to deal with the former, although they have made possible our modern civilization with all its benefits and its dangers. The latter are sometimes included under the general term of thinking machines, but this is an unfortunate expression, for they do not think, they merely aid man to do so. They are of two sorts, analytical machines and data-handling machines, and these are sometimes combined.

The great example of the first sort is the digital machine. It is often called a computer, but this is a misnomer, for the machine does far more than to compute. A single large unit costs several million dollars. Our present business organizations could not operate without it. Properly instructed, it can do about anything a man can do using pencil and paper, and do it a million times as fast. The only things it cannot do are those which distinguish a man from a machine.

It is told what to do by the insertion of a coded tape, and the preparation of this tape is called programming, of which more will be said later. When the computer has completed its job, it delivers its results by rapidly operating a typewriter, or sometimes by drawing them on a screen. It works entirely by using numbers, although these may also represent letters or instructions, and these numbers are in the binary system, that is, to a base two instead of the usual base ten. It gets the numbers it works on from the input tape, or from its own memory, where great masses of data are stored. The tape, and subsidiary instructions stored in the memory, tell it how to manipulate numbers for all its purposes.

Its main element is an elaborate network of electric circuits. These can manipulate numbers by addition, subtraction, multiplication, and division. Thus far it is indeed a computer. But it has, importantly, other circuits which can perform the operations of logic, and it is these which give the digital machine its great power. As a simple example, these can examine a set of numbers and pick out the largest. Or they can follow one set of instructions or another according to the results of the moment. The machine does all of these things very rapidly indeed, many million operations a second.

Another type of analytical machine is the analogue machine. These are nowhere near so precise as the digital machines, but they are far less expensive and are genuinely useful for exploratory purposes, especially in engineering. The principal form is the differential analyzer which appeared some thirty years ago. To use one of these in examining a problem, say the problem of how a suspension bridge will behave in a gusty wind, one assembles an electric circuit which follows the same physical laws as the bridge, though usually with a different time scale, and which then moves a point of light on a screen in just the way in which the bridge will swing in the wind. One has set up an electrical circuit which obeys the same differential equations as the physical system under study, and which hence behaves in the same way, and then one watches it perform, usually by the pattern it produces on an oscillograph.

There are also special-purpose analytical machines which do not belong to either of these classes. An early one of these is the tide-predicting machine. There are also machines for statistical analysis, evaluating correlation coefficients and the like, and for solving integral equations, or interpreting x-ray diffraction patterns of crystals. Some of these have been crowded out by the great success of the digital machine, but they include ideas which should not be forgotten. Everything that can be done on analogue or special machines can also be done on a digital machine, although often not so neatly or flexibly or inexpensively.

Data-handling machines are also of various sorts, from the extremely simple card catalog up through the numerous ways of manipulating punched cards. The memory component of the digital machine is probably the most remarkable of the data-handling devices. Another should be mentioned as well. This is the rapid selector, which first appeared some twenty years ago. This would take a roll of photographic film containing 100,000 or so items in single frames, and select desired items from these in accordance with a code in the margin. It could do so while viewing the items at the rate of 1000 per second. And it printed out the selected items on a short piece of similar film.

Each item could consist of a page of print, drawings, or photographs. There are now a variety of modern forms of this device. Some of them combine the sorting and ordering facility of the punched-card equipment with rapid selection by code. The same sort of thing can of course be done with magnetic tape.

The evolution of data-handling equipment thus has involved two important features: compression, which allows great masses of data to be stored in a small space, and rapid access, by which a single piece of information can be located and reproduced in a very brief time.

The development of detailed devices or elements did not alone make this whole range of equipment possible. There is another, and very important, general consideration which should be noted:

Over three centuries ago Pascal constructed a calculating machine which embodied many of the essential features of recent keyboard devices, but it could not then come into use. The economics of the situation were against it; the labor involved in constructing it, before the days of mass production, exceeded the labor to be saved by use of it, since all it could accomplish could be duplicated by sufficient use of pencil and paper. Moreover, it would have been subject to frequent breakdown, so that it could not have been depended upon; for at that time and long after, complexity and unreliability were synonymous.

Only a century ago, Babbage, even with remarkably generous support, could not produce his great arithmetical machine. His idea was sound enough, but construction and maintenance costs were then too heavy. Inexpensive construction is a new thing. Had a Pharaoh been given detailed and explicit designs of an automobile, and the tools with which to work metal, and had he understood them completely, it would have taxed the resources of his kingdom to fashion the thousands of parts for a single car, and that car would have broken down on the first trip to Giza.

Machines with interchangeable parts can now be constructed with great economy of effort. In spite of much complexity, they perform reliably. It is this reliable complexity, attained at reasonable cost, produced by hard work and the rigors of competition over many years, together with the advance of basic science, and finally man's ingenuity, which has now made it possible to lighten the burden on man's mind, as earlier developments lifted the load from his muscles.

An excellent example of how the advance goes forward is the history of the thermionic tube and the transistor. The thermionic tube was, at its inception, largely a matter of ingenious tinkering, without much reliance on science. Edison, who was no scientist, noted a current from the filament of one of his electric lamps to a plate he put in, but he did nothing about it. De Forest, who probably knew still less science, added a grid between them, and the thermionic tube was born. For many years it was erratic in operation and likely to fail at any moment. Then engineers learned to make a really good vacuum and it became much better. Finally it became so reliable that it could be installed in an amplifier of a submarine cable at the bottom of the sea and expected to last for forty years. It became so rugged that, in the proximity fuzes of the war, it could be put into a shell, fired out of a gun, and still be expected to work as a sensitive electronic detector.

Then came the transistor, which has superseded the tube for most purposes. This certainly did come out of the application of science. A group of men, working on the theory of electric conduction in solids, soon saw how the phenomena they predicted, and checked in the laboratory, could be put to use. The transistor, which can be as small as the eye of a fly, requiring extreme precision of construction, rugged and long lived when once built, is perhaps the most versatile device man has yet produced. With the use of very little power, and in a small space, it will amplify, modulate, rectify, and do dozens of other things. It is one of a whole family of devices based on the use of semiconductors: photoelectric cells, rectifying valves, etc. When the transistor is combined with other elements, resistors and capacitors, sealed in a resin, an assemblage the size of a thimble will do all that used to be done by a radio receiver as large as a suitcase. More than this: by some very modern methods of depositing very thin layers of material in a vacuum, the whole thing can be reduced to a thin wafer the size of a flyspeck, and a thousand such can be produced identically in a single manufacturing operation.

A very great advance—possibly the greatest so far—as we look toward the future memex, is magnetic tape. We have known it for some time in dictating machines. It hit the market modestly soon after the war, and, around 1958, tapes appeared capable of carrying great detail, so much so that video tapes appeared carrying an entire television broadcast with its 70,000 or so complete pictures on a single reel. The idea is a simple one, and the tape is merely a plastic strip covered with magnetic material in finely powdered form. As it passes over an electromagnet, the voice, picked up by a microphone, causes the strength of that magnet to vary, and these variations become impressed on the tape in the form of its magnetization. A wavy form of air vibrations from the voice becomes an identically wavy form of magnetism on the tape. Then, when the tape is run in front of a coil, the voltages there produced can be amplified and fed into a loudspeaker, and a replica of the original voice appears as sound waves in the air.

All this is now ancient history. But it is relatively new to put on the tape the variation of light impinging on a photocell as an optical system sweeps its view over a scene, and to do this so that all the details of a complex scene are thus recorded in a small fraction of a second. And then to reverse the process and reproduce the scene to a viewer a thousand miles away.

In our living rooms, we watch a football game. A television camera is scanning the scene line by line, twenty-four pictures a second. The response of its photoelectric equipment, transmitted a thousand miles to our living room, controls the intensity of an electron beam which sweeps over our TV screen and reproduces the play as it occurs. But the output of the camera also sweeps over a fairly broad magnetic tape, and magnetizes it. Thus, a few moments after a play occurs, the tape record can be re-scanned, and the result transmitted to our TV set, so that we can see the play over again. To accomplish this, using a reasonable amount of tape, has required a great compression of the magnetic record. But it has been done and is now accepted by television viewers as a commonplace.

Another important feature of magnetic tape, for our future memex, is that it can be erased. Fortunately, this is easy. One merely sweeps a permanent magnet over the tape and the record is gone. When we take a photograph we are stuck with it; to make a change we must take another whole photograph. But with a magnetic tape which presents to us a picture one can cancel half a line, if he will, add a changed line, or put in a marginal note or code. The moving finger writes, but its record is not here irrevocable.

The advent of the laser may bring photography back into competition for memex storage. It can produce such a small spot of light that
there is a factor of 100 or more on compactness compared to magnetic
storage. The spot can be intense, so much so that it is used to bore small
holes in diamonds, and this means a photographic record can be made
in a very short interval, and read out equally rapidly for projection. The
film used can be of such low sensitivity that daylight will not affect it
appreciably, and the usual processes of development can be avoided,
which means parts can be obliterated and additions made to the record.

Beyond this the laser renders possible an exciting process called
holography, which may render it possible to project the record so that
it is three-dimensional. This is an utterly new form of three-dimensional
projection, for it is as though the original scene or model were actually
present, and one can move about and view it from various angles. There
are many tough problems to be solved before the use of the laser for such
purposes becomes practicable. But, for a long view ahead, it exhibits a
wholly new field of versatility in which ingenuity will certainly produce results.

There is a point here worth pausing to consider for a moment. For
the purposes of memex we need a readily alterable record, and we have
it. But alteration of records has a sinister connotation. We watch a girl
on the screen moving her mouth and someone else is doing the singing.
One can put into a man's mouth for all to hear words he never spoke.
The ingenuity which special-effects men use on television is often
amusing, sometimes powerfully dramatic, sometimes annoying, as
when a razor is seen to shave sandpaper. Advancing technology is
making it easy to fool people. It would be well if technology also
devoted itself to producing forms of records, photographic, printed,
sound-recorded, which cannot be altered without detection, at least to
the degree of a dollar bill. But it would be still more effective if the code
of morals accepted generally rendered it a universally condemned sin
to alter a record without notice that it is being done.

It is thus fairly clear that there is no serious problem today in
assembling, editing, and correcting the record, or in compressing it into
as small a volume as we may need for memex. If we wish it, a whole
private library could be reduced to the volume of a matchbox; similarly,
a library of a million volumes could be compressed into one end of a

desk. If the human race has produced, since the invention of movable type, a total record in the form of magazines, newspapers, books, tracts, advertising blurbs, correspondence, having a volume corresponding to a billion books, the whole affair, assembled and compressed, could be lugged off in a wheelbarrow.

Compression is important not only to keep us from being swamped, but also when it comes to costs. The material for a microfilm private library might cost a nickel, and it could be mailed anywhere for a few cents. What would it cost to print a million copies? To print a sheet of newspaper, in a large edition, costs a small fraction of a cent. The entire material of a private library in reduced film form would go on ten eight-and-one-half-by-eleven-inch sheets. Once that was available, with the reproduction methods now available, duplicates in large quantities could probably be turned out for a few cents apiece beyond the cost of materials.

Mere compression, of course, is not enough; one needs not only to make and store a record, to add to it at will, and to erase, but also to consult it. As things are now, even the modern great library is not generally consulted; it is nibbled at by a few. How to consult the new compressed record is a major question in selective analysis.

The great digital computers of today keep their extensive records in various ways. The records constitute their memory, which they consult as they proceed with computation. They use magnetic tapes or disks. But they also use great arrays of minute toroids of magnetic material, interlaced with fine wires. The reason for these latter is the necessity of rapid access. The fast access, in a computer, is fast indeed, and has to be. Times, for them, should be mentioned in nanoseconds, or billionths of a second. In a nanosecond light will move only about one foot. That is why it is important to keep the components of a computer small; its speed of operation is sometimes limited by the time necessary to get an electric pulse from one part to another. The storage in little toroids can respond in times like these.

No problem of speed of access need bother the future memex. Indeed, for memex we need only relatively slow access, as compared to that which the digital machines demand: a tenth of a second to bring forward any item from a vast storage will do nicely. For memex, the problem is not swift access, but selective access. The indication of a possible beginning here is to be found in the rapid selector mentioned earlier. When items on frames projected for viewing can readily have codes entered in their margins, by which they can automatically select other items, we have a significant step toward memex. But the access problem is by no means solved. The storage of memex will be huge, and all parts of it need to be promptly available.

Clearly, we need to study further how the human brain meets this puzzle. Its memory system consists of a three-dimensional array of cells, each cell very small compared to even the volume of magnetic tape used for a single impulse, and the magnetic tape is two-dimensional. We make three-dimensional storage, for example, by an array of toroids, but the units here are huge compared to a cell. Somehow the brain consults this full array and brings into consciousness, not just the state of one cell, but the related content of thousands, to recall to us a scene of a decade ago. We have very little idea as to how it is done. In fact we do not even know what we mean when we write "consciousness." If there is a roadblock in the path toward a useful memex, it lies in this problem of moderately rapid access to really large memory storage.

The heart of this problem, and of the personal machine we have here considered, is the task of selection. And here, in spite of great progress, we are still lame.

Selection, in the broad sense, is still a stone adze in the hands of a cabinetmaker. Yet, in a narrow sense and in other areas, something has already been done mechanically on selection. The personnel officer of a factory drops a stack of a few thousand employee cards into a selecting machine, sets a code in accordance with an established convention, and produces in a short time a list of all employees who are females, live in Trenton, and know Spanish. Even such devices are much too slow when it comes, for example, to matching a set of fingerprints with one of five million on file. Selection devices of this sort have now been speeded up from their previous rate of reviewing data at a few hundred a minute. The great computer will enter its active memory and select a desired item in a microsecond or less, if it is told just where to go for it, and in an interval which is still very brief if it has to hunt for it.

So much for the methods of storing record and of retrieving items from storage. But what about the making of the record? Is it possible that somewhere during this procedure we may find ways of anticipating the selective needs to be encountered later when one wishes to consult that record? Our record-making system of today should remind us of the covered wagon; we are bound to have to improve it, and in doing so we must have an eye to the possibilities of coding, cross-linking, and all else that will be requisite to selective access.

Today, to make a record, we still push a pencil or tap a typewriter. Then comes the business of digestion and correction, followed by an intricate—and largely cockeyed—process of typesetting, printing, and distribution. To consider the first stage of procedure, will the author of the future cease writing by hand or typewriter and talk directly to the record? He does so (indirectly) even now, of course, by talking to a stenographer or into a dictating machine. And there is also the steno-type, that somewhat disconcerting device encountered in court or at public meetings. The operator strokes its keys languidly and looks about the room and sometimes at the speaker with a disquieting gaze. From the machine emerges a typed strip which records, in a phonetically simplified language, what the speaker is supposed to have said. Later this strip is retyped into ordinary language, for in its nascent form it is intelligible only to the initiated. It would be fairly easy to rig a device to operate a stenotype as one talked. In short, if anyone wishes to have his talk directly produce a typed record, all the elements are here. All he needs to do is to take advantage of existing mechanisms—and alter his language.

Our present languages are not well adapted to mechanization. True, digital machines can be made to translate languages, Russian into English, for example. As with their writing of poetry or composition of music, one wonders, not that they do it badly, but that they do it at all. So far, machine translation has not become really useful. But it is improving, and the study that is being devoted to the problem is showing us much about the nature of languages themselves. It is strange that the inventors of universal languages, none of which have ever caught on, have not seized upon the idea of producing one which better fits the technique for transmitting, recording, and modifying speech.

The business of communication between men and machines thus is a complex affair. Men's language has grown without reference to machine use, and now, if we try to talk directly to a machine, it will not understand us. Even if we write or type our material, we have to be careful to put it in form that the machine can grasp.

We see a simple example of this in the numbers put on bank checks with magnetic ink, so that machines can sort them. They have a faint resemblance to figures as we ordinarily write them, but to the machine their altered form is entirely clear.

A better example occurs with the digital computers. These can do extraordinary things, but only if they are given explicit and detailed instructions on how to do them. The process of instruction, programming, uses a special language, incomprehensible to the layman, learned by a human operator only after careful study and experience, but lucid and unambiguous to the machine. There are several new languages under development for this purpose of telling digital computers what to do and how to do it. They are in terms of binary numbers, when they enter the machine, for that is the natural language of the computer.

We will not expect our personal machine of the future, our memex, to do the job of the great computers. But we can expect it to do clever things for us in the handling of the mass of data we insert into it. We particularly expect it to learn from its own experience and to refine its own trails. So our means of communication with it merits careful consideration. Usually we will tell it what to do by pushing a button or moving a lever. Pushing just one button will often call up a fairly complicated internally stored set of instructions. This will serve for ordinary use. But it would be nice, and easily arranged for, if the machine would respond also to simple remarks. If Fido will respond to "lie down," the machine ought to respond readily to such a remark as "hold it."

This matter of a memex learning from its own experience merits some discussion. A digital machine can now be caused thus to learn. Such machines, for example, can be set up to play checkers with a human opponent. Chess is too much for them, because of its complication, which merely means that it calls for an excessive amount of storage and time, but they do very well at checkers. In fact, they can learn to beat a good player. In the digital machine's memory is stored a large number of positions that may occur in a game, and possible following moves to be used. But positions and moves are rated in accordance with assumed values. Confronted with a position, the machine consults its memory and chooses the best-rated move to use. But now comes the real point. It continually alters the rating of the moves in accordance with its success or failure. If a move results in a more highly valued position, its rating goes up, and if it results in catastrophe, it goes down. In this way the machine learns. Playing at first a very poor game, it finally becomes expert.

A memex can be constructed to do similar things. Let's say its master is a mechanical engineer, and that he has a trail which he uses very frequently on the whole subject of heat transfer. The memex notices (we have to use such terms; there are no others) that nearly every time he pursues the trail there are a series of items on which he hardly pauses. It takes them out of the main trail and appends them as a side trail. It also notices that when he comes to a certain item he usually goes off on a side trail, so it proceeds to incorporate this in the main trail.

It can do more than this; it can build trails for its master. Say he suddenly becomes interested in the diffusion of hydrogen through steel at high temperatures, and he has no trail on it. Memex can work when he is not there. So he gives it instructions to search, furnishing the trail codes likely to have pertinent material. All night memex plods on, at ten or more pages a second. Whenever it finds the words "hydrogen" and "diffusion" in the same item, it links that item into a new trail. In the morning its master reviews the new trail, discarding most of the items, and joining the new trail to a pertinent position.

Does this sort of thing sound bizarre or far-fetched? Machines are doing more surprising things than this today.

Much needs to occur between the collection of data and observations, the extraction of parallel material from the existing record, and the final insertion of new material into the general body of the common record. For mature thought there is no mechanical substitute. But creative thought and essentially repetitive thought are very different things. For the latter there are already powerful mechanical aids. We shall need still more.

In particular we have delved far enough into the chemical processes by which the human body operates to grasp the fact that we shall never come to full understanding in this enormously complex field until our processes of reasoning have been greatly refined, and divested of all the clutter of repetitive acts which now take up most of the time that we consider we are devoting to thought. For this reason there will come more machines to handle advanced mathematics and manipulation of data for the scientist. Some of them will be sufficiently bizarre to suit the most fastidious connoisseur of the present artifacts of civilization.

The scientist, however, is not the only person who manipulates data and examines the world about him by the use of logical processes, though he sometimes preserves this appearance by adopting into the fold anyone who becomes logical, much in the manner in which a British labor leader is elevated to knighthood. Whenever logical processes of thought are employed—that is, whenever thought for a time runs along an accepted groove—there is an opportunity for the machine. In fact a machine which will manipulate premises in accordance with formal logic has already been constructed. Put a set of premises into such a device and turn the crank; it will readily pass out conclusion after conclusion, all in accordance with logical law, and with no more slips than would be expected of a keyboard adding machine.

Logic can become enormously difficult, and it would undoubtedly be well to produce more assurance in the use of it. The machines for higher analysis have usually been equation *solvers*. But we now have equation *transformers*, which will rearrange the relationship expressed by an equation in accordance with strict and rather advanced logic. Progress here is a bit inhibited by the exceedingly crude way in which mathematicians express their relationships. They employ a symbolism which grew like Topsy and has little consistency; a strange fact in that most logical field.

What might be the consequences of the developments we have been discussing? Assuredly they would *not* be limited to the men of science. It could be hoped that the writing of history and biography, for example, would improve, not just in accuracy, but in art, as the writer is able to turn the drudge part of his task over to a tireless assistant, always willing to work when he is, and never at a loss to divine what he wishes to remember. Wholly new forms of encyclopedias will appear, ready-made with a mesh of associative trails running through them, ready to be dropped into the memex and there amplified. The lawyer will have at his touch the associated opinions and decisions of his whole experience, and of the experience of friends and authorities. The patent attorney will have on call the millions of issued patents, with familiar trails to every point of his client's interest. The physician, puzzled by a patient's reactions, will strike the trail established in studying an earlier similar case, and run rapidly through analogous case histories, with side references to the classics for the pertinent anatomy and histology.

Another area in which new machine accomplishments are needed is organic chemistry. These accomplishments are just beginning to appear. There are millions of organic compounds that have been studied, and an unlimited number of possible ones, many of them no doubt useful. The organic chemist is in a tough spot. His memory is severely taxed, and much of his time is consumed in labor that does not call on his true skills. He ought to be able to turn to a machine with a specification of a compound, in terms of either its form or its properties, and have it immediately before him with all that is known about it. Moreover, if he then proposes a chemical manipulation on such a compound, the machine should tell him, within the limits of knowledge at the time, just what will happen. It would do so by using the known laws of chemistry, and the chemist should turn to experiment in the laboratory only for confirmation, or when entering unexplored territory. We are a long way today from such a situation. But machines can certainly do this, if we build them intelligently and then tell them what to do.

The historian, of whom I have spoken above, with his vast chronological account of a people, can parallel this with a skip-trail which stops only on the salient items; he can follow at any time contemporary trails which lead him all over civilization at a particular epoch. There will be a new profession of trailblazers, those who find delight in the task of establishing useful trails through the enormous mass of the common record. The inheritance from the master will become, not only his additions to the world's record, but for his disciples the entire scaffolding by which they were erected. Each generation will receive from its predecessor, not a conglomerate mass of discrete facts and theories, but an interconnected web which covers all that the race has thus far attained.

When the first article on memex was written, the personal machine, the memex, appeared to be far in the future. It still appears to be in the future, but not so far. Great progress, as we have seen, has been made in the last twenty years on all the elements necessary. Storage has been reduced in size, access has become more rapid. Transistors, video tape, television, high-speed electric circuits, have revolutionized the conditions under which we approach the problem. Except for the one factor of better access to large memories, all we need to do is to put the proper elements together—at reasonable expense—and we will have a memex.

Will we soon have a personal machine for our use? Unfortunately not. First we will no doubt see the mechanization of our libraries, and this itself will take years. Then we will see the group machine, specialized, used by many. This will be especially valuable in medicine, in order that those who minister to our ills may do so in the light of the broad experience of their fellows. Finally, a long time from now, I fear, will come the personal machine. It will be delayed in coming principally by costs, and we know that costs will go down, how much and how rapidly none can tell.

It is worth striving for. Adequately equipped with machines which leave him free to use his primary attribute as a human being—the ability to think creatively and wisely, unencumbered by unworthy tasks— man can face an increasingly complex existence with hope, even with confidence.

Presumably man's spirit should be elevated if he can better review his shady past and analyze more completely and objectively his present problems. He has built a civilization so complex that he needs to mechanize his records more fully if he is to push his experiment in its proper paths and not become bogged down when partway home by having overtaxed his limited memory. His excursions may be more enjoyable if he can reacquire the privilege of forgetting the manifold things he does not need to have immediately at hand, with some assurance that he can find them again if they prove important.

The applications of science have built man a well-supplied house, and are teaching him to live healthily in it. They have also enabled him to throw masses of people against one another with cruel weapons. They may yet allow him truly to encompass the great record and to grow in the wisdom of race experience. He may perish in conflict before he learns to wield that record for his true good. Yet, in the application of science to the needs and desires of man, this would seem to be a singularly unfortunate stage at which to terminate the process, or to lose hope as to the outcome.

From "Of Inventions and Inventors"
Vannevar Bush

This passage is taken from Chapter V, "Of Inventions and Inventors" in Pieces of the Action, *Bush's autobiography.*

As I NOTED EARLIER, there is a story to be told in connection with the differential analyzer, for it illustrates a number of things that I am anxious to clarify. There is no question that my young assistants and I developed the differential analyzer at M.I.T. during the twenties. But who invented it? Ah, that is hard to answer for it depends upon how we define invention.

First, what is a differential analyzer? It is the first of the great family of modern analytical machines to appear—the computers, in ordinary parlance. It is an analogue machine. This means that when one has a problem before him, say the problem of how a bridge that has not yet been built will sway in a gusty wind, he proceeds to make a combination of mechanical or electrical elements which will act in exactly the same manner as the bridge—that is, will obey the same differential equations—and then by noting how this combination acts he will be able to predict the performance of the bridge. The trick, in a really useful device, is so to construct this model that by shifting some mechanical connections, or better by switching some electrical circuits, one can make it possible to handle a wide variety of differential equations, and hence of practical problems. If one does not know what a differential equation is, perhaps I can make it clear by a very simple example. Suppose an apple drops from a tree. One is supposed to have done so, to have hit Isaac Newton on the head and thus cleared his mind, although I doubt it. The thing we know about that apple is, to a first approximation, that its acceleration is constant, that is, that the rate at which it gains speed as it falls does not vary. So we just write this fact down in mathematical symbols. That is a differential equation, one very easy to solve, and thus we are enabled to make a plot of the position of the apple at every instant. But suppose we want to include the resistance that air offers to the fall. This just puts another term in our equation but makes it hard to solve formally. We can still very readily solve it on a machine. We simply connect together elements, electrical

Reprinted from Vannevar Bush's Pieces of the Action, *(New York, 1970), pp. 181-195, by permission of William Morrow and Richard Bush, MD.*

or mechanical gadgets, that represent the terms of the equation, and watch it perform. Actually, we interconnect integrators, rather than differentiators, for we thus avoid some serious difficulties. I have already discussed an integrator in connection with my old surveying instrument. The integrator is the heart of the differential analyzer.

We actually built three successive analyzers. The first one was just a breadboard machine. That is, it was made out of pieces of steel and anything else that was handy, and the object of it was only to see if the idea was sound. The second one was a mechanical machine. An unusual thing about this was that the integrators were made to be fairly precise—not an easy task. The integrator, as I have noted, could be simply a disc revolving at a controlled speed and a roller that pressed on it, which could be moved controlled distances from the center. The job was to keep the roller from slipping. If it carried any appreciable load, it would slip, and then the integrator would be highly inaccurate. We overcame this by putting on what is called a torque amplifier, but this was itself mechanical. We finally made integrators that had a precision of about one part in 1000, which was fairly good.

This machine was the one that the press talked about. The Army made a duplicate for the station where trajectories were computed. Our machine was copied by Professor Hartree[1] in Manchester, England. He did quite a lot of work on it. The difficulty with it, of course, was that it took quite a little time to change from one problem to another; and of course it did not have the scope that was necessary for many equations.

Finally came the third machine which we got into use just before the war. This one was wholly electrical, except that the integrators were still mechanical. It had a very large number of thermionic tubes, was quite hard to keep cool, and occupied a big space. It did work that was of some use during the war. After the war, when the digital machines began to come along, it was rapidly made obsolete, and we finally tore it down.

Many differential analyzers of the electrical type are now built and sold, and there are lots of engineers who use them. They are not highly precise, but they change easily from one problem to another, they give qualitative results very rapidly, and they are very useful gadgetry. They supplement the digital machine. If you want precision on a problem, you go to the digital. But if you want to explore, if you want to see what happens to the solution of an equation when you change constants, as you often do when you are designing something, the present-day differential analyzers are very convenient indeed. They are made in units that can be plugged together by cables, and they are most versatile. (They also would make great teaching machines if they were not so expensive.)

Now, quite a long time after we had the differential analyzer running, and doing a fairly acceptable job, I found an appendix I had not seen before in a book on dynamics, something of a classic, by Thomson and Tait.[2] In it Tait described how to connect a pair of integrators to solve a particular differential equation. Was Tait the inventor? As far as I know, he was the first to express the basic idea involved. But he did not describe how to do it or what to use as an integrator, and there were no integrators known in his day that could drive one another without such errors as to be fatal from a practical standpoint. So I make my belated bow to Tait, but I cannot call him the inventor, for inventors are supposed to produce operative results.

I can name an inventor who made a differential analyzer long before I did, or rather who readily could have done so without question if he had put his mind on it. This was Hannibal Ford. He was about as ingenious an individual as I ever heard of. He made the devices, the computers, if you will, to aim the great guns of battleships, to take into account the flight of the shell, including the effect of the rotation of the earth upon its path, the air density at the time, the speed and direction of the enemy target, and so on. This he did principally by interconnecting integrators. And he made a new form of integrator which could do the job without the help of a servomechanism. The resulting mechanism was a marvel of precision and completeness. Just how extraordinary it was can be shown by one great example from World War II, for the Germans were by then far advanced on the subject of gun direction, although Ford's great work was much earlier. There was only one decisive battle between battleships during the war. The *Bismarck,* not only the most powerful battleship in the world but also equipped with the most advanced fire control apparatus, put out to sea to attack Allied commerce. Shadowed by British cruisers, it was found and attacked by two British battleships, *Hood* and *Prince of Wales.* The battle opened at a range of 50,000 yards, about fifteen miles. A single salvo from the *Bismarck,* aimed by a combination of integrators, penetrated the deck of

Hood, the magazine exploded, and a proud ship and three thousand men disappeared.

I knew of the existence of Ford's work, and that was all. I did come close to knowing a lot about it, and if I had, I could have built a far better differential analyzer than my first model, and I would have been honored to collaborate with him. Shortly after the first war I reported on board the battleship *Texas* in Newport harbor. I was in uniform as I was a lieutenant commander in the Naval Reserve, and a group of us went aboard to study the possible development of anti-aircraft fire control. We never did. We were supposed to work with the airship *Shenandoah* and she did not show up; she probably went to a county fair at the behest of some senator. We all had a good time; I won a handball contest with the electrical officer of the ship, much to the delight of those who bet on me, but we did not do much to advance the cause of national defense. So I did not learn about Ford's work, beyond generalities, until long after. I wonder what would have happened if we had gotten together, but he was not aboard. He was a fascinating individual. He loved gadgets; his house was full of them: doors that would open when one spoke to them and so on. He did not care a hang about recognition of his work outside Navy circles. He just liked to build ingenious precise devices for people who could appreciate them. Did he invent the differential analyzer? One can say merely that he not only could have, but that he could have been the leader in the whole movement toward the modern computer, if he had wanted to. And the only reason he did not is probably that he did not move about in academic circles to see the need and the opportunity. I hail his memory. It is too bad the Navy monopolized his talents.

The other aspect of the family of modern computers is the digital machine, which today takes the center of the stage, and nearly the whole stage. Who invented the digital computer? I can write at once that I did not, in fact I had little to do with that whole development. The antecedents are interesting. Pascal[3] is the first man who really did anything on computing machinery. In fact, he built a computer, and he wrote about computers quite a bit. He had most of the ideas involved in the ordinary desk-type adding and multiplying machine. He was a pioneer of a very strange type, because he was primarily a theoretical physicist and mathematician, and ended up devoted to theology.

Charles Babbage[4] was the fellow who took these ideas, and some of his own, and started to make a really comprehensive machine to do all sorts of things. That could have been a genuine forerunner of the digital machine of the present day, but the trouble with Babbage was that he bit off more than he could chew. At the time he was working, mechanical devices could not be turned out cheaply or made reliable. The advent of reliable complexity is an exceedingly important phase of modern development. The modern computer, or telephone system for example, could not function if the units out of which it is built were not exceedingly reliable. It is very easy to see why. Suppose there are a million units involved. Assume the functioning of all of them is essential to performance. Let us assume they are quite reliable: For any one the chance of its failing in the next year is only one in a thousand. Still this means we must expect about three failures of the system per day, which is intolerable. There are ways of reducing the grief. In automatic routing of telephone calls, if one path is busy or defective, the machine automatically picks another. In the big computers, if a unit is faulty, the machine will not use it and will report it. Also the big computer has very ingenious ways of checking itself to catch mistakes. What's more, the digital machine can learn from its own experience, and the full import of this fact has not yet been truly realized. I want to return to it a bit later in another connection. Here I merely cite an example. Let us set up a digital computer to play checkers against a human opponent. We store in the computer's memory a catalogue of positions that may occur in a game, and a battery of possible moves to follow them, positions and moves being rated in accordance with assumed values. Position A occurs: the digital machine selects from its memory the best-rated move and makes it. Here follows the critical action. If the move leads to a position of higher value, the machine raises its rating, and, conversely, if the move brings about a poorer position, the machine lowers its rating. Thus the machine learns and approaches expertness at the game. We will return to this after a bit of discussion of reliability, upon which it in no small measure depends.

The nature of reliability is shown by the way ball bearings are sold. The companies do not guarantee a certain life. Rather they will present data which show that, of many of a given design and rating and under specified speed and load, 10 per cent may be expected to fail in, say, five thousand hours of use. It is always a statistical matter. We come to the superlative in reliability when the telephone company puts a cable across the Atlantic, with a complicated amplifier every forty miles, imbedded in the mud at the bottom of the ocean, and expects it to operate without a failure for twenty years.

The present-day reliability of components has been brought about by steady improvement of the design and materials of condensers, resistors, coils, relays, thermionic tubes, transistors, largely because of keen competition. In a socialistic economy, it probably would not happen at all rapidly.

As it is, I can buy a relay and expect it to operate for millions of cycles without fail. Also important, if I am a large customer, I can buy it for very little money. This fact has allowed many things, automation for example, to go forward rapidly.

Consider the automobile. When I drove fifty miles forty years ago, I fully expected something to quit. Now I complain if something goes wrong after ten thousand miles. And I am right—for the automobile companies press their suppliers so hard on prices that they do not even get the best that could be provided. On an automobile selling for $4000 they will cut the cost of the thermostat for the choke from twelve cents to eleven cents, and the $4000 car goes poof.

Babbage had no access to such reliable complexity as I have been talking about. Moreover, he was much too ambitious; instead of making a moderately complex machine which would work and give results (and that would attract attention), he started right in to make a machine that would be comprehensive indeed. And of course he never finished it. Babbage added some of his own ideas to those of Pascal, but primarily he was building rather than inventing. His conception of what he was trying to do fell short of practicality.

There are several somewhat distinct aspects of the whole revolution being brought about by the employment of machines to do man's mental drudgery for him, a development as significant for his future welfare as was the introduction of machines to perform his physical labor.

One such aspect is the handling of data, and this breaks into two parts. First, there is the storing and retrieval of figures and coded instructions. The modern computer has extensive memories for this purpose, and consults them very rapidly indeed. Second is the storing and finding of letters, sheets of figures, diagrams, all the complex records on which the conduct of business and libraries depends. This second phase of data handling has moved forward relatively slowly, but is now speeding up.

Just before World War II I got into this affair and, with the late John H. Howard, at M.I.T. built what we called a rapid selector. It had a somewhat strange history. I include it here because it illustrates well the type of invention which is almost inevitable once the technical elements it combines have advanced to the point where they are adequate for the purpose.

The way it worked was this. A reel of movie film had photographed on it a mass of data, perhaps 200,000 frames, each of some sort of document. The edge of this record film had a set of transparent dots on a black background which coded the adjacent frame. One set up the code of an item to be searched for by depressing a number of keys. As the roll of record film progressed through the machine, every time the set code coincided with the code of a frame a group of photocells triggered a flashing lamp, and that item was photographed onto a new strip of film—the reproduction film. Thus one could run through the reel and receive promptly a reproduction of every item in the collection called for by the set code. To accomplish this several things were necessary. First, the record film had to move rapidly as it left one reel and was wound up on another. This was easy. In a movie camera the film moves at only twenty-four frames per second. But it has to stop at each frame for an exposure and then start again. With continuous motion—no stops—the film could readily travel forty times as fast.

Second, when a desired frame was located, a photograph of it had to be made, without stopping the film, and without blur. Harold Edgerton[5] had solved this problem. His flash lamp gave intense light pulses of very brief duration. Exposures could be made in microseconds instead of centiseconds as in an ordinary camera. Thus no blur occurred in a picture of a fast moving film.

Finally, the coding had to be worked out so that only desired items would be selected and photographed. For this good sensitive photocells were then available. Several methods of coding were developed. The one easiest to describe, though not finally used, was as follows:

Opposite each frame in the long film were the transparent dots, say a hundred of them, arranged in groups of ten each. At a keyboard one punched out the code of the item desired, producing a small card with ten holes punched in it, arranged in a pattern according to the keys that had been pressed. The card was inserted in the selector so that the fast film ran close under it and was strongly illuminated. As the record film moved, light passed through the card and the film and impinged on a photocell whenever a hole in the card and a dot in the film registered in position. If nine or fewer such coincidences occurred, the photocells remained inactive, paid no attention. But if there were ten such coincidences, indicating that the frame then in position corresponded exactly to the impressed code, the photocell triggered the flash lamp to take a picture. Since, at the exact instant this occurred, the chosen frame was not in a position to be easily photographed, a delay circuit was introduced, and the flash lamp fired when the fast moving film had advanced two frames, to bring the chosen frame in front of the camera lens. The camera was an ordinary movie camera, with its shutter always wide open. Every time the flash lamp operated, it advanced the sensitive reproduction film one frame. There was some tricky gadgetry, which need not be described, to catch chosen frames that happened to be close together on the record film, and there was a rig so designed that, after a run, the short piece of exposed reproduction film, containing only a few frames, could readily be cut off and developed.

Suppose one had a roll of film containing a million pictures of checks, all duly coded, and wanted to find a check made out for $1036.48. One would punch this number on the keyboard, adding zeros to fill out the ten places. One would then run the film through, taking about sixteen minutes (or less if one stopped as soon as the camera clicked), and would have a picture of the sought check. One could get several pictures if there were coincidences in amounts.

Of course the coding would usually be more complicated than this. For a library, for example, the individual frames of the record film might be summaries of technical articles, coded in accordance with the subject matter, author, date, and so on.

The whole device was not much bigger than a typewriter. Of course it was crude compared to the equipment that can be built today. It was an early step along a path that has now become elaborate indeed. That step had no more than been taken when the war came along, and several things happened. First, the patent application on the device, with its assignment to M.I.T., somehow got lost, or not followed up. Second, the machine itself was taken over by the group working on enemy codes, and that was the last I saw of it. One does not worry much about long-range problems during a war.

After the war the Department of Commerce wanted such machines to handle some of its data. No company could be found to introduce the device into commercial use, for there was no patent to protect them. Commerce finally had one or two made and put to work. But an art like this moves rapidly, and there were soon better machines available. Today there are a wide variety of ways of going about this job of finding a needle in a literary haystack. With magnetic tapes, transistors, printed circuits, there is a whole family of machines for handling data. The Eastman Kodak Company has made an especially interesting one called Minicard. It combines the sorting features of the old punched-card machines with the searching ability of the rapid selector. It is not very fast as yet, but no doubt soon will be.

All this is a long way from a girl digging through a file cabinet. Some day libraries will be fully mechanized. Then, without leaving one's office, it will be possible to pick up the phone, dial in a code, and have the actual paper one is looking for almost instantly at hand. Something of the sort has got to happen, or our libraries will become buried in the mass of books and articles now being printed, and searching in the old way will become hopeless.

Something more than thirty years ago, pondering these latter problems in the light of the work in the selector as well as the analytical machines, I conceived the idea of a machine that should be an extension of the personal memory and body of knowledge belonging to an individual, and should work in a fashion analogous to the working of the human brain—by association rather than by categorical classification. I called the device a memex, and published a discussion of it in the *Atlantic Monthly* in July 1945. Essentially, a memex is a filing system, a repository of information, and a scheme of searching and speedily finding a desired piece of information. It utilizes miniaturization, high-speed photography, memory cores such as computers embody, and provisions for the coding of items for recall, the linking of code to code to form trails, and then refinement or abandonment of trails by the machine as it learns about them. It is an extended, physical supplement for man's mind, and seeks to emulate his mind in its associative linking of items of information, and their retrieval as a result.

No memex could have been built when that article appeared. In the quarter-century since then, the idea has been with me almost constantly, and I have watched new developments in electronics, physics, chemistry, and logic to see how they might help to bring it to reality. That day is not yet here, but has come far closer, as I set out in an essay, "Memex Revisited," published in 1967.[6]

The heart of the idea is that of associative indexing whereby a particular item is caused to select another at once and automatically. The user of the machine, as he feeds items into it, ties them together by coding to form trails.

For the usual method of retrieving an item from storage we use a process of proceeding from subclass to subclass. Thus in consulting a dictionary or an index, we follow the first letter, then the second, and so on. The rapid selector worked this way. Practically all data retrieval in the great computers follows this method.

The brain and the memex operate on an entirely different basis. With an item in consciousness, or before one, another allied item is suggested, and the brain or the memex almost instantly jumps to the second item, which suggests a third, and so on. Thus there are built up trails of association in the memory, of brain or machine. These trails bifurcate, cross other trails, become very complex. If not used they fade out; if much used they become emphasized. Thus a desired item may be found far more rapidly than by use of a clumsy index.

Millions of items are stored in man's brain, memories, sheets of data. Suppose I wish to recall what Aunt Susie, whom I haven't seen for twenty years, looked like. I don't start by turning to all of the pictures in my mind or storage where the name begins with S, and so on. Not at all. My brain runs rapidly—so rapidly I do not fully recognize that the process is going on in some cases—over when I saw her, what was the occasion, what were her mannerisms, and suddenly her picture is before my mind's eye. The goal of a memex is comparable—the use of the associative trail. Although we cannot hope to equal the speed and flexibility with which the mind follows an associative trail, it should be possible to beat the mind decisively in the permanence and clarity of the items resurrected from storage.

Here is where the ability of the digital computer to learn from its own experience—of which I spoke earlier—comes into play. Suppose that a memex has as its master a mechanical engineer and that he has a trail which he uses very frequently on the whole subject of heat transfer. The memex notices (we have to use such terms; there are no others) that nearly every time he pursues the trail there are a series of items on which he hardly pauses. It takes them out of the main trail and appends them as a side trail. It also notices that when he comes to a certain item he usually goes off on a side trail, so it proceeds to incorporate this in the main trail.

It can do more than this; it can build trails for its master. Say he suddenly becomes interested in the diffusion of hydrogen through steel at high temperatures, and he has no trail on it. Memex can work when he is not there. So he gives it instructions to search, furnishing the trail codes likely to have pertinent material. All night memex plods on, at ten or more pages a second. Whenever it finds the words "hydrogen" and "diffusion" in the same item, it links that item into a new trail. In the morning its master reviews the new trail, discarding most of the items, and joining the new trail to a pertinent position.

To leave the memex, there is one more story to be told about how secrecy can hide an inventor. In this case I was the one that got hid. Not that I minded at all; in fact it was a joyous excursion.

Along in the thirties the Navy got hold of me and asked me to look into a plan they had before them. By that time I was supposed to know something about machine analysis, and I was vice-president at the Massachusetts Institute of Technology, so I was taken in the front door instead of the back door. The plan was to mechanize their cryptography section, that is, to use machinery to break an enemy's secret cipher. They proposed to use punched-card machinery as originated by Hollerith[7] and then produced for use in business by the International Business Machines Company, the now great I.B.M. Now this breaking of a cipher was, and is, a far more complex matter than one would gather by reading Poe. It is not just a matter of shifting the letters about in accordance with a short key. Enciphering is done by a machine, and deciphering the same way. The key is very long. If it were indefinitely long the cipher would never be broken, except by capturing one of the machines, but then there would be no way of getting a distant station back into step if it ever fell out, and so a compromise is made. The job of breaking an enemy cipher consists of examining thousands of messages by statistical methods, combined with a canny sort of intuition possessed by some individuals. I could readily get intoxicated on the subject.

I made my study and reported that punched-card methods were not nearly fast enough, that they needed a special machine with at least one hundred times the speed. After a while they asked me if I could build such a machine, and I told them I thought I could. So we made a contract.

It was at this point that I derived my only benefit from the undertaking. I learned something about government contracts with universities, and this stood me in good stead later, in the days of N.D.R.C.

I told them I would do the work if they would pay just my out-of-pocket costs, that M.I.T. would contribute the cost of the overhead, that we would turn the whole thing over to the Navy and wished for neither profit nor credit, and that I wanted a simple contract which provided for just that, with no frills or inconvenient clauses. They soon laid before me a draft contract with all sorts of fancy clauses in it, provisions for accounting, rules regarding employment, and so on. It was brought to my hotel by a pleasant Navy captain. I read it, gave it back to him, told him to tell his boss to go to hell, and started to pack my suitcase. But he was back after a bit with a nice simple contract, and I went back home and started work. I think I still have a copy of that contract, and I do not know how they did it, that is, how they avoided all the constraints that fool legislation had imposed on them. They probably just ignored them and took a chance. It is too late to court-martial anyone about it now. And, later on, when I was on the other side of the fence and representing the United States Government, I did just the same thing, of course in a nice way and quite legally.

I went to work at M.I.T. and developed a device. When I got the thing built, I delivered it to the Navy. While this was going on, only four people at M.I.T. (Karl T. Compton[8], two young fellows I had working on it, and myself) knew anything whatever about it, or even knew the work was going on. When I delivered the machine to the Navy, they took over the whole thing—all the records, all the drawings, the machine itself, and the two men who had worked on it—so that nothing whatever was left at M.I.T., and I kept no copies of anything involved in it except that unusual contract.

Then the war came along, and this machine was undoubtedly used in connection with the breaking of the Japanese code. I cannot judge how instrumental it was in that regard—I certainly know it was used. Some of the young fellows who had worked with me said, in their enthusiasm, that it alone broke the code. I know this is not true, but I certainly know the machine was useful.

This led to incidents that were amusing. I remember one day some of the intelligence people over in the Army got me into a room, shut the door, and began to talk hush-hush. I do not think they looked under the pictures to see if there were any bugs present, but it was evident that they were going to introduce me to something very secret. So I interrupted them to say, "Are you gentlemen going to tell me about the breaking of the Japanese code?" They went up in the air about a foot, because that achievement was being held very secret indeed, and quite properly so, for the fact that we had solved that code gave us an enormous advantage in the Pacific for a long while. We were very careful not to use the information that came out of the intercepts in a way that would give away to the Japs the fact that we knew their code. The military forces had given up some very tempting opportunities rather than reveal this, so no wonder the people in the Army were a little disturbed. They wanted to know how I happened to know about it. I told them, "Well, inasmuch as I built one of the machines you are using, and inasmuch as I trained some of the young fellows who are working for you on this thing, it would be very strange if I did not know something about it."

The next incident took place after the war. Robert A. Lovett[9] was then Secretary of Defense, and the section on cryptanalysis made a request for funds in the budget. It was very hard for anyone to evaluate this request, because an accounting officer could not be told what that section was doing. Secretary Lovett asked me to look over the program and tell him whether the budget request seemed to make sense. I went out and visited the section. When I went in, there was my machine running. I told them I thought they were quite alert, that they had not known that I was coming out to see them until ten o'clock that morning, and in the meanwhile they had got that machine out of the attic, dusted it off, and got it running, and I thought that was pretty fast work. They took me around the corner, and there were six more machines just like it, all running. Then I said that now I was sure there was something the matter with them, that they were using obsolete machinery. As a matter of fact, of course, I looked over the rest of the program and told Lovett I thought it made sense, and the section got its money in the budget.

Visiting this section and talking with those fellows got me to thinking again about the subject, and I came to the conclusion that my machine was indeed obsolete. By that time the whole art had progressed to a point where it was questionable whether anything more could be done. Certainly far more speed was necessary if they were really going to have any success. So I wrote a memorandum and made some suggestions for a very much faster machine of a very different kind. As usual on any such matters, I wrote that memorandum in longhand, made no copies, sealed it, and sent it to the section by special messenger. A day or two later, a young lieutenant commander came down to see me. And I said, "Hope I did not burden you too much by giving you that memorandum in longhand, but I think that is the way to do it. I hope you did not have any trouble reading it—my handwriting is pretty bad." He said, "You forget, sir, that our business is cryptanalysis."

Endnotes

1. Douglas Rayner Hartree, 1897-1958. British theoretical physicist; professor, University of Manchester, from 1929; known for work in solid-state physics, one-electron approximation (Hartree-Foch method).
2. Thomson, Sir William, and Tait, Peter Guthrie, *Treatise on Natural Philosophy*. Cambridge University Press, 1890, Part I, pp. 488ff.
3. Blaise Pascal, 1623-1662. French scientist and philosopher; mathematical genius.
4. Charles Babbage, 1792-1871. English mathematician. Devoted much of his life and fortune to development of a calculating machine for which he was unable to obtain acceptance. Author of *On Economy of Machines and Manufactures* (1832) and *Ninth Bridgewater Treatise* (1837).

5. Harold E. Edgerton. Electrical engineer and inventor noted for the modern stroboscope which made stop-action and ultra-high-speed multiple-action photography possible. Graduate of University of Nebraska. With M.I.T. as student and teacher since 1926. Institute professor since 1966. Involved in underwater exploration since 1953, inventing special cameras and sound devices for ultra-sonar research.

6. See "Memex Revisited," pp. x-x of this volume.

7. Herman Hollerith, 1860-1929. Inventor. Instructor in mechanical engineering, M.I.T., 1882. With U.S. Patent Office, 1884-1890. Invented tabulating machine which worked on principle of punched holes in non-conducting material. His machine used for U.S. Census of 1890.

8. Karl Taylor Compton, 1887-1954. Physicist and educator. President, Massachusetts Institute of Technology, 1930-1948, Chairman of the Corporation, 1948-1954. Member National Defense Research Committee, 1940-1947; Chief, Office of Field Services, 1943-1945, Director Pacific Branch, 1945; Member Science Intelligence Mission to Japan, 1945; Special representative Secretary of War in S.W. Pacific Area, 1943-1944; Chairman, Research and Development Board, 1948-1949.

9. Robert A. Lovett. Secretary of Defense, 1951-1953. Special assistant to the Secretary of War, 1940-1941; Assistant Secretary of War for Air, 1941-1945; Undersecretary of State, 1947-1949; Deputy Secretary of Defense, 1950-1951. Since 1953, general partner, Brown Brothers Harriman & Co.

Part 3
The Legacy of Memex

Letter to Vannevar Bush and Program On Human Effectiveness

Douglas C. Engelbart

Stanford Research Institute
Menlo Park, California

May 24, 1962

Dr. Vannevar Bush
Professor Emeritus
Massachusetts Institute of Technology
Cambridge, Massachusetts

Dear Dr. Bush:

I wish permission from you to extract lengthy and definitely acknowledged quotes from your article, "As We May Think," that appeared in *The Atlantic Monthly*, July, 1945. These quotes would appear in a report that I am writing for the Air Force Office of Scientific Research, and I am sending a parallel request to *The Atlantic Monthly*.

For your information I am enclosing a relatively brief and quite general writeup describing the program that I am trying to develop here at Stanford Research Institute. The report which I am writing (and for which I am requesting quotation permission from you) is a detailed description of the conceptual structure that I have developed over the years to orient my pursuit of this objective of increasing the individual human's intellectual effectiveness. It will also contain a number of examples of the way in which new equipment can lead to new methods and improved effectiveness, to illustrate my more general (but non-numerical) framework, and your article is quite the best that I have found in print to offer examples of this.

I might add that this article of yours has probably influenced me quite basically. I remember finding it and avidly reading it in a Red Cross library on the edge of the jungle on Leyte, one of the Phillipine [sic] Islands, in the Fall of 1945. Subsequently, I went back and finished my B.S. in E.E. after the war (Oregon State), and worked for the NACA at Moffett Field (near here) until 1951, when I got fed up with my goal-less role. I formulated then the goal for which this program represents the pursuit vehicle, spent years in graduate school at the University of California (Berkeley), taught there a while, and finally ended up here—choosing SRI as a place where I would have a good chance to work toward developing such a program. I had had almost nothing but negative reactions from people up to then, and for several years here, too.

But the climate has changed of late, and for two years I have personally been able to spend almost full time trying to lay the concep-tual groundwork for launching a serious research program on "human intellectual effectiveness." I think I have a good approach developed for such a program, and we are trying to get it supported and started. Our OSR support has been for half of my time in this pre-program study, and the report for them will hopefully lay out considerations and reasoning that can show most readers where the promise and possibili-ties are for future improvement of our intellectual capability, and what is a reasonable approach to pursue these possibilities.

I re-discovered your article about three years ago, and was rather startled to realize how much I had aligned my sights along the vector you had described. I wouldn't be surprised at all if the reading of this article sixteen and a half years ago hadn't had a real influence upon the course of my thoughts and actions.

If you still have interest in this area and have the time and energy to give it some occasional consideration, I would be most happy to send you a copy of the report. (It is more than just a report to a government agency. For me it is more the public debut of a dream, and the overdue birth attests to my emotional involvement.)

Thank you for your consideration.

Sincerely,

Douglas C. Engelbart
Senior Research Engineer

Program On Human Effectiveness

I. Introduction

Human beings face ever more complex and urgent problems, and their effectiveness in dealing with these problems is a matter that is critical to the stability and continued progress of society. A human is effective not just because he applies to a problem a high degree of native intelligence or physical strength (with a full measure of motivation and purposefulness), but also because he makes use of efficient tools, methods, and strategies. These latter may be directly modified for increased effectiveness. A plan to systematically evolve such modifications has been developed[1] at Stanford Research Institute. The plan is a long-range one and is based on the premise that a strong, coordinated attack is necessary if significant progress is to be made.

The possibilities we are pursuing involve an integrated man-machine working relationship, where close, continuous interaction with a computer avails the human of radically changed information-handling and -portrayal skills, and where clever utilization of these skills provides radical changes in the way the human attacks problems. Our aim is to bring significant improvement to the real-life problem-solving effectiveness of individuals. It is felt that such a program competes in social significance with research toward harnessing thermonuclear power, exploring outer space, or conquering cancer, and that the potential payoffs warrant a concerted attack on the principal problem areas.

The basic concept of utilizing technological aids in close cooperation with an individual's detailed problem-solving activities is not new. Indeed, our books, pencils and typewriters attest to a long evolution of the concept. In recent years, however, a number of basically new approaches to the problem have been initiated. Several researchers[2-8] have pointed out the gains offered by close integration of modern information-handling equipment with the human problem solver. Many contributions have been made in different disciplinary areas—e.g. human engineering, problem-solving and educational psychology, linguistics, computer programming, electronic display systems, computer time sharing, operations research, management science, systems engineering, and industrial engineering—all of which appear to form part of a normal evolutionary development toward increased understanding of man-machine integration problems. Also, a number of efforts[9-13] are under way that bear more directly upon the type of man-computer cooperation envisaged in our program; however, none of these has revealed as basic an approach as that proposed herein. Perhaps the most useful work to guide our early activities is that in artificial intelligence and heuristic programming[14-16], where problem-solving processes and methods of approach have been developed for totally man-made systems.

II. Background

For other than intuitional or reflexive actions, an individual thinks and works his way through his problems by manipulating concepts before his mind's eye. His powers of memory and visualization are too limited to let him solve very many of his problems by doing this entirely in his mind. For most real-life problems, an individual needs to represent these concepts with numbers, letters, words, graphs, drawings, etc. (i.e., with symbols) that can be assembled and rearranged before his eyes in patterns that portray the conceptual relationships to be considered. We conventionally use marks on paper for thus augmenting our visualization and memory capabilities.

Thus, a large part of an individual's meaningful intellectual activity involves the purposeful manipulation of concepts; and of this concept-manipulation activity, a very important part is accomplished by the external manipulation of symbols. A fundamental hypothesis of the proposed approach is that the ability of a given human to control the real-time external manipulation of symbols, in response to the minute-by-minute needs of his thought processes, has a profound effect upon the whole structure of concepts and methods utilized in his intellectual activity. The approach can be succinctly described by saying that our aim is to use the best that technology can offer in providing increased symbol-manipulation power to the human, and then to explore the resulting possibilities for redesigning his structure of concepts and methods in order to make him significantly more effective in solving real-life problems.

For this application, the stereotyped image of the computer as only a mathematical instrument is too limiting—essentially, a computer can manipulate any symbol in any describable way. It is not just mathematical or other formal methods that are being considered. Our aim is to give help in manipulating any of the concepts that the individual usefully symbolizes in his work, of which those of mathematical nature comprise but a limited portion in most real-life instances.

Initially, at least, ours is an engineering approach toward the task of redesigning different parts of a functioning system in order to increase its performance. Our model stems from the picture of the "neuro-muscular" human, with his basic sensory, mental, and motor capabilities, and the means employed to match these capabilities to the problems he must face. These means have for the most part been evolved within the culture in which he is born, and he has been training in their use since childhood. We refer here to all of the tricks, tools, techniques, methods, strategies, special skills, etc., that the individual human can bring to bear upon his struggle with his problems. Our initial approach toward making the human more effective is to try to do a coordinated re-vamping of these means of augmenting basic human capabilities.

We have found four useful categories with which to divide these augmentation means:

(1) Language, which includes (a) the way the human's picture of his world is parcelled into the concepts that his mind uses to model that world, and (b) the symbols that he attaches to those concepts and with which he represents them when he does his concept manipulation (or "thinking").

(2) Artifacts, which we define as (a) the physical things designed to provide for his physical comfort and movements, (b) the tools and equipment that help him manipulate physical objects or materials, and (c) the tools and equipment that help him manipulate symbols (and therefore, concepts, or information).

(3) Methodology, which represents the methods, procedures, strategies, etc., with which he organizes his execution of a process.

(4) Training, which represents the conditioning needed by the human to bring his skills in the utilization of Items (1), (2), and (3) to the point where they are operationally effective.

We then have a functional model of a trained human, with his Language, Artifacts and Methodology, as the problem-solving system whose effectiveness we want to improve. Our aim is to make coordinated improvements upon the Language, Artifacts, and Methodology that he uses, and the Training that he is given.

III. The Plan

A. Objectives

1. Long Range

The long-range objective of this program is to increase significantly the effectiveness of human problem solvers. At any given stage of progress, our aim will be to recognize the controllable factors that limit the individual's particular level of effectiveness, and to develop means for raising that level.

We are concerned with an individual's ability to gain comprehension in complex problem situations, to recognize the key factors therein, to develop effective solutions to these problems, and to see that these solutions are successfully implemented. Problem-solving effectiveness is improved if solutions can be found to problems that previously were too "hard" to solve at all, or (for previously solveable [sic] problems) if the same solutions could be found in a shorter time, or if a better solution could be found within the same time.

2. Short Range (Two to Three Years)

The immediate objective of this program is to increase the effectiveness of individuals at special problem-solving tasks of our own designation, using the most sophisticated approach we can, and striving for comprehensive and integrated re-design of the individuals' means for working (see Section III B for discussion of these special tasks). We want to use this effort as a calibration of what *can* be achieved, as an introduction to the variety of difficulties associated with this particular type of an engineering approach to a human-capability problem and as an opportunity to develop sound research methods within a workably limited scope of activity.

B. General Approach

In view of the tremendous worth to society of any new development that could bring significant increase to the effectiveness of its planners, researchers, coordinators, arbitrators, etc., we feel that the approach offering the highest possible research payoff should be taken. This, together with the tremendous rate of development in the information-processing technology (hence the predictable widespread utilization of sophisticated equipment), impel us toward starting right out with the best that technology can offer now in the way of equipment to help the individual manipulate symbols.

A test subject will therefore have a digital computer whose capabilities are immediately available to his every call for service. He will communicate with the computer from a working station equipped with personal display and input devices that hopefully need make no compromise in giving him the best useable features that we can buy or develop. These facilities shall be continuously re-evaluated in light of other developments within the program, and it is expected that equipment modifications will be developed and tested as part of the program.

At any given stage of our research, we shall be making a coordinated development of both the special programmed-computer services that the subject can call upon, and the associated special methods for his using these services in manipulating symbols. Different sets of services and methods will be evaluated by measuring the subject's performance while using them on specially selected test tasks, until we have isolated a set of such services and methods that provide him with a significant degree of effectiveness at the given type of test task.

We plan a sequence of tasks, initially involving primitive but essential symbol-manipulation capabilities such as composing and modifying different forms of information portrayal (text, diagrams, etc.). This will lead progressively through developments for intermediate capabilities of personal "bookkeeping," composing or modifying computer-service designations (programming), calculating, planning, etc. Upon an integrated base of such human-controlled, machine-aided capabilities, we plan finally to develop the highest-ordered processes that real-world problem solvers can utilize.

The special problem-solving areas to which we first wish to apply our efforts toward increased effectiveness have been selected to satisfy the following criteria:

(a) The areas should involve a limited domain of information, and limited external-world interaction, to keep the system we are studying within a manageable scope.

(b) The areas should involve intellectually challenging problems of the same qualitative character as possessed by our more general real-world problems.

(c) The areas should be such that we can build upon our results if we are successful and decide to tackle a more general problem-solving area in a next stage of pursuit of our main objective. (i.e., the services and methods developed here can be extended to meet the needs of the problem solver of the succeeding stage of our program.)

(d) In general, the areas should be such that success could lead fairly directly to worthwhile real-world applications for bringing increased effectiveness to specialists in critical areas, in parallel with continued research work toward helping the solvers of more general problems.

(e) In particular, the areas should be such that success here could be applied to meaningful parts of our continuing research activity, to make significant increases in the effectiveness with which we do research on human effectiveness.

IV. Personnel and Facilities

It is estimated that eight to ten professional people representing a variety of disciplines will be required for successful pursuit of the objectives of the proposed program. Psychology, computer programming, and computer engineering comprise a set of essential disciplines; in addition, considerable benefit would be derived from personnel backgrounds in such fields as artificial intelligence, systems analysis, display engineering, time-and-motion study, management science, psycho-linguistics, and information retrieval. Since the program will be developing a new conceptual structure involving a number of disciplines, researchers from each discipline will to some extent tbe [sic] expected to adjust to this newly evolving structure and its terminology.

The heart of the experimental facilities will be a digital computer capable of working in real time with test subjects. The computer must be highly flexible with respect to the amount of internal high-speed storage and the type and amount of external storage that can be added.

In addition, the computer must lend itself readily to time-sharing utilization. The internal structure of the computer must be susceptible to ready modification as must also be the specially developed peripheral equipment with which it must work closely.

Two principal alternatives for realizing such experimental facilities exist. The first involves acquiring a small, fast medium-priced machine especially suited to the needs of this program. The second involves acquiring the basic computational service from a large machine whose use is shared (on a time-shared basis) with other users; in this case, only special-purpose matching and buffering equipment will be required for the particular needs of the program. In either case, the working station(s), with individual input and display provisions, will initially be composed of commercially available equipment but will undergo a fair degree of modification as the desired functional requirements evolve.

V. Development and Application Activity

There will be a progression of special problem-solving areas through which the program moves as we methodically build up the different capabilities which comprise the full and integrated repertoire needed for generalized real-world problem solving. It is planned to guide this progression so that within a few years we can begin to utilize our results in an associated Development and Application activity, where we develop special system designs (equipment, processes, methods, training, etc.) that can be applied practically to the tasks of real-world specialists. A computer programmer seems a natural candidate for the first such development, and cryptographers, information specialists, teaching-machine program composers, etc., can be considered subsequently. This type of activity is expected to provide very valuable feedback to the research work.

Ultimately the development work will progress toward even more general types of problem solvers, to lead us toward the researchers, the planners, the leaders, and the doers upon whom our society depends so critically.

Endnotes

1. Under SRI sponsorship, with the assistance, since March 1961, of the Air Force Office of Scientific Research under Contract AF 49(638)-1024.

2. Vannevar Bush, "As We May Think," *Atlantic Monthly*, (July 1945).

3. Simon Ramo, "A New Technique of Education," *Engineering and Science.* Vol. XXI (October 1957).

4. B.F. Skinner, "Teaching Machines," *Science*, Vol. 128, No. 3330 (October 24, 1958).

5. I.J. Good, "How Much Science Can You Have at your Fingertips?" *IBM Journal of Research and Development*, v. 2, no. 4 (October 1958).

6. J.C.R. Licklider, "Man-Computer Symbiosis," *IRE Transactions on Human Factors in Electronics* (March 1960).

7. D.B. Yntema and W.S. Torgerson, "Man-Computer Cooperation in Decisions Requiring Common Sense," *IRE Transactions on Human Factors in Electronics*, V. HFE-2, No. 1 (March 1961).

8. Douglas C. Engelbart, "Special Considerations of the Individual as a User, Generator, and Retriever of Information," *American Documentation*, vol. 12, no. 2, p. 121 (April 1961).

9. Merse, P.M. and Teager, H.M. "Real-Time, Time-Shared Computer Project," *MIT Fourth Quarterly Progress Report* Contract #Near-1841(69) DSR #8644 (October 31, 1961).

10. See Quarterly Progress Reports of Division 5 (Information Processing), Lincoln Laboratory MIT, especially the work of Group 58 under Bert F. Green. Yntema and Torgerson (see Item 7 above) are in this group.

11. RAND Corporation's Johniac Open Shop System currently under development. Private communication with Keith Uncopher.

12. Ramo-Woolridge, see A. Vazsonyi, "An On-Line Management System Using English Language," *Proceedings of the Western Joint Computer Conference*, Los Angeles, California (May 9-11, 1961).

13. Systems Development Corporation—see their brochure no. BR-2(2-61) entitled Automated Teaching Project.

14. The work of A. Newell, J.C. Shaw, H.A. Simon, "A Variety of Intelligent Learning in a General Problem Solver," RAND report P-1742, Mathematics Division, The RAND Corporation (July 6, 1959).

15. The work of J. McCarthy, "Programs with Common Sense," *Mechanisation of Thought Processes, Vol. I*, National Physical Laboratory Symposium No. 10 held in November 1958, London: Her Majesty's Stationery Office (1959).

16. The work of Marvin Minsky, "Steps Toward Artificial Intelligence," *Proceedings of the IRE*, vol. 49, No. 1 (January 1961).

As We Will Think

Theodor H. Nelson

This paper was presented at the International Conference on online interactive computing held at Brunel University, Uxbridge, England September 4-7, 1972.

Abstract

BUSH WAS RIGHT. His famous article is, however, generally misinterpreted, for it has little to do with "information retrieval" as prosecuted today. Bush rejected indexing and discussed instead new forms of interwoven documents.

It is possible that Bush's vision will be fulfilled substantially as he saw it, and that information retrieval systems of the kinds now popular will see less use than anticipated.

As the technological base has changed, we must recast his thesis slightly, and regard Bush's "memex" as three things: the personal presentation, editing and file console; a digital feeder network for the delivery of documents in full-text digital form; and new types of documents, or hypertexts, which are especially worth receiving and sending in this manner.

In addition, we also consider a likely design for specialist hypertexts, and discuss problems of their publication.

Beating Around the Bush

Twenty-seven years ago, in a widely acclaimed article, Vannevar Bush made certain predictions about the way we of the future would handle written information (1). We are not yet doing so. Yet the Bush article is often cited as the historical beginning, or as a technological watershed, of the field of information retrieval. It is frequently cited without interpretation (2,3). Although some commentators have said its predictions were improbable (4), in general its precepts have been ignored by acclamation.

Reprinted with permission from Online 72 Conference Proceedings, *Volume 1 (Uxbridge, 1972), pp. 439-454, by permission of the author.*

In this paper, an effort in counter-discipleship, I hope to remind readers of what Bush did and did not say, and point out what is not yet recognized: that much of what he predicted is possible now; the memex is here; the "trails" he spoke of—suitably generalized, and now called hypertexts—may, and should, become the principal publishing form of the future.

In July of 1945 an article entitled "As We May Think," by Vannevar Bush, was published in the *Atlantic Monthly*. It bristled with technical references but was actually fairly candid and simple.

It predicted many things. Bush, as director of Roosevelt's wartime Office of Scientific Research and Development, had seen the new ways in which technologies could be combined. In the urbane paragraphs of this article, Bush predicted a variety of useful future machines, including improvements in photography, facsimile systems, computers and miscellany. Depending on how you read it, he predicted, as well as you could hope, devices closely related to the Polaroid camera, the Xerox machine, computer transformation of mathematical expressions, and the telephone company's ESS switching system.

But the article is best remembered for its description of the new ways that scientists and scholars could handle and share their ideas, writing, reading and filing in a magical system at their desks. The system is the famous "memex."

> A memex is a device in which an individual stores all his books, records, and communications, and which is mechanized so that it may be consulted with exceeding speed and flexibility. It is an enlarged intimate supplement to his memory.

> It consists of a desk, and while it can presumably be operated from a distance, it is primarily the piece of furniture at which he works. On the top are slanting translucent screens, on which material can be projected for convenient reading. There is a keyboard, and sets of buttons and levers. Otherwise it looks like an ordinary desk. (106-7)

The memex will hold all the writings its master wants to read, and he can read them easily.

> If the user wishes to consult a certain book, he taps its code on the keyboard, and the title page of the book promptly appears before him,

projected onto one of his viewing positions. Frequently-used codes are mnemonic, so that he seldom consults his code book; but when he does, a single tap of a key projects it for his use. Moreover, he has supplemental levers. On deflecting one of these levers to the right he runs through the book before him, each page in turn being projected at a speed which just allows a recognizing glance at each. If he deflects it further to the right, he steps through the book 10 pages at a time; still further at 100 pages at a time. Deflection to the left gives him the same control backwards. . . . Any given book of his library can thus be called up and consulted with far greater facility than if it were taken from a shelf. (107, col. 1, para. 5-6)

Moreover, he can compare and annotate them.

As he has several projection positions, he can leave one item in position while he calls up another. He can add marginal notes and comments, . . . (107, col. 1, para. 6)

Not only ordinary documents need be held in the memex. The user may make connections between different parts of the things stored. He does this by

associative indexing, the basic idea of which is a provision whereby any item may be caused at will to select immediately and automatically another. This is the essential feature of the memex. The process of tying two items together is the important thing. (107, col. 2, para. 1)

By this associative technique he may create "trails," new documentary objects that are useful in new ways.

The patent attorney has on call the millions of issued patents, with familiar trails to every point of his client's interest. The physician, puzzled by a patient's reactions, strikes the trail established in studying an earlier similar case, and runs rapidly through analogous case histories, with side references to the classics for the pertinent anatomy and histology. (108, col. 1, para. 1)

These new structures, or trails, may be taken and given to other people.

Tapping a few keys projects the head of the trail. A lever runs through it at will, stopping at interesting items, going off on side excursions. It is an interesting trail, pertinent to the discussion. So he sets a reproducer in action, . . . and passes it to his friend for insertion in his own memex, there to be linked into the more general trail. (107, col. 2, para. 5)

And they may be published.

Wholly new forms of encyclopedias will appear, ready-made with a mesh of associative trails running through them, ready to be dropped into the memex and there amplified. . . . There is a new profession of trail blazers, those who find delight in the task of establishing useful trails through the enormous mass of the common record. The inheritance from the master becomes, not only his additions to the world's record, but for his disciples the entire scaffolding by which they were erected. (108, col. 1, para. 2)

It is strange that "As We May Think" has been taken so to heart in the field of information retrieval, since it runs counter to virtually all work being pursued under the name of information retrieval today. Such systems are principally concerned either with indexing conventional documents by content, or with somehow representing that content in a way that can be mechanically searched and deciphered.

This is indeed paradoxical. On the one hand, Bush did not think well of indexing.

The real heart of the matter of selection, however, goes deeper than a lag in the adoption of mechanisms by libraries, or a lack of development of devices for their use. Our ineptitude in getting at the record is largely caused by the artificiality of systems of indexing. . . . [between documents] one has to emerge from the system and re-enter on a new path. (106, col. 2, para. 3)

On the other hand, with regard to content retrieval, Bush merely hinted about the use of structured-data representations and calculi in storing ideas (105, col. 2, para. 3), and did not plainly relate them to his main exposition. The reason is plain: his real emphasis was on linkage, and new structures and activities that the automatic link-jump would make possible. While we might argue scripture about such matters, the fact is that Bush's most extensive concern has had few successors in the field called "information retrieval."

Transposition

The memex was to be a single screen console for handling the user's notes, writing and correspondence, for reading books and other writings created by others, and for creating new associative text structures, which may in their turn be read and distributed. All this I take to be the heart of Bush's prediction. This will happen. Such systems exist; they are approaching cost feasibility; and the world is readier than it thinks.

Bush's machine will not, of course, be built exactly as he foresaw. The complete description, which I omitted, involves microfilm cassettes, a photographic copying plate for adding new images to the microfilm file, and a telautograph stylus. Other machines he describes, such as the forehead camera and the direct-dictation typing machine, might or might not have been coupled to it as well. In the revised version of the article (5) his emphasis shifted to videotape. These impedimenta we ignore. There exist microfilm cassettes, copiers and so on, but the hardware ready to support a memex-class system will be something else.

The system will be built from existing computer equipment and peripherals. Physically it will be a computer display, with a keyboard, at the user's desk; a support computer system (at the desk or elsewhere) for handling various technical chores; and a library network of digital feeder machines. The written materials, when not shown on the screen, will be stored and sent digitally, as telegraphic symbols. They will be sent back and forth among these systems automatically, as programmed in the various devices. The trails, or associative text structures—more generally called "hypertexts"—will be stored in coded form, along with the more conventional documents in the various devices. The user will be billed automatically for the services and the delivery of copyrighted materials. The publisher, who maintains these copyrighted materials in the feeder machines, will be duly paid for their use.

Prototype units exist now. Appropriate console hardware can be purchased now for about $15,000.

Supply systems, however, are not quite ready. The best supply system may be a special-purpose computer or a general-purpose time-sharing system; which is better is not clear. While costs of either are presently in the tens or hundreds of thousands, they are coming down fast, and the use of a well-tailored system by many people at once should bring down the cost of such service down considerably. To name a figure arbitrarily, let us say that a service cost of $100 a month per user (exclusive of telephone lines and copyright) would be sufficiently low to draw many users. Such service at such a cost will surely be generally available between one and five years from now.

Various preoccupations have delayed us psychologically. We do not need direct dictation, optical scanning or the availabllity (sic) of vast libraries for such systems to be immediately practical and important to us.

The Console

We are speaking of a single console to handle notes, writing, much correspondence, much reading, and the creation of new kinds of texts. On it the user must be able to view, edit, file, and otherwise manipulate.

Let me now describe a system for various kinds of text handling, the Xanadu Parallel Textface™. XANADU™ is a system presently under development as a turnkey computer graphics console for non-technical users. A stand-alone system, it is built on a minicomputer with disk and/or cassette tape, vectoring display screen, and keyboard. A variety of unusual programming techniques permit various types of screen animation, as well as automatic retrieval and data-base editing in the undersystem; these automatically service different user front ends, faces or theaters. Foremost among these theaters is the Parallel Textface, a text system of some power and delicacy.

Many of its features exist in other text handling systems, notably that of Douglas C. Engelbart at Stanford Research Institute (6). The purpose of this description is to show parallelisms between memex and this general type of system, not to distinguish this system from its relatives.

I will speak of the Xanadu hypertext system, or Parallel Textface, simply as "the system," "the current system" or the like, to distinguish it from the memex. As its implementation is not yet complete, this description applies to the present specifications and not only the parts that are working. We will note some resemblances to the memex.

The user sits at a display screen with a typewriter keyboard, a light pen or other pointing tool, and various optional controls. With these he may read, explore, annotate, write and revise. Storage is of course digital rather than pictorial; the system may manipulate the words letter by letter, rather than as a single image.

In basic editorial operations, the system presents text materials on the screen; the user may command basic writing and editing actions by simple manipulations. Indeed, he may make these editorial changes tentatively, on copies or alternative versions of the material; and he may, at his option, have his actions recorded automatically in a cumulative editorial log, in case it is later necessary to retract any of them.

Bush did not really go into memex editorial operations, but of course there was that keyboard. It is interesting to note that the memex described in the revised version of Bush's article (5) kept a log of manipulations by the user. (95-6)

The system is generally geared to tentative and thoughtful operation. The alternative versions and editorial log are the strongest examples, but there are others. An editing command may be retracted if its results do not please. Another example: a section of text being tried in a new place is shown glowing more brightly, so you know its limits within the new setting.

The user of Bush's memex called its contents by means of a "code book" (107 *passim*)—but this too was actually stored in the system. From the code book the user was to choose contents for viewing "with a single tap of the key," as mentioned earlier. In the current system it is possible for the user to call something to the screen by picking the name from a screen menu or relational diagram with the light pen. He may do this not just with whole units, but also with subparts and different versions—separate copies—of documents being tentatively edited.

In the memex, the user could skip through a document at adjustable rates (107, col. 1, para. 5). In the current system he may zip forward through the text at whatever speed he chooses, watching it slide on the screen. (The necessity of smooth, incremental text motion for the CRT is not yet generally recognized.)

The memex user looked at several documents simultaneously through several screens or panels of the same screen (107, col. 1, para, 6). This simultaneous viewing will be possible for several documents on the Parallel Textface; indeed, explicit linkages between associated texts may be viewed on request. This is the notion of "parallel text," useful for commentaries, translations, intercomparisons of documents and much else. These facilities correspond rather well, I think, to Bush's "marginal notes and comments" between the "several projection positions."

The memex user created annotations by hand, or links between the things that were being viewed simultaneously. This is possible on the current system, which allows the user to create links between text sections regardless of whether or not they are parts of the same unit or otherwise related. These may be between parallel texts, or among free-floating paragraphs (discrete or "free" hypertexts), or in virtually any other useful arrangement.

For any system of this kind, design problems arise in the richer operations, such as creating and modifying connective structures. It is taken for granted that the console must be easy to use. That is no design problem for a small set of operations, such as text editing. But the design of the overall file handling elements and actions is more complicated. There are two problems. The first is how to achieve the desired performance values on available equipment and accepted software setting. This becomes a tradeoff. The grander problem, though, is conceptual unification for the system's filing structure and conventions.

In the current system there is presently only one type of connector. This restriction nevertheless permits a system sufficient to support real hypertext experimentation. Complex or annotated couplings are presently not defined. However, simple links are adequate for various possible forms of discrete-jump hypertexts, including Bush trails, and may in principle be extended to computer responsibility for link behaviors and complex coupling maintenance.

Hypertexts

While Bush's term, "trail," represents a very useful concept, we must generalize it. Bush's interest in microfilm led to his idea of the trail having a sequence.

By "trail," Bush appears to have meant a sequence of documents, document excerpts, and comments upon them.

> For [the user] runs through an encyclopedia, finds an interesting but sketchy article, leaves it projected. Next, in a history, he finds another pertinent item, and ties the two together. Thus he goes, building a trail of many items. (107, col. 2, para. 4)

This sequence would be established by making paired couplings.

> When the user is building a trail, he names it, inserts the name in his code book, and taps it out on his keyboard. Before him are the two items to be joined projected onto adjacent viewing positions. . . . The user taps a single key, and the items are permanently joined. (107, col. 2, para. 2)

Bush mentions two other types of trail. One is the "side trail," branching out from a main trail sequence.

> Occasionally he inserts a comment of his own, either linking it into the main trail or joining it by a side trail to a particular item. (107, col. 2, para. 4)

The other type of trail is the "skip trail," a subset of a main trail sequence that contains the highlights.

> The historian, with a vast chronological account of a people, parallels it with a skip trail which stops only on the salient items, and can follow at any time contemporary trails which lead him all over civilization at a particular epoch. (108, col. 1, para. 1)

In Bush's trails, the user had no choices to make as he moved through the sequence of items, except at an intersection of trails. With computer storage, however, no sequence need be imposed on the material; and, instead of simply storing materials in their order of arrival or of being noticed, it will be possible to create overall structures of greater useful complexity. These may have, for instance, patterns of branches in various directions. Such non-sequential or complex text structures we may call "hypertexts." (7)

"Hypertext" is the generic term; there are reasons, for which there is no room here, to rule out such other candidate terms as "branching text," "graph-structured text," "complex text" and "tree text."

The best current definition of hypertext, over quite a broad range of types, is "text structure that cannot be conveniently printed." This is not very specific or profound, but it fits best.

As Bush pointed out in his own terms, we think in hypertext (106, col. 2). We have been speaking hypertext all our lives and never known it. It is usually only in writing that we must pick thoughts up and irrelevantly put them down in the sequence demanded by the printed word. Writing is a process of making the tree of thought into a picket fence.

Hypertext structures are varied. For instance, they may be free-branching with only one type of link and backing up; they may have modal links with different meanings in a free structure; or have modal links and repetitive structure.

Discrete-jump hypertexts are not the only kinds. There is, for example, Stretchtext™. This is continuously variable text which never leaves the screen, but changes by small increments on user demand, growing longer and more detailed by a few words at a time, as required. Other continuous types are possible.

Just as items may be coupled, whole hypertexts may be coupled into books, or one another. An example of the first would be a hypertext with annotations coupling into the Bible. Such multi-couplings involve bundles of pointers between the texts, possibly with type codes or annotations. (In the current system the non-annotated multicoupler is the canonical case between files.) They may also involve alternative versions, which there is no room to discuss here. The structuring of these coupler types is a continuing design task for hypertext systems.

The creator of hypertexts may allow the user various options of jumping or branching. These options can lead the user to further reading in any pattern the author wants to make available to him. The only constraints on the author are usefulness, clarity, and artfulness.

There must, of course, be ways the reader may see, and choose among, possible branches from an item in the text. This problem was implicit in Bush's treatment. Since "any item can be joined into numerous trails" (107, col. 2, para. 3) there would have had to be some way of showing the user these options and their meaning. This is the case in general, and a standing aspect of hypertext system design.

Hypertexts may be casual rough notes, as described in Bush's extended example of the Turkish bow and arrow; or they may at the other extreme be finished units, editorially completed and organized. Such finished units would have many of the same properties as ordinary writing: intentional assembly, attempted clarity and expository structure of enumerable "points," and an overall comprehensible pattern whose interrelated parts may be in some way remembered or visualized. Finally, the concept of authorship applies to hypertexts as much as it does to an ordinary book or article.

As with ordinary texts, too, the editorial properties and "feel" of hypertexts may be quite distinct and varied. For hypertexts these are of course largely unexplored. It is also very hard to anticipate their possible administrative and social settings, and this will greatly affect their character and the modes of their use.

The Transmission Network

A general transmission network will carry requested documents from libraries to users, new documents from users to libraries, and communications and documents between users.

The network will consist of several computers or computer-like objects. In the user's own unit is digital logic, and possibly (as in our Xanadu) a small computer; if not, this unit is serviced or managed by a computer which stores the user's files and communicates with the library network. The user's requests for documents that are not available locally go out to a library network. These requests are sorted out to the appropriate repository machine; the repository machine returns the document and a bill or fee schedule.

Various fees are logged up to the user. These will include various basic costs, such as membership in the system, rental of the terminal and hookup. Additional fees may include logged-in time, per-usage costs of various facilities (such as average memory area occupied and quantities of text moved), storage charges for materials kept locally, and royalties to copyright holders. It should be noted that various grades of service may also exist, in which the user gets faster service by claiming larger buffers and higher priorities, and pays for the privilege.

Although this may sound like a formidable prospect, in general and with polishing there is reason to hope that the real costs of such a system will compete favorably with the real costs of the forms of publication and libraries we now employ. (Of course, in such "real cost" we must include the library services supplied "free" by various levels of govern-ment, including municipal libraries, grants to universities and the indirect subsidy of publishers by low postal rates. It is not unthinkable that similar encouragement will come about for this form of publishing and libraryship.)

Various technical design issues exist. These involve the feeder computers and their forms of memory. These hierarchies of memory are fairly clear. They will generally include disk (for working areas and directories), magnetic card or data cell (for the corpus), and magnetic tape (for rarely-needed materials and safety copies). Immense solid-state memories will never take over completely unless they are cheaper.

A more difficult question is, what should the feeder computers be? Their job in this system is the lookup and shovelling of text, plus book-keeping. One school of thought holds that a true general-purpose time-sharing system is necessary; another, that the correct machine is a dedicated computer with rich interrupts and comparatively little arith-metic capacity. The third school would point out the special character of the work and lean toward special designs and special tradeoffs, which could be anything from associative memory to the use of delay-line machines.

Similar issues exist for memory software and directory systems. There are complex technical problems of index and search techniques, and methods of their cross-tabulation. But they can be handled in some way or other.

A warning is necessary here, however. This area of console support is the area where things are not yet ready. The prediction of economic feasibility in five years, an eon in the computer world, is not the same as feasibility now. By devoting a whole computer, disk and tape to each user, the problem of console support can now be solved, in a manner of speaking; but the general problem of interleaved I/O and file manage-ment, with the efficient sharing of facilities, is another problem entirely, and the one that must be solved to make this whole thing go.

Publication: Redesign of the Technical Literature

Bush regarded his new text structures as transmissible between individuals, and publishable. The same is true of hypertext units, the generalized form of trails. I think it likely that once such systems are available, the creation of branching and complex text will become recognized as far more natural than the structures in which we now must write.

This will all follow naturally from the existence of consoles which permit multiple couplings between texts. Having created for personal use a hyper-document on one's console, it will seem only reasonable to press a button passing this on to a colleague in its hyper-form, without chopping and aligning it into conventional writing.

Various interesting possibilities follow. Private "journals" in a field may be started among co-workers merely by the pooling of their hyper-documents. The rental of memory space on magnetic cards is inconsequential next to what have been the costs of printing and mailing.

When professional and technical societies become interested in sponsoring hyper-publication, one of the most straightforward ways to begin would be with the creation of society-sponsored review articles. These could be like the ordinary review articles sponsored by such societies, save that the review article would open directly into the various materials it was reviewing, and footnotes could be more extensive and slanted to different categories of reader. (Figure 1.)

Figure One. Review Article

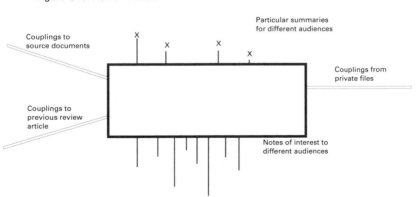

The next step is, of course, the creation of hyper-magazines or journals under the sponsorship and supervision of professional societies. Here the problem of organization would seem to become thorny. But this collection could be much like the journals of today, except for the direct availability of previous literature, working papers and various odds and ends. It should be observed that any of the "documents" noted in the illustration can themselves be hypertexts. (Figure 2.)

Figure Two Hyper-Magazine.

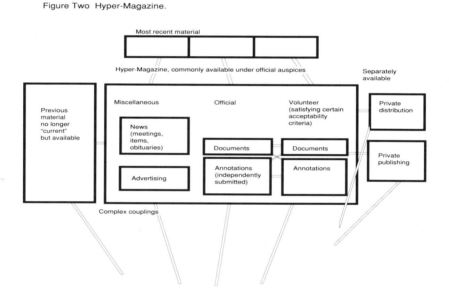

In this magazine, an arbitrary conjecture, all material of the past year is considered "recent" and embraced in a common lookup structure. New material enters the collection surreptitiously, at whatever time of day or night the editors release it; material one year old is formally expelled to a different file on the first of each month. (It may be just as accessible, but its nominal status changes, rather like that of a book taken off the "recent acquisitions" list of a library.) This magazine would hold most of what people were talking about in a field, and it would all be right there.

There are numerous technical complications to hypertext publishing. There is no room here to discuss the more esoteric technical ones, such as facilities, billing and copyright conventions, or possible techniques of encryption and validation to prevent pirating of works and to authenticate expeditionary versions.

How to Begin

How shall it begin?

Those contemplating massive retrieval systems commonly presume that they must begin with some massive corpus all accessible. The Library of Congress is often mentioned. Even Bush supposes regretfully (in the revised article, p. 100) that the personal system waits on large public establishments being automated first.

I do not believe this is so. It will be practicable and of considerable interest to begin on a small scale, having no grand corpus available. The grand corpus will come soon enough, as requests emerge. (We have a precedent: the prowess of University Microfilms, Inc. in rendering texts available to scholars in microfilm.)

The way to begin is to furnish supported consoles to small communities of users: key members of a "small" discipline, or specialists among whose work there is close connection. Suitable groups might be "early Egyptologists," or just plain "everybody at Woods Hole."

Such communicants, having been assured as well as possible of privacy and fail-safe design, will be encouraged to use the consoles fully. From the outset they may keep all their notes, manuscripts, articles, and copies of outgoing correspondence, on the system.

The rest will follow. I am fairly sure of the predictions so far, at least in broad outline, but I am just as sure that the first generation of hypertext users will invent twice as much as has been descried and described so far.

Who will support these beginnings? We have a choice, at the outset, of universities, publishing companies, computer companies (including service bureaux), research organizations or the government. Any of these might take such an initiative. Though such an initiative would seem severally unthinkable, it somehow seems collectively plausible and, of course, historically inevitable. If you believe in manifest destiny.

Endnotes

1. Vannevar Bush, "As We May Think." *The Atlantic Monthly* 176:1 (July, 1945), 101-108. References to "Bush" cite this article unless further specified, and all unexplained numbers and paginations in the text refer to it. Because the article is so tightly written and our interest in it so close, paginations are given to the column and paragraph.
2. Allen Kent, *Textbook on Mechanized Information Retrieval*, second edition. Wiley, 1966; pp. 7-9.
3. Joseph Becker and Robert M. Hayes, *Information Storage and Retrieval: Tools, Elements, Theories*. Wiley, 1963; p. 40.
4. John H. Wilson, "As We May Have Thought." In *Progress in Information Science and Technology: Proceedings of the American Documentation Institute 1966 Annual Meeting*. Adrianne Press, 1966, pp. 117-122.
5. Vannevar Bush, "Memex Revisited." In Vannevar Bush, *Science Is Not Enough*. William Morrow and Company, Inc., 1967, 75-101.
6. Douglas C. Engelbart, "Augmenting Human Intellect: A Conceptual Framework." AFOSR-3223 Summary Report, Stanford Research Institute, Menlo Park, California, October 1962. This expresses the philosophy, rather than the results, of the continuing project.
7. Theodor H. Nelson, "Getting It Out of Our System." In George Schechter (ed.), *Information Retrieval: A Critical View*. Thompson Book Company, 1967; pp. 191-210.

Memex as an Image of Potentiality Revisited

Linda C. Smith

Introduction

IN JULY 1945 AN ARTICLE BY VANNEVAR BUSH entitled "As We May Think" appeared in the *Atlantic Monthly* (Bush, 1945a). Bush had served as director of the Office of Scientific Research and Development during World War II and he now urged scientists in peacetime to turn to the task of making more accessible the growing store of knowledge. One device in particular that he proposed for development was the Memex, "a machine that should be an extension of the personal memory and body of knowledge belonging to an individual, and should work in a fashion analogous to the working of the human brain—by association rather than by categorical classification" (Bush, 1970b:190).

Bush's article generated considerable interest at the time it appeared. The 23 July 1945 issue of *TIME* summarized the major points of the article in a piece entitled "A Machine that Thinks," and the 10 September 1945 issue of *LIFE* carried a condensed and illustrated version of the article with the following heading: "A top U.S. scientist foresees a possible future world in which man-made machines will start to think." It is unlikely that Bush would have sanctioned these journalists' use of the word "think", for he later noted that the term "thinking machine" as applied to computers is "an unfortunate expression, for they do not think, they merely aid man to do so" (Bush, 1967b:82).

In addition to its appearance in *LIFE* (Bush, 1945b), "As We May Think" has been reprinted at least ten times since 1945: in 1946 as part of a collection of Bush's writings on problems and opportunities confronting science (Bush, 1946); in 1964 as a statement of the scientific information problem in a collection of readings on information retrieval (Bush, 1964); in 1967 as an example of the encyclopedia system idea in a collection of readings on the organization and retrieval of information (Bush, 1967a); in 1970 as a landmark article in the history of computers in a collection of readings entitled *Perspectives on the Computer Revolution* (Bush, 1970a); in 1986 in a collection of papers on CD ROM technology (Bush, 1986); twice in 1987, in a collection of papers tracing the evolution of an information society (Bush, 1987a) and as the end-piece in a collection of papers on the origins of information science (Bush, 1987b); twice in 1988, as a classic paper in the history of personal workstations (Bush, 1988a) and in a collection of readings relevant to computer-supported cooperative work (Bush, 1988b); and in 1990 as part of a text on hypermedia (Bush, 1990). The article has proved to be of continuing interest over the years, as shown by the following titles: "As We May Have Thought" (Wilson, 1966), "As We May Think—Information Systems Do Not" (Paisley, 1968), "As We Will Think" (Nelson, 1972), "As We May Think, Revisited" (Brunelle and McClelland, 1987), "As We May Learn" (Weyer, 1988), "As We May Think?: Psychological Considerations in the Design of a Personal Filing System" (Jones, 1988), and "As We May Think—Again" (Matheson, 1989).

Paisley and Butler (1977:42) have noted that "Scientists and technologists are guided by 'images of potentiality'—the untested theories, unanswered questions, and unbuilt devices that they view as their agenda for five years, ten years, and longer." The discussion thus far suggests that it is reasonable to view Bush's Memex as one image of potentiality which has guided work in information retrieval over the past 45 years. While it is known that Bush's article is often cited, there is a need for a detailed analysis if one is to assess the impact of Bush's ideas on the subsequent design and development of information retrieval systems. The study reported here, updating and extending a study first reported in 1981 (Smith, 1981), uses citation context analysis as a method to assess Bush's influence.

Citation Context Analysis

Small (1982) provides an explanation of the method of citation context analysis as well as a review of studies employing this method. A citation is any mention of a document by another document, and a citation context is "that particular passage or statement within the citing document containing the reference. A citation context analysis is any attempt to utilize these passages in a systematic fashion" (Small, 1982:288). Small identifies two principal approaches to the analysis of citation contexts: 1) classification of the types or functions of references in scholarly texts; 2) uses of the semantic content of the citing passage to characterize the cited work.

The content analysis scheme developed for this study identifies five categories that reflect citing authors' use of Bush's "As We May Think": 1) historical perspective; 2) hardware; 3) information store; 4) association and selection; 5) personal information system. Category 1 reflects the use of Bush's article as an event on a time line. Categories 2-4 reflect Bush's characterization of Memex (1970b:190) as "a filing system, a repository of information, and a scheme of searching and speedily finding a desired piece of information." They support the observation of Paisley and Butler (1977:42) that the properties of Memex "are so amorphous that information scientists construct it in their imaginations in many different ways. To some information scientists, it is elegant hardware. To others, it is information processing software whose algorithms rival those of the mind itself." Separate categories are needed because some citing documents focus on one aspect of Memex without considering the others. Category 5 applies to those citing documents which consider Memex as a whole. Each category is discussed in turn.

The search for citing documents encompassed a number of sources. All available volumes of *Science Citation Index* (with coverage from 1945), *Social Sciences Citation Index* (with coverage from 1956), *Arts & Humanities Citation Index*, and *CMCI CompuMath Citation Index* were examined, with a search of their online counterparts bringing coverage up through the end of 1990. Coverage of the citation indexes was supplemented by checking selected monographs and conference proceedings in such areas as information retrieval, library automation, and hypertext. Most citations identified were explicit (that is, associated with a reference number) but a few were implicit, involving statements about Bush and/or Memex in the text without a corresponding reference number to a list of references at the end of the book or article. Through these various steps, 375 citing documents were identified, of which 362 were available for examination. Almost half were published in the period 1981-90. As will be explained in the content analysis, the continuing high level of citation of the 1945 article into the 1980s can be attributed at least in part to the association of Bush with concepts similar to those underlying hypertext. In addition, the availability of several reprints of the paper in various texts has made the content of the original paper more accessible.

The citation context analysis is based on examination of the 362 documents; those citing documents mentioned in the body of this paper appear in the reference list at the end. Omitted from the discussion are citing documents that mention "As We May Think" only in passing and add little to one's understanding of the subsequent use of this article. Occasionally when reviewing citation contexts, one finds that the statements made by citing authors lead to questioning whether they have in fact read the paper they are citing. Examples include the observation by Barrett and Paradis (1988a:156) that "Vannevar Bush in 1945 developed a computer program, *memex*, to mimic the associational leaps of the mind" and Ball's (1981) reference to "mimix" as the name of the device, rather than "memex". While citing authors often used variant capitalizations, e.g., Memex or MEMEX, Ball's was the only misspelling encountered.

Historical Perspective

> There is a growing mountain of research. But there is increased evidence that we are being bogged down today as specialization extends. The investigator is staggered by the findings and conclusions of thousands of other workers—conclusions which he cannot find time to grasp, much less to remember, as they appear. (Bush, 1945a:101)

As one would expect, the majority of citations to Bush's article are used to provide a historical perspective. Publication of the article represents an event in time that the citing authors are noting. As such, many of these citations are "perfunctory" in the sense of Moravcsik and Murugesan (1975)— dispensable and not essential to the main point of the citing document. As Bottle (1981) has commented, the article is "oft quoted, but seldom read."

What emerges from a review of many of the citing articles that treat "As We May Think" from a historical perspective is the conviction, particularly among American authors, that its publication was the starting point of modern information science. Thus, one finds references to "As We May Think" (in chronological order) as "the beginning of the literature on mechanized information retrieval" (Joyce and Needham, 1958); "an inspiration to many later workers in the field" (Marden and Koller, 1961); "the manifesto of information science" (Paisley, 1968, 1990); "the start of modern documentation" (Dugan and Minker, 1969); "the beginning of an interest in information storage and retrieval" (Senko, 1969); "the earliest, and perhaps the most important, single description of the potential uses of computers for information processing" (Hayes and Becker, 1970); "the blueprint for the new field of information science" (Leimkuhler, 1972); a "seminal paper in modern information science" (Davis and Rush, 1979); "the real spark for online information retrieval" (Kent, 1979); and "the founding article of information science" (Bates, 1986). Memex, in particular, has been referred to as "a strong motivational force in information research" (Leimkuhler, 1973), "the first automated information retrieval project to be widely publicized" (Dammers, 1975), and the "vision of the knowledge worker's workstation" (Wigington, 1987). Vannevar Bush can thus be considered "the father of information science" (Donohue and Karioth, 1966) and "an early spokesman to catalyze interest" in information retrieval (Smith, 1976). He has "presaged a whole new field of study: the use of automated techniques to aid man in exploiting the fund of acquired knowledge" (Borman and Hay, 1977). Given Bush's prominence in World War II, "by the very writing of his article, he conveyed importance and prestige to this nascent, dimly appreciated field" that came to be called information science (Herner, 1984).

During the 1980s, "As We May Think" is cited most often as a significant publication in the history of hypertext. Nielsen (1989) indicates that "Vannevar Bush is normally considered the 'grandfather' of hypertext, since he proposed a system we would now describe as a hypertext system as long ago as 1945." The review of citing documents uncovered none which dissented from the view that the concept of hypertext is traceable to Memex as described by Bush. Consistent with Conklin (1987), who wrote a widely read introduction and survey of hypertext, many authors credit Bush with the initial description of hypertext. More specifically, Trigg and Weiser (1986) credit Bush with the notion of a path through hypertext, and Garg (1989) notes Bush's interest in filtering information in hypertext. Rorvig (1988) recalls that Bush's vision of the field of information retrieval included images as well as text, and Cawkell (1989) and Thornburg (1988) both credit Bush as the originator of the idea of hypermedia. Knuth and Brush (1990) view Bush as among the first to envision the information retrieval aspect of hypertext.

The critics of ideas set forth in "As We May Think" are few, but their concerns deserve some attention. The first identified was Fairthorne (1958). He suggests that the paper considered what machines *could* do rather than what they *should* do. Neglect of the second consideration then "sometimes allowed absurdity to undermine ingenuity" in information retrieval. Shera (1971) elaborates on the danger of placing too much faith in the machine: "What we failed to perceive in the 1950s and early sixties was that we had fallen into the error that Abraham Kaplan calls the Law of the Instrument. Simply stated his principle holds that the machine makes its own ends, the device determines what we shall do."

This fascination with the technology also troubled Wilson (1966), who titled his critique "As We May Have Thought." He notes that "Bush takes the engineer's delight in solving the engineering problem of Memex, minimizing the human difficulties that have to be dealt with." This concern is echoed by Mikhailov and Giljarevskij (1971), who observe that "some people still overestimated the role to be played by machines in solving information retrieval problems, and this attitude still survives today despite the fact that information retrieval problems can obviously be solved only through a profound study of man's thought processes." Shera (1970) makes a similar argument: "Since we do not understand the process of cognition, we cannot hypothesize with any degree of accuracy the pattern of recourse to recorded knowledge." As Maron (1965) observes, the problems of information retrieval do not relate primarily to hardware; ". . .they are *intellectual* problems, and they have remained unsolved because the proper framework within which to view them has not been firmly constructed." Rosenberg (1974, 1975) urges information science researchers to pay more attention to the social, cultural, and spiritual aspects of human communication. In an article entitled "Library Technology—The Black Box Syndrome," Stevens (1983) cites the need to regain skepticism toward mechanical solutions to information problems; "we should not expect miracles."

Hardware

> But there are signs of a change as new and powerful instrumentalities come into use. Photocells capable of seeing things in a physical sense, advanced photography which can record what is seen or even what is not . . .—there are plenty of mechanical aids with which to effect a transformation of scientific records. (Bush, 1945a:102)

For this category more than any other, what Memex symbolizes has changed over time as the technology available to the information system designer has changed. The first citation identified dealt with Bush's mention of dry photography among the many technologies briefly discussed in "As We May Think." Land (1947), in a paper describing a "new one-step photographic process," which would form the basis of Polaroid camera film, observed that while the photography literature failed to discuss such a system even in the ideal, Bush had identified the need for a dry and approximately instantaneous means of taking photographs. The other early citations dealt with microfilm-based systems to help realize the Memex.

Beginning in the 1960s, authors proposed use of combinations of technologies, with growing interest in computers. Bush (1967b:99-100) had the satisfaction of reviewing the advances in technology since the publication of his original article.

> Great progress. . .has been made in the last twenty years on all the elements necessary. Storage has been reduced in size, access has become more rapid. Transistors, video tape, television, high-speed electric circuits, have revolutionized the conditions under which we approach the problem. Except for the one factor of better access to large memories, all we need to do is to put the proper elements together—at reasonable expense—and we will have a memex.

Commentators in the 1970s note the increasing availability of online retrieval systems, which allow interactive searching of several databases simultaneously by multiple users in remote locations. While discussions of the Memex in terms of online retrieval systems tend to emphasize remote computer capacity, recent developments in computer technology have led other authors to envision the Memex more in the terms that Bush originally described, as an "information desk" with local storage. As optical storage technology developed during the 1980s, reference to videodisc as the information storage device of choice was superseded by discussions of CD ROM as the replacement for microfilm in Memex. Several authors describe the personal computer as a device capable of supporting the functionality of Memex.

The 1980s also brought discussion of technologies to support enhanced interfaces between the human user and the computer system. The graphical user interface, with its graphic icons and multiple windows displaying documents or graphics, seems well suited to support the type of interaction with stored information that Bush imagined. Computers are now more capable of supporting access to multimedia rather than to text only. In addition, the possibility of connecting a personal computer to a telecommunication network allows the information stored locally to be supplemented by access to remote databases, electronic mail, and bulletin boards.

There has been a continuing interest in hardware, the mechanisms needed to implement a Memex. Discussion of developments in microform storage and retrieval devices has generally been superseded by concern for developments in computers coupled with telecommunications. Recent developments in mass storage make it feasible once again to return to the idea of a local information store, although one may still decide to retain the capability for network access.

Information Store

Most of the memex contents are purchased on microfilm ready for insertion. Books of all sorts, pictures, current periodicals, newspapers, are thus obtained and dropped into place. Business correspondence takes the same path. And there is provision for direct entry. (Bush, 1945a:107)

Wholly new forms of encyclopedias will appear, ready-made with a mesh of associative trails running through them, ready to be dropped into the memex and there amplified. (Bush, 1945a:108)

Of the categories used as a basis for the content analysis, that of the "information store," the contents of the Memex, was found to occur least often, although it has received more attention in the last decade. This increased attention may be due to the growing availability of machine-readable databases of all types. Shera (1967) observes that "for generations, the scholar has dreamed of a Utopia in which he would have access to the total store of potentially useful materials." Priest (1972:20) provides a more detailed description of the development of this concept:

> [It] has been called the "world brain" by Wells, "memex" by Bush, the "world box" by Calder, and most recently the "mass information utility" by Sackman. In general, it has been envisioned as a utopian dream—information on anything, for anyone, in any form—and has always been promptly put aside until later as being a fiscal nightmare and a technological impossibility.

Recognizing that the information need not be stored all in one location, Kranch (1989) has coined the term *memex effect* to describe the resources that would be available to a user as a result of the seamless interfacing of remote databases by gateways communicating across telecommunication networks.

Some authors have described resources in support of particular groups, as Bush envisioned. Badertscher (1982), in tracing developments in computer applications to the law, notes that in 1946 a Professor Kelso proposed LAWDEX, inspired by Memex. In medicine, Frisse (1988) describes the Dynamic Medical Handbook Project, designed to serve as the medical student's "peripheral brain." Weyer (1982) has also been concerned with the design of dynamic books that could potentially offer multiple paths through complex information and help the user actively in searching. Anderson (1988) describes the Online Reference Works Program of the National Library of Medicine. Hartley (1990) suggests that encyclopedias, dictionaries, and handbooks lend themselves to electronic presentation because of their organizational structure and the kinds of tasks for which they are used. Smith (1989) reviews the established characteristics of printed encyclopedias and suggests new design possibilities for such reference works in a hypertext environment. Kahn (1989) describes experiments in adapting published material into a hypermedia environment, focusing on how to create useful links between different published sources. In his discussion of expert systems, Waters (1986) also identifies the need to develop useful links between otherwise separate resources. Hjerppe (1986) has explored the design of a HYPERCATalog, which would handle document descriptions in ways suggested by Memex.

Another theme that has emerged in the 1980s is an interest in computer-supported cooperative work, the possibility that computers might be used to support group problem solving or research. While Soergel (1977) asserts that Bush was concerned with the structure of an individual's external memory rather than with a public data store, Stefik *et al.* (1987) observe that "Bush believed that a common encyclopedic database of information integrated from many areas of human activity would enhance the quality of social problem solving." Interactive computer networks create new opportunities for the cooperative structuring of information, if methods can be developed for cooperative indexing, evaluation, and synthesis of information (Lowe, 1985). Already hypertext is being used to support scholarship among scientists, with electronic transmission of hypertext providing a chance to share the results and context in which reasoning occurred (Schnase and Leggett, 1989). While Bush envisioned that trails would become literary constructs in their own right and that one could pass on a particularly useful trail to others for incorporation in their Memex structures (Parsaye, Chignell, Khoshafian, and Wong, 1989), recent work by Marshall and Irish (1989) indicates that there is "a need to distinguish between the formulation of a hypertext network for a user's own research or other use and the presentation of the same network to an audience." They caution that "the trail-blazing and path-following metaphors that have been proposed in earlier work such as Bush . . . may be insufficient for a reader to make sense of another's path in the absence of context-creating metainformation and narration." Nielsen (1989) also cautions that the current technology does not yet coincide with Bush's vision of sharing trails, "since it is almost impossible to transfer selected subsets of a hypertext structure to another hypertext, especially if the two hypertexts are based on different systems."

While in 1981 Smith concluded that "citing authors have thus not really explored in depth what Bush viewed as the possibilities for 'wholly new forms of encyclopedias'," the last decade has provided many more examples of studies of the content and structure of the information store, for both personal and group use. Although the information is stored in digital form rather than as photographic images on microfilm, the quantity and variety rival that which Bush envisioned for Memex. But it is not enough to have large quantities of information in machine-readable form; techniques must be developed to support organization, search, and retrieval.

Association and Selection

> Selection by association, rather than by indexing, may yet be mechanized. One cannot hope thus to equal the speed and flexibility with which the mind follows an associative trail, but it should be possible to beat the mind decisively in regard to the permanence and clarity of the items resurrected from storage. (Bush, 1945a:106)

The category of association and selection is used here to denote the intellectual aspects of information retrieval, the organization of information, and the procedures for search and retrieval. Much of the citing literature over the years has tried to explore in some depth Bush's notion of "selection by association." Roberts (1984) states that Bush's "speculations about 'associative indexing' soon influenced a profession short on original ideas, but wishing mightily for the trappings of modernity." Tague (1969:55-56) has provided a useful summary of this research:

> In the years since Bush's article, and particularly since the late 1950s, there have been many attempts to mechanize association mapping within a large corpus of documents. These have produced the so-called statistical association methods in information retrieval. While nothing has yet been developed which will flit from topic to topic in the style of Bush's Memex, this research has stimulated a consideration both of the types of concept connections which are meaningful in an information retrieval context and the most effective and efficient methods for producing these connections.

But these approaches to retrieval were not without their critics. In particular, Bar-Hillel (1957) felt that the idea of approximating the association of ideas in the human brain by a co-occurrence chain of indexes to be traced by machine held very little promise. He notes that while remarks by Bush on this matter showed "a great deal of vision," they were also "unfortunately rather vague and indefinite." In spite of this criticism, work on association methods continues. Doszkocs, Reggia, and Lin (1990) provide a review of the place of connectionist models in information retrieval. Bates (1986) argues that information retrieval researchers should "stop trying to design systems that will *target* the desired information through perfect pinpoint match on the one best term; rather, design systems to *encompass* the answer by displaying and making it easy to explore a variety of descriptive terms." She sees the need to make available the means to facilitate the searcher's own rich associational tendencies. Frei and Jauslin (1983) describe one system for the graphical presentation of information to support retrieval by associations.

While it is evident that some researchers were intrigued with Bush's notion of the "associative trail," Nelson in a series of papers (1965, 1967, 1972, 1973, 1974) has criticized the approach taken in most computer-based information retrieval systems, asserting that what Bush really said has been largely ignored. His proposals for using the electronic medium to full advantage center on the notion of hypertext— that is, nonlinear text that could not conveniently be presented or represented on paper. Hypertext may differ from ordinary text in (1) its sequence—it may branch into trees and networks; (2) its organization— it may have multiple levels of summary and detail; and (3) its mode of presentation—it may contain moving or manipulable illustrations. Nelson believes that "As We May Think" is most notable for its clear description of various hypertext techniques—that is, linkages between documents, which may be brought rapidly to the screen according to their linkages.

Although there was some development of software tools for creating hypertext prior to 1980 (e.g., van Dam and Rice (1970) describe the Hypertext Editing System), there has been considerable activity in the past decade both in research and in the development of commercial products. They vary in their capabilities, but all seek to support the making and following of links. While Hall and Papadopoulos (1990) comment that "with an absence of any underpinning theory, hypertext systems have a strong flavour of 'a solution looking for a problem'," the availability of many more software tools means that developers are gaining experience with a much wider range of applications and a better understanding of the problems for which hypertext is well suited.

One theme in the literature discussing hypertext development is the relation between thinking and computing. Jones (1988) suggests that many constructs found in models of human memory may have application in computer-based systems of information retrieval. Gray and Shasha (1989) note that the use of links between information fragments is consistent with theories in modern psychology such as spreading activation. They have tried to answer the question "to link or not to link?" through experimentation, finding that links may be more useful when searches are undirected. Smith, Weiss, and Ferguson (1989) also have a concern with the relationship between WE (a hypertext writing environment) and the cognitive processes of its users, and Barrett and Paradis (1988b) comment that programs for teaching writing may attempt to model intellectual processes. But the relationship between thinking and computing still requires more study, as Neuwirth and Kaufer (1989:319-320) explain.

> The basic vision that Bush described for creating associative links, representing them, and following them has been pursued in many actual implementations of hypertext systems. An implicit assumption shared by such systems was that a good representation for performing the process of retrieval from an external memory would be one that provided a mechanism to mimic the associative links of human memory. This assumption has been called into question by the problems of users "getting lost in hypertext", a disorientation problem in which users forget where they are in the hypertext network, forget how to get to another place in the network, or forget what is in the network.

One aspect of hypertext systems that has received special attention is Bush's notion of a trail, sequences of links that users would construct and subsequently consult. Any location could appear in multiple trails. This concept has been implemented in various forms with various labels, such as paths (Conklin and Begeman, 1989; Zellweger, 1989) and guided tours (Trigg, 1988). Utting and Yankelovich (1989) describe a related notion of a hypermedia roadmap in the form of a web view to provide context and orientation in Intermedia. Fraase (1990) has coined the term "hyperliterate" to characterize users who are learning to build their own reference links, navigational trails, and indexes through large amounts of data.

The discussion of hypertext suggests that bibliographic retrieval systems, now the most common form of computer-based information retrieval systems, need not be viewed as the principal use of computers for handling ideas, but rather as accessories in support of other information-handling tasks, which can also be computer-based. This theme of computer assistance in information work is explored further in the discussion of Memex as a personal information system.

Personal Information System

> Consider a future device for individual use, which is a sort of mechanized private file and library. It needs a name, and, to coin one at random, "memex" will do. A memex is a device in which an individual stores all his books, records, and communications, and which is mechanized so that it may be consulted with exceeding speed and flexibility. It is an enlarged intimate supplement to his memory. (Bush, 1945a:106-107)

The previous sections on hardware, information store, and association and selection have considered the components of Memex separately. A number of authors, however, have looked at the system as a whole and discussed the prospects for implementation. The emphasis among these authors is the system as a personal tool in support of broadly defined "information work." Cady (1990) suggests that the articulation of the need for a scholar's workstation "demonstrated a growing recognition of the dilemma posed for the scholarly community in utilizing research materials requiring a reading machine, usually housed only in a library."

Commentary began in 1961 with a plea from Heumann: "What I want is a small, personal, mechanized storage and retrieval device that can store and search my personal files and will cost less than $1000." He concluded with, "I hope some engineer who reads this finds the problem intriguing." Proposals and some actual systems were soon forthcoming. Kochen (1964, 1965) describes a system which he identifies variously as an adaptive concept processing machine and an adaptive man-machine, non-arithmetic, information processing system. It was to extend and amplify the user's memory in the manner of Bush's "ingenious memex." Engelbart and co-workers in a series of papers (Engelbart, 1961, 1963; Engelbart, Watson and Norton, 1973) describe efforts to use machines to augment man's intellect, increasing the capability of a user to approach a complex problem situation, gain comprehension to suit his particular needs, and devise solutions to problems. They have explored in particular the technology of computer time-sharing and telecommunications.

The 1980s brought technology that could build an affordable personal workstation, with capabilities for storing, indexing, and retrieving information (Brooks and Bierbaum, 1987). With a microcomputer equipped with a database management system and communications capabilities, the user can log on to online catalogs and other remote databases and download records to create a personal electronic desktop library (Rice, 1988).

While some authors recognize Memex as a useful starting point for thinking about the functions which a personal information system can serve, they indicate some of the additional functions that a Memex of the future should encompass. Caruso (1973) notes that the scholar's desktop library will continue to exist, but that it will be augmented by access to machine-searchable stores of document references, full text, data, subject maps, and lists of individuals interested in particular topics. Lewis (1988) and Lynch and Preston (1990) all emphasize that connectivity with other resources is essential; a standalone workstation is inadequate. Paisley and Butler (1977) identify a number of limitations in the Memex concept as developed by Bush:

1. Memex has no networking or communication capability either with other information resources or with other users directly.
2. Memex supports the exploration and learning tasks of information work, but fails to provide equal support for subsequent tasks such as analysis, decision making, and report production.

3. Memex lacks transformative power over the symbols in its
    store, such as the ability to extract features for purposes of
    compression or comparison.

Turoff's (1977) view of the future 10-20 years later suggests how one
might avoid some of these limitations, coupling personal information
storage and editing systems with computerized conferencing systems.
His approach to the communications network of the future envisions
abstracting services, journal and book publishing, word processing,
computer conferencing, and information retrieval systems evolving
into a single system serving the needs of a community of users. Case
(1986) argues that by examining the ways in which information is stored
in scholars' offices, one can better understand the kinds of materials and
types of organizational problems scholars have and therefore better
design tools for scholarly work. Moon (1988) feels that the personal
information system should not only help scientists to manage their
document collections, but also allow them to represent the structure of
the literature by creating and storing links between document records.
In addition, the personal information system should be integrated with
other personal software, such as electronic mail and word processing
packages.

Some authors are interested in enhanced educational systems,
effectively exploiting the full range of multimedia—text, audio, and
graphics (McClintock, 1986). While Bush envisioned Memex in service
to the scholar, Weyer (1988), in an article entitled "As We May Learn,"
presents the need to go beyond Memex and explore how to aid the work
of learners of all ages and abilities. He argues that, instead of focusing
on hypertext and browsing, system designers should consider developing "hyperknowledge assistants." He notes that "the name Memex
suggests memory and storage; perhaps we should call our system
Mimex to emphasize simulation and learning from examples." Such a
system would be a partner with the learner in searching, interpreting,
and creating knowledge. Weyer asserts that "the powerful vision
typified by Memex can be made even more compelling by transforming
information into knowledge, by elevating the needs and importance of
the learner, and by evolving a flexible tool in the direction of becoming
an adaptive partner."

Among the examples cited by Bush (1945a) was support for the physician, who "puzzled by a patient's reactions, strikes the trail established in studying an earlier similar case, and runs rapidly through analogous case histories, with side references to the classics for the pertinent anatomy and histology." Some new systems are being designed to support at least some of these capabilities. For example, GUIDON-WATCH (Richer and Clancey, 1985) has a graphic interface that uses multiple windows and a mouse to allow a student to browse through a knowledge base and view reasoning processes during medical diagnostic problem solving. Work at Johns Hopkins University (Matheson, 1986, 1989; Lucier, Matheson, Butter, and Reynolds, 1988) will allow the user of the knowledge workstation to do more than recall and display information. Plans for the workstation are outlined as follows:

> Workers will be able to move easily between clinically oriented and literature databases to retrieve facts, refresh memory, record relevant data as part of a patient's management record, access authoritative information from online texts and reference works, review the literature, prepare and administer an examination, compose a book chapter, develop and maintain a knowledge base, and communicate with colleagues. (Lucier *et al.*, 1988:249)

Conclusion

> The problem is how creative men think, and what can be done to help them think. It is a problem of how the great mass of material shall be handled so that the individual can draw from it what he needs— instantly, correctly, and with utter freedom. (Bush, 1967b:75-76)

This study provides an assessment of the impact of Bush's ideas in the 45 years since "As We May Think" was first published. Counting citations is one measure of influence, but an imperfect one when at least some of the citations are perfunctory, making mention of the cited work only in passing. In addition, the fact that a work is cited provides no guarantee that the citing author has actually read the cited work, as was evident from some of the citing passages that were analyzed. Although there are now some testimonials regarding Bush's influence on subsequent research (e.g., Engelbart as reported by Rheingold, 1985), additional instances of influence must be inferred from discussions citing the article in the published literature. The citation context analysis demonstrates that the article has been used as a symbol for a number of different concepts. Although most citing authors affirm various viewpoints presented by Bush, there have also been critics.

Tracing citations to Bush has proved to be a convenient device for revealing trends in information retrieval as well as for raising questions that must be addressed as one considers future directions. Can information retrieval include greater emphasis on what is known about human information processing? Do interactive information retrieval systems take full advantage of the electronic medium? Should information retrieval systems be designed with regard to how they fit into "information work" as a whole? Is it possible to develop systems which can be directly searched by end users? Answers to these and related questions will suggest what "images of potentiality" will be created to guide future research and development in information retrieval.

Revisiting this topic after a decade allows one to make some assessment of what has been learned in the past ten years. Although each prior decade had at least some commentators asserting that the technology had caught up with Bush's vision, the 1980s saw the emergence of technologies—e.g., personal computers, mass optical storage, hypertext, full text and image databases—that make it much more feasible (both technically and economically) to realize the vision of Memex. Researchers and system developers can now ask and begin to answer a new set of questions: How does one build trails? How does one share trails? To link or not to link? What are wholly new forms of encyclopedias? What is the best design for a personal workstation? What is required for computer-supported cooperative work?

Acknowledgements

The assistance of Virgil Diodato (in 1980) and Carol J. Elsen (in 1990) in gathering many of the sources used in this paper is gratefully acknowledged.

References

This list is divided into two parts. The first includes articles consulted as background for this chapter, including the original Bush article, reprints, and discussion of methodology. The second part includes the citing documents mentioned in this paper.

Background

Bush, V. (1945a). As We May Think, *Atlantic Monthly*, *176*(1), 101-108.

Bush, V. (1945b). As We May Think: A Top U.S. Scientist Foresees a Possible Future World in Which Man-Made Machines Will Start to Think, *LIFE*, *19*(11), 112-114, 116, 118, 121, 123-124 [condensed and illustrated version of 1945a].

Bush, V. (1946). As We May Think, in *Endless Horizons* (pp. 16-38), Washington, DC: Public Affairs Press.

Bush, V. (1964). As We May Think, in H.S. Sharp (editor), *Readings in Information Retrieval* (pp. 19-41), New York: Scarecrow Press.

Bush, V. (1967a). As We May Think, in M. Kochen (editor), *The Growth of Knowledge: Readings on Organization and Retrieval of Information* (pp. 23-35), New York: Wiley.

Bush, V. (1970a). As We May Think, in Z. W. Pylyshyn (editor), *Perspectives on the Computer Revolution* (pp. 47-59), Englewood Cliffs, NJ: Prentice-Hall.

Bush, V. (1970b). *Pieces of the Action*, New York: Morrow.

Bush, V. (1986). As We May Think, in S. Lambert and S. Ropiequet (editors), *CD ROM The New Papyrus* (pp. 3-20), Redmond, WA: Microsoft Press.

Bush, V. (1987a). As We May Think, in A. E. Cawkell (editor), *Evolution of an Information Society* (pp. 165-178), London: Aslib.

Bush, V. (1987b). As We May Think, in A. J. Meadows (editor), *The Origins of Information Science* (pp. 254-261), London: Taylor Graham.

Bush, V. (1988a). As We May Think, in A. Goldberg (editor), *A History of Personal Workstations* (pp. 237-247), Reading, MA: Addison-Wesley.

Bush, V. (1988b). As We May Think, in I. Greif (editor), *Computer-supported Cooperative Work: A Book of Readings* (pp. 17-34), San Mateo, CA: Morgan Kaufmann.

Bush, V. (1990). As We May Think, in M. Fraase, *Macintosh Hypermedia, Volume I: Reference Guide* (pp. 5-21), Glenview, IL: Scott, Foresman.

Moravcsik, M. J., and Murugesan, P. (1975). Some Results on the Function and Quality of Citations, *Social Studies of Science*, *5*, 86-92.

Small, H. (1982). Citation Context Analysis, *Progress in Communication Sciences*, *3*, 287-310.

Citing documents

Anonymous (1945). A Machine That Thinks, *TIME*, *46*(4), 93-94.

Anderson, P. F. (1988). Expert Systems, Expertise, and the Library and Information Professions, *Library and Information Science Research, 10*, 367-388.

Badertscher, D. G. (1982). An Examination of the Dynamics of Change in Information Technology as Viewed from Law Libraries and Information Centers, *Law Library Journal, 75*, 198-211.

Ball, A. J. S. (1981). Videotex: Chimera or Dream Machine, *Canadian Library Journal, 38*(2), 11-15.

Bar-Hillel, Y. (1957). A Logician's Reaction to Recent Theorizing on Information Search Systems, *American Documentation, 8*, 103-113.

Barrett, E., and Paradis, J. (1988a). Teaching Writing in an On-line Classroom, *Harvard Educational Review, 58*, 154-171.

Barrett, E., and Paradis, J. (1988b). The On-line Environment and In-House Training, in E. Barrett (editor), *Text, ConText, and HyperText: Writing with and for the Computer* (pp. 227-249), Cambridge: MIT Press.

Bates, M. J. (1986). Subject Access in Online Catalogs: A Design Model, *Journal of the American Society for Information Science, 37*, 357-376.

Borman, L., and Hay, R., Jr. (1977). The Information Transfer Process on the University Campus—The Case for Public Use Files, *Drexel Library Quarterly, 13*, 82-99.

Bottle, R. T. (1981). Legislation, Technology and Curriculum Requirements for Open and Closed Information Systems, *Journal of Librarianship, 13*, 75-82.

Brooks, T. A., and Bierbaum, E. G. (1987). Database Management Systems: New Homes for Migrating Bibliographic Records, *Library and Information Science Research, 9*, 327-339.

Brunelle, B., and McClelland, B. (1987). As We May Think, Revisited, *Proceedings of the 8th National Online Meeting*, 41-46.

Bush, V. (1967b). Memex Revisited, in *Science Is Not Enough* (pp. 75-101), New York: Morrow.

Cady, S. A. (1990). The Electronic Revolution in Libraries: Microfilm Déjà Vu?, *College and Research Libraries, 51*, 374-386.

Caruso, E. (1973). Interactive Retrieval Systems, in E. M. Arnett and A. Kent (editors), *Computer-based Chemical Information* (pp. 125-138), New York: Marcel Dekker.

Case, D. O. (1986). Collection and Organization of Written Information by Social Scientists and Humanists: A Review and Exploratory Study, *Journal of Information Science, 12*, 97-104.

Cawkell, T. (1989). From Memex to MediaMaker, *The Electronic Library, 7*, 278-286.

Conklin, J. (1987). Hypertext: An Introduction and Survey, *Computer, 20*(9), 17-41.

Conklin, J., and Begeman, M. L. (1989). giBIS: A Hypertext Tool for Exploratory Policy Discussion, *ACM Transactions on Office Information Systems, 6,* 303-331.

Dammers, H. F. (1975). Economics of Computer-based Information Systems—A Review, *Journal of Documentation, 31,* 38-45.

Davis, C. H., and Rush, J. E. (1979). *Guide to Information Science,* Westport, CT: Greenwood Press.

Donohue, J. C., and Karioth, N. E. (1966). Coming of Age in Academe—Information Science at 21, *American Documentation, 17,* 117-119.

Doszkocs, T. E., Reggia, J., and Lin, X. (1990). Connectionist Models and Information Retrieval, *Annual Review of Information Science and Technology, 25,* 209-262.

Dugan, J. A., and Minker, J. (1969). Automatic Data Processing, Library and Information Center Applications, *Encyclopedia of Library and Information Science, 2,* 184-230.

Engelbart, D. C. (1961). Special Considerations of the Individual as a User, Generator, and Retriever of Information, *American Documentation, 12,* 121-125.

Engelbart, D. C. (1963). A Conceptual Framework for the Augmentation of Man's Intellect, in P. W. Howerton and D. C. Weeks (editors), *Vistas in Information Handling: I. The Augmentation of Man's Intellect by Machine* (pp. 1-29), Washington, DC: Spartan Books.

Engelbart, D. C., Watson, R. W., and Norton, J. C. (1973). The Augmented Knowledge Workshop, *AFIPS National Computer Conference Proceedings, 42,* 9-21.

Fairthorne, R. A. (1958). Automatic Retrieval of Recorded Information, *Computer Journal, 1,* 36-41.

Fraase, M. (1990). *Macintosh Hypermedia, Volume I: Reference Guide,* Glenview, IL: Scott, Foresman.

Frei, H. P., and Jauslin, J.-F. (1983). Graphical Presentation of Information and Services: A User-Oriented Interface, *Information Technology: Research and Development, 2,* 23-42.

Frisse, M. E. (1988). Searching for Information in a Hypertext Medical Handbook, *Communications of the ACM, 31,* 880-886.

Garg, P. K. (1987). Abstraction Mechanisms in Hypertext, in *Hypertext '87 Proceedings* (pp. 375-395), New York: ACM.

Gray, S. H., and Shasha, D. (1989). To Link or Not to Link? Empirical Guidance for the Design of Nonlinear Text Systems, *Behavior Research Methods, Instruments, & Computers, 21,* 326-333.

Hall, P. A. V., and Papadopoulos, S. (1990). Hypertext Systems and Applications, *Information and Software Technology, 32,* 477-490.

Hartley, J. (1990). Hype and Hypertext, *Higher Education, 20,* 113-119.

Hayes, R. M., and Becker, J. (1970). *Handbook of Data Processing for Libraries,* New York: Wiley.

Herner, S. (1984). Brief History of Information Science, *Journal of the American Society for Information Science, 35,* 157-163.

Heumann, K. F. (1961). New Device Needed, *American Documentation, 12,* 157.

Hjerppe, R. (1986). Project HYPERCATalog: Visions and Preliminary Conceptions of an Extended and Enhanced Catalog, in B. C. Brookes (editor), *Intelligent Information Systems for the Information Society* (pp. 211-232), Amsterdam: North-Holland.

Jones, W. P. (1988). "As We May Think"?: Psychological Considerations in the Design of a Personal Filing System, in R. Guindon (editor), *Cognitive Science and Its Applications for Human-Computer Interaction* (pp. 235-287), Hillsdale, NJ: Lawrence Erlbaum Associates.

Joyce, T., and Needham, R. M. (1958). The Thesaurus Approach to Information Retrieval, *American Documentation, 9,* 192-197.

Kahn, P. (1989). Linking Together Books: Experiments in Adapting Published Material into Intermedia Documents, *Hypermedia, 1,* 111-145.

Kent, A. (1979). The On-line Revolution in Libraries, 1969-, *American Libraries, 10,* 339-342.

Knuth, R. A., and Brush, T. A. (1990). Results of the Hypertext '89 Design Survey, *Hypermedia, 2,* 91-107.

Kochen, M. (1964). Adaptive Mechanisms in Digital Concept Processing, *IEEE Transactions on Applications and Industry, 83,* 305-314.

Kochen, M. (1965). *Some Problems in Information Science,* New York: Scarecrow Press.

Kranch, D. A. (1989). The Development and Impact of a Global Information System, *Information Technology and Libraries, 8,* 384-392.

Land, E. H. (1947). A New One-step Photographic Process, *Journal of the Optical Society of America, 37,* 61-77.

Leimkuhler, F. F. (1972). Library Operations Research—Process of Discovery and Justification, *Library Quarterly, 42,* 84-96.

Leimkuhler, F. F. (1973). Operations Research and Information Science—A Common Cause, *Journal of the American Society for Information Science, 24,* 3-8.

Lewis, D. W. (1988). Inventing the Electronic University, *College and Research Libraries, 49,* 291-304.

Lowe, D. G. (1985). Co-operative Structuring of Information: The Representation of Reasoning and Debate, *International Journal of Man-Machine Studies, 23*, 97-111.

Lucier, R. E., Matheson, N. W., Butter, K. A., and Reynolds, R. E. (1988). The Knowledge Workstation: An Electronic Environment for Knowledge Management, *Bulletin of the Medical Library Association, 76*, 248-255.

Lynch, C. A., and Preston, C. M. (1990). Internet Access to Information Resources, *Annual Review of Information Science and Technology, 25*, 263-312.

Marden, E. C., and Koller, H. R. (1961). *A Survey of Computer Programs for Chemical Information Searching,* Washington, DC: National Bureau of Standards (Technical Note 85).

Maron, M. E. (1965). Mechanized Documentation: The Logic Behind a Probabilistic Interpretation, in M. E. Stevens, V. E. Giuliano, and L. B. Heilprin (editors), *Statistical Association Methods for Mechanized Documentation* (pp. 9-13), Washington, DC: National Bureau of Standards (Miscellaneous Publication 269).

Marshall, C. C., and Irish, P. M. (1989). Guided Tours and On-line Presentations: How Authors Make Existing Hypertext Intelligible for Readers, in *Hypertext '89 Proceedings* (pp. 15-26), New York: ACM.

Matheson, N. W. (1986). Libraries in the Clinic, *M.D. Computing, 3*(2), 6-7.

Matheson, N. W. (1989). As We May Think—Again, in W. D. Linton and N. J. Dunton (editors), *New Directions: Developments in Published Medical Information Transfer* (pp. 58-71), Oxford, England: Medical Information Working Party.

McClintock, R. (1986). Into the Starting Gate: On Computing and the Curriculum, *Teachers College Record, 88*, 191-215.

Mikhailov, A. I., and Giljarevskij, R. S. (1971). *An Introductory Course on Informatics/Documentation,* The Hague: International Federation for Documentation.

Moon, C. (1988). Computerized Personal Information Systems for Research Scientists, *International Journal of Information Management, 8*, 265-273.

Nelson, T. H. (1965). A File Structure for the Complex, the Changing and the Indeterminate, *Proceedings of the ACM 20th National Conference,* 84-100.

Nelson, T. H. (1967). Getting It Out of Our System, in G. Schechter (editor), *Information Retrieval: A Critical View* (pp. 191-210), Washington, DC: Thompson.

Nelson, T. H. (1972). As We Will Think, in *Online 72 Conference Proceedings Vol. 1* (pp. 439-454), Uxbridge, England: Online Computer Systems Ltd.

Nelson, T. H. (1973). A Conceptual Framework for Man-Machine Everything, *AFIPS National Computer Conference Proceedings, 42,* M21-M26.

Nelson, T. H. (1974). Dream Machines: New Freedoms Through Computer Screens—A Minority Report, in *Computer Lib,* South Bend, IN: Ted Nelson.

Neuwirth, C. M., and Kaufer, D. S. (1989). The Role of External Representations in the Writing Process: Implications for the Design of Hypertext-based Writing Tools, *Hypertext '89 Proceedings* (pp. 319-341), New York: ACM.

Nielsen, J. (1989). *Hypertext and Hypermedia,* Cambridge: Academic Press.

Paisley, W. (1968). *As We May Think—Information Systems Do Not,* Stanford: Stanford University, Institute for Communication Research (ERIC Document Reproduction Service No. 037095).

Paisley, W. (1990). Information Science as a Multidiscipline, in J. M. Pemberton and A. E. Prentice (editors), *Information Science: The Interdisciplinary Context* (pp. 3-24), New York: Neal-Schuman Publishers.

Paisley, W., and Butler, M. (1977). *Computer Assistance in Information Work,* Palo Alto, CA: Applied Communication Research (ERIC Document Reproduction Service No. 146900).

Parsaye, K., Chignell, M., Khoshafian, S., and Wong, H. (1989). *Intelligent Databases: Object-oriented, Deductive Hypermedia Technologies,* New York: Wiley.

Priest, W. C. (1972). Restructuring Communication in Science and Technology, *IEEE Transactions on Professional Communication, PC-15*(2), 20-22.

Rheingold, H. (1985). *Tools for Thought: The People and Ideas Behind the Next Computer Revolution,* New York: Simon and Schuster.

Rice, J. G. (1988). The Dream of Memex, *American Libraries, 19,* 14-17.

Richer, M. H., and Clancey, W. J. (1985). GUIDON-WATCH: A Graphic Interface for Viewing a Knowledge-Based System, *IEEE Computer Graphics and Applications, 5*(11), 51-64.

Roberts, N. (1984). The Pre-History of the Information Retrieval Thesaurus, *Journal of Documentation, 40,* 271-285.

Rorvig, M. (1988). Psychometric Measurement and Information Retrieval, *Annual Review of Information Science and Technology, 23,* 157-189.

Rosenberg, V. (1974). The Scientific Premises of Information Science, *Journal of the American Society for Information Science, 25,* 263-269.

Rosenberg, V. (1975). The Scientific Study of Information—Its Nature and Impact, in A. Debons and W. J. Cameron (editors), *Perspectives in information science* (pp. 221-232), Leyden: Noordhoff.

Schnase, J. L., and Leggett, J. J. (1989). Computational Hypertext in Biological Modeling, in *Hypertext '89 Proceedings* (pp. 181-197), New York: ACM.

Senko, M. E. (1969). Information Storage and Retrieval Systems, *Advances in Information Systems Science, 2*, 229-281.

Shera, J. H. (1967). Librarians Against Machines, *Science, 156*, 746-750.

Shera, J. H. (1970). What Is a Book, That a Man May Know It?, *Bulletin of the Cleveland Medical Library, 17*(2), 32-43.

Shera, J. H. (1971). The Sociological Relationships of Information Science, *Journal of the American Society for Information Science, 22*, 76-80.

Smith, J. B., Weiss, S. F., and Ferguson, G. J. (1987). A Hypertext Writing Environment and Its Cognitive Basis, in *Hypertext '87 Proceedings* (pp. 195-214), New York: ACM.

Smith, L. C. (1976). Artificial Intelligence in Information Retrieval Systems, *Information Processing and Management, 12*, 189-222.

Smith, L. C. (1981). "Memex" as an Image of Potentiality in Information Retrieval Research, in R. N. Oddy *et al.* (editors), *Information Retrieval Research* (pp. 345-369), London: Butterworths.

Smith, L. C. (1989). "Wholly New Forms of Encyclopedias": Electronic Knowledge in the Form of Hypertext, in S. Koskiala and R. Launo (editors), *Information * Knowledge * Evolution; Proceedings of the 44th FID Congress held in Helsinki, Finland, 28 August-1 September, 1988* (pp. 245-250), Amsterdam: North-Holland.

Soergel, D. (1977). An Automated Encyclopedia—A Solution of the Information Problem?, (Pt. 1, Sections 1-4), *International Classification, 4*, 4-10.

Stefik, M., Foster, G., Bobrow, D. G., Kahn, K., Lanning, S., and Suchman, L. (1987). Beyond the Chalkboard: Computer Support for Collaboration and Problem Solving in Meetings, *Communications of the ACM, 30*, 32-47.

Stevens, N. (1983). Library Technology—The Black Box Syndrome, *Wilson Library Bulletin, 57*, 475-480.

Tague, J. (1969). Association Trails, *Encyclopedia of Library and Information Science, 2*, 55-81.

Thornburg, D. D. (1988). From Metaphors to Microworlds: The Challenge of Creating Educational Software, *Computers and Education, 12*, 11-15.

Trigg, R. H. (1988). Guided Tours and Tabletops: Tools for Communicating in a Hypertext Environment, *ACM Transactions on Office Information Systems, 6*, 398-414.

Trigg, R. H., and Weiser, M. (1986). TEXTNET: A Network-based Approach to Text Handling, *ACM Transactions on Office Information Systems, 4*, 1-23.

Turoff, M. (1977). An Online Intellectual Community or "Memex" Revisited, *Technological Forecasting and Social Change, 10*, 401-412.

Utting, K., and Yankelovich, N. (1989). Context and Orientation in Hypermedia Networks, *ACM Transactions on Information Systems, 7*, 58-84.

van Dam, A., and Rice, D. E. (1970). Computers and Publishing: Writing, Editing, and Printing, *Advances in Computers, 10*, 145-174.

Waters, S. T. (1986). Answerman, the Expert Information Specialist: An Expert System for Retrieval of Information from Library Reference Books, *Information Technology and Libraries, 5*, 204-212.

Weyer, S. A. (1982). The Design of a Dynamic Book for Information Search, *International Journal of Man-Machine Studies, 17*, 87-107.

Weyer, S. A. (1988). As We May Learn, in S. Ambron and K. Hooper (editors), *Interactive multimedia* (pp. 87-103), Redmond, WA: Microsoft Press.

Wigington, R. L. (1987). Evolution of Information Technology and Its Impact on Chemical Information, *Journal of Chemical Information and Computer Sciences, 27*, 51-55.

Wilson, J. H. (1966). As We May Have Thought, *Proceedings of the American Documentation Institute Annual Meeting, 3*, 117-122.

Zellweger, P. T. (1989). Scripted Documents: A Hypermedia Path Mechanism, in *Hypertext '89 Proceedings* (pp. 1-14), New York: ACM.

Hypertext — Does It Reduce Cholesterol, Too?

Norman Meyrowitz

Introduction

IF YOU LOOK BACK JUST TWO YEARS AGO to the Hypertext '87 conference, there were literally only two books available with any great mention of hypertext. These were Ted Nelson's *Computer Lib/Dream Machines* and *Literary Machines*. By 1989 there were a dozen books fundamentally about hypertext that I could gather from my office in under three seconds. And there are literally scores of others that purport to be about hypertext that are sprouting up like dandelions. One hypothesis is that all the books that were supposed to be about cold fusion were reprinted with new covers about hypertext.

So what's happening with the field? I wonder and I worry that hypertext may be the oat bran of computing, that we may be so excited about perceived potential that we miss some of the real advantages and some of the real impact that hypermedia and hypertext could have amidst all of the hype. What I want to do today is look at the impact of hypertext and hypermedia and how it can survive and be something nutritious for us all.

What Is Hypertext, Really?

First we have to figure out what hypertext is. To some of us it's graphical programming à la HyperCard. To others it is outline processing à la More or Acta. To others it is multimedia presentations that you make to the board of directors containing a lot of dancing dollar signs and so forth. And to others it's simply glitz replacing substance: no longer do I have to think because now these pictures are moving, and moving pictures look interesting.

One can glean, by reading the conference proceedings and tracking the press, that other people think that hypertext is fundamentally a tool for teaching writing. There are people who think that hypertext is a

This essay is based on a talk delivered as the keynote address for the Hypertext '89 Conference in Pittsburgh, PA, November 1989.

reference tool, a way to put encyclopedias or dictionaries online. Some are focusing on hypertext as a way to do argumentation, as a way to focus and connect the different parts of an argument. Some are looking at hypertext fundamentally as a backbone for group decision support, as a way to put together all the disparate decisions of an organization.

Others are excited about hypertext for interactive fiction, as a means for creating new types of novels. Others are looking at hypertext as a way to do annotations, commentary, and criticism. Still others see it as the library of the future, a grand vision where hypertext replaces the current public libraries. Others who are represented at the conference see hypertext as the physician's dream, where all the medical textbooks are online with immediate access to the information that is needed, or the attorney's dream where all case law, all briefs, and all citations are immediately accessible. And still others see hypertext as a funding mechanism now that their object-oriented programming grants have run out.

Hypothesis

My hypothesis is that hypertext is all of that, but hypertext is more. Down deep, we all think and believe that hypertext is a vision that sometime soon there will be an infrastructure, national and international, that supports a network and community of knowledge linking together myriad types of information for an enormous variety of audiences. So when we speak of hypertext and hypermedia in terms of our dreams and our passions, we're talking about having information at our fingertips in all the natural ways. Hypertext may be too narrow a term — we're envisioning this exciting information environment of the future.

A Roadmap

To give you a roadmap of the talk, or a trail or a path, what we're going to do first is take a hypermedia tour through some of the Vannevar Bush papers — "As We May Think" and "Memex Revisited" — looking at what he said and trying to correlate what he was talking about with where technology is today, how far we've advanced, and where we yet have to go. Then we'll look at the Memex of the 1990s, at what a potential information environment might look like given the context of today's machines, marketplace, and where things are going. Finally, we'll look at some challenges in the field, what I think the major challenges are for all of us if hypermedia is to have the payoff that we all hope it will.

Touring Vannevar Bush

Bush's Vision

The first thing we have to look at is Bush's vision. His vision, as we all know, is the Memex. The following illustrations are based on the actual pictures from the September 1945 issue of *Life* magazine, in which an artist rendered Bush's ideas with Bush's approval.

The Memex (below), as Bush coined it, was a future device for individual use. It was an individual's private library, private file system, and as he called it, "an enlarged intimate supplement to his memory." And that was key — intimate supplement to memory. It was something personal, something with which you were truly engaged. As we move forward, these are very difficult goals to strive for, having something in which you can store all your records, store all your communications, and yet be so speedy and flexible. It's a big vision to live up to.

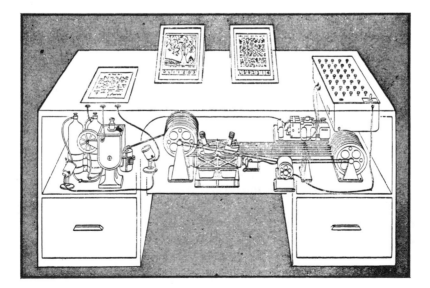

Technology

Pictures and Photos. As we look at some of the technology that Bush envisioned, we see that he thought that pictures and photos would be of great importance, that the "camera hound of the future would wear on his forehead a lump a little larger than a walnut" (Bush, 1945:102). It would take pictures that would be projected, enlarged, and stored. In Bush's vision, one would take a lot of pictures for the record.

Where are we today? This is a picture of Bush's camera (below).

The closest we have to this right now in the hypermedia field is Ben Shneiderman taking pictures at conferences. But there **are** some tech-

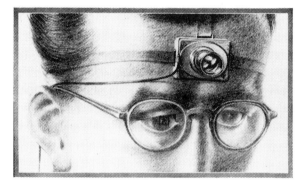

nologies that are starting to look very, very promising. Instead of using film, which no longer is a fast enough technology for the magnetic-digital era, the Sony Mavica still video camera and the Canon still video camera allow you to take and capture photographs on a two-inch magnetic floppy disk. You can take those pictures and eventually display them on a computer screen. Right now it's cumbersome. It's not Bush's vision of taking a picture, plugging it into the Memex and having it stored. Today you have to put the image up on a TV set, use a frame-grabber, and download the image to your computer. So it's a pain in the neck, but the basic technology is there to make photography much more integral, to be able to take pictures and have them go right into your record. Kodak's recently announced Photo CD promises to put one hundred very high resolution copies of your color prints onto a compact disc for later display and manipulation on a computer or TV screen.

Similarly, the Sony 8mm Video Handycams are as tiny as a Japanese passport, with zoom, autofocus — the whole bit — and you can get four hours of video on a $5 videotape. So we have the technology for recording, but we still need the technology for storing and playing that back via computer. We're only halfway there, but we've made a lot of progress.

Voice. The next thing that Bush talked about was voice. Bush said that the author of the future would cease writing by hand and would instead talk directly into the record. But where are we right now? This was his picture of a Vocoder (below).

We actually don't have anything that looks like this right now, fortunately, but we are making some strides on voice recording. There's the Xerox PARC Etherphone experiments. Polle Zellweger and others

have incorporated hypermedia paths into a system using voice recording that is quite nice. That's available right now on a research basis. There are now commercial products like Farallon's MacRecorder for the Macintosh and a new product that will do voice annotation. There's LipService, a voice electronic mail system on the NeXT machine, and there are the ubiquitous digital telephone voice mail systems that we all use, in which our voices get digitally recorded when we try to call somebody. (It's a little-known fact that nobody really exists in Silicon Valley, there are only digital telephone systems taking messages.)

But we haven't yet solved the automatic transcription problem. There are many research projects that have realized basic voice understanding, but this isn't an area that has of yet been terribly fruitful. Physicians and lawyers, for instance, make great use of dictation, but until they can have a machine that converts dictation automatically into text, they're going to think this computer and hypertext technology is all a second-order effect. So if hypermedia is going to be provocative, and we want to have a permanent record, you have to be able to speak the record, rather than type the record.

Wireless Networks. Bush also talked about wireless networks. He said "One can picture a future investigator in his lab. His hands are free and he's not anchored. . . . He moves about and observes. . . . Times are recorded automatically. . . . If he goes into the field he may be connected by a radio to his recorder" (Bush, 1945:104). How close are we to that vision?

There are currently a variety of portable computers you can get containing cellular phone modems. Without having to be near a telephone, you can log in at 2400 baud. There is also an intriguing technology coming from a company called Agilis — a DOS and UNIX portable computer with a packet radio Ethernet connection. By using the airwaves, without even the need for an FCC permit, you can now link at 10 megabits per second back to a server. This starts to become exciting. So we're potentially within a couple of years of having whole wireless networks where you are not tethered to your machine.

Handwriting. Handwriting recognition was another very appealing technology that Bush thought about. He said that the individual using the Memex "can add marginal notes and comments. . . .can take advantage of dry photography. . .and can [write handwriting] using a stylus scheme" (Bush, 1945:107). We've replaced dry photography with scanning, but where is handwriting recognition right now? Essentially, we're again within a couple of years of having some breakthroughs. Grid has a new portable computer with a stylus mechanism. You can actually write on the portable's screen and it will translate into text. IBM's T. J. Watson Research Center has shown versions of a stylus mechanism where you can actually fill in a Lotus 1-2-3 spreadsheet with a stylus, and it will automatically convert it to numbers. And there are indications that pen-based computing may be an interesting battleground in the 1990s, with GO Corporation's Penpoint and Microsoft's PenWindows squaring off in the marketplace. If we can incorporate this very promising capability into our hypermedia environments, we will start to get the information environment that people envision.

Scanning. Scanning — where are we with mass data input? Bush wrote that "On the top of the Memex is a transparent platen. On this are placed longhand notes, photographs, memoranda, all sorts of things. When one is in place, the depression of a lever causes it to be photographed onto the next blank space. . ." (Bush, 1945:107). That sounds like a great vision, but where are we? Scanners exist, but by and large they're not personal yet. They're still shared, except for little hand scanners which are fairly cumbersome to use. The software for scanners is still cumbersome beyond belief. Bush talked about putting a piece of paper on a platen, pressing a lever, and it was done, like a copying machine; it went somewhere in the Memex automatically. The way you use most scanners is that you open up an application, you preview the scan, you change the threshold, you scan it three times, you finally get it, you have to name it as a file, you forget the name, you can't find the scan anymore. Scanning is something you can't do with abandon. You have to do it very carefully because it takes a long time and a lot of storage. So we're not there yet, but we're close.

Similarly with optical character recognition (OCR). There are many personal OCR programs that are pretty good, except they still take too long, two or three minutes per page, there's still too much intervention, and the accuracy isn't good enough. What you want to be able to do, if you're going to have this information environment, is take all the paper that you get in the mail, throw it in a hopper like your copy machine hopper, press a button, have it automatically scanned, timestamped, named and put in a folder for you. Later on you can do some information retrieval on it to see if there is anything of interest to you or browse through it very quickly. You can't do that today. If you want to OCR something, you're very explicit about wanting to get one particular article. You'd really like to be less explicit, have the system just read in all of your mail, first class or junk, and later only present to you the items that pass a particular filter. So we have some work to do here.

Bush also said "if the user inserted 5000 pages of material a day it would take him hundreds of years to fill the repository, so he can be profligate and enter material freely" (Bush, 1945:107). Where are we in terms of that vision? I took a little liberty to do some experiments. If you look at bitmap scanning today, it's about 1 minute per scan; you can only do about 480 per day in an 8 hour day if you don't eat or anything like that. At 3 minutes per page for an OCR scan, you can do about 160 OCR scans per 8 hour day. So we're off Bush's projections by a factor of somewhere between 10 and 50.

Storage. Now let's look at storage. If we do 5,000 pages at 2,000 bytes per page for machine-readable text, we're talking about 10 megabytes a day, or 3.65 gigabytes per year. We can do this with optical disk or magnetic disk storage, but it's not all that inexpensive, though it's close. When we start getting into digitized graphics — if we're talking about low-resolution monochrome, 75 dots per inch, which is what a Macintosh screen is, for example — an 8 1/2 x 11 inch page or picture takes 64 kilobytes per picture. You now need about 320 megabytes a day, or 100 gigabytes a year, which is a lot of storage. And when you talk about hi-resolution color — 150 dots an inch with 8-bits per pixel, or the Macintosh 75 dot per inch resolution, but with 32-bits per pixel for true color — that's about 2 megabytes per page, 10 gigabytes a day, or 3.65 terabytes a year. If you're using twenty 500-megabyte optical disk cartridges, which will give you 10 gigabytes, you have about a $5,000 a day optical disk habit. There are some compression schemes that can get these numbers down significantly, but this is still an area where we need several orders of magnitude improvement. Today's optical disks are just not as big or inexpensive as we might want them to be. So Bush was being somewhat optimistic, I think, in terms of where would be. Though we have made great strides in digital storage, there's still further to go.

In terms of storage, Bush said, "The *Encylopædia Brittanica* could be reduced to the volume of a matchbox. A library of a million volumes could be compressed into one end of a desk" (Bush, 1945:103). I did some calculations, and I'm happy to report that the matchbox right here — and I believe these are the same matchboxes that Bush had in 1945 — is 27.24 cc and the CD ROM right here is 13 cc. Encyclopedias like the *Brittanica* text, the *Compton's Encyclopedia, Grolier's,* and some other encyclopedias have been put on the CD ROM medium, so we have reached Bush's desired storage density and solved one of his problems.

Access. Bush also said, "A record, if it is to be useful to science, must be continuously extended, it must be stored, and above all, it must be consulted" (Bush, 1945:102). One of the problems we have here is that even if we have the storage density — the CD ROM matchbox containing the *Encyclopedia Brittanica* — CD ROM is not necessarily the medium that is most appropriate. First of all, you typically can use only one reference work at a time because you have only one CD ROM drive, and swapping CD ROMs is a pain in the neck. The retail price of the CD ROM is still largely prohibitive. The price is at least $200 per CD ROM for volumes that often cost much less in print (even though the CD ROM medium itself costs under $5 to produce, even in limited quantities). Accessing the same information over slow national networks at large amounts of money per minute is not the right way of handling this storage problem, either. Just because we have the density of CD ROM or optical disk doesn't mean we've solved the access problem.

Use

Selection. Besides technology, Bush talked about use, and he was very interested in selection and association. He said, in a famous quote, "Selection [of that day]...is a stone adze in the hands of a cabinet maker" (Bush, 1945:105). It was so hard to find something in the library, to find information, because we weren't giving people the appropriate tools.

Where are we now? Today, manual selection of things is the paradigm that we use in desktop computing — pointing at something and selecting it as our focus. Trying to find the focus by actually browsing through entire works is a very labor-intensive, manual effort. Search by content, finding information by its attributes or its semantic content, is still haphazard. And we still have the same filename problem that we've had for 20 or 30 years. Unless you are a very disciplined or compulsive user, it's very difficult to think of a name for something when you're first creating it. Later on when you want to find it, you can't recall it because you didn't have the proper name for it in the first place. We are still locked into that mechanism today.

Association. In terms of selection and association, Bush had this vision of "two items to be joined, projected onto adjacent viewing positions. At the bottom of each are a number of blank code spaces, and a pointer is set to indicate one of these on each item. The user taps a single key, and the items are permanently joined" (Bush, 1945:107).

That sounds about as close to hypertext as we've been in this tour. This was his vision of the system circa 1945 (below). Interestingly, even to this day there are an inordinate number of hypertext systems out there whose designers still haven't realized that when you want to link

two things it is often essential to see them both at the same time. So multiple windows and multiple viewing surfaces are quite important, and it is unfortunate that they aren't seen as fundamental to all hypertext systems.

Furthermore, is creating links that easy? Is it so seamless in our systems? Is it done in the context of daily work? Bush was talking about being able to create links at will. Right now, with most of our systems you have to get into your hypermedia application, import the text from your text processor, import images from your graphics editor, and wade through a lot of dialog boxes. By the time you're done making links you've forgotten your original context. So we have a problem with the way hypertext systems are implemented today: they are not and cannot be used easily in people's daily work. They are used as special-purpose applications rather than as the primary tools with which people operate.

Automatic links. Bush also talked about automatic links. He said that, "we can expect it [Memex] to do clever things for us in the handling of the mass of data we insert it into it. We particularly expect it to learn from its own experience and to refine its own trails" (Bush, 1967:94-95). There has been some work in that, but there are not very many hypertext systems that people can actually use to make automatic links. There's been some work on similarity measures at the University of Strathclyde. Jim Coombs at IRIS has done some work on using text patterns to link together various articles (Coombs, 1990). There's work on Bayesian inferencing by Mark Frisse at Washington U. (Frisse, 1989) and by Croft at U. Mass. (Croft and Turtle, 1989) and work on clustering by Crouch at the University of Minnesota (Crouch *et al.*, 1989). It's worthwhile to look into this area and see how we might put automatic linking into our systems and have them learn for us.

Social Issues

Contents/Materials. Bush talked about some of the social and cultural implications of the Memex, of hypermedia. He said, "most of the Memex contents are purchased on microfilm ready for insertion. Books of all sorts, pictures, current periodicals, newspapers, are thus obtained and dropped into place" (Bush, 1945:107). Again, where are we right now? I think we're not very far on that. By and large we have specialized, hard-wired content which you can buy, that comes along with specialized, hard-wired applications. You can get *Grolier's Encyclopedia*, or *MedLine*, or Ziff-Davis's *Computer Select*, but they all have their own idiosyncratic interface. They're all very functional in and of themselves, but they're all very separate, and it's impossible just to buy data. You have to buy data and some program to read that data. So every time you buy another piece of data that's interesting to you, you have to learn a whole other interface and a whole other retrieval mechanism. Will we ever get to the point where we're not selling software, but we're actually selling just the content? That's a question we must ask ourselves.

Funding. Finally, Bush talked about funding. In his 1967 paper, "Memex Revisited," he said, "The libraries still operate by horse-and-buggy methods, for there is no profit in libraries. Government spends billions on space since it has glamor and hence public appeal. There is no glamor about libraries, and the public do not understand that the welfare of the children depends far more upon effective libraries than it does on the collecting of a bucket of talcum powder from the moon" (Bush, 1967:81-82). He didn't think that the Memex would be done soon, but that eventually it would be created. So where are we to this day? Perhaps it's not the space program that's the scapegoat in the 1990s, but there are other programs that are taking over the funding that we should be using for building up our intellectual infrastructure, and it is still a real problem.

Why is this? Is hypertext so difficult to get funding for? There is no money and there is no glitz in creating an information network, but we need to have significant government leadership and scientific strategic leadership to make this a primary effort in our country, and internationally as well.

So What's Wrong?

This picture is not so bleak. A lot of the technology is just around the corner for putting this all together. So what's wrong with hypermedia? What do we have to do?

Does everyone remember the rotary telephone? You may not, but this was part of the desktop infrastructure for 30 years, and it did not change very much. It stayed virtually the same for years and years and years. Only recently did you get telephones like today's feature-phone. It took a long time to get these new handsets, which have much more functionality. Why was that? One possible reason was the whole notion of monopoly, thus the phone company did not need to innovate. But I think another reason was that instead of working on the handsets, the "end-user applications," the phone companies spent much of the 1960s, 1970s, and early 1980s building the infrastructure, building the connectivity that allows you to make a call now virtually anywhere in the world, so that you can have long distance services that are virtually error-free and ubiquitous. Building the infrastructure is incredibly important.

The real question we have to ask ourselves is how do we build the infrastructure for hypertext? Where is this information environment going to come from? What is it going to look like so that we're not simply building fancy handsets but building handsets that connect to other handsets and give us this vast information environment that Bush was talking about?

The Desktop of Tomorrow

My contention is that if hypermedia is to catch on and secure its place in the computing repertoire, we have to integrate hypermedia features into the standard desktop environment that we are all used to today. The infrastructure has to be integrated into the standard computing environments and standard networks of today and tomorrow. There's an installed base of 30 million IBM PCs and compatibles and 3 or 4 million Macintoshes. It is fairly egocentric to have anyone in the field of hypermedia say "We're just going to create a new environment, and it's going to be a wholesale replacement for all the existing environments that people are using." Instead we have to work somewhat "within the system" to create an exciting environment. But I think existing personal computer systems are set up so that we **can** create stimulating information environments. The next third of this discussion looks at how all of this might work, how we might integrate hypermedia technologies into the desktop of tomorrow.

Requirements. What do people want to do, in terms of what Bush was talking about and in terms of hypermedia? They want to create content — graphics, text, and so forth. They want to reference things. They want to associate content. They want to have references not only to static media but to dynamic media. They want to have tools that tell them where they are in a vast information space. They want to do some filtering and querying and searching on that information. They want information processed automatically. They want to work in groups. They'd like to have some semantics to their information so it has some intelligibility. And they'd like to have some standard information services. I want to go through each of these topics and talk about how they might be addressed in the desktop of tomorrow.

Content. One of the things that we have to wrestle with is that the content that people want to deal with is diverse. The following are some of the different types of information in which people are interested:

Rich Text	3-D/Rendered Graphics
Structured Graphics	Voice
Bitmap Graphics	Audio
Timelines	Music
Tables	Statistical info
Video	Modeling info
Animation	CAD/CAM
Spreadsheets	External databases
Calendars	Reference materials
Cartographics	Symbolic math

There are many more. The information that people want to link together ranges from CAD/CAM drawings to animations, from symbolic math to voice, from bitmap graphics to timelines, and to other things I have not even put down here. One of the questions we must ask is "Can any hypermedia system provide all of these types of content?" Can Intermedia provide all of those kinds of applications? Can NoteCards? Can KMS? Can any? No. Why not? Can any application developers, can any third-party developers, provide all the applications that are out there? If you look at the big players, Microsoft and Claris and Lotus, you'll see that they can't provide all the applications. So it stands to reason that if they can't provide all the applications, neither will they be able to provide all the applications and provide a hypermedia environment, too. The only way we are going to get all the content editors that people want **and** all the hypermedia functionality they want is to have third-party developers create applications that handle appropriate content, while hypermedia functionality is built into the desktop system just like cut, copy, and paste, so that all application developers can participate. Then you'd be able to link together documents from all the applications, all the content that you normally deal with.

Anchors. So how is this done? First, we have to add the concept of *anchors* to the desktop environment. People are very familiar with selection. Everybody seven years old and up knows how to select things on a Mac or on a PC with Microsoft Windows. So we have to extend the notion of selection to an *anchor* — a persistent or "sticky" selection. People already know how to create a selection, so you say to users, "hey, if you do this special thing, the system will remember your selection next time, as if you had run over the item with a yellow highlighting pen in your text." That's the first thing we have to do. Any entity now, which users already know how to select, can be an anchor, a selection that's persistent, that's stored over time. The system can remember an insertion point or a word or a paragraph in text, or an object or a group of objects in graphics, or a cell or a row or a range of cells in a spreadsheet. If we have anchor functionality as a fundamental part of our system, then we have the basis for hypermedia. Anchors are essentially the next level of desktop integration; they're the next stop after selection and cut, copy, and paste. We want to be able to have anchors that have names, that have attributes so that we can do queries on them, and that can be the source or destination of links. So you'd be linking to very fine-grained things, not the very coarse card or document, but to whatever you had actually pointed out. Even if you didn't want to have links to them, you could store these anchors as bookmarks, as important areas that you wanted to highlight permanently in your document.

Navigational links. The next thing we want to do, now that we have anchors, is to introduce the notion of *navigational linkage* into the desktop. Previously, we've had cut, copy, and paste. Everybody knows how to do that now. What we want to do next is have navigational linkage, where you can have a persistent tie between two anchors. If we have a user interface similar to cut, copy, and paste —where instead of saying "cut" you say "start link," instead of saying "paste," you select something and say "complete link," and a link is created between the two — it will be very easy to teach people, because they already know how to do cut, copy, and paste. In this desktop architecture, we should make sure that links are bidirectional so you can both follow forward references and also find out who references you. Since any anchor may be a very significant anchor, like the beginning of the Gettysburg Address, for instance, you want to make sure you can have more than one link emanating from that anchor, so it can be linked to many things. You want to have a very rich structure down at the desktop level, not a very basic one, so that users can model as many things as they like.

Warm links. From navigational linking we want to go to *warm linking.* We want not only to be able to follow a link from source A to destination B, but also to exchange data over that link. We want to be able to push data that's in a selection in document A into document B, or vice versa. If we're in document A and there's something significant at the other end of the link, we want to be able to pull that data in and have it replace our current selection. This allows us easily to create updates of information that everyone links to. If you have a central paragraph or list of telephone numbers that often changes, you can pull the new information in. The important part is that we can use the same mechanism that we use for navigational linkages for these warm linkages (Catlin *et al.*, 1989).

Hot links. Similarly, we want to use the same architecture to support *hot linkage*. Hot linkage is the automatic synchronization of anchors at two ends of a link, such that when you edit the information in one anchor, the altered information automatically is broadcast to all the other anchors that are linked to it and is typically editable everywhere. That's currently being done partially in some individual applications such as Lotus' Jazz and Modern Jazz (which actually never was released) for the Macintosh. In Apple's System 7.0 there's a publish and subscribe mechanism, for Microsoft Windows on the PC there's DDE (Dynamic Data Exchange) and OLE (Object Linking and Embedding), as well as Hewlett-Packard's New Wave. So we're beginning to have mechanisms that allow us to have this hot linking, this hot copy and paste. One very difficult problem is editing any type of element in any other document. If you want to be able to paste the bottom line of a spreadsheet into a word processing document and be able to edit the bottom line of the spreadsheet in the word processing document, suddenly you have to have editing capabilities for spreadsheets in your word processing application, or you have to have some object-oriented protocols and building blocks such that when a piece of spreadsheet data gets put into a word processing document, all the editing facilities and all the capabilities come along with it. Carnegie-Mellon's Andrew system and HP's New Wave begin to have these capabilities, but are not in widespread commercial use. Yet as object-oriented programming and those type of architectures become more prevalent in the systems that we all use, they hopefully should become common commercially within the next two or three years.

Active Anchors. After you have this hot linking, again using the same basic mechanism as navigational linking and warm linking, you have to start looking at dynamic links, or links to *active anchors*. Today's applications, by and large, are passive applications. You essentially bring something up, you edit it, it immediately gets updated, and the control is returned to the user. Newer applications like animation, video, music, and voice are temporal in nature. They exist in time; they're not static. Creating links to them and creating links from them are a very complex problem. Anchors now have to represent time spans, and one has to start creating standard mechanisms and standard policies so that when a user follows into an active anchor, the appropriate thing happens. For example, when the user follows into a video clip, do you want the clip automatically to start running? Do you want the software to pause at the beginning of the clip and wait for the user to issue the play command? Do you want the author to be able to specify that option? These are all issues that need to be worked out, but we have to have some consistency and some policy that works the same for all temporal applications. There is some work going on in this area. We've done some work (Palaniappan *et al.*, 1990), Randy Trigg has done some in the VideoNoter project (Roschelle *et al.*, 1989), and Tim Oren has been looking at some of those issues in the HyperCard context (Oren *et al.*, 1990).

The dynamics in anchors are not only limited to the temporal axis. Especially for model-driven animation and rendering, the anchor has to reference not a temporal span, but a set of viewspecs that will allow the destination view to be computed at follow time with the same parameters as were used when the link was made.

Wayfinding. Wayfinding capability is the next thing that we have to put in the desktop environment, and this is not simply for hypermedia. It's for all the desktop, because separate from hypermedia, people still have these same questions: What's my current state? What have I done right now? What have I done in the past 5 or 10 minutes? And what can I do next? Where can I go? What's available to me?

History. Those wayfinding questions can be answered by a variety of mechanisms. We need to add *history* and *paths/trails* to the desktop environment. For history, even separately from hypermedia, the system should remember all of the windows you have on the desktop and all of the ones that you've opened that session. If you look at the PC and the Macintosh, every application typically has its own "window" menu that tells you all the open windows for that application, but not for the other applications. You spend a lot of time switching between applications and then switching between window menus finding what is open and what's not. I'd like to have a standard mechanism: one window that gives you the history of everything that's been opened, everything that's been closed, everything that's been followed into, everything that's been activated and so forth. This history window should be included as part of the desktop environment and should include hypermedia information, but not just hypermedia information. That's very, very important.

Paths/Trails. Paths and trails are very important, too (Zellweger, 1989; Marshall and Irish, 1989; Trigg, this volume). There have been some nice breakthroughs in how to do those paths. Paths are essentially histories that have been captured, edited, shortened, and made into concrete desktop objects that can be played back. Again, we're trying to look at keeping within the desktop metaphor. The important thing about paths is that we'd like users not to have to program these paths but to be able to create them by actually doing the traversals and editing out events that they don't necessarily want to keep.

Maps. The next type of wayfinding that we need is mapping. There has been some work done on maps, and the general conclusions are that global maps of large hypermedia systems don't give people particularly useful information. If you have a binary tree approach that spreads out visually, you don't see enough of the information, because the information isn't topological and you can't create a global map that has any continuity; the information is all over the place. So rather than spending a lot of time trying to create global maps, which become unwieldy with massive amounts of information, we should concentrate on creating local maps. These give you the details of your local environs and how you can branch one level or two levels out from your local environs. It's easy to generate these local maps, and they give people good cues as to where they can break out of their current environment. If you are in a city, you typically do not take out a world atlas to find out where the open restaurants are; you take out the local city map. Again, these maps should be an intrinsic system structure. They should be generated as you open the desktop, and as you open new documents, they should automatically be updated. People get familiar with them;

they're there all the time. This is not something that you have to batch compile, or make on the fly, or draw yourself; it's done for you by the system.

Filtering. We want to make sure that with hypermedia we do not fall into the trap of thinking that it can solve all problems. We have to have a nice, tight coupling between hypermedia linkage–browsing technology and information retrieval technology. We want to be able to apply filters to our hypermedia on system attributes such as author, creation date, and modification time and on user-supplied attributes and values, so that you can start issuing some complex queries. We need to have *collection filtering* where we can run a query over an entire hypermedia web yielding a list of all the hits that fulfill the criteria, and *exposure filtering* where we hide or display the icons that indicate anchors and links based upon the filtering criteria. So it's the Engelbart *viewspecs* notion, where we can have various things exposed based upon criteria that we issue. We have to have these notions of filtering in the desktop so that all of our information can be filtered, hypermedia information being just one of the types of information that we care about.

Queries. We need to do something about queries. We need to have easier to use interfaces for creating queries. The state of queries for end users is a total mess. Not because there aren't good interfaces. In fact, there are a hundred good interfaces, and that's the mess. When you get any database program or any full-text retrieval program or any large database that's out there on a Macintosh or a PC, it comes with its own idiosyncratic interface and its own strategy for doing boolean expressions and for specifying keywords. It's time there was a standard, system-provided query sheet that individuals could fill out, save as a concrete object on the desktop, and open up to have a query issued automatically, accessing a diverse set of databases with the same user interface. You no longer would need separate interfaces for every type of database you had. One of the problems with such a strategy, however, is determining how much power one needs in the query interface. One ends up in large arguments: Do we have to give the users all the power of SQL? Do they have to have nested queries — "give me all the documents with this keyword that have anchors in them with that keyword that have links in them with this other keyword"? Or do we need to have much simpler queries that allow users to get better feedback very quickly? These are the very knotty issues we have to tackle. We have to start standardizing on some of these things so **users** can actually start using our systems.

Content Searching. We have to start looking at *content searching* as well as the keyword-type filtering that I talked about. We must see that full-text searching is compatible with hypertext, and together they are much more synergistic and useful than they are separately. Again, you want to have full-text indexing as a system function. So for any application, as long as it has some text in it, whether it be a graphics document, or a spreadsheet, or a text document, the text is indexed. And it's indexed behind your back. There is no full-text database into which you have to force your documents. Behind your back the system is reading documents as you change them and computing an index for you, so that you can find all the documents that have particular words in them. Having that system anticipation, where it indexes things before you explicitly ask, is liberating. You get some positive fallout from having full-text retrieval that helps in the next feature that I'll discuss, *virtual linkages*.

Virtual Links. One of the things that Frank Halasz mentioned in his Issues paper at Hypertext '87 is the notion of virtual linkages (Halasz, 1988). Often you don't want to explicitly, manually create the anchors at both ends of the links. Often you'd like to anchor something at the source, but what if the resultant documents and anchors at the other end of the link are going to be the result of a query? Well, if you have full-text indexing you can suddenly have a link anchor to some source that, when followed, a query is issued saying, for instance, "find me all the documents that have the word 'lipid' in them." The system then does a full-text search on all the documents, system-wide, to find those that meet the criteria. Well, if you don't have full-text indexing, if you want to have a virtual link like that, the system has to painstakingly search through or *grep* through (for all you Unix hackers) the content of each document in the system. If you have a full-text index, you can start to have virtual linkages that occur instantaneously, because the system simply looks at the index, not the actual content of all documents. That becomes very, very exciting. The synergy between full-text indexing and virtual linking is quite significant. Again, we want to have these virtual linkages in the desktop environment as part of the linking technology that all applications participate in, with full-text in there as base functionality as well.

Automatic links. Automatic linkage is something else that we'd like to have in the desktop environment, though this might be a little further out than the previous features. You'd like to have the system, while you're gone for the evening, bring new information into the system (from mail or newswire, for instance), forge links in the background based upon patterns or Bayesian inferencing, or clustering, and notify you in the morning. You'd like to have different options for this. The system might just do the whole process automatically. Or perhaps it should allow the user to review each link as it is created. Or perhaps it should make all the links but replay them through a history mechanism and let you get rid of the ones that you don't like.

Group Work. Finally in terms of some additional hypermedia features, we'd like to have some group work technologies. We'd like annotations, like notes — the Post-It™-like notes that have become prevalent in a lot of hypermedia systems. We're seeing a little of this already. Applications like MacDraw, spreadsheets like Excel, all have little note facilities. Rather than having a hundred different application-specific note facilities that work differently, let's have note facilities for leaving little pop-up notes as something that's standard on the desktop, so you can create a note on any application with the same user interface. Importantly, and this doesn't occur with all note implementations today, you want the notes to keep track of their anchors in the document as you edit the document. You want to make sure that your annotations stay in synch with all of your content. A lot of the annotation programs you can buy in the market turn your document into a bitmap, and you can attach notes to the document. But you're not attaching notes to a live document, you're creating notes to a dead document. While behind your back somebody else is editing the real document, your annotations no longer reflect the state of the real document. We have to use hypermedia technology that keeps our anchors correlated with our notes as we edit the document and create annotations.

Similarly, we want to have annotations that allow us to draw or write notes on top of documents much like we would use an acetate sheet, and again, we want those acetate marks — those proofreader's symbols or whatever — to work on editable documents. As a document is edited, the marks would move about the acetate to keep in synch with the content to which they are anchored.

As I mentioned earlier, we'd like to integrate voice as a desktop medium. NeXT has done that in its mail system. We want voice to be easily used in the hypermedia context as well. Essentially, voice is an application, and you want to link to and from voice just like any standard application, using the standard, system–provided linking protocols. Another area to explore in hypermedia and group work is using hypermedia linkages in the desktop environment to handle the threads in mail and conferencing systems.

Semantic Markup. Beyond pure hypermedia issues, there are other things we want in the desktop to support this information environment. Semantic markup is one of them. Right now, our WYSIWYG (what you see is what you get) interfaces are by and large procedural. There is a lot of manual labor in changing rulers, moving objects around, changing patterns, and so forth. We'd like to start moving away from that, still using a direct manipulation interface, but beginning to have more semantics of document style. Just as Scribe had in batch systems, you'd like to have, in all direct manipulation systems, standard document style sheets so that documents of a particular type can be created from templates that are already filled out. You can start having object-oriented document classes, where you have, say, a Personnel document, and you can create subclasses of that for UnionEmployee or NonUnionEmployee. Now where does hypertext come in? We'd like to have hypermedia templates as classes. This is similar to the notion of composites that Frank Halasz discussed in 1987 (Halasz, 1988:843). You want to have links set up automatically between different documents, so you can create a class of document that already is prelinked to another class of document, and when you instantiate a class you get an entire web of empty template documents, but with all the links pre-made. Once we can start doing that, you won't have to manually forge every link that you create, but rather have the system understand some of the inherent linkages between documents.

Services. Finally, we want to have some *services* in the desktop of tomorrow. Besides *linking* services, other services that are important are *reference* and *linguistic* services. You want to have the reference tools that you're used to, like dictionaries and glossaries, integrated into the system in a standard way, with a standard dictionary protocol so that all dictionaries can be accessed through the same type of interface. You'd like to be able to have multiple dictionaries and set up a dictionary path so that when you select a word and issue the "look up" command, the system follows a path you have set and tries to find the word in all the dictionaries you have put in your dictionary path, your virtual bookshelf. You want to have a way for people to make their own glossaries. Often work groups have their own terminology, their own acronyms, and people should be able to create glossaries in a group, and have them work just like the real *American Heritage Dictionary* or the real encyclopedia. You want the glossaries to use the same protocols and the same mechanisms, so your personal dictionary is part of the dictionary path you normally use. Of course, we want thesauri to use that same mechanism.

We'd like to have spelling correctors and grammar correctors in the desktop. Today all the spelling correctors that exist are application-specific, and you have to learn 27 different spelling correctors to use all of the different applications you normally run. All of these utilities and reference tools should be part of the base system, with third parties supplying the actual data and specialized extensions.

We'd like to have morphology services. Right now, when you do information retrieval and type in a word like "filter," you will typically get "filter," and sometimes "filtering." We want to start using morphology, linguistic analysis where you can get "refilter," and "unfilter," and all of the morphological derivatives of that word, which will give much better hits from information retrieval queries. It might be nice to have standard pattern-search mechanisms. Again, if you look at today's applications, every single application that's around has a different interface for doing pattern searches, but by and large each is doing the same thing. We'd like that interface to be a standard in the desktop.

Challenges

Hypermedia fits very well in the desktop as the next level of integration, but it needs a lot of support if it is going to be exciting and important. So as we enter the final part of this discussion, we want to look at the challenges.

Challenge 1: Let's start putting the theory into practice. Let's build and analyze the systems that we create, especially at appropriate scales, and test them out on users, not just ourselves.

One of the challenges we have is that our field is very compelling to ponder. Many fields have too little vision, and in some sense, our field has too much. We can hear and see and taste and smell the future so well that sometimes we forget to build it. Just as the perfume that comes in the airline magazines isn't the real thing, we have to make sure that when we're talking about having large, multi-user hypertexts, that we are building those things, and not just doing proofs of induction where $n = 1$ and that's it.

Challenge 2: Input and ouput mechanisms must be central to my daily work for hypertext to take hold.

The next challenge is the technology challenge of input and output. As we saw, scanning, OCR, handwriting recognition and annotation, and voice input and recognition are all getting there. We have to start working with the developers of these technologies to get them to recognize that these devices need to be intrinsic and integral to our system, so that they work seamlessly. You can't create systems that have all of the peripherals working as if they just met the CPU today. They have to be intimate, so the scanner, the OCR, and the handwriting recognition work well with the system. It's a matter of having hardware developers and peripheral developers work closely with the hardware platform developers and system software developers. So "peripheral" is a misnomer. Input/output technologies must not be peripheral to the system, but rather central to an integrated environment.

Challenge 3: Make the screen display exceed paper. Until individuals choose a computer over paper for reading, hypermedia will not catch on.

Richard Saul Wurman is one of my favorite graphical information designers. A page from his *London Access* guide is dense with information represented by text, graphics, icons, symbols, maps, and color. A page from the new *U.S. Atlas* he just did provides new clarity for road atlases by using crisp graphic images coupled with sound organization. One of the interesting things about the atlas is that it was done entirely on the Macintosh, using desktop publishing. But it was done in a way such that you could never present this density of information on the screen. You can print it out to get color separations and so forth, but the technology just isn't there to completely display this sophisticated information on the screen. One of the challenges is to make the screen display meet or exceed that of paper output.

Right now desktop presentation is still pretty lousy. Computer graphics folks typically focus on and get their jollies over how **long** a time it takes to make one screen, rather than how short a time it takes to generate a screen of information, and we have to try to change that attitude around.

The low density of screens, even though they're much higher than they used to be, still is not good enough to present information like the Wurman atlas pages. We need to have flatter screens and much higher resolution, at least 150 dots an inch, better color, and so forth. We need to have portable screens that have better resolution. We're not there yet. Hypermedia is only going to catch on if the screen exceeds paper.

Challenge 4: We need a removable storage medium of the 1990s. We need cheap, random access, exchangable, ubiquitous storage — the gigabyte floppy.

We must not think that we have all the storage problems solved. CD ROM and CD-I technology is a weak technology for interactive computing. It's a great technology for transmitting information because CD duplication simply involves stamping out injection-molded plastic, which is much cheaper and much faster to do than recording magnetic or optical media. But we don't want to be condemning all data to be read-only and non-malleable. We want individuals to be able to annotate and manipulate the information. We need to start making sure that we have a ubiquitous medium that is as dense as CD ROM but is also very interactive. We need to have removable medium of the 1990s just like the 3 1/2" disk of the 1980s. But it has to be a 1 gigabyte floppy disk that is cheap and with which everyone can transmit information, store information, and link information.

Challenge 5: We need a common anchor model. Just as all applications now handle selections, all applications must handle anchors.

As the next challenge, we have to devise a common anchor model. We have to start seeing anchors as fundamental parts of the system. We have to come up with standard ways in which to train users to create anchors, and standard ways to indicate the existence of anchors, just as we came up with ways to indicate non-persistent selections.

Challenge 6: We need to work on multi-user issues. As researchers, we need to better formulate the requirements and solutions for sharing.

We have to look at multi-user issues. Hypertext has been going through the emperor's new clothes syndrome, where we talk about it as a multi-user technology and a wide-area technology but typically the systems are single-user systems that aren't networked and don't solve many of the multi-user problems. We have to move from workgroup to local-area network to wide-area network and concentrate on the problem of shared hypertexts. We need to look at a problem that has not adequately been addressed: that of shared keyword indices and authority lists, and how to handle conflicts. Most indexing done today is done by professionals, using large authority lists, who typically divide up a large corpus and work on separate parts. If you look at the results, there are many inconsistencies between indexers. If we now have shared hypertexts, and we want to have multiple individuals create a single index, we need to provide a model for all individuals to see the shared keyword taxonomy, to notice conflicts, to manage synonyms, and to create their own private taxonomies when the group taxonomy doesn't meet their needs.

Similarly, it's still unclear how we should deal with document transfer and exchange. If I create an item here, and create a link from it and send you a diskette, do you have a copy of the information that was linked to it or just a reference? As for the source document, is there any way to know what the genealogy of the information is, where that document was first created, so that if I receive a modified version of my original it can be automatically merged back in? These multi-user problems have not yet been solved even at the small group level, much less at the local-area or wide-area level, so there is much challenge ahead.

Challenge 7: We need transferability and sharing through a national and international file system, with transparent internetwork addressing, file addressing, and anchor addressing.

We also have to address the multi-user issues from the wide-area perspective. How do we begin to manage document addressing and uniqueness? Do we use a model like the proposed Nelson/Xanadu back-end byte stream protocol? There is a new project called the Collaboratory that Bill Wulf at the National Science Foundation is getting underway. It proposes to create a national collaboration network, a "center without walls," hooked together through a transparent national and international file system. Regardless of the base technology that is used, we have to begin to deal with the creation of a national and international infrastructure allowing true addressing to the anchor level.

Challenge 8: Apply object-oriented techniques to hypertext.

How do we make hypertext be something other than unstructured programming, a melange of gotos with no coherence? Structured programming helped slow down the proliferation of spaghetti code by introducing a stricter notion of subroutine calls and a standard "methodology" of entering and exiting routines. Object-oriented programming went a step further by allowing users to model objects that pointed to other objects, and coupled the notion of data structure with data *behavior*. Classes serve as templates from which objects of like structure and behavior are manufactured, and from which objects with similar structure and behavior can be refined/subclassed. We need to look at object-oriented techniques for hypermedia. Documents are the end-user objects, and links are the pointers connecting objects. We need to look at document classes and webs from which linked structures can be spawned and refined. And we have to look at knowledge lattices and taxonomies as ways to organize such classes in an intelligible fashion.

Challenge 9: We need funding for long-term research in the hypermedia and information arenas.

There are some social challenges. How do we get funding for this area? It's a massive research project of national and international import, but government research support for this area is tiny. There's been a bill before Congress sponsored by Al Gore, for a $1.9 billion high-speed national network largely for supercomputing. How do we make sure that this is not only for supercomputing, but forms the basis for a national network that is speedy enough to support a hypermedia information environment?

How do we convince those with the funding of the need for longer-term research? Right now you can get funding for short-term work in hypermedia, but that's largely from companies saying "We'll give you some money to port Intermedia to the X Window system on our Bazinga Workstation in the next three months" or "Can you create an electronic version of this particular manual by next quarter?" That's not going to further the field, that's just going to help some companies gain visibility or produce a product with a very short shelf life.

Challenge 10: We must encourage trailblazers and allow the scaffolding and rhetoric of hypertext to evolve by rewarding such work professionally.

Bush talked about the profession of trailblazers, those who would create the links between records and be the modern-day editors in the hypermedia world. You'd be able to see not only the content that an expert creates, but the scaffolding from which it was created.

The problem is that there are few experts today who are actually making those linkages, because there aren't hypertext systems they can use in their daily work. The rhetoric of hypertext still isn't all that well understood, although there are beginning to be some good efforts.

The other problem is that junior faculty members do not get tenure for creating hypertext linkages, and so the freshest scholars, and often the people with the most creativity, do not get rewards for creating hypertexts, and in fact are strongly discouraged from doing so. How do we allow the scaffolding and the rhetoric to flourish, to be rewarded, and to be a professional activity?

Challenge 11: Re-examination of copyright laws to achieve parity between rights of author/publisher and needs of community.

Will copyrights be replacing ambulances as the thing that lawyers chase? The copyright issues have just not been addressed. I don't have any particular details about how the laws need to be changed, but there needs to be a concerted effort to re-examine these issues by those people who have both the necessary technical expertise and the legal expertise. They need to examine the copyright law and make sure that the owners of information have their rights, but that the community of people who need to use that information, without profiting directly from it, can have their rights, too.

Challenge 12: Let's understand the policies we are trying to capture before standardizing on a mechanism to capture them.

There are the challenges of hypermedia standards. Standardization is a good thing at appropriate times, but we shouldn't standardize on something if we don't know what it is. We shouldn't standardize on hypermedia until we understand hypermedia policy. A lot of people standardize on mechanism, and then soon realize that it was the policy — how you use things — not the mechanism for storing or representing them, that they needed to standardize on. X Windows is a great piece of technology, but they standardized on the wrong problem. Everyone has agreed on X Windows as the mechanism for display windows and graphics, but there is total discontent about which user interface package, which policy, should go on top of that. They haven't standardized on anything because they're all fighting about what package is going to sit on top of X Windows. We shouldn't do that in hypermedia.

SGML is an important standard, but we should make sure that we don't stretch it too far. We should make sure that it really works. Often standards get created but don't get used. A lot of applications can write out SGML subsets, but very few of them can read full SGML back in. We need to make sure that standards are fully operational, and easy enough to be widely implemented.

And then there are other standards organizations that are downright dangerous. They just like making standards. If they perceived an inkling of a "ransom note" standard, they would be gathering a committee right now.

So we should standardize, but we should first make sure that we're standardizing the policy, and not just the mechanisms, of hypertext.

Challenge 13: Publishers should make available, for the next 2 years, machine readable copies of their holdings for non-commercial research in hypermedia by qualified institutions.

Publishers own materials and copyrights on those materials, but there is little research in building hypermedia versions of the materials. Publishers are primarily interested in creating real products immediately. If we don't have material for hypermedia researchers, or hundreds of big works which researchers can put into a large hypermedia corpus, we're never going to understand the issues of generality and scale, and we're never going to be able to push our systems forward. It is to the publishers' advantage to let researchers have access to a wide range of materials for research purposes so that researchers can push, not only the technical attributes of hypermedia systems, but can foster breakthroughs in the process of creating and linking materials as well. So I challenge all the publishers here, and all the publishers who are not here, to make available over the next two years, at no cost to qualified hypermedia researchers, large amounts of content, so we can actually experiment with what we need to sustain long term hypermedia development from the system side and the materials development side.

Challenge 14: Linking protocols from all major vendors within the next 2 years. By Hypertext '91, all major platform vendors (IBM, Microsoft, Apple, NeXT, Sun, Digital, HP, etc.) should supply application-independent protocols for hypermedia and the information environment.

The final challenge is the "missing link." This is a summary of what I've been trying to propose throughout the talk.

Today's monolithic hypermedia systems are compelling, they're reasonably easy to build and design — as we can see from the more than 20 demos scheduled this evening — but in some sense, they're doomed to failure because they're just one more application off to the side.

The current level of integration is the desktop metaphor and cut/copy/paste. It is prevalent and has caught on because it's easy to learn. It was functionality that everyone wanted, just as hypermedia functionality is desired today, and it was integrated deep in the system with a protocol provided to application developers in system-level toolboxes that allowed them to add cut, copy, and paste to their applications at very low cost.

If hypermedia is to survive and blossom, the major vendors need to provide system-level hypermedia support where there are standard linking protocols that all developers can participate in, providing support for anchors (navigational, warm, and hot linking), wayfinding support for maps, paths and history, support for keyword, content search and filtering, automatic links, and virtual links.

We no longer want separate hypermedia applications. We want a linking protocol deep in the system. We want the applications that everyone uses today to be the nodes of the hypermedia system. We want to move from the era of the clipboard to the era of the linkboard, where documents from the regular applications that we use every day — Lotus 1-2-3, Excel, Microsoft Word, AutoCAD, MacDraw, WordPerfect, etc. — are the entities that we can link to and from.

So the challenge is for all major platform vendors, the IBMs, the Microsofts, the Apples, the Suns, the NeXTs, the Digitals, the HPs, whoever, to supply application-independent protocols for hypermedia in their systems, so that we can have the current system architectures as the basis for the information environment of the future.

Conclusions

That bring us to the question "Hypertext — Does It Reduce Cholesterol, Too?"

There are a couple of answers. One is that sources tell me that yes, in fact, HyperCard Version 2.0 will have a cholesterol reduction feature. I'm not sure how reliable those sources are.

Another way to answer that question is to say that just as oat bran is important for reducing cholesterol, so is hypermedia important for reducing information clogging and information glut. But just as a diet of nothing other than oat bran is not the ultimate key to health, neither is a diet of nothing other than hypermedia the key to our information well-being. What we need is an information environment, in which hypermedia is an important and fundamental element, but is just one of a balanced diet of elements that, together, bring us towards the vision that Vannevar Bush set out for us in 1945.

References

Bush, V. (1945). As We May Think, *Atlantic Monthly*, 176(1), 101-108.

Bush, V. (1967). Memex Revisited, in *Science Is Not Enough*, (pp. 75-101), New York: William Morrow.

Catlin, T., Bush, P. E., and Yankelovich, N. (1989). InterNote: Extending a Hypermedia Framework to Support Annotative Collaboration, *Hypertext '89 Proceedings* (pp. 365-378), New York: ACM.

Coombs, J. H. (1990). Hypertext, Full Text, and Automatic Linking, *International Conference on Research and Development in Information Retrieval (SIGIR '90)*, Brussels, Belgium.

Croft, W. B., and Turtle, H. (1989). A Retrieval Model Incorporating Hypertext Links, *Hypertext '89 Proceedings* (pp. 213-224), New York: ACM.

Crouch, D. B., Crouch, C. J., and Andreas, G. (1989). The Use of Cluster Hierarchies in Hypertext Information Retrieval, *Hypertext '89 Proceedings* (pp. 225-238), New York: ACM.

Frisse, M. E., and Cousins, S. B. (1989). Information Retrieval from Hypertext: Update on the Dynamic Medical Handbook Project, *Hypertext '89 Proceedings* (pp. 199-212), New York: ACM.

Halasz, F. G. (July 1988). Reflections on Notecards: Seven Issues for the Next Generation of Hypermedia Systems, *Communications of the ACM*, 31(7), 836-855.

Marshall, C. C., and Irish, P. (1989). Guided Tours and On-Line Presentations: How Authors Make Existing Hypertext Intelligible for Readers, *Hypertext '89 Proceedings* (pp. 15-26), New York: ACM.

Oren, T., Salomon, G., Kreitman, K., and Don, A. (1990). Guides: Characterizing the Interface, in Laurel, B. (editor), *The Art of Human-Computer Interface Design*, Reading, MA: Addison-Wesley.

Palaniapann, M., Yankelovich, N., and Sawtelle, M. (1990). Linking Active Anchors: A Stage in the Evolution of Hypermedia, *Hypermedia*, 2(1), 47-66.

Roschelle, J., Pea, R., and Trigg, R. (March 1990). *VideoNoter: A Tool for Exploratory Video Analysis* (IRL90-0021), Palo Alto, CA: Institute for Research on Learning.

Zellweger, P. T. (1989). Scripted Documents: A Hypermedia Path Mechanism, *Hypertext '89 Proceedings* (pp. 1-14), New York: ACM.

Memex: Getting Back on the Trail
Tim Oren

Bush's Changing Vision of the Trail

THE NOTION OF A TRAIL, OR SEQUENCE OF ASSOCIATIONS, is central to Bush's vision of the Memex. He believed that the human mind was organized with "some intricate web of trails carried by the cells of the brain" (Bush, 1945:106). The intent of Memex was to extend the human memory by building a device that acts by such associations rather than by "artificial" numerical, alphabetical, or hierarchical indexing schemes. In more modern terms, Bush believed that a Memex based on trails would provide a match between the cognitive structures of man and machine.

Bush was quick to admit that we could not "hope fully to duplicate this mental process artificially" (Bush, 1945:106). However, he believed that shortcomings of the mechanical implementation could be ameliorated by other advantages. It is a key point that Bush's estimation of the potential of the artificial Memex to mimic the trails of the mind shifted dramatically during his career. The watershed is marked by his exposure to early machine learning technology.

In Bush's 1940s vision of Memex "trails do not fade" (Bush, 1945:107). This is seen as a key advantage of an artificial system over human memory. The permanence and literal nature of artificial storage would be memex's advantage, to set against its lack of "speed and flexibility" in comparison to the brain.

By the time of his later writings, Bush accounted for developments in digital computers and had seen early examples of machine learning. In all of his later Memex works, he mentions (without explicit citation) Samuel's famous checkers playing program. This system learned to play at the level of a human expert due to a combination of careful choice of data representation and parameter adaptation to wins and losses in actual and archived games (Samuel, 1959; Jackson, 1974). This program raised expectations for machine learning in the professional community and became an object of notoriety in the popular press (Anon., 1959a; Anon., 1959b). In "Memex Revisited," Bush gives a popularized version of the parameter adjustment learning strategy used by the checkers player, so he was clearly familiar with the details of the work.

Bush's extrapolations from this early learning research as well as the advent of digital computing were incorporated into a revised vision of the Memex. Where before he thought that a (opto-mechanically-based) Memex would be slower than the mind, now "it will progress along trails at lightning speed" (Bush, 1967:22).

More significantly, Memex will now "learn from its own experience, refine its own trails, explore in unknown territory to establish trails" (Bush, 1967:22). In the earlier Memex, trails were immutable once entered, though the user could extend them manually. By the time of *Pieces of the Action, both* brain and machine trails have the property that "if not used they fade out; if much used they become emphasized" (Bush, 1970:191). Memex will now notice which items in a trail are seldom used and which digressions are commonplace, and automatically adjust the course of trail accordingly. Further, it will "explore in unknown territory to establish trails." I will refer to this later vision of Bush as the *adaptive Memex* or *adaptive trails*.

Impact of Bush's Changing Vision

It is Bush's earlier vision of Memex and trails, as documented in "As We May Think," which has become enshrined as an image of potentiality or concept symbol for later workers (Smith, 1981 and this volume; Small, 1978). It has been particularly influential on three fields that have direct bearing on constructing an adaptive Memex: hypertext, optical disc publishing, and information search and retrieval. This image has combined with the research agendas and historic technology limits of these fields to produce an emphasis on systems that are public, rather than personal, in nature and that emphasize the value of the static record over adaptivity.

Hypertext

Nelson's seminal description of hypertext, *Literary Machines*, is very explicit in its heritage from Bush; some editions reproduce the entire 1945 article. However, in citing Bush, Nelson states:

> The memex was a publishing system that would hold everything that is written, and allow each new user to add connections — Bush called them trails — to connect and clarify the material that's already stored. (Nelson, 1987)

Here Nelson has conflated Bush's individualized memexes into a centralized publishing system. The owner has become a user. Rather than individually inserting externally created trails into a personal Memex, the user now obtains them as part of this central system. The design of Nelson's proposed Xanadu hypertext system indeed revolves around a universal, standardized repository for all digital information. While private spaces may be maintained, once documents and links are explicitly published, they are part of a permanent record. While subsequent users (and the original author) may link to, annotate, or create revisions of the publication, the original is to remain fixed in order that others' links and annotations will not become rhetorically invalid.

Later in the same volume, Nelson is explicit in his suspicion of "advocates of Artificial Intelligence [who] would have computers decide what the reader shall see," further evidence of a stance in favor of immutability, as opposed to any sort of adaptive browsing mechanism.

While the Xanadu system has yet to be implemented, the heritage of hypertext as a medium for public discourse is still clear in the field. A number of researchers have emphasized that their systems' value is bringing explicit, public representations of rhetoric to the process of collaboration and argumentation (e.g., Conklin and Begeman, 1987; Smolensky *et al.*, 1987). The use of hypertext in externalizing personal knowledge and structuring public discourse continues to be pursued by many workers; see Streitz *et al.* (1989) for an example and survey.

Bush's idea of trails as means of orientation within an externally produced corpus is also being reflected in current practice. Trails in this role have also become known as paths and tours. An example in the domain of classical scholarship is given in Mylonas and Heath (1990), and a sample for legal argument is shown in Marshall and Irish (1989). Due to the lack of compatible, open hypertext systems, these trails have thus far been limited in scope to a single database and the hypertext system which produced it.

Optical Media

In the last five years, the advent of inexpensive, read-only optical discs capable of holding the content of several hundred conventional books has supported the beginning of an information publishing industry not tied to online access. Again, the Bush influence is very explicit, with an early volume of articles on optical media reprinting "As We May Think" in its entirety (Lambert and Ropiequet, 1986).

Bush had predicted that:

> Wholly new forms of encyclopedias will appear, ready-made with a mesh of associative trails running through them, ready to be dropped into the memex and there amplified. (Bush, 1945:108)

This and other visions of an encyclopedia of the future (Weyer and Borning,1985) were very conscious guides to pioneers in optical media. It was no accident that the first general audience optical disc product to be implemented and capture the public imagination was an encyclopedia (Foster, 1985; Caruso, 1985; Marchionini and Schneiderman, 1988). The notion of a "multimedia encyclopedia" was a feature of early CD ROM industry conferences and continues to be a central theme of the industry's marketing and product offerings.

The dominant optical disc technology, CD ROM, is mass produced and is not rewritable. Economies of scale mean that all users receive the same version of the data. Annotation and trail building are impossible on the base medium — a system must be specially engineered to store such personalized characteristics on a parallel, writable store (Carr, 1986).

The publication of "static" texts and hypertexts on optical disc has emphasized the issues of authority, editorial control, and layout that are common with public printed works (Oren, 1987). The metaphor of the electronic book has become common in both optical media and hypertext (Yankelovich *et al.*, 1985), and a number of hypertext systems have authoring modes that are explicitly separated from the browsing function (Shneiderman, 1987; Walker, 1987). The net effect, again, is to emphasize the permanent record aspect of the memex vision.

Information Retrieval

Smith (1981 and this volume) reports on a comprehensive survey of citations to Bush's 1945 article from works in the area of information retrieval. It is clear from this work that Bush's earlier vision of the Memex had a large role in shaping the research agenda of the field of information retrieval. It remains here to discuss the technological and conceptual issues which jointly shaped and reinforced that agenda. Textual information retrieval first became useful in the 1960s, an era of expensive processing and mass storage units that were centralized, and first batch operated and later timeshared among many users. User terminals of the time were electromechanical, and local memory and processing power were nonexistent.

In such an environment, all text and indexing information was perforce stored centrally. Given the high cost of such storage and the potential size of the data structures, one inverted index was built and consulted for queries from all users. This notion of a fixed document index against which queries would be tested for similarity became the central dogma of information retrieval (see for instance Croft, 1990). It persists to the extent that the common definition of "user relevance feedback" is to adjust the query so that it better fits the public index (Salton and McGill, 1983).

Existing online, full text retrieval systems suffer from poor performance in the hands of end users, even those trained in the information domain at hand (Blair and Maron, 1985). It proves impossible to find a large fraction of the relevant information without also retrieving much data that is essentially noise. The root of this difficulty may lie in variations of language use and meaning by individuals and in literary conventions such as using multiple words for one concept rather than repeating a single word within a passage. Testing has shown that the ability of multiple individuals to produce the same descriptors for common objects is quite limited (Furnas, 1983). The effect of pooling heterogeneous documents and queries in a public index may be to extract a "consensus reality," which is useful but forever limited in its performance for any one individual.

As we shall see, the advance of computing hardware has undermined many of the implicit technology assumptions built into the research agenda of information retrieval. However, one advance, the optical discs described above, has perpetuated the current situation by mass producing the indexing information along with data, though both are intended for individual consumption.

Only in the end of the period surveyed by Smith did those citing Bush's 1945 work begin to turn their attention to the personal aspects of Memex (e.g., Paisley and Butler, 1977). This theme occurs at the same time that personal computers begin to play an important commercial role. Bush's later works, in which the adaptive theme emerged, are seldom cited. A search of the Citation Index shows only two references to "Memex Revisited" from the hypertext and information retrieval technical literature (Meyrowitz and van Dam, 1982; Utting and Yankelovich, 1989). No citations to *Pieces of the Action* (Bush, 1970) were found in these literatures. Clearly, Bush's later vision of the Memex has had a minor impact on retrieval research compared to the concept symbol status of the 1945 article.

Characteristics of the Adaptive Memex

From Bush's first vision, Memex was to be a private device into which public encyclopedias and colleague's trails and information might be inserted to be joined with the owner's own work. In the adaptive Memex, the owner's trails are to be mutable, with the possibility of change and fresh creation by the Memex itself. Clearly the locus of such an evolving index of trails is personal. The union of all the permuted trails of all owner's memexes into a public space could be Babel indeed.

The adaptive Memex is acting on behalf of its owner, who delegates partial authority to make correlations or adjust the weight of those already made. This adaptation proceeds in parallel with the owner's work, for his or her habits of association must be observed, but without interference in the tasks at hand. Actions taken by the Memex are reflected in its storage for later observation and possible correction by the owner.

The adaptive Memex is acting as what has been termed an "agent": the owner has delegated the authority to make observations of use habits and effect corresponding changes on the storage and presentation of the Memex contents (Kay, 1984). The remainder of this paper examines the technological and representational issues in creating such agents within a personal, adaptive Memex.

Toward the Adaptive Memex

The Future of Personal Computing

Though Bush's first notion of a Memex was extrapolated from optical-mechanical technology, his later work reflects the advent of digital computing, which has now reached the power and compactness for true personal systems. At the time of this writing, a researcher's personal computer commonly has several hundred megabytes of magnetic disk memory, 4 to 16 megabytes of RAM, and several MIPS of processing power. As noted above, these capabilities already exceed those of entire mainframes of the 1960s; however, their effective utilization is very low. Unlike centralized mainframes, where every expensive cycle was timeshared if at all possible, today's personal computers largely spend their time running idle processes, even when the user is seated in front of them. An adaptive Memex based on today's machines could make effective use of this wasted resource and greatly increase the utility of personal computers at little additional cost. The hardware potential to construct adaptive personalized data stores already exists.

The projected computing environment of the next decade will put increasing resources even closer to the individual. Portable computers will free this power from the desktop to travel wherever the owner goes. Wireless interconnect will make the physical location of the owner's storage irrelevant as well as give access to numerous public databases. Parallel processing will greatly increase the power of computers and make it even easier to compute intensive tasks without disrupting the user's work. These trends in performance may make some currently impractical adaptive algorithms feasible.

The dominant paradigm of interaction with today's personal computers is the so-called "desktop metaphor," invented at Xerox PARC, commercialized at Apple and since widely imitated. While this has allowed great advances in usability, it was originally designed for systems with a few hundred files on 5 to 10 megabytes of storage. The purely user-directed browsing style of the desktop is approaching its limits of utility, with the number of files on a single user's machine often reaching 10,000 and with easy access to even more information across networks. The increasing popularity of products such as On Location™, which allow very simple searching of a user's files, indicates a recognition by many users that the desktop metaphor alone is insufficient for organizing personal information.

Existing interfaces and personal computers are largely directed toward the task of creating text, graphics, and integrated media documents. In a computing environment that is increasingly interconnected and information rich, the user's role will shift from author toward analyst. Rather than creation *de novo,* more attention will be paid to the problems of selection, comprehension, and integration of existing pieces of knowledge. As this description strongly resembles the task of the scientist, a job which was Bush's design center for the Memex, we may have some confidence that his ideas will be relevant to the next generation of personal computing.

Getting from the current state to a system which approaches Bush's latter vision of the Memex will require advances in both our notions of user interface and in underlying algorithms. We need interfaces that effectively mediate between the user and complex underlying algorithms, and we need new data representations and adaptive algorithms that make effective use of massive computing power in the hands of end users.

Adaptivity and Agents

In an adaptive Memex, the owner has delegated to the machine the ability to propose or effect changes in the stored information. By analogy to business practice, the Memex is said be functioning as an agent (Kay, 1984). The machine is playing an autonomous role within a restricted charter: to attempt a more effective organization of the information based on observations of actual use and topical similarities.

In current user interface practice, predictability is valued over autonomy and adaptivity. Interfaces such as the desktop metaphor represent the state of the information contained, but they do not initiate actions. In the pure "direct manipulation" paradigm, actions leading to a change of state are always initiated by the user. The task of the interface is to reflect continuously the change back to the user until the manipulation is completed (Shneiderman, 1983). The changes are to remain until the user again acts.

Introducing agents, hence the possibility of autonomous change in the user's absence, upsets the basic assumptions of this interface style and the expectations that users have formed about their computers and stored information. New representations will have to be found that lead users to accept and effectively utilize adaptivity and form correct models of its utility and limits. Though this problem is inherent in Bush's technological vision, he did not explore its ramifications.

There are many examples of static information organization from the real world: desktops, file cabinets, card boxes, and so on. Natural sources of metaphor for autonomous, directed action are more scarce. For many people the easiest model of an entity with these abilities is another person—anthropomorphization of mechanical devices of even limited autonomy is a well-known phenomenon.

The simplistic reaction to this observation is to equate the entire functionality of the computer with a single human figure, as has been done in a number of design studies and promotions of future technologies, e.g., Apple's Knowledge Navigator video (1987). However, the current state of the art is unable to support the expectation of flexibility and conversational ability that may be raised by such a figure. The introduction of the human image sets expectations of character and associated coherent action, which must be carefully examined and designed (Laurel, 1990).

The functionality of an autonomous system may be divided among several characters, each with a limited but consistent set of abilities and a portrayal strongly associated with these capabilities. Results from such experiments indicate that users are willing to accept artificial figures that are not fully conversational, but fill other known roles such as storytellers (Oren *et al.*, 1990; Laurel *et al.*, 1990). Such characters acting through time can make up stories, and efforts are being made to apply dramatic and narrative theory to the construction of frameworks for agent representation (Don, 1990; Laurel, 1991).

The technologies currently in prospect for implementing agents are fallible and will probably err at times in suggesting items to examine, possible reorganizations of information, and other functions likely to be delegated in an adaptive system. When dealing with a human agent, such breakdowns can be repaired through conversation leading to changed behavior. The methods available for direct repair of computer agents may be limited, since the underlying data structure may be unintelligible to most users. The chosen representations will need to establish the possibility of error and suggest what methods of critique are available. For instance, one system has represented agents as newspaper reporters, suggesting flexibility but shallow understanding — a reporter may occasionally "blow an assignment" (Erickson and Salomon, 1991).

Though the use of character to represent agency may seem a natural step, there will be many occasions when it is inappropriate. In some data and task domains, there may be no character representations that correspond intuitively to the abilities of the agent to be represented. Many users have strong preferences against the use of the human figure. We may also find that character is a naive metaphor, temporarily required to introduce the possibility of action to users who have heretofore assumed that information is static.

Dynamic Information

In Bush's original Memex, the user would create a trail, name it, and place the name in a code book. Though there is a problem of remembering and retrieving this name later, the creator at least has the advantage of recognizing its significance and recalling the original thread of association and argument that made the trail coherent. Trails received from colleagues and public sources have the additional burden of names whose connotations may not be so obvious. Since the user did not create these trails, they must contain a good deal more annotation or comment for the discourse to be clear.

With the introduction of adaptive, Memex-generated trails, further problems are faced. The computer must construct a meaningful name or other representation of the trail to indicate its presence and purpose to the user. Within the trail, the Memex may need to indicate and elaborate the rationale for construction if it is not obvious to the user. Neither of these issues was examined by Bush, but current work in dynamic assembly and layout of text and multimedia documents, as well as investigation into the generation of explanatory text, may offer approaches to what amounts to an issue of machine-generated rhetoric.

By associating a collection of documents, a trail effectively creates a view of their contents different from that originated by the author. Furnas (1986) proposes the "fisheye view" as a generalized mechanism for emphasizing points of interest within a structured document or collection. This notion was applied in the Superbook system, which alters the view of a document's outline or text stream based on the results of user queries (Egan *et al.*, 1989). Kohda (1991) also proposes that the presentation of documents, for instance the font face and size, be distorted to emphasize salient features.

What appears to the user to be a single document might actually be assembled dynamically. A number of systems have taken the approach of composing items retrieved from news wires and other information sources into a single "newspaper" to be browsed by the user (Lippman and Bender, 1987; Erickson and Salomon, 1991; Bender *et al.*, 1991). Xerox's Tioga editor, among others, allows the creation of active documents where portions of the text may be computed or transformed during the display or editing process. Recent advances in commercial operating systems, such as Window's DDE and Macintosh's publish/subscribe will make it feasible to add such features to widely available applications, increasing users' awareness that a document need not be a static entity.

When the user's information contains elements such as sound and video, the layout problem gains a temporal dimension (Tonomura and Otsuji, 1991). Just as a user's sensitivity for the conventions and meaning of page layout must be taken into account in text, so principles of cinematic composition must be considered when dynamically assembling temporal elements (Rubin and Davenport, 1989). While currently the markup that would enable such composition must be manually logged and attached (Davis, 1991), some progress has been made in automatic segmentation of time-based material (Ueda *et al.*, 1991).

All of these approaches attempt to convey coherence by knitting the linked or assembled information into an apparent whole. Perhaps more in the spirit of Bush is to maintain the separate identity of the information elements while providing active guidance to the user who is browsing the trail. Some approaches to guidance create a single trail using procedural programming (Zellweger, 1989), while others use statistical techniques to generate a range of choices which are biased toward coherent next moves (Oren *et al.*, 1990). Frisse and Cousins (1990) provide a survey of approaches to implementing and representing guidance.

In both the layout and guidance approaches to dynamic information, the computer may be called upon to render an explanation of the correlation that has been made. If the information was assembled in direct response to a user request, this may be done by reference to this query. In the case of adaptive behavior, which may be occurring as a result of a user's acts over an extended period, this easy referent is not present, and the adaptive Memex will have to generate a more elaborate justification. There is a large literature on automatic text generation (see Paris *et al.*, 1989 for an example). Recent work has begun to explore the specific issues of generating explanation (Suthers and Woolf, 1990) and automatically laying out text to convey meaning (Arens and Hovy, 1990). However, all of these approaches presently rely on the existence of knowledge representation structures, which must be manually coded and are unlikely to be available for most documents.

Adaptive Technologies

To support the adaptive Memex, software technologies that respond to the individual must be developed. There is currently no single candidate that is both general and scalable. However, we can lay out a number of the requirements for adaptive software technology for information access and explore the current state of progress in each direction.

Individual Data Collections

Search and retrieval methods using weights based on the aggregate statistics of word occurrence in databases have been in use for some time (Salton, 1983). A simple step is to employ the same statistical methods when dealing with an individual's collection of data. However, most retrieval schemes make the naive assumption that the occurrences of words within documents are independent distributions. This is obviously not the case, and it is possible to take advantage of covariances to find term to term relationships implicit in the stored data. For instance, the Latent Semantic Indexing technique (Deerwester *et al.*, 1990) employs singular value decomposition of a document vs. word array to find an optimal subspace to represent the total feature distribution.

Applied to one person's pool of information, such a technique has the potential to find patterns in vocabulary that are idiosyncratic or peculiar to that person's work. This knowledge may make personal retrieval more effective. It could also be applied to construct interest profiles for external information filtering or to suggest search terms when dealing with external databases.

Conventional retrieval deals primarily with similarity, that is, finding documents that are known to have in common their resemblance to a query. In dealing with personal information, it is just as important to deal with distinction, meaningful difference between classes of documents that define the range of the personal data and may suggest new organizations. Such distinctions are supported by clustering techniques.

It was observed early that techniques such as factor analysis could be used for clustering in a retrieval environment (Baker, 1962; Borko and Bernick, 1963; Ossorio, 1966). In many cases, clustering has been employed to improve the efficiency of storage and retrieval of document indexes, but has not been represented to the user. Recent work suggests the utility of presenting the inferred structure to the user (Crouch *et al.*, 1989). Kohonen's neural network organization has been used to construct diagrams showing the meaningful clusters within a personal space (Lin *et al.*, 1991). Hidden layer neural networks can also incrementally compute the principal factors of their inputs (Lelu, 1988). Such methods may lead to systems that propose new filing organizations for personal information that represent distribution and concentration of data along thematic lines.

Integrating Heterogeneous Information

In a real Memex, clues to what items are associated for the user, or which should be presented next, will arise from multiple sources. These may include topical similarity, explicit hypertext links, evidence from expert systems or taxonomies, and task and activity models of the user. In current systems, such information may be stored in forms as diverse as semantic nets, absolute pointers, vectors, weighted inferences, or even procedural code. Drawing these together into one system presents enormous problems of data integration and scaling.

It may be better to look for some uniform representation that may be applied to these different information sources. An attractive possibility is belief networks, which employ a uniform metric of probability with consistency maintained by Bayesian rules (Pearl, 1988). This technique has been applied to the problem of retrieval in hypertexts by Frisse and Cousins (1989) and Croft and Turtle (1989) with some success, but poses challenges in knowledge acquisition and computing performance.

Relaxing the requirement of Bayesian consistency results in a spreading activation network. Such networks suffer from the difficulty of weights and activities often being "magic numbers" with relative scaling being rather arbitrary, but are potentially easier to construct and compute. Belew (1989) and Rose (1991a) have constructed spreading activation networks using edge weighting schemes derived from conventional information retrieval practice.

Suggestions and Feedback

The core function of an adaptive Memex is to suggest new trails and take the owner's feedback on their validity. Authoring aids, which use retrieval techniques to find potentially related documents and suggest them to database creators as possible endpoints for links, are beginning to appear in hypertext systems. Bernstein (1990) describes an "apprentice" that uses a simple hash-coded signatures scheme to suggest links. Coombs (1990) has integrated similar functionality into the Intermedia hypertext environment.

The majority of current retrieval systems allow the user to give feedback only by modifying the query. However, the retrieval process can also be modeled as a man-machine dialog, where the user directly critiques the appropriateness of documents suggested (Oddy, 1977). Recent advances in computer performance have made this approach more practical (Oddy and Balakrishnan, 1988), and user testing has shown that feedback through critique is superior to feedback through restatement for a large majority of users (Dumais and Schmitt, 1991). While these systems deal with large collections of unlinked documents, Frisse and Cousin's (1989) dynamic medical handbook applied critique to the display of a hypertext structured document.

Adaptive Databases

If the Memex is truly to adapt and learn, it must make changes in the underlying information based on user feedback. An early experiment modified the contents of a vector model retrieval system based on critique by multiple querents (Brauen, 1971). One of the stated goals of the research was to adapt the database to changes in scientific vocabulary over time. Though this experiment was successful, there was little follow up, perhaps due to computing hardware limits. More recently, Furnas (1985) has modified the contents of a public database by attaching users' initial query terms to the documents they eventually find and adjusting weights of indexing terms based on the frequency of retrieval accomplished via the term.

Progress in neural networks has suggested other means of accomplishing adaptation. The AIR system constructed a spreading activation network among terms and documents and adjusted edge weights based on the feedback of a community of users (Belew, 1987; 1989). The Memory Extender project (with an obvious heritage from Bush) applied the notion of spreading activation to filing in a personal computer (Jones, 1986). The SCALIR system uses an extension of Belew's techniques, but is specifically designed for adaptation to an individual's habits of association (Rose, 1991a; 1991b).

User Modeling

A final area for progress is in forming models of the user's task and organizational contexts bearing on informational associations and needs. While modeling of this sort has had some success in instructional systems where the task and desired information result are well defined, there are no systems available that approach the flexibility needed for a Memex, which might literally be put to any task in the world. From experiences in cooperative work systems, users can also be very hostile to even the most general task frameworks, if they become prescriptive of how the work is done (Erickson, 1989). If models must then be obtained from the actual user at work, how can they be solicited, explained, and critiqued without the Memex becoming intrusive and obnoxious?

Getting Back on the Trail

While Bush's later views of trails have found little note in the research literature, many recent investigations in basic technologies and representation bear on the problem of constructing the adaptive Memex. Progress in computing hardware, networking, and information publishing will continue to be a driver for such studies, whether or not the adaptive Memex becomes an image of potentiality. Agenda setters in the hypertext community have also begun to take note of Bush's later work (Meyrowitz, this volume), and the time appears ripe for a synthesis.

References

Anonymous (1959). Dr. A. L. Samuel Discusses Checker Playing Test with IBM 704, *New York Times,* July 20, 1959, (2), 27.

Anonymous (1959). Heuristics; Checker Playing Machine, *New Yorker, 35*(32).

Apple Computer (1987). *Knowledge Navigator Videotape* [#VID-041], Cupertino, CA: Apple Computer.

Arens, Y., and Hovy, E. H. (1990). Text Layout As a Problem of Modality Selection, *The RADC Conference on Knowledge-based Specification Assistance,* Rome, NY.

Baker, F. B. (1962). Information Retrieval Based upon Latent Class Analysis, *J. Assoc. Computing Machinery, 9,* 512-521.

Belew, R. K. (1987). *Adaptive Information Retrieval: Machine Learning in Associative Networks,* Ph.D. diss., University of Michigan, Ann Arbor.

Belew, R. K. (1989). Adaptive Information Retrieval: Using a Connectionist Representation to Retrieve and Learn about Documents, *Proc. 12th Intl. Conf. R&D in Info. Retrieval (SIGIR),* June 25-28, 1989, Cambridge, MA (pp. 11-20).

Bender, W., Lie, H., Orwant, J., Teodosio, L., and Abramson, N. (1991). Newspace: Mass Media and Personal Computing, *USENIX Summer '91,* Nashville (pp. 329-348), USENIX Association.

Bernstein, M. (1990). An Apprentice That Discovers Hypertext Links, in A. Rizk, N. Streitz, and J. André (editors), *Hypertext: Concepts, Systems and Applications* (pp. 212-223), Cambridge: Cambridge University Press.

Blair, D. C., and Maron, M. E. (1985). An Evaluation of Retrieval Effectiveness for a Full-Text Document-Retrieval System, *Communications of the ACM, 28*(3), 289-299.

Borko, H., and Bernick, M. (1963). Automatic Document Classification, *J. Assoc. Computing Machinery, 10*(3), 151-162.

Brauen, T. L. (1971). Document Vector Modification, in G. Salton (editor), *The SMART Retrieval System: Experiments in Automatic Document Processing* (pp. 456-484), Englewood Cliffs: Prentice-Hall.

Bush, V. (1945). As We May Think, *Atlantic Monthly, 176*(1), 101-108.

Bush, V. (1967). Science Pauses, in *Science Is Not Enough* (pp. 14-30), New York: Morrow.

Bush, V. (1970). *Pieces of the Action,* New York: Morrow.

Carr, R. (1986). New User Interfaces for CD ROM, in S. Lambert and S. Ropiequet (editors), *CD ROM: The New Papyrus* (pp. 185-193), Redmond, WA: Microsoft Press.

Caruso, D. (1985). Optical Storage: Hot Item or a Dud?, *Electronics*, September 16, 1985:26-29.

Conklin, J., and Begeman, M. L. (1987). gIBIS: A Hypertext Tool for Team Design Deliberation, *Hypertext '87 Papers* (pp. 247-252), New York: ACM.

Coombs, J. H. (1990). Hypertext, Full Text, and Automatic Linking, *International Conference on Research and Development in Information Retrieval (SIGIR '90)*, Brussels, Belgium.

Croft, W. B., and Turtle, H. (1989). A Retrieval Model Incorporating Hypertext Links, *Hypertext '89 Proceedings* (pp. 213-224), New York: ACM.

Croft, W. B. (1990). Hypertext and Information Retrieval: What Are the Fundamental Concepts?, in A. Rizk, N. Streitz, and J. André (editors), *Hypertext: Concepts, Systems and Applications* (pp. 362-366), Cambridge: Cambridge University Press.

Crouch, D. B., Crouch, C. J., and Andreas, G. (1989). The Use of Cluster Hierarchies in Hypertext Information Retrieval, *Hypertext '89 Proceedings* (pp. 225-238), New York: ACM.

Davis, M. (1991). Director's Workshop: Semantic Video Logging with Intelligent Icons, *Position Paper for AAAI-91 Intelligent Multimedia Interfaces Workshop*, Anaheim, CA.

Deerwester, S., Dumais, S. T., Furnas, G. W., Landauer, T. K., and Harshman, R. (1990). Indexing by Latent Semantic Analysis, *Journal of the American Society for Information Science*, 41(6), 391-407.

Don, A. (1990). Narrative and the Interface, in B. Laurel (editor), *The Art of Human-Computer Interface Design*, Reading, MA: Addison-Wesley.

Dumais, S. T., and Schmitt, D. G. (1991). Interative Searching in an Online Database, *Proc. Human Factors Soc.* (forthcoming).

Egan, D. E., Remde, J. R., Gomez, L. M., Landauer, T. K., Eberhardt, J., and Lockbaum, C. C. (1989). Formative Design-Evaluation of "SuperBook", *ACM Transactions on Office Information Systems*, 7(1), 30-57.

Erickson, T. (1989). Interfaces for Cooperative Work: An Eclectic Look at CSCW '88, SIGCHI *Bulletin*, 21(1), 56-64.

Erickson, T., and Salomon, G. (1991). Designing a Desktop Information System: Observations and Issues, *CHI '91 Conf. Proceedings*, New Orleans.

Foster, E. (1985). CD ROM: Megabytes into Minispace, *InfoWorld*, September 23, 1985, 27-29.

Frisse, M. E., and Cousins, S. B. (1989). Information Retrieval from Hypertext: Update on the Dynamic Medical Handbook Project, *Hypertext '89 Proceedings* (pp. 199-212), New York: ACM.

Frisse, M. E., and Cousins, S. B. (1990). Guides for Hypertext: An Overview, *Artificial Intelligence in Medicine 2*, 303-314.

Furnas, G. W. (1983). Statistical Semantics: Analysis of the Potential Performance of Key-Word Information Systems, *Bell System Technical Journal*, 62(6), 1753-1806.

Furnas, G. W. (1985). Experience with an Adaptive Indexing Scheme, *Proceedings of the CHI '85 Conference on Human Factors in Computing Systems* (pp. 131-135).

Furnas, G. W. (1986). Generalized Fisheye Views, in M. Mantei, and P. Orbeton (editors), *Proceedings of the CHI '86 Conference on Human Factors in Computing Systems* (pp. 16-23).

Jackson, P. C. (1974). Introduction to Artificial Intelligence, New York: Petrocelli/Charter.

Jones, W. P. (1986). The Memory Extender Personal Filing System, *CHI '86 Proceedings* (pp. 298-305).

Kay, A. C. (1984). Computer Software, *Scientific American, 251*(3), 53-59.

Kohda, Y. (1991). Toward the Semi-Meaningful Interface: Beyond the Direct Manipulation Interface, *Proc. Intl. Conf. Multimedia Info. Syst.*, Singapore.

Lambert, S., and Ropiequet, S. (1986). *CD ROM: The New Papyrus*, Redmond, WA: Microsoft Press.

Laurel, B. (1990). Interface Agents: Metaphors with Character, in B. Laurel (editor), *The Art of Human-Computer Interface Design*, Reading, MA: Addison-Wesley.

Laurel, B., Oren, T., and Don, A. (1990). Issues in Multimedia Interface Design: Media Integration and Interface Agents, *CHI '90 Conference Proceedings* (pp. 133-139).

Laurel, B. (1991). *Computers as Theatre*, Reading, MA: Addison-Wesley.

Lelu, A. (1988). Browsing through Image Databases via Data Analysis and Neural Networks, *Proceedings of the Conference on User-Oriented Content-Based Text and Image Handling (RIAO 88)*, MIT, Cambridge, MA: Centre des Hautes Etudes Internationales d'Informatique Documentaire.

Lin, X., Soergel, D., and Marchionini, G. (1991). A Self-organizing Semantic Map for Information Retrieval, *Proc. SIGIR '91*, Chicago.

Lippman, A., and Bender, W. (1987). News and Movies in the 50 Megabit Living Room, *Proc. Globecom '98, IEEE Global Telecomm. Conf.* (pp. 1976-1981).

Marchionini, G., and Shneiderman, B. (1988). Finding Facts vs. Browsing Knowledge in Hypertext Systems, *IEEE Computer, 21*(1), 70-79.

Marshall, C. C., and Irish, P. (1989). Guided Tours and On-line Presentations: How Authors Make Existing Hypertext Intelligible for Readers, *Hypertext '89 Proceedings* (pp. 15-26), New York: ACM.

Meyrowitz, N. (1989). Hypertext—Does It Reduce Cholesterol, Too?, *IRIS Technical Report* (89-9), Providence, RI: Brown University.

Meyrowitz, N., and van Dam, A. (1982). Interactive Editing Systems: Part II, *Computing Surveys, 14*(3), 353-415.

Mylonas, E., and Heath, S. (1990). Hypertext from the Data Point of View: Paths and Links in the Perseus Project, in A. Rizk, N. Streitz, and J. André (editors), *Hypertext: Concepts, Systems and Applications* (pp. 324-336), Cambridge: Cambridge University Press.

Nelson, T. H. (1987). *Literary Machines, Edition 87.1*, (self-published).

Oddy, R. N. (1977). Information Retrieval through Man-Machine Dialogue, *Journal of Documentation, 33*(1), 1-14.

Oddy, R. N., and Balakrishnan, B. (1988). Adaptive Information Retrieval Using a Fine-grained Parallel Computer, *Proceedings of the Conference on User-Oriented Content-Based Text and Image Handling (RIAO 88)*, MIT, Cambridge, MA: Centre des Hautes Etudes Internationales d'Informatique Documentaire.

Oren, T. (1987). The Architecture of Static Hypertexts, *Hypertext '87 Papers* (pp. 291-306), New York: ACM.

Oren, T., Salomon, G., Kreitman, K., and Don, A. (1990). Guides: Characterizing the Interface, in B. Laurel (editor), *The Art of Human-Computer Interface Design*, Reading, MA: Addison-Wesley.

Ossorio, P. G. (1966). Classification Space: A Multivariate Procedure for Automatic Document Indexing and Retrieval, *Multivariate Behavioral Research*, 479-524.

Paisley, W., and Butler, M. (1977). *Computer assistance in information work.* Palo Alto, CA: Applied Communication Research (ERIC Document Reproduction Service No. 146900).

Paris, C. L., Swartout, W. R. and Mann, W. C. (1989). *Natural Language Generation in Artificial Intelligence and Computational Linguistics*, Kluwer Academic Publishers.

Pearl, J. (1988). *Probabilistic Reasoning in Intelligent Systems: Networks of Plausible Inference*, San Mateo, CA: Morgan Kaufmann.

Rose, D. E. (1991a). *A Symbolic and Connectionist Approach to Legal Information Retrieval*, Ph.D. diss., University of California, San Diego, La Jolla.

Rose, D. E., and Belew, R. K. (1991b). A Connectionist and Symbolic Hybrid for Improving Legal Research, *International Journal of Man-Machine Studies*, (forthcoming).

Rubin, B., and Davenport, G. (1989). Structured Content Modeling for Cinematic Information, *SIGCHI Bulletin, 21*(2), 78-79.

Salton, G., and McGill, M. J. (1983). *Introduction to Modern Information Retrieval*, New York: McGraw Hill.

Samuel, A. L. (1959). Some Studies in Machine Learning Using the Game of Checkers, *CT*, 71-105.

Shneiderman, B. (1983). Direct Manipulation: A Step Beyond Programming Languages, *IEEE Computer, 16*(8), 57-68.

Shneiderman, B. (1987). User Interface Design and Evaluation for an Electronic Encyclopedia, *Proceedings of the 2nd International Conference on Human-Computer Interaction*, Amsterdam: North-Holland.

Small, H. G. (1978). Cited Documents as Concept Symbols, *Social Studies of Science, 8*, 327-340.

Smith, L. C. (1981). 'Memex' as an Image of Potentiality in Information Retrieval Research and Development, in R. N. Oddy (editor), *Information Retrieval Research* (pp. 345-369), London: Butterworths.

Smolensky, P., Bell, B., Fox, B., King, R., and Lewis, C. (1987). Constraint-based Hypertext for Argumentation, *Hypertext '87 Papers* (pp. 215-246), New York: ACM.

Streitz, N. A., Hanneman, J., and Thuring, M. (1989). From Ideas and Arguments to Hyperdocuments: Travelling through Activity Spaces, *Hypertext '89 Proceedings* (pp. 343-364), New York: ACM.

Suthers, D. D., and Woolf, B. P. (1990). Accounting for the Epistemological Structure of Explanation, *AAAI-90 Spring Symposium on Knowledge-based Environments for Learning and Teaching*, Stanford, CA.

Tonomura, Y., and Otsuji, K. (1991). Structured Video Handling for HyperMedia Systems, *Proc. Intl. Conf. Multimedia Info. Syst. '91*, Singapore.

Ueda, H., Miyataka, T., and Yoshizawa, S. (1991). IMPACT: An Interactive Natural-Motion-Picture Dedicated Multimedia Authoring System, *CHI '91 Conference Proceedings*, New Orleans.

Utting, K., and Yankelovich, N. (1989). Context and Orientation in Hypermedia Networks, *ACM Transactions on Information Systems, 7*(1), 58-84.

Walker, J. H. (1987). Document Examiner: Delivery Interface for Hypertext Documents, *Hypertext '87 Papers* (pp. 307-324), New York: ACM.

Weyer, S. A., and Borning, A. H. (1985). A Prototype Electronic Encyclopedia, *ACM Transactions on Office Information Systems, 3*(1), 63-88.

Yankelovich, N., Meyrowitz, N., and van Dam, A. (1985). Reading and Writing the Electronic Book, *IEEE Computer, 18*(10), 16-30.

Zellweger, Polle T. (1989). Scripted Documents: A Hypermedia Path Mechanism, *Hypertext '89 Proceedings* (pp. 1-14) New York: ACM.

Aristotle's Library: Memex as Vision and Hypertext as Reality

Gregory Crane

Pieces on the design and implementation of hypertext systems are not noticeable for their shelf life, but those essays by Vannevar Bush collected under this title have laid claim to a position in the small "canon" of texts on hypertext. Nevertheless, many of those who remain skeptical of electronic "hypertexts" in general will very probably apply those same doubts to Bush's vision of the Memex. The experience of editing a hypertext project collecting a large multimedia database on Ancient Greek civilization has given my colleagues and me a chance to explore a number of the ideas advanced in this collection of essays (for more on this hypertext, the Perseus Project, see Crane, 1988; 1990; 1991; Crane *et al.*, 1991; Crane & Mylonas, 1991).

The modern research library, as we know it, is a creation of the nineteenth century and, as such, is a fairly recent phenomenon. Many scholars, however, underestimate the extent to which the research library, in its function as a clearinghouse for information, affects the questions that they pose and the organization of the universities in which they work. Access to relevant information is not trivially achieved, and graduate students spend much of their energy learning how to move from point to point through a maze of research materials. Yet despite (or because of) the influence that logistical considerations exert, many scholars minimize such factors. They would contest the "thesis is that gadgetry is not necessarily trivial, and that in particular it may contribute substantially to man's mental development in the future as it has in the past" (Bush, 1941:1). This piece will begin with two points drawn from the study of Classical antiquity to recall how scholarship functioned before *gadgets* (to use one of Bush's favorite terms), which appeared in the late nineteenth century, affected very traditional scholarly work. This look back to earlier conditions will lead into a discussion of Bush's ideas and of the extent to which we have in our experience found them applicable.

The Books of Aristotle and the "Common Library"

Bush takes up, at several points in these essays, the figure of Aristotle — or, to be more precise, the Aristotelian corpus and the slavish way in which European intellectuals adhered to these texts until the Renaissance. "The only science admitted was the science of Aristotle—including its absurdities. The only reasoning permitted about men or nature followed the strict logic of Aristotle — including its fallacies. The scholastics argued learnedly about angels. But they did not open an egg and observe the growth of a cell" (Bush, 1967:16). And yet the immediate fate of Aristotle's real work provides an insight into one of Bush's primary arguments, that the changes in our material condition are massive and profound, but that the technology by which we represent and exchange our ideas is by far the most important.

The philosopher Theophrastus, Aristotle's student, colleague, and successor, was responsible for founding a school of philosophy to continue on the research that he and his more famous mentor had begun. Theophrastus managed to acquire property at Athens — not an easy thing to do since Theophrastus was not an Athenian and could not normally own real estate in that city. Equally important, however, Theophrastus possessed, in addition to his own books, the hand-written texts of Aristotle himself. At his death Theophrastus jointly bequeathed the real estate associated with his school to a group of scholars, but the library he bequeathed solely to a certain Neleus, presumably as sign that Neleus should succeed him as director of this institution. Instead, another scholar, a man by the name of Strato, became the new head, and Neleus, presumably in high dudgeon at the slight, decamped for his home city on the West Coast of Turkey, taking with him all of his books.

The effect was just what Neleus had intended, for in one stroke he deprived his former colleagues of the primary materials on which their work was largely based. Those who followed Theophrastus had only a few minor books at their disposal. The geographer Strabo, writing at the time of Augustus Caesar, is our source for this story, and he observes that the loss of these books had catastrophic consequences for the school as an institution. After Theophrastus, the Aristotelians could no longer "carry on the search for knowledge in a pragmatic fashion" but could only "pompously declaim platitudes." Only much later, when many of the lost works reappeared did Aristotelian research improve (Strabo, 1933:13.1.54; Canfora, 1987:26ff).

Roughly nine megabytes of Aristotle have survived — an enormous amount by ancient standards and a fair sampling of his work, and yet a tiny collection by modern standards. A few dozen modern textbooks could probably have contained every word in Neleus' whole library, and yet the loss of this cache brought virtually to a halt the research at a great academic institution, where, one source informs us, 2,000 people might attend a single lecture.

The books that Neleus took with him to Asia Minor were not books in any modern sense. Of course, they were papyrus rolls, not books (which did not appear until much later), but Neleus' *biblia* differ less in the form and material than in their social (one might say economic) significance. These scrolls were far closer in their value and their limits to works of art, which can be in only one place and which, once destroyed, are gone forever. Neleus' descendents buried the books in a kind of trench, and a combination of mold and insects damaged the texts, destroying sections of the texts forever. These texts could be (and, centuries later, were) copied, but only by hand, an expensive process that inevitably introduces errors into the text. In making off with these scrolls, Neleus had done even more damage to his colleagues than a deranged thief who systematically made off with every original known painting by Rembrandt. The art historian limited only to photographs is still in a better position than the discomfited Aristotelians with essentially nothing to read.

"Generations Old"

Access to common ideas, as Bush emphasizes, is the foundation on which communities are based, and communities, by their values and priorities, determine the directions to which they will apply their energies. It is perhaps easy to smile or to shudder at the thought of the desolated philosophers in Athens, trying to get on without their texts and "laboratory notebooks," but the example, quaint as it may seem, is not so very distant. When Bush declared that "professionally our methods of transmitting and reviewing the results of research are generations old" (Bush, 1945:101), he was quite right, but, at least as far as American scholarship is concerned, just barely so. Only a little more than two generations had elapsed since the modern research university, with all of its scholarly apparatus, had assumed recognizable shape in the United States.

Shortly after the Civil War, Daniel Coit Gilman, first president of Johns Hopkins University, set about to create a modern university, one that pursued the European goal of research and the production of knowledge (rather than simply the production of students). In 1876, he lured Basil Lanneau Gildersleeve from his position at the University of Virginia, "put him in an empty room and told him to radiate" (Flexner, 1946:67). The resulting waveforms attracted a steady stream of students and colleagues over the coming decades.

Gildersleeve had a pronounced vision, at once far-sighted and retrospective, for the place of scholarship within America. Greek and Latin had been studied in North America since the earliest European settlers arrived — the first commencement at Harvard College in September 1642 included a Greek oration (Morison, 1963: 259). And yet, just over a century ago, little or no research in this area took place; all energy was focused upon teaching. At Saratoga in July of 1878, Gildersleeve addressed the American Philological Association's annual convention. The classicists who had come vast distances by rail to attend this convention understood the problems well enough: "the isolation from other workers" was "chilling" (APA, 1878:22), and no one in North America could compete with the libraries of the great German universities (at which the most ambitious Americans did their advanced work).

Yet, for all that, classicists had a peculiar, but profound advantage:

> The field of antique literature is vast, but it is a narrow range compared with the continent of commentary and dissertation, and any competent man can survey with his own eyes large stretches of the original sources of all our knowledge and so gain new points of view as well as new illustrations for the work he may have in hand. Let any man try what can be done by close study of a text, and a wide range of reading in cognate directions, before he says that Americans have nothing to do except to repeat the references in German books, or at most to run over the indexes of German editions. (APA, 1878:22)

Readers scattered throughout the United States, with their limited access to expensive European books, could nevertheless reasonably expect to collect in a few hundred, even in a few dozen books, the primary materials around which their field was built. The "Classics" of ancient literature exerted an enormous influence on European and American thought, not only because of their intrinsic qualities but because they were reasonably finite in number. These texts were especially valuable precisely because they could be accessible not only to the learned professor in Europe but to the schoolmaster on the frontier. And because these texts were accessible, they could provide the basis for a larger community, which could transcend the vicious political quarrels of the period. In this, Gildersleeve looks backwards, towards the tradition of the few, critical great books. If Neleus' spite illustrates the danger of such an environment, Gildersleeve understood as well its strengths.

Journals and the Academic Community

One major idea that Gildersleeve radiated from his empty room was the creation of an academic journal, based on the European model, for *philology*, a loose term that may be broadly defined as the study of language, and which (at least according to philologists) can include linguistics and literary criticism. The creation of a journal was a critical idea, for if scholars were to produce "knowledge" and not simply trained students, they needed a regular medium in which to send their knowledge. Books would not do (if only because men like Gilman wanted yearly publications, and few were ready to produce a book each year). The first volume of the *American Journal of Philology* in 1880 was an historic milestone for the study of antiquity in America, and it was one of the first major academic journals published in this country. The journal's pages created a common intellectual space, which scholars shared and in which they could exchange ideas. An academic journal, now so common and natural, is an extremely recent development. It represents the best of nineteenth-century information technology— inexpensive, acid-filled (and thus ultimately self-destroying) paper. Those who ponder Memex would do well to cast their imaginations back and conceive of those scholars who opened American universities at the far end of the railhead a century or so ago, with their few books and with the awesome space that separated them from each other. The nineteenth century journal, inexpensive, regularly produced, and easily distributed, was a strategic tool. Because of the journal, scholars throughout the North American continent, rather than in a few imperial university cities, could explore the outer edges of their subjects.

And yet, two generations after Gildersleeve addressed his sweltering colleagues on a hot July night of 1878, Vannevar Bush surveyed a huge and institutionally mature university system. Gildersleeve's colleagues had struggled to collect the sum of its knowledge, and they succeeded all too well. Academic society had become so finely developed, widely articulated, and efficient that the flow of information had begun to inundate individual scholars. All of this took place in a single lifetime. Some of those who had begun their careers as students in the burgeoning universities of the 1870s were still active when Bush began in the 1930s drafting the ideas that would coalesce in Memex. Or, to put the matter in another perspective, Bush was about as far removed from the founding of Johns Hopkins University as we are from the time when Bush first sat down to draft his ideas on Memex. The extra two generations that have elapsed since the conception of Memex have eliminated all living memory of that even earlier period, and it is tempting (even for classicists) to view the problems and possibilities of modern research as an eternal concern, rather than the recent product of the previous century. People began studying much Greek literature, for example, as soon as it was composed (the fifth century B.C. comic playwright Aristophanes gives us, in his plays, one of the best and most perceptive commentaries on his contemporary Euripides), but the study of classical antiquity as now practiced is a fairly recent phenomenon. The complex web of dictionaries, scholarly editions, commentaries, professional journals, specialized monographs, bibliographies, and massive "card catalogues" through which we now thread our way in the study of antiquity, only assumed its present form in Germany during the nineteenth century. And of course virtually all scholarship focused on the written record. The same year Gildersleeve addressed his scholarly colleagues in Saratoga, Heinrich Schliemann would publish "Mycenae: A Narrative of Researches and Discoveries at

Mycenae and Tiryns," and thus effectively invent the field of classical archaeology.

Resistance to Memex as an "Institutional" Idea

I have purposely dwelled upon this point at some length. Bush concluded his memo on Memex (1941:6-7) with the cautionary statement: "It is certain, however, that, if it [the story of Memex] is to be anything more than an amusing tale, it needs to be revamped to bring it in line with changed times. . . . My hearn [yearn] to influence the attitude toward science would then have to be approached from an entirely new direction when and if it were possible to do so." The fact that his Memex did not materialize had as much to do with technological limitations as with the social conditions of the university. Both Marxists and cultural anthropologists point out that institutions resist change by implying that their current form (whatever that may be) has been stable since the dawn of history (or at least the dawn of civilization — which usually coincides, in the minds of those who run an institution, with the dawn of the institution). Change is harmful and unlikely, since things have always been as they are, and the current order reflects, in fact, the "natural" order of things. Nowhere does such an institutional "false consciousness" exert a stronger influence than in great universities, where the complex network of specialization is now inscribed in the adamantine form of faculties, schools, departments, and discipline specific professorships. A library system in which hundreds of employees haul paper up and down flights of stairs more relentlessly than Sisyphus rolled his stone has stupendous institutional momentum and clamors for stability. The faculty is trained to produce students who reproduce their teachers as closely as possible. Within two or three generations, bold pioneers in learning begin to resemble a guild of hereditary priests, all charged with promulgating the mysteries peculiar to their faiths.

Society and technology are as tightly bound together as two fugitive convicts linked by a heavy chain. Technology opens up possibilities that lead in one direction, but a quick jerk on the chain, and society knocks technology off its feet. Society points in yet another direction and technology stumbles and is unable to follow. Every so often, if only by the laws of probability, technology and society do in fact move, if not in an identical situation, then at least in two directions close enough together so that the two actually move somewhere. Bush's vision of Memex the machine was a great vision, but it was not his most important contribution. When Bush declared that our minds are being deadened by specialization, he spoke eloquently, but his views were orthodox. What distinguishes Bush's work is that he put the two together: he not only condemned specialization and the crushing effects of massive paper publications, he also outlined a reasonably practical machine that would have addressed the issue. A machine such as Memex would not only have changed the day-to-day work of every active scholar, but would have sent shock waves throughout the vast infrastructure of publishers and libraries that support research.

Bush is fond of the self-deprecating term *gadgetry*, but this term is revealing, for its lightly mocking tone locates the popular role for a machine. With a slightly comical flavor, the term "gadget" reflects the unease of society, which fears machines and badly wishes to keep them in a subordinate, easily dismissed role. The choice of this term implies the argument which Bush explicitly outlines in "Man's Thinking Machines" (Bush, 1963), that machines, even machines that can think, must — and can — only be servants to man. Gadgetry, however useful, can be dismissed and ignored. In the end, we shall be like Bush's idealized mathematician:

> [He] is skilled in the use of symbolic logic on a high plane, and especially he is a man of intuitive judgment in the choice of the manipulative processes he employs. All else he should be able to turn over to his mechanism, just as confidently as he turns over the propelling of his car to the intricate mechanism under the hood." (Bush, 1945:105)

The machine is a black box, useful to us, but silent and apart.

The problem with Bush's vision is that it goes both too far and not far enough. The rhetoric is reassuring throughout. Machines are "docile servants which do as they are told " (Bush, 1963:9). They will serve and will support human beings. They will liberate them from "laborious detailed manipulation" so that people may "free their brains for something more than repetitive detailed transformations in accordance with established rules." And yet, a world with a Memex in every office, and especially a world in which scholars actively used the Memex to branch out beyond their narrow specialty, would be vastly different, more challenging, and more difficult. Research universities system had, in Bush's day, for generations rewarded specialization and had constructed departments that bound their faculty tightly in academic pigeon holes. They cannot expect faculty to branch off into some new specialized area overnight. The modern university does, in its own perverse way, give its inhabitants one great freedom—which Bush hopes to receive from Memex—the freedom to possess selective and restricted knowledge and to remain ignorant of what they do not need to know for their immediate work. Sherlock Holmes shocked Dr. Watson when he professed no knowledge of whether the earth revolved around the sun or the sun around the earth. Holmes pointed out, however, that such knowledge was of no value to him as it did not affect his work, and he would promptly forget what he had just learned from Watson. Holmes would have made a wonderful professor.

Bush acutely knew that no human being could contain in his or her mind more than a microscopic fragment of our collective experience. But where the university insulates and protects its inhabitants, Bush, in a still unpublished essay (Bush, 1939:5) looked to the bold mariner, using compass and astrolabe, "to sail the seas and plunge into the unknown." He imagines a world in which his scientific colleagues would freely turn to the detailed study of the short Turkish bow vs. the English longbow. The scholar works through books, articles, an encyclopedia, and even sidles off into "textbooks on elasticity and tables of physical constants" when it becomes clear that "the elastic properties of available materials had a great deal to do with the bow" (Bush, 1945:107). Bush does not concern himself with what would have happened when the scientist's colleague in history ridiculed his effort, pointing out that the books and articles were long out of date and superseded by newer material (much of it in German), while the analysis made no direct use of source documents (many of them in Greek or Arabic) from the period of the Crusades.

The ability to cross disciplinary boundaries is just as much a social as it is a technological phenomenon. It does not matter whether one travels by foot or by air if one's neighboring countries will interdict this travel by Turkish bow or air-to-air missile. Every scholar on earth could have a Memex, but the impact on specialization would be small unless scholars as a group decided that they would actively help outsiders to cross their special domains of learning. The simple and unassuming rhetoric of "gadgetry" and "docile servants" is true enough, for the machines will always be subordinate to man. But the unthreatening stance which Bush took masked the much more difficult and challenging changes that a Memex would demand in the relationship of human beings to one another. A massive and interdisciplinary system such as Memex may not turn the intellectual world into a "global department," but it can certainly challenge the barriers which, even now in an age that prides itself on interdisciplinary research, insulate different disciplines from one another. The academic is likely to face the same stresses and opportunities as the nineteenth-century European, for example, who must work not only with his traditional rivals across the frontier, but with people from lands that not long before had existed in his mind as exotic travellers' tales.

Conclusion: Memex, Technology and Change

Now that we have begun to build large, multidisciplinary systems that aspire to the functionality of a Memex, we are in a better position to advance Bush's insights. The vision that animates Bush's writings is deceptively simple and conflates two very different kinds of use. Neither kind necessarily excludes the other, but they are not automatically linked.

On the one hand, Bush is clearly concerned with the practical problems that scientists faced already in his day. He chose as an example Mendel's concept of the laws of genetics, "lost to the world for a generation because his publication did not reach the few who were capable of grasping and extending it," as the "sort of catastrophe" which a Memex should help to avoid (Bush, 1945:101). Elsewhere he cites the lawyer, the physician, and the chemist using Memex "trails" to pursue their particular researches (Bush, 1945:108). In these passages, Memex is portrayed as a boost to efficiency, but it becomes ultimately the black box that resides, as Bush puts it, underneath the hood and drives an automobile—just another tool that lets us pursue our daily work quicker and more conveniently. The difference may occasionally be enormous (e.g., access to Mendel's thoughts), but progress here would advance linearly within the well-defined tracks of existing specialties.

On the other hand, many of the most eloquent and moving passages in these essays have their gaze fixed upon a very different kind of usage.

> Presumably man's spirit should be elevated if he can better review his shady past and analyze more completely and objectively his present problems. He [Man] has built a civilization so complex that he needs to mechanize his records more fully if he is to push his experiment to its logical conclusion and not merely become bogged down part way there by overtaxing his limited memory. His excursions may be more enjoyable if he can reacquire the privilege of forgetting the manifold things he does not need to have immediately at hand, with some assurance that he can find *them again if they prove important.* (Bush, 1945:108, empahsis mine)

Here, the scientist, confronted with new and crushing responsibilities, is forced to pull back from his immediate specialty and to survey human civilization as a whole. Bush observes at the conclusion of "Science Pauses":

> Young men who will formulate the deep thought of the next generation, should lean on science, for it can teach much and it can inspire. But they should not lean where it does not apply. . . . As always he [the young man] will build his own concepts, and his own loyalties. He will follow science where it leads, but will not attempt to follow where it cannot lead. With a pause, he will admit a faith. (1967:29-30)

Now, more than a generation later, we have begun to encounter some of the problems that complicate Bush's program. Behind this image of the thoughtful scientist lies Memex, with its trails winding through the disparate records of human experience. And yet, what good does Memex serve if the materials, once collected, are opaque and incomprehensible to the untrained eye? How far can scientists get if the trails blazed take them to untranslated tablets covered with cuneiform? Herakles and the Nemean Lion is one of the most common scenes that appears on painted Greek vases, but this fact is not obvious to anyone gazing at the scene for the first time. If the author of a trail assumes the viewer will realize that this is a typical scene, the untrained wayfarer may not be able to make a vital connection that leads from one part of the argument to another. It does not matter how many specialists build trails through their databases of material. Unless the basic materials published in the database are designed for both specialist and non-specialist, all readers will be able to find more material within their specialties, but will be unable to widen their intellectual range. The point of a Memex is not to make more widely available the well-digested summaries of an Encyclopedia. Rather, a Memex should enable the general reader to push past neat and dull conclusions and survey with comprehension the actual evidence on which particular conclusions are based.

There is no reason to believe that electronic tools will, of necessity, decrease the specialization that separates us from each other. The research library has a deceptive structure, for while most of its holdings are physically open to any user, most of the materials are so abstruse and assume so much background knowledge that they are of little use to anyone but the specialist. If scholars in their separate disciplines simply continue to create information that serves the dozen or so others working on the same arcane problem, then little qualitative change will take place. We can anticipate more and better, but essentially the same, materials to appear.

A Memex-like system offers two quantitative advantages over its static counterpart, and these two quantitative advantages combine to enable scholars to interact with materials in a qualitatively new way. Bush imagined that scholars would have the ability to store far greater amounts of information than before, and he also foresaw that this would require new tools for what has come to be called "information retrieval." Bush did not, however, anticipate that electronic hypertext systems could make information more useful on the screen than it had been on the page of a book. Animations can simplify complex problems. Basic linguistic tools can identify Chinese ideograms or analyze complex word forms, allowing those who are not specialists to make more intelligent use of linguistic documents. Geographical information systems can allow scholars to see interrelationships between complex factors. At an even more basic level, one can tailor the support materials for a document to match the needs of different levels of users: the specialist might be directed to more complex and technical analysis, while the system might present a more general reader with a list of basic references or with a simple glossary. The expert who has spent years working on the Athenian playwright Aeschylus will inevitably see many more things in the text than his or her colleague who specializes in Elizabethan Drama. Nonetheless, the Renaissance scholar can certainly make good use of an electronic Aeschylus text that can be largely decoded with software tools appropriate to his or her level of expertise. Hypertext can allow scholars to work with many more kinds of information, and it can thus stimulate interdisciplinary thought. Hypertext is, however, a necessary, but not sufficient, condition for such an advance in our habits of thought. If, then, the guardians of a discipline decide to allocate a part of their time and energy to generalizing their basic publications, and if they invest effort in designing documents that lead the general reader more deeply into their subject, we can reasonably expect that many disciplines will be able to touch directly a wider audience than ever before.

References

The American Philological Association 1877-8, (1888), minutes.

Bush, V. (1939). *Mechanization and the Record,* [Vannevar Bush Papers, Library of Congress], Box 138, Speech Article Book File.

Bush, V. (1941). *Memorandum regarding Memex,* [Vannevar Bush Papers, Library of Congress], Box 50, General Correspondence File, Eric Hodgins.

Bush, V. (1945). As We May Think, *Atlantic Monthly, 176*(1), 101-108.

Bush, V. (1963). *Man's Thinking Machines,* [Vannevar Bush Papers, MIT Archives], MC78, Box 21.

Bush, V. (1967). Science Pauses, in V. Bush, *Science Is Not Enough* (pp. 14-30), New York: William Morrow.

Canfora, L. (1987). *The Vanished Library,* Berkeley: University of California.

Crane, G. (1988). Redefining the Book: Some Preliminary Problems, *Academic Computing, 2,* 6-11, 36-41.

Crane, G. (1990). Formats of Print and Questions of Culture: *HyperMedia* and Scholarly Publishing, *Scholarly Publishing, 21*, 131-155.

Crane, G. (1991a). Composing Culture: The Authority of an Electronic Text, *Current Anthropology, 32*, 293-311.

Crane, G., and Mylonas, E. (1991b). Ancient Materials, Modern Media: Shaping the Study of Classics with Hypertext, in G. Landow and P. Delany (editors), *Hypermedia and Literary Studies* (pp. 205-220), Cambridge: MIT Press.

Crane, G., Mylonas, E., Morrell, K., and Smith, N. (1991). The Perseus Project: Data in the Electronic Age, in J. Solomon and T. Worthen (editors), *Computing and the Classics* (forthcoming), Tempe: University of Arizona Press.

Flexner, A. (1946). *Daniel Coit Gilman: Creator of the American Type of University*, New York: Harcourt, Brace and Company.

Morison, S. E. (1963). *The Founding of Harvard College*, Cambridge: Havard University Press.

Strabo (1933). Geography, H. L. Jones (translator), *The Geography of Strabo*, New York: G.P. Putnam's Sons.

From Trailblazing to Guided Tours: The Legacy of Vannevar Bush's Vision of Hypertext Use

Randall H. Trigg

Introduction

> There is a new profession of trail blazers, those who find delight in the task of establishing useful trails through the enormous mass of the common record. The inheritance from the master becomes, not only his additions to the world's record, but for his disciples the entire scaffolding by which they were erected. (Bush, 1945:108)

BUSH'S VISION MUST HAVE SOUNDED FAR-FETCHED to readers of the *Atlantic Monthly* in the late 1940's. Thousands of pages of microfilm stored in one's office desk? Access times counted in seconds? Built-in viewing screens and dry photocopying? In the years since Bush's vision of the memex first appeared, all this has been realized and more. Or has it?

In this essay, I consider the single most important process-related idea in Bush's memex, *trailblazing*. The notion itself is a complex one incorporating both trail creation and trail following and, in his later writings, overt attempts to model human mental processes. There is widespread agreement that the field of hypertext has its roots in just this notion of trailblazing, and it could be further argued that recent work marrying hypertext with AI and user modeling was largely anticipated by the extensions of trailblazing described by Bush in the 1960s.

I will argue, however, that one critical feature of Bush's original notion of trailblazing has yet to be realized, namely, the subsumption of linking under the activities of trail creation and following, or more simply, *linking as trailblazing*. When one uses the Memex, every link created is part of a named trail. Links do not primarily embody local relationships between nodes, but function as part of a coherent sequential context under continual development, the *trail*. Bush himself very rarely uses the terms "link" and "linking" in his descriptions of the

Memex. Rather he refers to the processes as building and following trails, and encompasses both with the single metaphorical term, trailblazing.

In what follows, I briefly review Bush's descriptions of trailblazing both in his early and later writings. I then follow one path through the legacy of these ideas, focusing primarily on my own work on the capture, representation, and recording of sequential motion through hypertext's inherently non-linear medium. Along the way, I'll visit Textnet paths; browsers, documents, history cards, and guided tours in NoteCards; and the time-based trails of VideoNoter, among others. Though only a small sample of work in this area, it is representative of the trail-related hypertext research of the past decade. Finally, I confront the question of why Bush's notion of trailblazing has yet to be fully realized.

Bush on Trailblazing

Bush saw trails and trailblazing as an alternative to traditional indexed, hierarchically structured information. His "operation by association" was instead based on a mental model of information organized as networks of intersecting trails. The Memex is the machine he envisioned as supporting access to information so organized. The basic constructive activity in the Memex is trail building. In particular, the creation of links is always in the context of a developing trail:

> When the user is building a trail, he names it, inserts the name in his code book, and taps it out on his keyboard. Before him are the two items to be joined, projected onto adjacent viewing positions. . . . The user taps a single key, and the items are permanently joined. In each code space appears the code word. Out of view, . . . on each item [is designated] . . . the index number of the other item. Thereafter, at any time, when one of these items is in view, the other can be instantly recalled merely by tapping a button below the corresponding code space. (Bush, 1945:107)

Although a link is represented "out of view" using the unique identifier of the destination item, user access is always provided in terms of the enclosing trail (named by "code word").[1] Just as link creation is subsumed under trail building, so is link traversal subsumed under trail following:

> On a new exploration one may often just follow one of these old trails, the machine stepping along slowsly [sic] and automatically from item to item as the user recalls what is there. But also he will at times move through the network in some novel way, following one trail for a time, branching off to another, taking false trails and promptly backing up, tying together on the path he traces through the maze a whole new association of ideas which has become of importance to him. (Bush, 1959:11)

"Side trails" are formed when the user builds new links (and possibly items) from a point in the middle of the current trail as opposed to attaching them to one of its endpoints. It is unclear exactly how users would choose among the side trails available at an item, but Bush hints at mechanical support:

> . . . this [item] has a code for a trail on a subject on which he has had correspondence with many people. So he alters the direction, in which he moves the lever, and steps along a trail that brings the thoughts of them all. (Bush, 1959:8)

Bush also mentions the use of color for trail selection, where older trails are marked with darker colors (Bush, 1959:7-8).

Interestingly, Bush even anticipated problems of simultaneous access to a shared trails database:

> Many individuals may thus consult the library store simultaneously. When they meet on trails there will need to be special means provided so that they can pass one another. (Bush, 1959:10)

The description of the original Memex focused on trails as manually created and accessed while the later writings emphasized automated trailblazing. In both cases, Bush blurred the distinction between creation and access. Indeed, his trailblazing metaphor suggests both the clearing and following of a trail. In "Memex II," for example, trails are created by a mix of active trail-making actions and automatic recording of the user's wanderings. As can be seen from the examples that follow, support for trail creation and following has appeared in many hypertext systems since the time of Bush's writings. However, the blending of the two that is so crucial to Bush's trailblazing notion has yet to be realized.

The Textnet and NoteCards Experience

My own work in the field of hypertext was strongly influenced by the Memex vision. In the projects I've been associated with, I've focused on using trails to support communication and collaboration and in each case have been able to realize the potential of some part of Bush's vision. At the same time, the confrontation of running systems with real use situations has raised research issues Bush did not anticipate.

Each hypertext facility described below embodies certain features of Bush's notion of trails. Textnet paths are most reminiscent of memex's mode of moving through a network along a trail, changing it as one goes along. In NoteCards, document cards specifically address the issue of generating hardcopy and begin to suggest some of the automated trail following Bush describes in "Memex II." History cards are directed toward collaborating researchers and writers and capture the idea of exchanging trails, records of work in a network, among collaborators. Finally, guided tour cards are a means of crafting online presentations of a portion of a hypertext network in the form of a branching "tour."

Textnet Paths

My interest in the field of hypertext started with a reading of Ted Nelson's *Computer Lib/Dream Machines* (Nelson, 1974) in which he used Bush's Memex and Doug Engelbart's NLS system (Engelbart and English, 1968) as jumping off points for a discussion of his own Xanadu hypertext design. My subsequent thesis work on hypertext attempted to combine the network-based linking style of Xanadu with the hierarchical "outline" structures of NLS (Trigg, 1983). The overall goal was to support communication and collaboration in an envisioned future online scientific community; in this way Textnet resembled a computer-based version of the Memex. Textnet differed from Memex in its focus on collaborative, distributed use of hypertext and on explicit support for link types and hierarchical structures.

Most directly relevant to our discussion here are Textnet's three means of hypertext "perusal": *vertical*, following hierarchical structures; *horizontal*, following paths and links to side paths; and *jumping*, using an index of keywords. Especially interesting with respect to Bush's trails is Textnet's support of horizontal motion via its "path" capability:

> [Having a default starting path] avoids the need for explicit link selection when moving between nodes. Rather a reader must explicitly choose a link only when the default path is undesirable at that point. The current path is modified accordingly as new choices are entered. At any time, the user can save this current path to reuse later or give to other readers desiring a similar walk through the given material. (Trigg and Weiser, 1986:12)

This description recalls Bush's trailblazing notion, but there are two significant differences. First, Textnet explicitly confronted the issue of branching paths and the means by which readers make choices at branch points. Second and more importantly, Textnet did not assume a huge starting body of largely unlinked nodes. Rather, the image was of a working scientist connecting nodes together as she created them. In this way, linking was a key part of writing. Textnet did support annotation of a colleague's hypertext, but even in that case, the predominant activity involved the simultaneous creation of nodes and links rather than pure linking among an existing set of nodes. The Textnet vision had scientists using hypertext in their daily work where link creation was no more fundamental than node creation.

Although like the Memex user, a Textnet scientist could peruse the extant literature in a field, this was under the assumption that that body of literature was created in or translated to Textnet.[2] The Memex user, on the other hand, blazes trails through existing unlinked materials created for the most part outside Memex. Later, we'll return to the "open systems" issues this raises.

Document Cards

The design of the NoteCards hypertext system (Halasz *et al.*, 1987) was driven less by visions and more by the concrete needs of users and usage situations. This continuing accountability to use offers us the chance to see which of Bush's ideas one is driven to in an effort to support the day-to-day activities of people working with hypertext.

This concern with the practical realities of hypertext use led us to see the importance of supporting a gradual changeover from the current state of affairs to an envisioned future. For example, how can one work in an online medium but continue to publish in offline linear form? Bush says almost nothing about translation from the Memex to hardcopy, and yet such translation is an obvious application for trails, precisely because they embody linearizations of a hypertext. (For this reason, paths in Textnet were used in part to generate hardcopy of portions of the network.)

In NoteCards, the functionality of linearization was judged important enough to warrant special support. The result was the "document card," a means for traversing the network under user control, copying the contents of all nodes encountered into one combined linearized node. In effect, the document card automatically computes and follows a path specified by the user. The specification includes a starting node and options dictating how to traverse node hierarchies, which non-hierarchical links to follow, etc. Document cards have been used primarily to linearize the network for "publication" rather than as a viewing mechanism as in Textnet and Memex.

Document cards hearken back to Bush's ideas on user-controlled automatic trail creation and traversal. However, once document cards became widely used in the NoteCards community, we encountered a variety of trail-related problems unanticipated by Bush:

1. Linearization of a portion of the network requires "flattening" any existing structure. Subsequent access to the document card's contents cannot generally make use of the original structure.[3]
2. A "copying versus viewing" problem arises involving whether and how the document card should be kept up to date with the cards from which it was formed.
3. Finally, there is a problem involving the coherence of the linearized information. We found that the contents of a node often needed different phrasing or transitions (sometimes called "smoothing") depending on the particular sequential context.

Choosing a viewer-based approach to document cards in addressing problem (2) obviates the need for copies but exacerbates the problem of ensuring coherence in multiple contexts. Further discussion of our experience with these problems can be found in Trigg and Irish (1987).

History Cards

Although NoteCards was originally intended as a single-user system, the importance of supporting collaborative use soon became clear to us (Trigg *et al.*, 1986). Taking seriously the idea of communication and collaboration in hypertext led to a simple problem: how to know what one's collaborator has recently done in the network. Unlike paper-based collaborations, one cannot just thumb through an online draft looking for red markup. To address this problem, we designed a trail-like facility called the *history card*. Like a Memex trail, it provides an annotated record of one's work in the network (though in NoteCards the work involved more building and less browsing than Bush's use scenarios for Memex II). In their first incarnation, history cards were manually constructed by each collaborator at the end of a session of work in NoteCards (Trigg and Suchman, 1989). Later, however, we semi-automated the process of history card construction (Irish and Trigg, 1989) and so began to approach the automated trailblazing Bush describes so eloquently in "Memex II."

Again, the confrontation of these ideas with the contingencies of usage raised issues unanticipated by Bush. First, we quickly recognized the need to support discussions *about* the work in the shared hypertext network (the "notefile"). Such discussions concerned the *process* of working as well as the content of the work, for example, whether to use different fonts to quickly indicate a card's author, or how best to title new cards. Such procedural discussions took place in the medium of the notefile and thus also appeared in history card trails.

Second, in semi-automating history card creation, we ran a risk of reducing the intelligibility of the history card. When the card is manually created, annotations are composed explicitly for one's collaborator. In contrast, the history card generator writes standardized textual annotations for each hypertext operation recorded. Though these can be modified or augmented by the user, there is a risk that history cards could lose their previously "personalized" character. It is an open question how important such personalization is to the activity of collaboration.

Guided Tours

Much hypertext research has focused on ways to address the reader's "lost in hyperspace" problem. In the NoteCards project, we believed that a little work by the network's author could go a long way towards helping its future readers. Guided tour cards (Trigg, 1988) capture a trail through the network, but unlike history cards, they are more than a record of work done and nodes visited. Rather, guided tours are hand-crafted branching hypertext presentations. The intended communication is not between collaborators working in the same network, but between the network's author and future unknown readers. The facility includes a graphical tour editor, which can also be used by the reader as an overview when stepping through the tour.

Bush imagined two uses of trails for communication: (1) trails and parts of trails could be exchanged privately among colleagues, and (2) librarians could create publicly available trails through the standard literature in a field. "Wholly new forms of encyclopedias will appear, ready-made with a mesh of associative trails running through them, ready to be dropped into the memex and there amplified" (Bush, 1945:108). By the term "amplified," Bush was referring to the process by which an existing trail is extended into both existing and new material. "So he sets a reproducer in action, photographs the whole trail out, and passes it to his friend for insertion in his own memex, there to be linked into the more general trail" (Bush, 1945:107).

We found, however, that trail "amplification" is not so simple. Our first experiences with guided tours indicated the importance of annotation and "meta-structural description" accompanying the tour in order for it to make sense. For example, when taking advantage of the overlapping window bitmapped display, each stop on a guided tour is actually a set of cards, called a "tabletop." This gives a certain freedom to the tour's author, but in return can require, for example, directing the reader's perusal *within* the tabletop (Marshall and Irish, 1989). Though Bush discusses trail annotations, it is only in the practical realization of the idea that the crucial nature of presentation issues arises.[4]

Multi-media Trails

The possibilities for incorporating non-textual media were anticipated by Bush; his Memex scenarios included pictures and sound. Recent work in hypermedia has realized much of his vision and is moving further into issues surrounding linking and anchoring in multi-media nodes.

Sound

> On some of the letters appear his own comments, and he adds to these from time to time, speaking his thoughts, which the machine then inscribes on the item in its phonetic shorthand. (Bush, 1959:8)

> He speaks a summary, and some of his conclusions, and tacks it on at the head of the trail. (Bush, 1959:13)

Like NoteCards guided tours, Polle Zellweger's Scripted Documents system (1989) supports online presentations through information spaces. But perhaps more than any other dynamic hypermedia system, Scripted Documents directly addresses the issue of sound annotations in a hypermedia trail. Scripted Documents also provides direct support for the crafting of automatic trail playbacks. By means of a simple paradigm, users can program a wide variety of dynamic events. Especially important is the fact that the nodes in a scripted document are often constructed outside the system. In this way, a scripted document approaches Bush's idea of a trail through an existing mass of information.

Video

My own work in this area in collaboration with Jeremy Roschelle led to an object-oriented hypermedia system we called VideoNoter (Roschelle *et al.*, 1990). VideoNoter primarily supports the work of social scientists analyzing videotapes of activity, although the system provides general support for linking to and from time-based media. For example, a trail in VideoNoter can be followed under control of the video. Such time-based trails are created and manipulated using proxy graphical representations of the videotape aligned with annotative text and graphics.

Just as with automated Memex trails, one can sit back and watch the trail play itself, intervene and make modifications, or step manually through links along the trail.

VideoNoter resembles Memex in its intention of supporting scientists in their daily work. Building and reviewing trails is one way of coming to better understand the time-based materials one is analyzing. Those same trails (properly annotated) can subsequently be used to communicate and present research results.

Automating Trails

> The machine will learn from its own experience, refine its own trails, explore in unknown territory to establish trails there. (Bush, 1967a:22)

Recently, several hypertext systems have appeared that explicitly support system-constructed trails. The ideas behind these systems overlap significantly with Bush's automated trailblazing described in "Memex II."

At the simplest level, many hypertext systems provide an historical trail facility, where nodes recently visited (or links recently followed) are logged by the system and made available to the user. HyperCard, for example, provides an interface that presents the last 42 cards visited. A similar idea, but under closer user control, is the notion of "bookmarks." In Document Examiner, for example, the user can mark certain visited nodes as being of importance; these are then saved in an easily accessed list (Walker, 1987). Intermedia's *web view* (Utting and Yankelovich, 1989) presents both recently visited nodes and nodes that are one link away from the current node in a constantly updated graphic overview window.

Other research has involved the automatic creation of trails that include nodes yet to be visited. For example, StrathTutor (Kibby and Mayes, 1989) uses similarity measures to compute a virtual path starting from the current node and including all unvisited nodes. The user is presented with the first three nodes from that list as options for a next node to visit. The guided tours of Hammond and Allinson (1988) provide customized subtours based on reader responses to "quizzes." The petri-net-based approach of Trellis (Furuta and Stotts, 1989) allows the specification of prerequisite relationships among nodes out of which paths can be constructed.

Finally, the IDE hypermedia system (Jordan *et al.*, 1989) creates entire sets of nodes and links based on preexisting template structures at the click of a button. In this case, one is not just blazing a trail, but also building the forest! As with the other NoteCards-based facilities discussed earlier, IDE's *auto-link* feature was derived primarily from the needs of users. It thus indicates the degree to which link (and trail) creation needs to occur together with node creation, at least in this case. Unlike Memex users, IDE users are not blazing trails through existing corpi of online information, but creating it as they go along.

One form of automatic trail creation suggested by Bush that (as far as I'm aware) is still to be realized in a working system could be called *trail creation by example* (Bush, 1959:17-20). Here, the Memex user wanders through a maze of trails, stopping occasionally to add new material. Memex then replays the trail, allowing the removal of side trips that turned out to be dead ends. Interestingly, the end result is not actually a new named trail, but rather a weighting of this one. "Then when he is satisfied he presses the button which says 'repeat that trail ten times' and he goes about other business" (Bush, 1959:18).

Trailblazing: Present and Future

As we have seen, many of Bush's trailblazing notions are realized in today's hypertext systems. We can support sequential renderings of non-linear information, or trails, which can be time-based, include multi-media materials, and to some degree be created and followed automatically. What we have not seen are examples of Bush's sense of trailblazing as fundamental to linking. Instead, trails are generally added to today's networks on top of existing webs of links. I believe this is a direct result of the two primary ways we build hypertexts: (1) by transporting existing offline document sets into hypertext, and (2) by starting from scratch, generating linked materials online.

In the first case, the offline source documents are usually homogeneous. That is, though the materials (e.g., system documentation) may come in different forms, they are generally created by a single person or organization for a given application area. Because of this, online links

can be established according to "rules" inherent in the original documents or the field of practice from which they are derived. In the second
case, we do not start with a mass of unlinked, externally created
materials, but build both nodes and links as we go along. The links thus
tend to be locally coherent and only later become part of sequentially
consistent trails.

Thus, we either work with a homogeneous set of materials or we
make our own materials (and links among them) as we go along.
According to this reading, Bush's essential trailblazing notion has not
yet materialized precisely because we lack trailblazable forests—namely,
large corpi of heterogeneous online material. Indeed, it is often easier
to create and link new material than to gain online access to existing
materials. Here is one of the few cases where Bush, the futurist, guessed
wrongly:

> Will we soon have a personal machine for our use? Unfortunately not.
> First we will no doubt see the mechanization of our libraries, and this
> itself will take years. Then we will see the group machine, specialized,
> used by many. This will be especially valuable in medicine, in order
> that those who minister to our ills may do so in the light of the broad
> experience of their fellows. Finally, a long time from now, I fear, will
> come the personal machine. (Bush, 1967b:100)

Bush just had it backwards. Today, we have the personal machine (or
"workstation"), but we have yet to see the "mechanization of our
libraries" or even a proper "group machine."

Why haven't things turned out as Bush expected? Here are three
possible reasons why we still lack large corpi of heterogeneous online
information: (1) problems of security and copyrights, unanticipated by
Bush, have made it difficult to gain legal access to materials created by
others; (2) the technology of optical scanning hasn't come along fast
enough—only a few users have streamlined, online access to offline
materials; and (3) monolithic environments, closed systems, propri-
etary black-box editors, and a lack of standards have technically made
it nearly impossible to integrate information from different sources.

Though there has been recent progress along all three of these
dimensions (societal, technological, and technical),[5] it may be some
time before Bush's deep vision of trailblazing becomes a reality. And

this, I believe, is to our collective detriment. In an important sense, Bush's complaints about the conduct of research in the 1940s still apply today. Though current hypertext systems provide support for the creation of new associatively linked information, we still have little access to the vast storehouses of existing documents. When that situation finally changes, we would be well advised to look back to Bush's original trailblazing notion for help in designing the next generation of hypertext tools.

Acknowledgements

I am grateful to Liam Bannon, Kaj Grønbæk, Paul Kahn, and Jim Nyce for comments on earlier drafts of this essay.

Endnotes

1. Finding a trail in the first place can either be done by simple name lookup or by associated keyword lookup. As described in "Memex II" (pp. 16-18), the keywords are organized in hierarchical, thesaurus-like lists with trails starting at the leaf nodes.
2. See Trigg (1983:118) for a discussion of linear document conversion.
3. For the case of hierarchical structuring, this problem is addressed by systems that support *outline processing*, an idea with roots in the early NLS/Augment systems (Engelbart and English, 1968).
4. Another need that emerged from concrete use was for a "collection" capability for guided tours readers; or as Kaj Grønbæk interprets the metaphor: "to pick up post cards and leaflets in kiosks that I pass on the guided tour" (Grønbæk and Bannon, 1991).
5. One recent example is the Perseus project, which is developing research and educational hypertexts in the area of classical studies, and has augmented HyperCard with support for user-definable trails. "Unlike many systems, where the information is added incrementally as new links are created, Perseus is starting out with a large database of extant materials" (Mylonas and Heath, 1990:326).

References

Bush, V. (1945). As We May Think, *Atlantic Monthly*, *176*(1), 101-108.

Bush, V. (1959). *Memex II*, [Vannevar Bush Papers, MIT Archives], MC78, Box 21.

Bush, V. (1967a). Science Pauses, in *Science Is Not Enough* (pp. 14-30), New York: William Morrow.

Bush, V. (1967b). Memex Revisited, in *Science Is Not Enough* (pp. 75-101), New York: William Morrow.

Engelbart, D. C., and English, W. K. (1968). A Research Center for Augmenting Human Intellect, *AFIPS Conference Proceedings, 1968 Fall Joint Computer Conference*, *33* (pp. 395-410), Montvale, NJ: AFIPS Press.

Fountain, A., Hall, W., Heath, I., and Davis, H. C. (1990). MICROCOSM: An Open Model for Hypermedia with Dynamic Linking, in A. Rizk, N. Streitz, and J. André (editors), *Hypertext: Concepts, Systems and Applications* (pp. 298-311), Cambridge: Cambridge University Press.

Furuta, R., and Stotts, P. D. (1989). Programmable Browsing Semantics in Tellis, *Hypertext '89 Proceedings* (pp. 27-42), New York: ACM.

Grønbæk, K., and Bannon, L. (1991). Personal communication.

Halasz, F. G., Moran, T. P., and Trigg, R. H. (1987). NoteCards in a Nutshell, in J. M. Carroll and P. P. Tanner (editors), *Proceedings of the CHI and GI '87 Conference on Human Factors in Computing Systems* (pp. 45-52), New York: ACM.

Hammond, N., and Allinson, L. (1988). Travels Around a Learning Support Environment: Rambling, Orienteering or Touring?, *Proceedings of the ACM Conference on Computer Human Interaction (CHI '88)* (pp. 269-273), New York: ACM.

Irish, P. M., and Trigg, R. H. (1989). Supporting Collaboration in Hypermedia: Issues and Experiences, *Journal of American Society for Information Science*, *40*(3), 192-199.

Jordan, D. S., Russell, D. M., Jensen, A. S., and Rogers, R. A. (1989). Facilitating the Development of Representations in Hypertext with IDE, *Hypertext '89 Proceedings* (pp. 93-104), New York: ACM.

Kibby, M. R., and Mayes, T. (1989). Towards Intelligent Hypertext, in R. McAleese (editor), *Hypertext: Theory into Practice* (pp. 164-172), Norwood, NJ: Ablex Publishing Corporation.

Marshall, C. C., and Irish, P. (1989). Guided Tours and On-Line Presentations: How Authors Make Existing Hypertext Intelligible for Readers, *Hypertext '89 Proceedings* (pp. 15-26), New York: ACM.

Mylonas, E., and Heath, S. (1990). Hypertext from the Data Point of View: Paths and Links in the Perseus Project, in A. Rizk, N. Streitz, and J. André (editors), *Hypertext: Concepts, Systems and Applications* (pp. 324-336), Cambridge: Cambridge University Press.

Nelson, T. H. (1974). Dream Machines: New Freedoms through Computer Screens—A Minority Report, in *Computer Lib: You Can and Must Understand Computers Now*, South Bend, IN: Hugo's Book Service.

Roschelle, J., Pea, R., and Trigg, R. (1990). *VideoNoter: A Tool for Exploratory Video Analysis* (IRL90-0021), Palo Alto, CA: Institute for Research on Learning.

Trigg, R. H. (1983). *A Networked-based Approach to Text Handling for the On-line Scientific Community*, Ph.D. diss., University of Maryland, College Park, MD.

Trigg, R. H. (1988). Guided Tours and Tabletops: Tools for Communicating in a Hypertext Environment, *ACM Transactions on Office Information Systems*, 6(4), 398-414.

Trigg, R. H., and Irish, P. M. (1987). Hypertext Habitats: Experiences of Writers in NoteCards, *Hypertext '87 Papers* (pp. 89-108), New York: ACM.

Trigg, R. H., Suchman, L., and Halasz, F. G. (1986). Supporting Collaboration in NoteCards, *Computer-Supported Cooperative Work (CSCW '86) Proceedings* (pp. 153-162).

Trigg, R. H., and Suchman, L. (1989). Collaborative Writing in NoteCards, in R. McAleese (editor), *Hypertext: Theory into Practice* (pp. 45-61), Norwood, NJ: Ablex Publishing Corporation.

Trigg, R. H., and Weiser, M. (1986). TEXTNET: A Network-based Approach to Text Handling, *ACM Transactions on Office Information Systems*, 4(1), 1-23.

Utting, K., and Yankelovich, N. (1989). Context and Orientation in Hypermedia Networks, *ACM Transactions on Information Systems*, 7(1), 58-84.

Walker, J. H. (1987). Document Examiner: Delivery Interface for Hypertext Documents, *Hypertext '87 Papers* (pp. 307-324), New York: ACM.

Zellweger, P. T. (1989). Scripted Documents: A Hypermedia Path Mechanism, *Hypertext '89 Proceedings* (pp. 1-14), New York: ACM.